Contents

THE ARCHITECTURAL HISTORY OF SCOTLAND

General Editors
CHARLES MCKEAN
and
DEBORAH HOWARD

SCOTTISH ARCHITECTURE

From the Accession of the Stewarts

to the Reformation

1371–1560

RICHARD FAWCETT

with best wishes

Richard

EDINBURGH UNIVERSITY PRESS
in association with Historic Scotland

For Sue

© Richard Fawcett, 1994

Edinburgh University Press Ltd

22 George Square, Edinburgh

Typeset in Lasercomp Perpetua
by ROM-Data Corporation Ltd, Falmouth, and
printed and bound in Great Britain by The University Press, Cambridge

A CIP record for this book is available from the British Library

ISBN 0 7486 0465 0

The publisher gratefully acknowledges subsidy from
the Scottish Arts Council towards
the publication of this volume.

List of Illustrations

ABBREVIATIONS

A series of views . . . of Elgin Cathedral	Isaac Forsyth, *A series of views . . . of Elgin Cathedral* London, 1826
Billings	R. W. Billings, *The baronial and ecclesiastical antiquities of Scotland*, Edinburgh, 1845–52
Collie	J. Collie, *Plans, elevations . . . and views of the cathedral of Glasgow*, London, 1835
Gordon of Rothiemay	James Gordon of Rothiemay, *Four views of buildings in Edinburgh* (engraved by F. de Wit), *c.* 1649
Grose	F. Grose, *The antiquities of Scotland*, London, 1789–91
MacGibbon and Ross	D. MacGibbon and T. Ross, *The castellated and domestic architecture of Scotland* and *The ecclesiastical architecture of Scotland*, Edinburgh, 1887–97
Memorabilia of Perth	J. Cant, *Memorabilia of the city of Perth*, Perth, 1806
National Art Survey	National Art Survey of Scotland, *Examples of Scottish architecture*, Edinburgh, 1921–33
Registrum . . . Sancti Egidii	D. Laing, *Registrum cartarum ecclesie Sancti Egidii de Edinburgh*, Edinburgh, 1859
Robertson	J. Robertson, 'Notice of a deed . . . to complete . . . the church of Midcalder', *Proceedings of the Society of Antiquaries of Scotland*, vol. 3, 1857–60, pp. 160–71
Slezer	John Slezer, *Theatrum Scotiae*, London, 1693
Walker	J. R. Walker, *Pre-Reformation churches in Fifeshire*, Edinburgh, 1885

Preface

I was asked to write this book as one of a series intended to present the current state of understanding of Scottish architectural history. But there are many areas in the period covered by this book where there is still no real consensus, and consequently the survey that is offered here is at least partly a personal view. Nevertheless, in attempting to cover a wide range of architectural types over a period of almost two centuries, I have inevitably drawn heavily on the work of many others. I have tried, so far as possible, to acknowledge my specific debts to published work through the footnotes; but I cannot believe that I will have always succeeded in this and, where I have failed, I must hope it will be accepted that my sins have been those of omission rather than of commission. Having completed my task, I am acutely conscious that the time is not yet near when more than a provisional account of the late Gothic and early Renaissance architecture of Scotland can be offered. However, on the secular architecture of the period at least, there is much work in progress, and I am aware that parts of what I suggest here will soon require revision.

Having almost forgotten the pains of staring into a word-processor screen that doggedly refused to give coherent expression to the thoughts I wished to convey, it is a great pleasure to remember the help and kindness that have been given by so many during and after the period of gestation. In this respect, my warmest thanks are due to the late Professor Gordon Donaldson, to Mr John Dunbar, Dr Deborah Howard, Mr Iain MacIvor and Mr Charles McKean, all of whom read through the whole text and gave me advice and encouragement which I found invaluable – even if on some points I chose to persevere in my chosen path. I additionally owe a considerable debt to several people who read through and commented on sections covering areas in which they have specialist interest, including Dr Mark Dilworth, Mrs Doreen Grove, Mr Aonghus MacKechnie, Dr Denys Pringle and Mr Christopher Tabraham. But, despite the great help I have received from them, responsibility for all faults and errors must, of course, be laid at my own doorstep.

I have also discussed aspects of the areas this book covers with many other people. Among those I especially wish to thank in this respect are Dr David Breeze, Dr David Caldwell, Mr Neil Cameron, Dr Ronald Cant, Mr Gordon Ewart, Professor Eric Fernie, Mr Nicholas Holmes, Mr John Lewis, Mr Geoffrey Stell, Dr Alexander Stevenson and Dr Christopher Wilson. All of these have, perhaps not always knowingly, helped me on a wide range of matters. At another level I owe a particular and two-fold debt to my employer, Historic Scotland: in the first place because my work has allowed me to come into close contact with many of the buildings discussed below, and in the second place because I have been permitted to make use of photographs held in its fine collection for this book. On the latter point I am grateful to Mr Michael Brooks, Mr David Henrie and Mr Christopher Hutchison for practical help and advice on photographic matters. Thanks for practical help are also gladly acknowledged to the Society of Antiquaries of London and the British Academy for grants that made it possible for me to visit the Low Countries and France when I was looking into the architectural debts that Scotland owed those areas. But, at the risk of seeming to end this preface with an obligatory cliché, I must truthfully state that above all I am indebted to my wife, Sue, and my children, Tim and Clare. My debt to the latter is partly for being invariably at hand when scapegoats were needed, but largely for accepting with disconcerting readiness that I had to spend less time with them than I should; to my wife I offer thanks for unfailing support at what was a rather difficult period for a number of reasons.

RICHARD FAWCETT

Introduction

The following chapters cover the period from the accession of the Stewart dynasty in the person of Robert II in 1371, up to the Reformation of the church, which was given legal status by the parliament of August 1560. After an initial chapter which looks at the great resurgence of building activity in all categories of architecture between the later fourteenth century and the first decades of the fifteenth century, the rest of the book is divided into chapters which consider the main building types individually from the earlier fifteenth century onwards. Arranging the material in this way has disadvantages when trying to discern the underlying trends in architectural thought, but it was felt that the sheer number of buildings to be covered at what was a highly productive period would make any other approach over-complicated.

Within the inevitable constraints of reconciling the breadth of material to be covered with the publisher's word limit, space has been made for some assessment of the design of the buildings as an expression of their function, and for seeing them within their historical context. But it must be said at the outset that the book has been planned primarily as a survey of later medieval and early Renaissance architecture as an art form. One consequence of this is that, for much of the book, there is greater concentration on ecclesiastical than on secular architecture. This is because, before the sixteenth century, it was generally the more lavishly-funded church-building operations that allowed the greatest scope for the evolution of new ideas. While there are certainly highly important developments in the secular architecture of the fifteenth century, except in the more prestigious projects masons were more inclined to rely on variations on established formulae than were the designers of church buildings. It is therefore possible to make generalisations which can be applied to significant numbers of secular structures, whereas many of the surviving church buildings show such individual characteristics that they need separate discussion. However, this balance shifts in the sixteenth century, when a number of magnificent royal palaces were among the most prestigious projects then in progress.

Following almost two centuries during which Scottish architecture – in the Lowland areas at least – had been closely linked with developments south of the Border, the later Middle Ages was a period when patrons and masons tended to follow a different path. Although it is always debatable how far 'national' qualities can be identifiable in any art form, in following this new path a synthesis of ideas progressively emerged in Scotland which is arguably of a more distinctive character than that of any other period before or since. Among the various elements which underlay this synthesis was what appears to have been an increased openness to direct inspiration by continental architecture, although any imported ideas were usually modified to attune them to Scottish usages; it may be mentioned that those usages seem also to have involved some renewed interest in earlier architectural solutions that had been current within Scotland itself. Towards the end of the period covered by this book – and particularly from about the 1530s onwards – yet another spirit influenced by continental ideas began to emerge, especially at first in the royal palaces. This is the herald of the new architectural era of the Renaissance and provides an important foretaste of themes to be dealt with more fully in the next volume in this series.

At this point it may be helpful briefly to place our architecture within a broader context by saying a little about the wider cultural picture within Scotland. It would be very wrong to devalue the national achievement by over-estimating its importance in relation to what was happening in the leading continental centres; it is salutary, for example, to remember that only three years after the beginning of our period the Italian poet Petrarch had already died, and that in England Chaucer was to be writing his *Canterbury Tales* towards the end of the next decade. Nevertheless, there is little doubt that at this period our small and relatively poor nation towards the northern fringes of Europe was beginning to play an ever more significant part among its fellow nations. Scotland was, after all, a maritime state enjoying commercial, cultural and political contacts with all parts of the Continent, and it naturally became an increasingly receptive beneficiary of the main steams of European thought. (It may be, indeed, that Scotland had even wider contacts than that, because the first Sinclair Earl of Orkney, who succeeded to the title in 1379, is said to have crossed the Atlantic a century before Columbus!)

The wars with England had fostered an enhanced sense of national identity that found strongly patriotic expression in a number of histories. Among these were John Barbour's *Bruce* of 1375, John of Fordoun's history, which was written before his death in about 1387 and continued by Walter Bower to form the *Scotichronicon*, Andrew of Wyntoun's *Orygenale Cronykil* of the 1420s, and Hector Boece's history of 1527. All the writers of these works were churchmen: Barbour was archdeacon of Aberdeen, Fordoun a chantry priest in Aberdeen, Bower was abbot of Inchcolm, Wyntoun was prior of Lochleven, and Boece was the first principal of King's College in Aberdeen. This reminds us that the church continued to be the chief promoter of artistic and intellectual activity at this time, and certainly the three medieval universities – at St Andrews, Glasgow and Aberdeen – were founded by prelates and remained under the control of their successors. Among the finest minds in the service of the church were a number of notable theologians, like Laurence of Lindores – a leading figure in the new university of St Andrews – and, towards the end of our period, John Ireland, John Major and Hector Boece – all of whom had distinguished careers in the famous schools of Paris before returning to give their talents to Scotland. The church's patronage of the arts is, of course, most clearly seen in the architecture that is one of the main themes of this book, and that architecture provided the matrix for the best sculpture and painting that was produced. The churches were also the setting for the superb music composed to beautify their services, by such as Robert Black and Robert Carver.

However, much of Carver's finest work was composed for the Chapel Royal in Stirling Castle, and this reminds us that the crown was itself playing an increasingly important role in the patronage of the arts in the later Middle Ages. In assessing the artistic achievements and patronage of kings it is essential to allow for the hyperbole of contemporary descriptions, but there is ample evidence of the interests of several of Scotland's monarchs. James I may have been the author of the *King's Quair*, a movingly introspective poem recounting his courtly passion for Joan Beaufort in a manner influenced by Chaucer, while one of the complaints apparently levelled against James III was that he gave more attention to his artists than his nobles. Impressive evidence for the artistic and cultural tastes of James IV and James V is provided by the buildings produced for them, but it should also be remembered that the printing press set up by Walter Chapman and Andrew Millar in 1507 was under royal patronage, although one of its main tasks was to print service books to meet the growing demand for religious observances suitable for Scottish tastes.

Having mentioned the *King's Quair*, reference must also be made here to the fine tradition of poetry which flourished in later medieval Scotland, on both sides of the Highland line. Its highest achievements are perhaps heard in the works of Robert Henryson, William Dunbar and Gavin Douglas. Henryson, who died in 1500, was a schoolmaster in Dunfermline and possibly a teacher at Glasgow University; Dunbar, who died in 1514, was a priest; Douglas, who died in exile in 1522, was Bishop of Dunkeld. At their hands we see how the new humanist learning together with a knowledge of classical antiquity were brought into the service of a thriving taste for vernacular poetry.

Here it may also be useful to move on and say a little about the architectural scene within the rest of Europe. The start of our period was generally one of great attainments, although the effects of the Hundred Years War, which had broken out in 1337 when Edward III of England renewed his claim to the French throne, were still then limiting possibilities in France. But in Italy work was well in hand on the second phase of Florence Cathedral, whose construction had restarted around 1357, and building at Milan Cathedral was to be initiated in 1386. In the German states one of the most important campaigns at this time was on the choir of Prague Cathedral, of between 1344 and 1385, while in the Low Countries the choir of Mechelen was to be completed in 1375 and that of Utrecht was under construction throughout the period which concerns us here. England was increasingly choosing to follow an independent course from that of the rest of Europe, and this divergence is perhaps best epitomised in the restrained and rather cerebral 'Perpendicular' architecture of the nave of Canterbury Cathedral, started in about 1378.

Most European countries were to continue actively developing the range of possibilities inherent within the various late Gothic idioms throughout the fifteenth and into the sixteenth centuries. In France there was a growing taste for a counterpoint between a complex flamboyant treatment of many exteriors – as seen at the remodelled nave at Louviers of around 1510 – and a more restrained treatment of interiors – as exemplified in St Ouen at Rouen, started in 1469. In parts of Germany one of the most satisfying achievements was to be the development of more unified spatial modelling in a number of great hall churches, such as St George at Dinkelsbühl of 1448–92. Such hall-churches were to be found throughout Europe, but nowhere else was the idea carried to so high a level of attainment.

The great majority of the churches mentioned above were far larger than anything that was attainable in Scotland, and it is sobering to contrast the scale of the English Chapel Royal at Windsor, of between 1475 and 1511, with that of the contemporary Scottish Chapel Royal at Restalrig (see Figure 5.5). But this is at least partly an illustration of the differing resources available rather than of disparity of artistic potential. Moving on to the Low Countries, one of the great achievements of the late Middle Ages there was the large number of ambitious town churches, especially in the prosperous coastal provinces. These probably offered a more attainable goal for Scottish patrons and masons to aim at, especially since there were such close commercial, artistic and intellectual links with the area, and also since Scotland was itself rebuilding many of its burgh churches at this time.

By contrast with northern Europe, in Italy Gothic had always been an exotic growth, and memories of classical antiquity were never far beneath the surface. There, change was in the air, and between 1419 and 1424 the first phase of the Renaissance in architecture was given articulate expression in Brunelleschi's Foundling Hospital in Florence. Except perhaps for some very muffled echoes, however, the Italian Renaissance was to have little identifiable impact in Scotland before the very end of the fifteenth century, though soon after then it is worth remembering that the Piedmontese scholar Joannes Ferrerius spent five years teaching at the Cistercian abbey of Kinloss in the 1530s. Nevertheless, it is not always easy to be conscious of the fact that the momentous achievements of the Italian High Renaissance were taking place during the very period that concerns us here, and that by the time the Scottish Reformation severed the links of our church with papal Rome, Palladio was already building some of his palaces and villas around Vicenza.

The first impact of the Renaissance on Scottish architecture is more likely to have come through the medium of France, and to a lesser extent from England, rather than from Italy. Cardinal Georges d'Amboise had started his extraordinary castle of Gaillon in 1502, though it was probably not until six years later that Italianate elements were evident in its design. Soon after, a more regular approach to planning became apparent in Florimond Robertet's château of Bury, started in 1511. But before that was far advanced, the architectural lead in France had passed firmly to the crown. The magnificent series of châteaux built for François I included Blois, started in 1515, Chambord, begun in 1519, Madrid, started in 1528, and works at Fontainebleau and the Louvre, begun in 1528 and 1546 respectively. The influence of the French Renaissance was increasingly strong on the secular architecture of Scotland towards the close of our period because of the active political and dynastic contacts with that country, and we know that several masons were attracted here from France – though they may not necessarily have been the best available. There was less influence in ecclesiastical architecture and, although at St Eustache in Paris we find classical forms bonded on to a Gothic plan in a way that might have been attractive to Scottish churchmen, nearly all of our churches continued to be resolutely medieval in character.

With that necessarily cursory attempt at a *mise-en-scène* for the architecture of late medieval Scotland, we must now move on to consider developments within Scotland itself around the turn of the fourteenth century.

PART ONE

From the Late Fourteenth to the Early Fifteenth Century

CHAPTER ONE

The Resurgence Of
Building Activity

The period embraced by the last quarter of the fourteenth and the first quarter of the fifteenth centuries was one of the most seminally creative in the history of Scottish Gothic architecture. Yet it was also an unsettled period, partly because of a lack of strong leadership between the accession in 1371 of Robert II – the first monarch of the Stewart dynasty – and the return of James I from English captivity in 1424.

Robert Stewart had been recognised as Robert I's heir presumptive in 1318, being the king's grandson by his daughter Marjory Bruce, though the birth of the future David II in 1324 had then blocked his succession. But when David himself died in 1371 without issue, Robert again came into his own, though he was by then fifty-five years old and little inclined to kingship. He progressively transferred as much responsibility as possible to his eldest son, John, Earl of Carrick, but Carrick was himself to prove a broken reed and, after a kick from a horse in 1388, became a permanent invalid and as unfitted to rule as was his father. This vacuum was filled by Carrick's younger brother, the Earl of Fife and Menteith and eventually Duke of Albany who, from 1388 onwards, was in effective control of the kingdom until his own death in 1420. Robert II himself preferred to be away from the main centres of activity, and it was at his favourite castle of Dundonald in Ayrshire that he died in 1390 (see Figure 1.1).

In the north of the country the chronic disorder at this time was most forcefully expressed in the depredations of Robert II's fourth son, Alexander, who became Earl of Buchan by marriage in 1382. His activities resulted in a period of near anarchy across and beyond the province of Moray, which earned him the sobriquet of 'the Wolf of Badenoch'. For our purposes his activities are most graphically represented by his burning of Elgin Cathedral in 1390.

In the south renewed outbreaks of hostilities with England created another form of disorder. By 1384 the truce of 1369 had expired, and the Earls of Douglas (Archibald the Grim) and March attacked the English forces occupying Annandale and Teviotdale, whose galling presence reminded the Scots of the English King's claims of overlordship. In the same year a group of French knights joined Borderers in forays into northern England, as the unofficial prelude to the arrival of a larger French force in 1385. This led to the strengthening of the English-held castles of Roxburgh and Berwick, and major retaliatory campaigns in 1384 and 1385;

further waves of Border warfare followed in 1388, 1400, 1402 and 1417. Architecturally, the renewed warfare had a particularly disastrous impact on the vulnerably situated Border abbeys. To add to Scotland's misery, from about 1400 one of England's most effective weapons was a blockade of the Scottish ports, resulting in a devastating decline in exports, with inevitable consequences for the nation's economy.

By this stage Scotland had come to see France as its best ally against the English, despite indications that France could take a cynical view of its obligations and might not honour them when to do so could be disadvantageous. There were renewals of treaties with France in 1371 and 1391, and it was there that the future James I was being sent for his safety when captured by the English in 1406.

An indication of Scotland's loyalties at this time is provided by its alignment in the great schism of the church which developed in 1378, following the election of Pope Clement VII as a rival to the authoritarian Urban VI. England supported Urban, who was based in Rome, while Scotland joined France in supporting Clement, who was based in Avignon. The situation changed in 1409, when a third pope, based at Pisa, was elected. Both France and England gave their support to this new pope, leaving only Scotland out on a limb with Aragon in its continued support of Clement. Eventually yet another pope, Martin V, was elected in 1417, and Scotland joined the rest of Europe in accepting him. Faced with such rapidly changing international situations, a small and geographically peripheral country like Scotland could easily find itself in an unenviable position, whatever its alliances.

Scotland's European contacts were not confined to France. There were commercial contacts with the German states, although hostility from the Hanseatic League eventually led to a prohibition of trade with Scotland between 1412 and 1436. Links with the Scandinavian nations also developed, while trade with southern states, such as Spain and Italy, was additionally of some significance.[2] But the strongest commercial links which Scotland developed were with the Low Countries, and enduring cultural relationships were also established with that area.[3] Even as early as the twelfth and thirteenth centuries trading links had been built up, and by the first half of the fourteenth century a Scottish staple – the channel through which all trade had to be directed – was established at Bruges, in Flanders. Relationships with the area were occasionally fraught, as when Scottish goods at Bruges were seized in 1347, or when in 1410 Brouwershaven was given permission by the Count of Holland to attack Scottish traders. The inability of Scotland's rulers to control the activities of Scottish pirates was a particular periodic source of friction. Yet despite these difficulties there was continuing competition for trade with Scotland and, when breaches developed with one city, others – including most notably Middelburg and Veere in Zeeland – were eager to step in. The closeness of the links which grew up between Scotland and the Low Countries is illustrated by the marriages of a daughter of James I to the Lord of Campvere in 1444, and of James II to a daughter of the Duke of Guelders in 1449.

SOME CASTLES BUILT FOR THE ROYAL HOUSE

The architectural patronage of the royal house during the reign of Robert II is documented at the major castles of Edinburgh and Stirling. At the former, amongst other works he completed the tower-house started around 1368 by David II,[4] and added the gatehouse known as the Constable's Tower, between 1375 and 1379. Together with the linking perimeter wall these created an outer line of defence along the castle's most vulnerable face, and it is unfortunate that so little remains of them other than the shattered lower walls of David's Tower within the Half-Moon Battery of 1574. At the other major royal castle of Stirling, there are records of works between 1380 and 1390,[5] which can perhaps be linked with the much-altered North Gate. But if Edinburgh and Stirling have only fragmentary remains we do still have much of Robert II's castle at Dundonald, at the heart of the Stewart family's Ayrshire barony of North Kyle (see Figure 1.1).[6]

Excavations there between 1986 and 1988 revealed an unexpectedly long history of site occupation, stretching back as far as about 3000 BC.[7] The lands were specifically granted – or possibly formally regranted – to Alexander, fourth High Steward of Scotland (who died in 1283), by Alexander III.[8] It was presumably after this that a major castle was built, with a lozenge-shaped courtyard entered through two twin-towered gatehouses; a plan which suggests analogies with Edward I's north Welsh castle of Rhuddlan, started in about 1277. With the accession to the throne of the Stewart dynasty in 1371, Dundonald became a royal castle, and it was after this that the great block which now dominates the site was built. Heraldry, which includes both the royal arms of Scotland and the family arms of the Stewarts, shows it was built for one of the royal Stewarts, and Robert II's known love for the place allows little doubt that he was the builder.

Dundonald had almost certainly suffered in the Wars of Independence, and there is a tradition that Angus, Lord of the Isles wrested it from the English for Robert I. Damage then caused could have necessitated rebuilding by Robert II. The new building, which partly incorporated the western of the two thirteenth-century gatehouses at its lower levels, is a rectangle of about 25 by 12 metres, aligned on a north–south axis. The main entrance to the principal accommodation was towards one end of the courtyard façade. The building was covered at two levels by pointed barrel vaults, the lower one embracing a basement and a first-floor hall with an entresol floor over one end. But the most impressive internal space was on the top floor, which was presumably the king's privy hall, and which was covered by its own vault. Such a building can be classified with equal validity either as an elongated tower-house, or as an imposing hall-house, and provides a salutary warning of the difficulties inherent in exclusive terminology. It is worth mentioning here that Dundonald shows significant links of planning and arrangement with another late fourteenth-century western castle, that of the Campbells of Lochawe at Carrick in Argyll.

Although only its springings remain, the upper vault at Dundonald is of some importance for the development of Scottish later Gothic architecture (see Figure 1.2). As Scottish masons began to pursue a course increasingly independent of

FIGURE I . I (*above*)   Dundonald Castle, the west face. The bases of the thirteenth-century gatehouse towers may be seen at the foot of the wall.

FIGURE I . 2 (*below*)   Dundonald Castle, the springing of the hall vault.

England, a new approach to vaulting is to be seen at a number of buildings. Many of these vaults were of the pointed barrel – or tunnel – form, which was employed in the lower storeys of Dundonald, to provide both strength and fire-proofing. But in the grandest projects the austerity of the vaults might be palliated by a decorative veneer of ribs. Frequently these ribs were set out as a series of closely spaced parallel arches along the vault, as had been done in earlier buildings like the so-called 'Goblin Hall' at the castle of Yester.[9] But in the high hall at Dundonald the ribs were set out on a diagonal cross pattern, imitating the ribs which defined the intersections of quadripartite vaulting. Other early examples of this approach to vaulting will be considered in the context of church building, and particularly at Edinburgh St Giles and Melrose, since it was in churches that the most ambitious variants were developed (see Figures 1.20 and 1.21). It is likely, however, that such vaults have their origins as much in domestic as in ecclesiastical architecture, and the importance of Dundonald must not be forgotten. It is particularly interesting to see there a residual reference to the lateral intersections of quadripartite vaulting in the segmentally arched wall ribs.

DOUNE CASTLE

Another important castle of at least semi-royal status from this period is at Doune, in Perthshire, which has survived with remarkably few changes (see Figure 1.3).[10] The builder of Doune was Robert Stewart, third son of Robert II and brother of

FIGURE 1.3 Doune Castle from the north, before the restoration of its roofs.

Robert III who was, as has already been hinted, the most ambitious member of his immediate family. By 1361 he had become Earl of Menteith through marriage, and ten years later also became Earl of Fife through agreement with that countess. In 1388, he was appointed Guardian of the kingdom when Robert II submitted himself to a general council because of his own indisposition and his heir's infirmity. In 1398 Robert III, in an attempt to reduce antagonism between his own eldest son, David Earl of Carrick, and his brother, made them both dukes; Carrick became Duke of Rothesay and Fife became Duke of Albany. However, in 1402 Rothesay died while in Albany's custody at Falkland, leaving only the King and his next surviving son, the future James I, between Albany and the throne. In 1406 James was sent to France, but was intercepted *en route* by the English and lodged in the Tower. Robert III died soon after, and Albany was appointed Governor of the kingdom. To what extent this reveals Fate working out its inexorable purposes unaided by Albany is incalculable; nevertheless, he would hardly have been averse to ascending the throne occupied first by his father and then by his brother, and to which two of his nephews were successively heir apparent.

A major castle built by such a man, therefore, must have reflected current ideas of what was appropriate for a royal castle, and perhaps more than does a castle like Dundonald, which was built for a king who may have preferred not to be one. Set within the ancient province of Menteith, at what is almost the central point of Scotland, Doune could have been started for Robert Stewart at any time after 1361, though it was probably some years before work was initiated. The first reference to it is in a charter of 1381, suggesting it was already partly habitable, and the flow of charters signed there by Albany from 1406 onwards indicates it became a favoured residence.[11] The architecture shows both that the design of the castle was altered in several respects in the course of construction, and that it was never completed as first intended. Nevertheless, those ranges which were built within the curtain walls seem to have been erected relatively quickly, if the distribution of the same masons' marks can be taken as an indicator that some masons were at work throughout much of the operation.

Doune straddles a narrow neck of land, above the confluence of the River Teith and Ardoch Water; the Romans had already recognised the strategic advantages of the area when they built a fort nearby in the later first century. The main enclosure of the castle was an irregular pentagon, around which are traces of outer lines of defence which either completely encircled the castle or cut across its more vulnerable northern and southern sides (see Figure 1.4b). Possibly with an eye as much to effect as to defensibility, the main living quarters of the castle were concentrated across the entrance front on the north. The gateway passed through the four-storeyed block at the north-east corner of the courtyard, where it was flanked by a drum tower. Extending westwards from this entrance block was a lower two-storeyed range. Despite this concentration of buildings along the north front, however, other structures were originally planned around the perimeter of the whole courtyard, and the windows which pierce the south curtain are of a type which would only have been intended for high-quality accommodation.

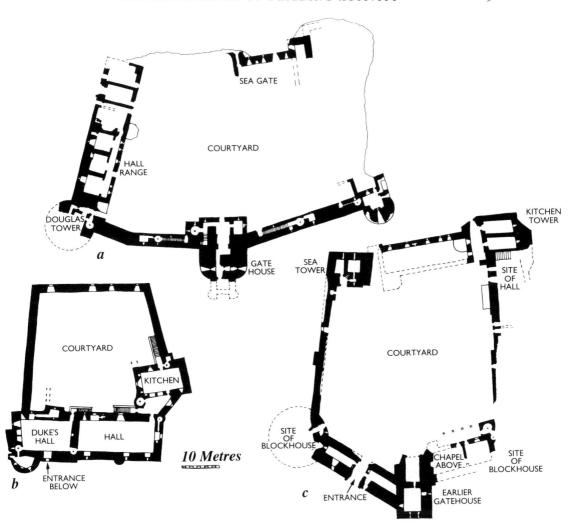

FIGURE 1.4   Plans of major courtyard castles: a. Tantallon Castle; b. Doune Castle; c. St Andrews Castle.

As might be expected, the main living quarters of the castle are above a stone-vaulted ground floor, which afforded them greater dignity and enhanced security. The main hall occupies the two-storeyed range in the western part of the entrance front, and is approached from a forestair which opens into a triangular vestibule between the hall and the kitchen. The latter – one of the best appointed in medieval Scotland – is in a block on the west side of the courtyard, which has spacious lodgings on the upper floors, and there were also chambers above the vestibule. Idiosyncrasies in the levels of windows in the vestibule and hall, together with an arch below the vestibule apparently designed to support something never built, all show the planning of these parts was modified during construction.

The duke's own hall was on the first floor of the gatehouse block (see Figure 1.5), from where he had some control over access to the gate in times of emergency: there is a machicolation in the north window embrasure which looks down into the entrance passage, and trap doors open into the ground floor of the chambers flanking the gate. This inner hall could be approached either by a protected stairway from the courtyard, or through a small doorway in the north-east corner of the great hall, which also opened on to a spiral stair. The duke's hall was a handsome barrel-vaulted space, the main architectural focus of which was a double fireplace in the end wall. Opening off it is a side chamber in the drum tower, and a mural closet in a projection above the courtyard side of the entrance passage.

There was a room similar to the duke's hall on the floor above, which could have been the hall of a separate lodging for his duchess. This upper room had an oratory in a projection above the closet on the floor below, which was evidently screened off from the main space. From this level there was also access to the wall-walk around the curtain wall. The wall-walk owes its present form partly to repairs of 1580, but with parapets on both sides, it must have provided a valued promenade, as well as a line of defence in times of emergency. There were other chambers on the floor above, where the main spaces were probably subdivided.

The living quarters of Doune were planned on a generous scale, and as much thought was given to domestic convenience and vice-regal splendour as to defensibility.

FIGURE 1.5   Doune Castle, the duke's hall.

It has been suggested that its planning presents a parallel with that of the castle of Pierrefonds in France. The same writer argued that it should be understood as an architectural expression of bastard feudalism, a system by which late medieval magnates are thought to have supported their military activities with paid mercenaries rather than feudal vassals, and thus also had to provide for defence against potentially unruly followers.[12] Neither of these views would now find support, and in fact the juxtaposition of what is essentially a vertically arranged tower-like residence with a more horizontal hall range is not dissimilar from what we shall see was built for the Earls of Douglas at Tantallon and Bothwell. This combination of elements, which evidently so ideally met the main needs of Scottish aristocratic households, was to continue at varying scales and in different forms as one of the enduring themes of castle design throughout the later Middle Ages.

As part of the restoration of 1883 by the Earl of Moray, the roofs of the main parts of Doune were reinstated; but by then the evidence for the original construction had been lost. The most impressive evidence for the feats of roof carpentry possible at this period is now afforded by the splendid roof over the hall of one of the principal residences of the medieval Earls of Moray, at Darnaway Castle (see Figure 1.6). That hall was unusual for its period in being at ground-floor level, though it was remodelled in 1809–10 to the designs of the architect Alexander Laing, and its original form may have been transformed more than we know. At some stage the lower timbers of the roof have been enveloped within the wall-head masonry, thus partly obscuring some details of its construction. The main structure, however, is a hybrid between hammer-beam and arch-braced construction; even more extraordinary is the variety of additional decoration applied to the principal rafters in the form of great curved cusps. The Exchequer Rolls apparently refer to roofing here in 1456–8, but dendro-chronological analysis has shown that the timbers used in the roof were cut in about 1387.[13] In view of this it was presumably constructed for one of the Dunbar earls, who held the title between 1372 and 1455.

THE GREATER CASTLES OF THE LATER FOURTEENTH CENTURY

The later fourteenth century was a period when a number of ambitious castles were constructed for the Scottish magnates, and when there were also major operations of reconstruction at several of those castles which had been built earlier but damaged or destroyed in the wars with England. It should be added that the English were themselves active at some of the castles they continued to occupy in the Borders. At Roxburgh Castle, for example, major works were carried out by the mason John Lewyn, who is also known to have worked on several northern English castles and religious houses.[14] Roxburgh was one of the two most important English strongholds in Scotland, until recaptured at the siege of 1460,[15] and it was in 1378 that Lewyn contracted to carry out large-scale rebuilding. This consisted of a thirty-foot-high wall running along the castle from north to south, with three fifty-foot-high towers, the central one having a gate and barbican.[16] It is possible that the results of this campaign are still represented in the fragmentary fortifications along the east side of the site, overlooking the Teviot.

FIGURE 1.6   Darnaway Castle, the hall roof.

Among the castles remodelled for Scottish patrons was the Maxwell family's stronghold of Caerlaverock in Dumfries-shire, where slighting in 1312, and again in 1355 or 1356, necessitated much rebuilding.[17] Considerable parts of the two drum towers which define the southern angles of the triangular main enclosure must be of the later fourteenth century, as must parts of the gatehouse towers and of the curtain walls which run between all of these. An approximate period for this work is suggested by tree-ring dating of around 1370 for the timbers from the replacement bridge across the moat.[18]

In East Lothian the Halyburton family extensively remodelled their castle at Dirleton,[19] which had passed to John Halyburton through marriage with the heiress of the de Vaux family in the mid-century (see Figure 1.7). The castle had almost certainly suffered badly in the wars and, over the following century and a half, successive heads of the family progressively rebuilt much of the entrance front on the south side, and the hall range on the east side. At the entrance to the castle a formidable new gatehouse was formed, flanked to one side by the lower storeys of the only survivor of the massive towers built at the angles of their castle by the de Vaux family in the thirteenth century. The drawbridge, which spanned the last section of the approach to the new gate, was operated from a superstructure carried on an arch between massive buttresses projecting out on each side of the entrance passage. These buttresses also supported turrets flanking the platform, the corbels at the base of which were pierced by machicolations so that missiles might be dropped on anyone who approached too closely. Within the drawbridge the passage was further defended by a machicolation and a portcullis.

One of the most costly of the later fourteenth-century campaigns of rehabilitation of a major castle was at Bothwell, superbly sited on a high bank above a loop of the River Clyde in Lanarkshire (see Figure 1.8).[20] This magnificent later thirteenth-century castle of the Moray family had never been finished as originally planned. It had also been slighted by the Scots themselves on two occasions during the wars, first after Bannockburn, and again in 1337 when it was recaptured from the English by its owner, Sir Andrew de Moray, Guardian of the Kingdom. In 1362 Bothwell passed through marriage to Archibald the Grim, the future third Earl of Douglas, and it was he who started the rebuilding process. As a first stage he probably reduced the size of the castle by constructing a high northern curtain wall half-way across the courtyard, thus leaving an unfinished gatehouse outside the main enclosure. He also rebuilt the curtain along the east side of the courtyard, possibly together with the square tower at its northern end.

FIGURE 1.7   Dirleton Castle, the entrance front.

FIGURE 1.8   Bothwell Castle from the south-east.

The reconstruction was continued after his death in 1400 by his son, the fourth earl. To the latter are attributed the curtain along the south side, the spacious hall and chapel range along the east side adjacent to the existing rectangular north-east tower, and a round tower at the south-east corner of the courtyard commanding the external angle. The arched machicolations of that tower, carried on three-stage corbels have a rather French appearance, probably resulting from the fourth earl's French connections, culminating in his elevation to the dukedom of Touraine.

Another Douglas stronghold which was extended around this time was the Border stronghold of Hermitage, where a manor house built by the Dacre family after about 1358 formed the core (see Figure 1.9).[21] The first Earl of Douglas had re-established his family's claim to Hermitage by 1371, after which the manor house was incorporated into a rectangular structure of about 23 by 14 metres, with a small wing to contain a first-floor entrance near the south-west corner. When in 1388 the earldom of Douglas passed to the side of the family represented by Archibald the Grim – a branch that came to be known as the Black Douglases – the lands which included Hermitage stayed with a rival branch. The head of that branch, known as the Red Douglases, inherited the earldom of Angus through his mother. It was probably he who added the wings which project from the four angles of the main core, before his death in 1402. An attractive feature of the additions is the arches spanning the heads of the wings on the short ends of the castle, which were probably placed here to simplify the construction of wall-head timber hoarding. (It may be mentioned in passing that one of the few parallels for this arrangement of corner towers and linking wall-head arches is at the Irish castle of Bunratty in County Clare, although this similarity is likely to be coincidental.[22])

FIGURE 1.9   Hermitage Castle from the south-east.

The piecemeal development of Hermitage could have resulted in visual disharmony, yet its final appearance is remarkably homogenous. In part this homogeneity results from a Draconian restoration by the fifth Duke of Buccleuch in the 1820s, though clearly the process of expanding around the original nucleus in the later fourteenth century involved consideration not just of military expediency and domestic convenience, but also of architectural appearance. Scotland's greater magnates were evidently already alive to the need for buildings to offer comprehensible statements about the power and dignity of their owners.

The rebuilding campaigns just discussed were conceived on a grand scale; but such operations can give only a partial idea of the architectural potential of the generation which produced them. To understand that potential more fully we must look to works in which the approach of the patrons and masons was less conditioned by what was already on site.

The castle which most magnificently epitomises the spirit of the second half of the fourteenth century is yet another Douglas stronghold, at Tantallon in East Lothian (see Figures 1.10 and 1.4a).[23] Massively constructed across a high promontory on the coast east of North Berwick, Tantallon offers one of the most memorable images of the power of a great late medieval magnate. Its builder was probably the same Earl William who instigated rebuilding at Hermitage and, like Hermitage, it later passed to the Red Douglas Earls of Angus. Douglas's inheritance of Tantallon had been confirmed by David II in 1354, and he was created first Earl of Douglas in 1358. Construction of the castle may have been started soon after, and enough was complete by 1374 for the earl to be able to sign correspondence at 'our Castle of Temptaloun'.

FIGURE 1.10   Tantallon Castle from the south-west.

The main element of the castle is a wall about 15 metres high and 3.7 metres thick running north–south across the neck of the promontory, with a drum tower at each end and a strong gatehouse at the centre. There were lean-to ranges along the back of at least part of the curtain wall. The defences around the other sides of the courtyard would have been less strong, and may never have been finished, since on three sides there were high cliffs. But it is likely the castle was intended to be fully enclosed, and on the east side a start was made on building a sea gate. On the landward side was a large outer courtyard of uncertain date, which was less formidably enclosed, but nevertheless served as an important part of the system of defences, as well as providing space for ancillary structures.

The castle has undergone various modifications, particularly after being seized from the sixth Earl of Angus by James V in 1528;[24] the most obvious relic of the changes then made is the present frontispiece of the gatehouse, with its small doorway, curved corners and polychromatic banding. Nevertheless, the basic form of the castle is still essentially as designed in the third quarter of the fourteenth century. The gatehouse was planned on similar principles to that at Dirleton, albeit on a larger scale. Flanking the approach to the entrance passage were deeply projecting buttresses, capped by turrets with machicolations through their corbelling and connected by a flying bridge. The passage itself was defended by a drawbridge, a portcullis and three sets of doors, and above the entrance passage were four storeys of chambers which it seems were for the earl's constable. Outside the gatehouse itself there was originally an outer defensive pocket or barbican.

In the round tower at each end of the cross wall were sets of chambers. The east tower – the smaller of the two – had five storeys of chambers before the post-1528 changes, each with a fireplace and a garderobe, and individually reached from a spiral stair within the thickness of the curtain wall. This suggests each chamber was occupied separately by a member of the earl's household. The west tower, known as the Douglas Tower, had six storeys of chambers above a vaulted basement, and probably served as the lodging of the earl and his family. As such, in its vertical stacking of rooms and its relationship with an adjacent hall, it shows kinship of arrangement with the north-east tower at Bothwell, and the gatehouse tower at Doune. It also shows parallels with the tower-houses which were increasingly being built as the main residential element at castles elsewhere. At Tantallon the hall was on the first floor of a range along the north side of the courtyard; it had an open-timber tie-beam roof on the evidence of the seating provided for the timbers.

A slightly later building than Tantallon which shows some analogies with it is the castle of the bishops of St Andrews, to the north-west of their cathedral there (see Figures 1.11 and 1.4c).[25] Like Tantallon, it occupies a cliff-top site, though at St Andrews there are steep drops on only two sides. As at Bothwell, the castle had been captured from the English by Sir Andrew Moray in 1337, and had then been slighted to prevent its being held again for the English. According to the *Scotichronicon* the castle was rebuilt by Bishop Walter Traill, who had been elected in 1385 and who died within it in 1401.[26] Traill laid out the castle as a shield-shaped pentagon, with towers – probably all originally of square plan – at the five angles, and ranges running between some or all of the towers behind the curtain walls. The main entrance was through the tower at the centre of the south front, in which the gateway jambs and a slot for one of the drawbridge gaffs survive. That tower was the only part of the structure in which earlier work was retained, but it is uncertain if that earlier work predates the English occupation of 1336, or is part of the work then carried out.

St Andrews Castle was so extensively rebuilt, both before and after a siege of 1546–7, and is now so ruined that there are many uncertainties about the original planning. But the north-west tower had at least one residential chamber, complete with fireplace and garderobe, above prisons at ground-floor and basement levels. The north-east tower had a first-floor kitchen to serve the hall in the adjacent range, and may also have had chambers in the upper storeys. In its final state the lodging for the archbishops probably extended along the south side of the castle, overlooking the main entrance (see Figure 8.40), but we do not know if this perpetuated the initial arrangement. By the sixteenth century – if not before – there were outer courtyards to the west and south of the castle, the latter protecting the main entrance. As at Tantallon, the structurally upstanding parts of such a major castle probably represented only the more permanently constructed core, beyond which requirements of defence, domestic convenience and architectural prestige would call for other enclosures. At St Andrews excavation has revealed a complex history of uses for the area

FIGURE 1.11   St Andrews Castle gatehouse tower. The windows and wall-head date from later modifications.

covered by the western of the outer courts which is shown on a sixteenth-century drawing.

At Mugdock, in Stirlingshire, there is a castle which could have been a smaller prototype of Traill's work at St Andrews (see Figure 1.12).[27] Possibly attributable to Sir David de Graham, who died in 1376, Mugdock also seems to have had a shield-shaped plan with square towers at the angles, one of which served as a gatehouse, and with ranges running between the towers. Unfortunately, the eastern side of the courtyard has been lost beneath later rebuilding, and it is unclear how far it was a symmetrical reflection of the western side. The most complete surviving part is the tower at the south-west angle, which still stands to full height, albeit remodelled at the top. It is on the basis of the details of this tower that it seems the work was earlier than St Andrews. These details include a shoulder-lintelled doorway and ogee-headed windows, though it is true that such details had a relatively long history in Scotland.

FIGURE 1.12   Mugdock Castle, the south-west tower.

LATER FOURTEENTH-CENTURY DEVELOPMENTS OF THE TOWER-HOUSE

Castles like Tantallon and St Andrews were exceptional since by this stage the majority of castles and fortified houses in Scotland had a tower-house as their most prominent residential element. Within the British Isles tower-houses as a type of residence – in so far as they are a type – are most commonly found in Scotland, Ireland and northern England.[28] They have therefore tended to be regarded a little dismissively as the response of a 'Celtic fringe' to the problems of providing some limited measure of domestic defence without undue expenditure. There is some truth in this idea; but David's Tower in Edinburgh Castle reminds us that tower-houses could be impressive structures associated with strong defences, and we have only to look at later examples like Craigmillar, Spynie and Craignethan to understand that the idea could be developed to provide powerful expressions of the social standing of their owners (see Figures 8.13, 8.9 and 9.4). Indeed, recent re-evaluations have shown that the tower-house was sometimes revived in the later Middle Ages as a symbol of seigneurial – or even royal – authority, as is splendidly demonstrated by English or

Welsh examples at Tattershall, Warkworth, Raglan and Warwick, or in Scotland by James V's tower at Holyrood.

At another level, investigations throughout Europe are demonstrating that tower-houses are more widespread than has been generally appreciated in Britain. In parts of the Netherlands, for example, *woontorens* (living towers) were particularly common between about 1275 and about 1325, and in more remote areas there they continued to be built into the fifteenth century.[29] Without invoking direct comparisons, it is instructive to see how the severely plain lower walls of these *woontorens* were often relieved by more decorative treatment of the wall-heads, with open rounds or bartizans at the corners, foreshadowing an approach that became usual in Scotland.

It is essential that we do not visualise tower-houses as having stood in isolation. In the majority of cases they represented only the main residential unit for their owner and his immediate family within a larger complex. As such, they would usually be more permanently constructed, more architecturally imposing and more defensible than most of the other buildings, and have thus usually survived better. But without the other structures which once surrounded them, both within and beyond the confines of the defensible courtyard, they could hardly have supported the way of life of which they were the main focus. More often than not, even the kitchens were outside the tower.

The extent to which the tower-house was physically linked with the other buildings varied. At many larger castles residential towers were an integral element in the architectural massing around the perimeter of the site, like David's Tower in Edinburgh Castle. Elsewhere, and particularly in the castles of the smaller landholders, the tower might have been given a more dominantly expressed form, though it was usually linked with the defensive courtyard wall and often abutted by other buildings.

There is still no consensus on the emergence and early development of the tower-house type in Scotland, though its roots could lie in the later thirteenth century. One of the most impressive tower-houses to date from later fourteenth century is at Threave, in Kirkcudbrightshire, which was built by Archibald the Grim, whom we have previously encountered in connection with the rebuilding of Bothwell Castle (see Figure 1.13). It was through marriage to the heiress of the Moray estates in about 1362 that Archibald had acquired those lands of Bothwell, and in 1369 David II had granted him the lordship of eastern Galloway, with which in 1372 he was able to unite western Galloway. In 1388 – following the death of the second Earl of Douglas at the battle of Otterburn – Archibald succeeded to that title, and added to his already vast estates the lands of Douglasdale, Lauderdale, Eskdale and the forest of Selkirk.[30]

As befitted so important a magnate, the third earl was a prolific patron of architecture, and consideration will be given below to other works produced for him. But the gaunt tower-house of Threave, on an island in the River Dee about fifteen kilometres north of Kirkcudbright,[31] symbolises particularly vividly both his architectural and political aspirations. The first reference to Threave relates to the death

FIGURE 1.13   Threave Castle, the tower-house rising behind the later curtain wall.

of Earl Archibald within its walls on Christmas Eve 1400, but a date for its construction around the third and fourth quarters of the fourteenth century is most likely.

Threave has a simple rectangular plan (see Figure 8.1c), measuring 18.5 by 12 metres, but was designed for a more positive approach to defence than was to be usual in tower-houses, as is evident from the design of its top floor. Its walls at that level are pierced by an array of arched windows and a doorway, with a large number of small holes in the outer face, all of which were designed to allow the construction of timber hoarding around the wall-head as a covered fighting gallery in times of emergency. The small holes were the slots for the supports of the timber platform, while the windows allowed the garrison to look out from the greater safety of the main body of the tower. Such an arrangement was most unusual, though we have already seen something like it at the Douglas castle of Hermitage. Behind this hoarding the roof was relatively flat, perhaps to serve as a platform for military equipment.

The tower at Threave was of five storeys, with the entrance at first-floor level and with communication between the upper floors by a spiral stair at the north-west corner. Latrines were stacked at the south-west corner, in a way that allowed the waste chutes to run together. The ground floor, which was entered only by hatches from above, was used for storage and had a well at one corner, though it also had a prison enclosure at another. The first floor was covered by a stone vault, and was divided into two compartments, one of which was the entrance vestibule, while the other could serve as a kitchen. The way in which this floor was tucked in beneath a vault was to be reflected in the entresol – or mezzanine – floors of many later castles, but at Threave greater headroom was allowed at this level than was to be common. The hall, the main living-room of the tower, was on the second floor. The third floor had two fireplaces and must have been divided into two parts by a cross partition of timber. From the way the first of these subdivisions was entered directly from the stair and the other only through the first, it seems they formed the outer and inner chamber of a single lodging, presumably for the earl himself, with the garderobe serving the latter.

The tower-house did not stand alone, and excavation between 1974 and 1978 located the foundations of a number of contemporary structures in other parts of the island.[32] Except when they had to take refuge in the tower in times of siege, most members of the earl's household, his servants and guests would be housed in the scattering of less substantial but still carefully built structures beneath its walls. One of these was probably the main hall of the castle, a more public room than the hall in the tower. Also found through excavation was a walled harbour, immediately to the west of the tower, a reminder – if any were needed on an island site – of the importance of communications by water at a time when roads tended to be execrable.

Variants on a basically rectangular plan were to remain common for tower-houses of all sizes up to the end of the Middle Ages, though more complex plan types were also quick to emerge (see Figure 8.1). Indeed, the eventual range of types which is generally comprehended by the portmanteau term 'tower-house' can seem so wide as to make the term lose much of its sense. Most common of the variants were those in which a small wing projecting from the end of one of the longer faces created an L-shaped plan.

Such a plan had earlier been employed for David's Tower at Edinburgh Castle as early as 1368. Fourteenth-century dates have been suggested for other examples of L-planned towers at Dunnottar in Kincardineshire, and for Craigmillar on the outskirts of Edinburgh (see Figure 8.12).[33] For the former the Earl of Sutherland was granted a license in 1346, and the latter has been thought closely to post-date the grant of the lands to the Preston family in 1374. In fact both of these are more likely to date from the fifteenth century, though there are others which do sit happily in the fourteenth century.

One of these is the tower built at Neidpath near Peebles for the Hay family (see Figures 1.14 and 8.1g).[34] Its most likely builders are Sir William Hay or his son Sir Thomas, which would place it between 1335 and 1397, but more probably towards the end of that period. Neidpath was to prove itself so adaptable that it continued to provide first-rate accommodation well into the eighteenth century, and was consequently much modified. Major changes were carried out for the second Earl of Tweeddale around the 1660s, and the interiors of that date are a fine feature of the castle; nevertheless, we can still broadly understand its original dispositions.

FIGURE 1.14   Neidpath Castle.

The position chosen for Neidpath, on a ledge above the Tweed, must have been a factor in the rhomboidal rather than rectangular plan of both main block and wing. In later L-plan castles the entrance was usually placed in the angle between the main block and the wing, so that it could be afforded some protection by flanking fire. Yet at Neidpath, perhaps because of the configuration of the site, the entrance was placed at one end of the main block; the narrow path along which it had to be approached was probably considered protection enough. Immediately inside the doorway, within the thickness of the wall and conveniently at the junction of the main block and wing, was the main stair, which connected all the floors. Unusually for this period two other stairs were provided, at diagonally opposite corners of the main block, each of which only led to certain of the floors.

The lofty stone-vaulted hall of Neidpath was itself above another stone vault which embraced both the ground and entresol levels. The thought given to convenience of planning in this tower is shown by the placing within the wing, at the same level as the hall, of a spacious kitchen. Nearly half of this kitchen was taken up by a large fireplace, since most cooking was carried out over an open fire. Doorways from the kitchen opened on to both the main stair and the servery area – which would have been enclosed by a timber screen – at the entrance end of the hall. The upper floors have been extensively remodelled, but there must certainly have been ample provision of chambers both within the wing and in the main block.

THE START OF THE REVIVAL IN CHURCH BUILDING

For much of the first three quarters of the fourteenth century church building had been sporadic. But, despite the troubled times, there is evidence of the beginnings of a resurgence of operations well before the end of the century, and by the early fifteenth century there were several major documented campaigns. There may also have been a revival of monumental sculpture, and it is significant that, in the earlier years of Robert II at least, the royal house was prepared to look to England for the production of some of its tombs, despite the fact that Robert I's tomb had been brought from France in 1329.[35] In 1372 the mason William Patrington, who had worked on the English Chapel Royal of St Stephen's at Westminster, was licensed to travel to Scotland to make the tomb of David II at Holyrood.[36] Some years later Robert set about preparing his own tomb and those of other members of his family. These were being decorated by Andrew the painter in 1378–9,[37] but the stone for them was English alabaster. Unfortunately we know nothing of the appearance of these tombs.

Among the building campaigns pointing to renewed activity are works at Brechin and Aberdeen Cathedrals, and at St Giles Parish Church in Edinburgh. Discussion of Edinburgh will be postponed to a later chapter, but at Brechin stones were being delivered for the building of the belfry in the time of Bishop Patrick de Leuchars (1351–c.1383).[38] This reference could be to the building of the upper parts of the north-west tower, the lower stages of which are of the mid-thirteenth century on the basis of the stiff leaf foliage of the vaulting shafts (see Figure 2.1). At Aberdeen Cathedral Hector Boece's history of the bishops says that work on the new nave was started by the second Bishop Alexander de Kininmund (1355–80), and that he built the cylindrical arcade piers to a height of six cubits as well as starting work on the towers (see Figures 1.24c and 2.11).[39] However, the evidence of changes of base courses and pier types in the shell of the transepts and at the east end of the nave shows the start of work on the nave was more piecemeal than Boece suggests, and the final design probably took some time to evolve. More will be said about Aberdeen below (see pp. 40 and 73).

A smaller building of this period is the collegiate church of Maybole, in Ayrshire (see Figures 1.15 and 5.1a). John Kennedy of Dunure established this as a chapel within the parish churchyard in 1371, and in 1382 permission was given to found a college of priests, when it was said that building was almost complete.[40] The aim behind the foundation of such colleges was to ensure salvation for the founder and his family by providing for prayers to be offered in perpetuity by a succession of priests. As we shall see later, many of the great families of Scotland were to found colleges of priests in the course of the later Middle Ages and Maybole is one of the first of the type to survive (see Chapter Five).

FIGURE 1.15   Maybole Collegiate Church.

The church at Maybole is a rectangle of about 16 by 5.5 metres, the eastern part of which is divided into bays by buttresses, and there is a barrel-vaulted sacristy on the north side.[41] The nave apparently occupied less than half the structure, and the position of the screen which separated it from the choir is probably indicated by small lancet windows to the west of the mid-point of the side walls. Internally there is a tomb recess in the north wall, close to the site of the high altar, which was presumably for the founder and which bears some similarities with tomb recesses in the nave of Whithorn Cathedral. In this position a tomb could also serve as an Easter Sepulchre or Tomb of Christ, in which the consecrated host was ceremonially entombed together with a crucifix between Maundy Thursday and Easter Sunday; such supplementary use was felt to confer benefits on the soul of the tomb's occupant.[42]

The windows around the high altar, in the east wall and at the east end of the south wall, have reticulated tracery, and illustrate a revival of types of ultimately English origin which were no longer current there but which were to enjoy a renewed vogue in Scotland. Revival of earlier forms can also be seen in the main doorway, and the tomb recess in the north wall, which have dogtooth mouldings of essentially thirteenth-century type. Early moulding types were to enjoy a limited revived fashion in many parts of Scotland in the later Middle Ages, although nowhere more than in the west of the country; however, if these mouldings are a primary feature at Maybole, they represent a particularly early example of such revival.

Another church likely to be of this period is at Temple, in Midlothian (see Figure 1.16).[43] The ecclesiastical history of this site, earlier known as Balantradoch, began in the reign of David I, when the main Scottish house of the Knights Templars was founded here, and from their presence the site took its later name. It is possible that part of their domestic buildings underlies the modern manse. At the suppression of the Templars in about 1309 the site passed to the Knights Hospitallers, with all other Templar properties. But at some date before 1426 the church became parochial, with both the parsonage and vicarage appropriated to the Hospitallers, and it remained in use until a new church was built in 1832.

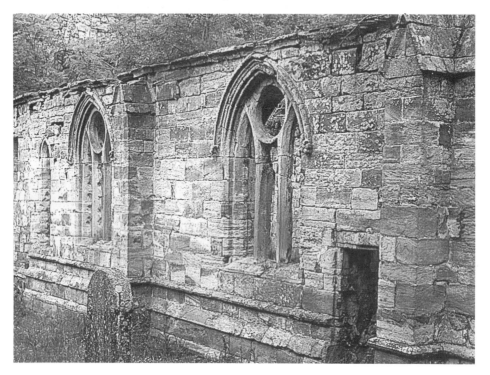

FIGURE 1.16   Temple Church, the south flank.

The roofless shell of the church is of rectangular plan, though this could represent a remodelled fragment of a larger structure because its western end has been rebuilt since the Reformation. The most highly finished parts now surviving are the east end and the south flank, which are of ashlar above a well-proportioned base course, and which have single-stage buttresses capped by gablets. The windows are the finest feature, and have unusually complex arch mouldings for a church of such modest scale. The east window has tracery of circlets within intersecting arcs, while those on the south flank have a central circlet between the two side lights, with no arch to the central light. There are no precise parallels for the south windows, but the east window is related to examples at a group of churches to be discussed below, which includes Elgin, Fortrose and Tain (see Figures 1.37, 1.38 and 1.40). Such comparisons indicate a date around the last decades of the fourteenth century. This would suggest that the church was partly rebuilt by the Hospitallers, either for their own use or to adapt the church for parochial worship.

In this context reference must also be made to the tower of Inverkeithing Parish Church in Fife,[44] a much-modified four-storeyed structure, with a polygonal stair turret at its south-east angle (see Figure 1.17). A corbelled parapet was constructed above it in the fifteenth or sixteenth centuries; a new door was slapped through its west face when the rest of the church was rebuilt by James Gillespie Graham after a fire in 1825; and a spire was placed on it in 1835, which was augmented by ungainly lucarnes for clock faces in 1883. The sturdy two-stage buttresses with chamfered angles to the upper stage, and the belfry windows with three or four circlets within a larger circlet, suggest a date in the late fourteenth century for the original structure.

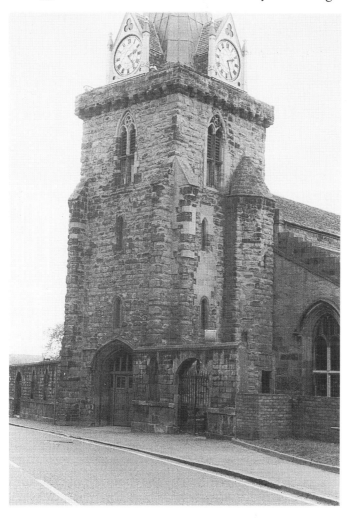

FIGURE 1.17   Inverkeithing Church, the west tower.

THE FIRST CAMPAIGN OF REBUILDING MELROSE ABBEY

The minor church-building operations considered so far are valuable indicators of increasing activity at this period, but to understand the shift in architectural attitudes that was beginning to take place we must look to a number of major structures. Several of the most creative building campaigns started at this seminally important phase in the history of Scottish late Gothic architecture were necessitated by military activities. One of these was the invasion led by Richard II and the Duke of Lancaster in 1385, which ravaged the Borders and Lothian before being driven back to England by the Scottish scorched earth policy. The religious differences resulting from the great schism in the church meant there was even less compunction in attacking church property than in earlier stages of the wars with England. The abbey churches of Melrose and Dryburgh among others were thus yet again devastated, as was the burgh church of St Giles in Edinburgh. At all of these rebuilding soon followed, the most ambitious and influential campaign being at Melrose, where work started soon after the English attack, but was still only partly complete by the Reformation.[45] In the protracted course of rebuilding Melrose there were two major changes of design which, within the same building, provide us with an invaluable barometer of the shifting architectural climate of their time.

Melrose was probably under construction by 1389, when Richard II granted in compensation a reduction of 2s. on the customs payable on wool sent by the abbey to Berwick-on-Tweed, and in 1398 arrangements were made for paying feudal casualties to the new work (see Figure 1.18).[46] As first started, the new abbey church is a fascinating amalgam of the traditional and the contemporary, which says much about the ambivalence in architectural attitudes at this period. There may be an adherence to the early austere principles of the Cistercian order in the relatively low central tower, but it is in the plan that loyalty to earlier ideas is most evident, since excavation in 1923 showed that the church as laid out after 1385 was essentially a larger version of the original building (see Figure 3.14e). Like the first church it has a rectangular presbytery – albeit more elongated than previously – and three rectangular chapels on the east side of each transept, with the monastic choir in the eastern bays of the nave. Also as in the original plan, the chapels flanking the presbytery project further east than the others, an echelon arrangement possibly inspired by the two first stone-built phases of the twelfth-century church at the Cistercian house of Fountains in Yorkshire.

A church that is still a variant on the classic 'Bernardine' Cistercian plan is a little unexpected so late as the 1380s. It is true that the Scottish Cistercians were rather conservative in such matters, because the last house of the order – founded at Sweetheart in 1273 – still had the characteristic Cistercian plan. Nevertheless, of the other Scottish churches of the order whose plans we know, Kinloss and Newbattle already had more complex layouts.[47] Those churches reflected a movement within the order towards planning which allowed more altars to be housed without indulging in the more elaborate plan types developed in the wider world; but at Melrose there was still to be none of that.

Although the plan must have been a matter of deliberate choice, construction of the new church at Melrose was also conditioned by the buildings already on the site. The north aisle, for example, is narrower than its southern counterpart, presumably because the new north arcade was kept to the line of the original foundations, while northward expansion was limited by the cloister on that side (see Figure 3.15). It is also likely that the earlier church was only progressively demolished a little ahead of the new work. The old west front still stands to a height of about one metre, showing that the new nave, which was to have extended two bays further westwards, never was completed. The incompleteness of the nave may have been relatively easy to cope with at Melrose because in the traditional Cistercian plan the western bays of the nave housed the choir of the *conversi*, the illiterate lay brethren responsible for the physical work of the community. Although there are references to *conversi* as late as 1389, by the fourteenth century it is unlikely they could be recruited in any numbers, and there was thus a reduced urgency for building this part. Nevertheless, there is evidence that lay folk came to have rights of worship in the church, and it is not known where they were accommodated if not in the western bays of the nave.

The failure to complete the church suggests it was planned on such a grand scale, and with so high a level of architectural enrichment, that the community simply could not afford it. But that was in the future and the first campaign was initiated with the highest aspirations and with great vigour. This phase included the walls of the presbytery, together with parts of the transepts; on the evidence of the continuity of base types and of foliate capital types from the transepts to the piers of the first three bays of the western limb, it also seems that it extended to the arcades of the monastic choir (see Figure 3.16). The first phase thus embraced the shell of those areas of the church which were essential for the monks' daily services: the presbytery and the monastic choir. Also as part of this campaign the tracery must have been built into some of the windows, including those in the east and south sides of the presbytery, the north presbytery clearstorey, two of the south transept chapels and the eastern clearstoreys of the two transepts. Once that had been done, there was evidently a change of master mason, and the second phase of works will be considered in a later part of this chapter.

The architectural evidence suggests the mason of the first phase of the rebuilding was sent from England, (see Figure 1.18), at a period when this part of Scotland was still under English control – the abbey being afforded the special protection of Henry IV even after the deposition of Richard II in 1399. It has been suggested by one writer that this mason could have been John Lewyn, who has already been referred to at Roxburgh,[48] though the evidence is insufficient to regard this as more than a possibility. It is the window tracery which most clearly marks out the first work at Melrose from preceding Scottish buildings. In its use of a grid of strong vertical and horizontal lines it is in step with contemporary English Perpendicular designs, which had been developed under the aegis of the royal works since the earlier years of the fourteenth century, and which were to remain current in England up to the end of the Middle Ages.[49]

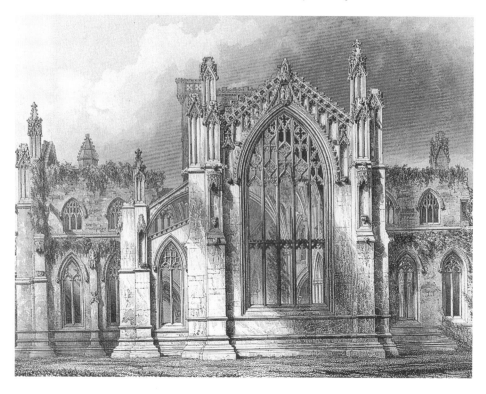

FIGURE 1.18   Melrose Abbey, east end.

Used in so important a building it might have been expected that tracery of this radically new type in Scotland would be highly influential; but in fact it was to have very little following. In the chapel of St John on the north side of the crossing at St Giles in Edinburgh, of about 1395, there is an area of walling which has a rather English panelled treatment, and we may suspect the tracery above it was similarly Perpendicular in its detailing. But among the few other buildings in which such tracery was definitely installed at this period were chapels adjacent to Carnwath Church in Lanarkshire and Corstorphine Church on the outskirts of Edinburgh (see Figures 1.19 and 5.7). The former was probably built in advance of the foundation of a college there by the Somerville family in the 1420s, while the south chapel at Corstorphine may date from about 1425 (see p. 150). Yet at both Carnwath and Corstorphine the English elements were little more than a decorative extra, and both chapels were covered by characteristically Scottish pointed barrel vaults with either parallel or diagonal ribs. The general rejection of Perpendicular tracery in Scotland was probably symptomatic of a growing distaste for all things English, although lack of familiarity with the rationale behind it must also have been a factor at buildings where English masons were not actually in charge of the work.

At Melrose it has long been suspected that a mason from eastern England was responsible for the first phase of works. Most of the first tracery designs are permutations on standard Perpendicular types, but the east window – with its

FIGURE 1.19   Carnwath Collegiate Church.

unbroken verticals, its triangular or flat light-heads and the prominent diamond shapes in the tracery field – is a remarkable essay. The hard angularity of this window finds some reflection in a roughly contemporary group of churches centred on St Nicholas at King's Lynn, in Norfolk, showing that such ideas were in circulation in eastern England at this time.[50] However, the diamond-shaped forms probably show greater kinship with details in the west window of St Mary's Church at Beverley, in the East Riding of Yorkshire, which dates from about 1400, having survived a rebuilding operation in 1520. Inside Melrose there is perhaps also something of the feeling of another Beverley church in the heavily plastic modelling of the arcade piers. Both the basically eight-lobed section of these piers and the deeply moulded capitals of some may show parallels with those built some decades earlier in the nave of the minster there, although Melrose's elaborately corbelled-out vaulting shafts towards the central spaces are more complex.

Eastern English influences are also apparent in external detailing such as the deeply modelled tabernacle work across the gables of the presbytery and south transept. Parallels might be drawn with the Lady Chapel at Ely Cathedral, which was completed by 1353. But, again, there are perhaps even closer analogies with work in the East Riding – such as the east gable of the choir of the collegiate church of Howden, started around the 1320s, although at Howden the window tracery, being earlier, was curvilinear rather than Perpendicular.[51] At both Howden and Melrose the tabernacle work and blind tracery extends to the buttresses and pinnacles, and is combined with a decorative secondary arch through the gable above the window arch. The east Yorkshire approach to two-storeyed internal design represented at Howden could also have influenced Melrose in the elevation of the aisled section of the presbytery

FIGURE 1.20   Melrose Abbey, the presbytery.

(see Figure 1.20). At both there are rear-arches and traceried balustrades on the inner plane of the wall, though Melrose is more enriched, with its inner skin of skeletal tracery.

Without providing precise prototypes for Melrose, these eastern English buildings offer a possible ambience within which the first Melrose mason could have received his training. But there are few buildings which can prepare one for the full range of delights at Melrose. The way in which the finely jointed pink and yellow polished ashlar creates a foil for the extraordinary range of carved decoration is particularly memorable, as is the elegant restraint of details such as those buttress tabernacles which are sunk within deep rectangular recesses.

Another fine feature of the first campaign at Melrose is the stone vaulting with which it was covered throughout, and which shows how lavishly funded was this stage of the work. The strangest of the various types was that over the north presbytery chapel which, on the evidence of the wall ribs, must have been almost completely flat. Although flat vaults can be found over small spaces, where the distances to be bridged meant that the stones were little more than lintels, larger flat vaults usually had to be supported by flying ribs, or were of a more domed profile than can have been the case at Melrose.

THE EARLY DEVELOPMENT OF THE CROSS-RIBBED POINTED BARREL VAULT

The most significant vault from this first campaign at Melrose is that over the presbytery, of which only the eastern bay survives. It is likely the design of this vault was modified during construction because, except for those which are part of the wall ribs, the carved bosses at the intersections of the ribs seem to have been adapted for use in their present positions (see Figure 1.20). Usually the blocks from which bosses are carved incorporate the springings of the ribs which spread out around them, but in the presbytery at Melrose the edges of the bosses are rather crudely cut at angles which allow the ribs simply to abut against them. The most striking feature of this vault, however, is that it is basically of tunnel section, having only shallow lateral intersections with the depressed arches framing the clearstorey windows. In this it shows some kinship with the vaulting over the upper hall at Dundonald Castle discussed above (see Figure 1.2). At Melrose, however, the patterning created by the ribs is very much more decorative. The lines of the basic tierceron configuration are projected across the bay to create a complex sequence of intersections which also extended across the adjacent bays, thus emphasising the unity of the vault as a whole rather than the individuality of the bays.

Although there are no precise parallels for this vault, it shows a similar approach to design as in the net-vaults of a number of churches in the English West Country. Starting in about 1298 at Bristol Cathedral, they attained a high point in the vault over Gloucester Cathedral choir, which was completed by about 1357.[52] At this stage such vaults represented a particularly English approach to vault design, though they were soon to be developed further in other parts of Europe. Rather surprisingly for an otherwise highly accomplished building, however, the Melrose vault offers only a pale reflection of such high achievements. Even compared with a less ambitious essay like that over the choir of Nantwich Church in Cheshire, which was ready for consecration in 1405 but which may have been started well before, the Melrose vault has a faltering quality. Significantly, it was never copied and even at Melrose more orthodox tierceron vaulting was preferred for the later parts. Nevertheless – like that over the hall at Dundonald – Melrose's presbytery vault has an important place in the development of Scottish ribbed tunnel vaults.

An approximately contemporary experiment in vaulting was made over the aisles of the three western bays of the choir and over the original south transept at St Giles' Church in Edinburgh (see Figure 1.21). There, the tunnel section of the vault, with a simple cross pattern of diagonal ribs in each bay, is made even more obvious by the absence of arched wall ribs, and it is only the window or arcade arch to each side

FIGURE 1.21   Edinburgh St Giles' Church, the vaulting over the north choir aisle.

which creates even a minimal sense of lateral intersection. What we have at St Giles, therefore, is the Scottish late medieval cross-ribbed tunnel vault in an almost fully developed state. The precise date of the St Giles' vault is uncertain, though it is likely to post-date Richard II's attack of 1385, but to predate a first unsuccessful attempt by the burgh to establish a college in the choir in 1419.

THE EARLY STAGES OF CONTINENTAL INFLUENCE ON SCOTTISH ARCHITECTURE

If the first phase of rebuilding at Melrose demonstrates renewed English influence on one Scottish building, at a number of other operations started around this time there is reason to think that stimuli from further afield were beginning to have an impact. One of the first of these operations was at St Andrews Cathedral, following a fire recorded by Bower in 1378, and referred to in Wyntoun's *Chronicle*, as well as in papal correspondence and the Exchequer Rolls.[53] We know that several of the nave arcade piers had to be rebuilt, presumably with the superstructure they carried, together with the upper parts of the west front. The rebuilding was started virtually immediately, because Robert II paid for two masons between 1381 and 1384. The earliest work may have been within the eastern limb (see Figure 2.3), but repair of the nave was sufficiently advanced for the roof to be replaced during the priorate of James Bisset (1393–1416).

The sub-bases of the replaced nave arcade piers, which are all that survives of them, hint at work of considerable modernity for their time in the way they have a continuous horizontal ogee moulding of late Gothic type, and even more in the way they are elongated towards the central space as if to carry wall shafts which articulated the bays through their full height. But the most important key to the character of the new work is the window design at mid-height of the west front which, allowing for distortion through compression of the window arches, appears to have had tracery consisting of a triplet of large cusped circlets (see Figure 1.22). Despite previously having been a relatively common tracery type in England, as in the aisles of the Angel Choir at Lincoln Cathedral started in 1256, such tracery had generally been abandoned south of the Border by the later thirteenth century. Its use at St Andrews, therefore, could point to a revival of well-established but out-moded types, and there certainly were to be cases of such revival from the later fourteenth century onwards – as at Maybole.

However, the way the design is handled at St Andrews is rather un-English, particularly in the stilting of the main arch and tracery field above the light heads; such treatment was far more characteristic of French window design. In this connection it should also be remembered that tracery with triplets of circlets had itself first been a French development of the years around 1230,[54] and that it continued in use there considerably longer than in England – as in the apse clearstorey of Nevers Cathedral of around 1331.

Considering the strengthened political links which were being forged with France around this time, it is tempting to see this as an example of Scottish patrons encouraging their masons to look beyond England to France for their ideas, and we do know that one mason of French birth did some work at St Andrews (see p. 43).

FIGURE 1.22   St Andrews Cathedral, the west front.

In further support of this it should be remembered that both of the two bishops likely
to have witnessed the partial rebuilding of the west front had stronger ties with France
than with England. Bishop William Landallis's election to the diocese in 1342 had
been supported before the Pope by Philip VI of France,[55] while Bishop Walter Trail,
who was elected in 1385, had been a student at the universities of Paris and Orleans.[56]
Of course, the tentative evidence for a realignment of Scottish architectural attitudes
provided by St Andrews can be no more than a straw in the wind. Yet, considered
along with the purchase of Bruce's tomb in Paris in 1329, it forms part of an
accumulating body of evidence to which we shall shortly have to give further
consideration in connection with the second phase of Melrose.

Nevertheless, a note of caution must be sounded here. In considering possible
French borrowings for Scottish buildings in the fourteenth century it must be

reiterated that the outbreak of the Hundred Years War in 1337 meant church building had been disrupted as much in France as in Scotland, and there were thus relatively few immediately contemporary French buildings for Scottish masons to see. It is also true that, for some time to come, the French architectural repertoire was not so very different from that of other parts of north-western mainland Europe. It can therefore be difficult to differentiate between ideas brought from France and those which could have been inspired from elsewhere at this time, particularly when those ideas have undergone reinterpretation by Scottish masons.

Further light on the ferment of ideas emerging in Scotland in these decades is afforded by the nave of Dunkeld Cathedral (see Figure 1.23). Abbot Alexander Myln tells us this part of the structure was started on 27 April 1406 by Bishop Robert Cardeny,[57] who was eventually buried below the canopied tomb he provided for himself in the chapel of St Ninian at the east end of the south aisle. Cardeny was able to complete the work as far as the triforium stage before his death in 1437, and the

FIGURE 1.23   Dunkeld Cathedral, the nave from the east.

work was eventually completed and dedicated by Bishop Thomas Lauder in 1464. The information provided by Myln can be supplemented from analysis of changes in moulding types, and there is no reason to doubt his accuracy in this.

The plan of the new seven-bay nave, with an aisle down each flank, was partly conditioned by the way the eastern walls of the aisles had been built during the mid- and later thirteenth-century operation which raised the choir (see Figure 1.24b). Yet in other respects Cardeny presumably had a free hand and, despite his cathedral being small by European standards, he evidently had high ambitions for it. There are signs, however, that economies were necessary, and the corbels and vault springings suggest stone vaulting was planned in the south aisle but only timber vaulting in its northern counterpart. There was certainly no more than a timber roof above the main space, although this is only to be expected in any but the most ambitious operations.

Cardeny's hopes of making a grand architectural impression are most clear in the internal elevation. Its three completely distinct storeys, arranged with a strongly horizontal emphasis which creates something of the appearance of an aqueduct, were perhaps a little old-fashioned by this date – although for many Scottish patrons the three-storeyed elevation was to be the *sine qua non* of a major church up to the end of the Middle Ages. Even more seemingly old-fashioned were the subdivided

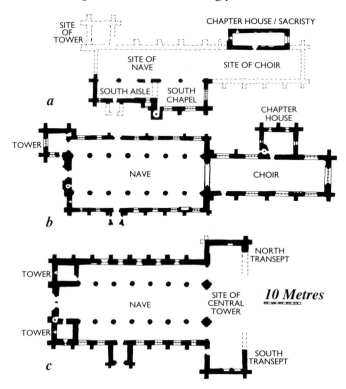

FIGURE 1.24   Plans of cathedrals: a. Fortrose Cathedral; b. Dunkeld Cathedral; c. Aberdeen Cathedral.

semi-circular arches of the triforium stage which, together with the cylindrical piers of the arcades, might almost invite comparison with Romanesque work at such as Dunfermline Abbey. But it would be wrong to regard the design of Dunkeld as representing a form of Romanesque revival. Round arches were beginning to enjoy a revived vogue, as may be seen from the processional doorway from the east cloister walk into the north aisle at Melrose. Close inspection of Dunkeld also shows that Cardeny's mason was seeking inspiration from contemporary work. In particular, the arcade bases are of clearly late Gothic type in their deep profile and in the marked separation of circular base from polygonal sub-base.

The same is equally true of a related fragment at St Andrews Cathedral, which was the result of yet another misfortune at that church (see Figure 1.25). There, a semi-circular respond in the south transept, which was rebuilt following the collapse of the south transept gable in 1409,[58] is of a form analogous to the Dunkeld arcade,

FIGURE 1.25   St Andrews Cathedral, the south transept arcade respond.

FIGURE 1.26   St Machar Cathedral, Aberdeen, the south-west crossing pier.

and was presumably part of an arcade of cylindrical piers. Together, the piers at Dunkeld and the respond at St Andrews clearly show that Scottish masons were developing an interest in such piers at this time.

It will also be remembered that the second Bishop Kininmund (1355–80) had started building cylindrical piers in the nave of Aberdeen Cathedral (see p. 24 and Figure 2.11). A difficulty in understanding the chronology of what remains of Aberdeen, however, is that the two western piers of the central tower – now embodied in the nave east wall – are different from the others (see Figure 1.26). They are of freestone and in the form of massive cylinders with four attached smaller half-cylinders towards the cardinal directions; they also have finely carved capitals rather than the simplified mouldings of the other piers. It cannot be ruled out that they were inserted by Henry Lichton (1422–40) when he started the central tower and rebuilt the north transept, in which he was eventually buried. But on balance it is more likely they represent a completion by Kininmund of Chene's work on the choir, and thus slightly predate the start of work on his granite cylindrical nave arcade piers, which must therefore date from well into the third quarter of the fourteenth century.

Since cylindrical piers were almost unknown in major English churches of the later Middle Ages, it is unlikely it was from there that the idea was taken. On the Continent, however, there had been a renewed interest in cylindrical piers in a number of areas, including France, Germany and the Low Countries, although it was in the last of those that piers most like those of Dunkeld, St Andrews and Aberdeen were common.

The architectural revival first centred on the duchy of Brabant, and signalled by the new choir of St Rombout's Church at Mechelen in 1342, led to the widespread use of such piers across the Low Countries.[59] In some of those churches the rather heavy proportions of the piers, together with the broad, flat arch soffits, come quite close in spirit to the Scottish examples. By comparison, in other parts of Europe the proportions of cylindrical piers tend to be more attenuated, and there is often a subtle interpenetration of piers and arches which is alien to what we find in Scotland – as at Caudebec-en-Caux in Normandy, started in about 1426.[60] In the Netherlands, examples with proportions closer to those at Dunkeld and Aberdeen are to be seen in the choir of St Bavo at Haarlem in the county of Holland, started not long before 1400, or at Sts Peter and Paul at Brouwershaven in Zeeland, where the choir was started at about the same time as Dunkeld.[61] The case for suspecting Netherlandish borrowings is reinforced by the way the more complex Aberdeen crossing piers are also of a type found more often in the Low Countries than elsewhere. Comparisons may be made, for example, with the crossing piers of St Gudule in Brussels. It might be added that the foliage carving of some of the Aberdeen crossing capitals could have been inspired by examples across the North Sea, particularly in the way some of the rather bulbous leaves are pressed closely up to the abacus, leaving the bell relatively bare.

In further support of the derivation of the Scottish architectural details from the Low Countries we must remember that trade with that area was well established by the time Dunkeld and Aberdeen were started. There is also evidence of the beginnings of that appreciation of Netherlandish art which soon led to the importing of considerable quantities of church furnishing, of which the Van der Goes altarpiece for Trinity College is the best-known surviving example.[62] When the monks of Melrose eventually went to law in 1441, for example, they said they had ordered their choir stalls many years earlier from the master of the Bruges carpenters' guild, Cornelius van Aeltre.[63] It is also significant that, as part of the eventual settlement, Cornelius was prepared to come to Melrose to fit the stalls, suggesting that such an international expedition for a craftsman was not out of the ordinary.

Nevertheless, the possible artistic debt of the arcade piers of Dunkeld and Aberdeen to the Low Countries should not be overstated without supporting evidence, since it could hardly be claimed that they look like those in Netherlandish churches except at a rather superficial level. All we can say is that it is likely it was some external stimulus which led to the adoption of this pier type, and the closest parallels are to be found in the Low Countries. But the case for foreign influences is strengthened when we look at the elegantly flowing tracery forms in the windows of Dunkeld. It could be argued that the inspiration for their design came from England, where flowing tracery had been first developed in the early fourteenth century; the reticulated tracery at Maybole was almost certainly ultimately English in origin, and there is also a window with reticulated tracery at Dunkeld. But the fashion for tracery with flowing patterns had passed in England, whereas it was being developed with new enthusiasm in continental Europe. Beyond this, several of the designs used at Dunkeld were of a type which was more common in Europe than it had been in England. Particular note should be taken of the frequent use of 'spherical' figures, that is, polygonal figures with curved sides. If we are to accept the likelihood of foreign influence being behind these designs, as was earlier suggested at St Andrews, it is again possible that the germ of the idea came from the bishop. Cardeny had spent some years in Paris,[64] graduating there in 1381, and he would probably also have known the Low Countries, since many people chose to travel to and from France through that area rather than running the risks of the channel ports.

The problem at both St Andrews and Dunkeld, however, is that, although we may suspect that foreign ideas had influenced native masons, and we also know that the patrons of the work had seen and worshipped in some of the buildings which could have provided these stimuli, we cannot see how the ideas could have been transferred. But when we return to the second phase of works at Melrose we find a documented case where it is almost certain that the new ideas were imported by the master mason himself.

THE WORK OF JOHN MOROW

As so often at this period, the change between the first and second phase work at Melrose is most obvious in the window tracery, and it is the change between the windows of the presbytery and south transept gable walls that is most striking (see Figures 1.18 and 1.27). These two gable walls are closely similar compositions in their lavish tabernacle work across the triangle of the gable and up the buttresses, and in the dominance of a large window. The two must certainly have been built to the same mason's design. Yet the contrast between the rectilinear grid of tracery of the east window and the flowing pattern of the south window could hardly be greater, and it is evident that a second mason must have inserted the south window. It is equally clear that a number of other windows had been left unfilled by the first mason, including that in the north wall of the presbytery and those in a number of the transept chapels. More than one mason may have contributed to the design of these secondary windows, since they show some variety, though it is likely a single master mason was in overall charge.

The most ambitious essays in this flowing tracery were those in the five-light window of the south transept and in the four-light window on the north side of the

presbytery. The latter has sinuously curvilinear foiled figures, which suggest comparison with windows in the collegiate church of Eu in Normandy, as rebuilt after a
fire in 1426, for example. The subsidiary tracery in the south transept, which is
contained within sub-arches to each side of the central light, is similarly sinuous. Yet
in general these tracery designs are relatively restrained, with some 'spherical'
figures, as at Dunkeld. This approach to tracery design shows parallels with what is
also seen in a number of areas of north-western mainland Europe at this time. In
many European buildings there is the same evidence of ambivalence between the
cool restraint of the prestigious French Rayonnant tradition on the one hand, and
the more extravagant freedoms encouraged by ogee curves on the other. (In France
itself, however, the latter was eventually to lead to the almost excessive liberty of
the Flamboyant.)

The parallels with contemporary European tracery make it even less likely than at
Dunkeld that the designer of this phase of works at Melrose was simply reviving
outmoded English types. But the supreme importance of the second phase of Melrose
for our understanding of Scottish late Gothic is that we know there was a French-born
mason in charge. We know this from two inscriptions inserted secondarily in the west
wall of the south transept (see Figure 1.28). One of these, which is simply cut into
the coursed ashlar around the lintel of the stair turret doorway refers to 'Johne
Morvo'. The second inscription, on an inset tablet, says this John Morow was a mason
who had been born in Paris. We are also told that he was responsible for masonwork
at St Andrews, Glasgow, Paisley, Nithsdale and Galloway.[65] We shall return later to
discuss how far his work can be identified in those other places; but for the moment
we must consider the implications of a French-born mason being responsible for the
change of architectural direction at Melrose.[66]

This change of personnel involved the insertion of high-quality European work
into a building of previously English character. But apart from the insertion of
tracery, it seems the scope of Morow's work at Melrose was limited. On the one
hand, the shell of the presbytery, much of the transepts and the arcades of the
monastic choir must have been largely complete by the time he arrived; on the other
hand, the fine tierceron vault of the transept was probably built only after he had
left. That vault bears the arms of Abbot Andrew Hunter (1444–71), whose arms are
also in another part of the building which plainly post-dates the period of Morow's
involvement. Possibly the only structural addition to the church made by Morow
was the commencement of a row of chapels against the south aisle (see Figures 3.14e
and 3.15).

It had become a major problem in Cistercian houses of traditional plan-type to
provide sufficient chapels without resorting to complications of planning regarded as
unacceptable by the order's earlier leaders. Additional space was also needed for the
lay folk who wished to enjoy the previously forbidden privilege of burial with the
Cistercians which, of course, carried financial advantages for the abbey.[67] A solution
adopted at several European houses about this time was to add a rank of chapels against
the nave aisle on the side away from the cloister, just as at Melrose. This was done,
among other examples, at Fontfroide in southern France, at the turn of the fourteenth

FIGURE 1.27 (*above*)   Melrose Abbey, the south transept.

FIGURE 1.28 (*left*)   Melrose Abbey, the secondarily inserted inscription around the head of the doorway in the south transept.

FIGURE 1.29 (*right*)   Melrose Abbey, the window tracery of the first nave chapel west of the south transept.

and fifteenth centuries, and at Maulbronn in Germany, in about 1420. (Although there was a Scottish precedent for ranks of chapels along the nave, in the post-1270 work at Elgin, differences of approach make it unlikely the work there was the stimulus for Melrose (see Figure 2.7).)

How far the idea of the additional chapels at Melrose originated with Morow himself, or how far it was the idea of the community, we cannot know. The attendance of representatives of all houses at the General Chapter at Cîteaux was one way for outlying houses to find out about what was happening elsewhere, and it could even have been through such contacts that the abbey had secured Morow's services in the first place. It is also significant that enough was known at Melrose about particular Cistercian houses on the Continent for the choir stalls at Ter Duinen and Thosan to be specified as the models for the new stalls which were commissioned in Bruges, through this knowledge could also have come through Melrose's long-established trade links with Flanders and the surrounding areas.

Whatever the origins of the idea for the chapels, however, Morow must have carried out the preliminary work on several of them, though it seems he was responsible for the windows in only the two next to the transept. It also seems he constructed the vaulting over only the eastern of those, which is of basically quadri-partite type, with a ring of lierne ribs around the crown that may have been like the ridge ribs in having suspended cusping; this was a type of vaulting which was to become relatively common in France, at such as the castle chapel at Thouars in the west of the country. But it is the tracery of these two chapels which best demonstrates the finesse Morow brought to his work; and it is the repetition of one of the tracery types which makes his work most clearly identifiable elsewhere. The tracery in the chapel west of the transept (see Figure 1.29) is a particularly valuable pointer to Morow's personal style, since it is of a design known to have been used in only two other churches: in the north nave aisle at Paisley Abbey (see Figure 1.30) and in the choir of Lincluden Collegiate Church, on the edge of Dumfries (see Figure 1.31).

FIGURE 1.30   Paisley Abbey, the window tracery in the two north nave aisle bays west of the transept.

FIGURE 1.31   Lincluden Collegiate Church, the south flank of the choir.

Significantly, both of those are probably included in the list of his works, Paisley under its own name and Lincluden as 'Nyddysdayll' (Nithsdale), the valley in which it is situated. Equally significantly, at all of these churches the windows in question are framed by similar highly unusual mouldings, the main feature of which is a wide segmental hollow.

This three-light window design – used with only very slight variations at Melrose, Lincluden and Paisley – has curved daggers rising around a spherical triangle at the head of the central light, and a second spherical triangle at the apex of the window. The other windows at Lincluden give us a more complete idea of the range of tracery design of which Morow was capable, and the south transept window there – which evidently had a triplet of spherical squares within a spherical triangle as its main motif – was also used at Paisley, though there some of the lesser tracery has been lost. It may be mentioned that the windows in this group of churches also show some links with those at Dunkeld, and – depending on how the evidence is interpreted – it is possible that one of the types seen there was also used at Lincluden in modified form.

As has been said, a feature of these windows is a balance between flowing forms and 'spherical' figures, and this is also a characteristic of some of the few windows known to have been designed in France in the rather unproductive period at the turn of the fourteenth century. Those of the chapels added along the flanks of Amiens Cathedral nave by Cardinal de la Grange in about 1375, for example, show a related approach, albeit on a much more expansive scale. The same is true of some of the tracery types used for the great west front screen at Rouen Cathedral, of around 1386–7. It could have been such works that Morow was reflecting, though it must be reiterated that similar forms were also to be found elsewhere. Some Low Countries buildings of the later fourteenth century, including the Halle aux Serges in Bruges, reveal a kindred spirit of tracery design, as do a number of German churches, such as the choir of the Heiligkreuzkirche at Schwäbisch Gmünd. This is said not to minimise the French origins of Morow's work, but to show that it must be understood within the larger context of a European development in which Scotland was now playing its own limited part.

At each of Morow's works the weight of evidence points to dates around the last years of the fourteenth and the early decades of the fifteenth century for his contribution. At Melrose it clearly post-dates the first phase of building which followed the destruction of 1385, and equally clearly predates the contribution of Abbot Hunter between 1444 and 1471. Beyond this, we know his work at Melrose post-dates at least the start of work on Lincluden and Paisley for those churches to be included on the list he gave there. The dating of Paisley is particularly difficult, since the relevant work is largely confined to the three eastern bays of the north nave aisle, and is part of a complex sequence of building operations dating variously from the thirteenth, fourteenth and fifteenth centuries (see Figure 3.14d).[68] However, we know work was in progress on some part of the church in 1389, since Robert II then made a contribution towards the cost of glazing.[69] It is tempting to see that as part of a building campaign which then moved on to the north aisle, since Abbot Lithgow appears to have chosen a position in the vicinity of the north porch as his future burial place in 1433, suggesting that he may have had a part in the rebuilding of this side of the church.[70]

Lincluden's date is the most problematic of the group. The college had been founded within a suppressed Benedictine nunnery in 1389 by the third Earl of Douglas,[71] and it is certainly possible he started work on it before his death in 1400. However, the person whose tomb occupies the prominent position usually taken by the founder is Princess Margaret, wife of the fourth Earl of Douglas and daughter of Robert III, who died in about 1451 (see Figure 1.33). She augmented the original foundation,[72] and it is the connections of herself and her husband which are displayed in the heraldry around the choir walls.[73] The masonry suggests construction of her tomb started after the lower walls of the chapel's eastern limb had been laid out, perhaps showing that she revived a project which had been languishing. Certainly, papal correspondence in 1406 refers to the chapel as unfinished,[74] and it is likely that construction of the church was protracted and never fully completed.

Since Morow's contribution to Melrose was so limited by what had already been built, it is the choir and south transept of Lincluden that offer the fullest picture of his abilities (see Figure 1.32). Its choir is an aisle-less rectangular structure of three bays, constructed of red sandstone ashlar which rivals that of Melrose in quality (see Figure 5.1k). It was covered by tierceron vaulting with a second vault of ribbed barrel type above. This shows a rare concern for completely fire-proof construction, and suggests the upper floor was put to some specialised use, such as a treasury. The choir was separated from the rest of the church by a stone screen pierced by a single door, and surmounted by a loft reached from a stair at the east end of the south aisle (see Figure 1.33). The internal lower walls of the prebendaries' choir, in the western bay of the eastern limb, were plain, to accommodate their canopied timber stalls, two of which survive in the National Museum of Scotland.

FIGURE 1.32 (*left*)   Lincluden Collegiate Church, the screen at the west end of the choir, looking into the choir.

FIGURE 1.33 (*right*)   Lincluden Collegiate Church, the interior of the choir.

The two eastern bays of Lincluden provide a display of architectural enrichment at its finest. On the north side is Princess Margaret's tomb, with a miniature arcade containing shields along the tomb chest; the canopy has a cusped arch enclosed first by an ogee containing arch, and then by a square frame decorated with arcading along the upper part. West of the tomb is the sacristy doorway, with a continuous band of foliage carving between two orders of engaged shafts; within the arch is a tympanum carved with shields and foliage. Facing these, on the south wall of the presbytery, are the piscina and sedilia, which echo on a smaller scale the essentially architectural forms of the tomb. Throughout the design of all these details there is a unified repertoire of forms and, despite the profusion of ornament, there is an extraordinary sense of one high-calibre creative mind having stamped his authority on the whole.

Much of the carved detail is sadly weathered, but still deserves scrutiny. Of special interest are some corbels with prophets carrying scrolls, which would once have been carved or painted with their key prophecies (see Figure 1.34). This was a relatively widespread motif in European sculpture and painting, but rather less common in Scotland. Similar corbels are, however, also to be seen at Melrose and, though not necessarily the work of the same sculptor, this suggests they were one of Morow's favoured motifs (see Figure 1.35). If they are indeed a pointer to his authorship, it is worth noting that one of the few other places where they are seen in Scotland is

FIGURE 1.34 (*above, left*)   Lincluden Collegiate Church, a prophet corbel.
FIGURE 1.35 (*above, right*)   Melrose Abbey, a prophet corbel.
FIGURE 1.36 (*centre*)   Glasgow Cathedral, a prophet corbel, possibly from the western towers.

Glasgow Cathedral, which was also included by Morow on his list of works (see Figure 1.36).

Unfortunately, at Glasgow the two corbels of this type are *ex-situ* fragments, but they are said to have been preserved from the demolition of the western towers,[75] raising the possibility that it was on one of them that Morow worked (see Figure 2.5). A connection between Lincluden and Glasgow is provided by John Cameron, who was provost of the former from 1425, and bishop of the latter between 1426 and 1446. There is also a tradition that Cameron was involved in building the south-west tower at Glasgow and, although another tradition links the work with his predecessor Bishop Lauder,[76] both could be right since construction was probably protracted. A date in the early fifteenth century for the Glasgow corbels finds additional support in the mason's mark carved on them, which is a cross saltire from which a half arrow emerges. A similar, if more crudely cut, mark is found inside the central tower at Glasgow Cathedral, a part of the building which will be discussed below, but which was started by Bishop Lauder (1408–25/6) and completed by Cameron. The greatest caution must always be applied when considering masons' marks; but this could suggest that, if Morow was the designer of the prophet corbels at Glasgow, it was a mason already working in the cathedral lodge who carved them for him.

Morow's work represents such a significant element in the opening-out of Scottish architecture to wider European influences that it has been discussed more fully than can perhaps be afforded in a book of this scale. It is now necessary to move on to look at other buildings under construction at this most stimulating period, which fill out the picture of the range of ideas being explored by our masons.

If the buildings considered so far show new influences being introduced into the Scottish architectural repertoire – from England, France and the Low Countries – it can hardly be surprising that for some time to come other buildings should show what are essentially permutations on the established stock of ideas. One of these more conservative operations is the first stage of rebuilding Elgin Cathedral after the fire of 1390, although in this case conservatism was probably partly because of a wish to have the new work sit comfortably with what already existed.

The cathedral and the canons' manses at Elgin were burnt by Alexander Stewart, Earl of Buchan. In 1370 he had undertaken to protect the bishop and his possessions, but by February 1390 his services had been rejected by Bishop Alexander Bur, who excommunicated him and turned instead to Thomas Dunbar, the sheriff of Inverness, for protection. In retaliation, Buchan descended on the cathedral on 17 June and destroyed all that he could.[77] The heart-broken bishop appealed to Buchan's brother, Robert III, for redress,[78] but matters were not helped by a further attack on the cathedral in 1402 by Alexander, a son of the Lord of the Isles.

Rebuilding took many years. The tomb of Bishop John Innes (1407–14) recorded that he was an active contributor to the earlier phases. He is said to have started reconstruction of the central tower, among other works, though that tower again collapsed and had to be rebuilt again in 1506. After Innes's death the canons agreed to raise funds on the basis that, if any of them were elected bishop, one-third of the revenues of the bishopric would be devoted to reconstruction. The earliest repairs were probably to the eastern limb, and within the presbytery the large circular window in the gable has stumps of the type of tracery likely to date from this period – with spherical triangles around the perimeter. The aisles flanking presbytery and choir also required considerable repairs. The tierceron vaulting inserted over the aisles after the fire of 1270 was retained, though some reconstruction was needed since a number of the bosses may be replacements. The greatest change in the aisles was the insertion of larger three- and four-light windows, with small cusped circlets set within intersecting arcs (see Figure 1.37). In choosing this design the mason was partly taking his cue from the one- and two-light post-1270 windows in the lower level of the aisle-less part of the presbytery, since those windows also had circlets within arcs. Nevertheless, as we shall see, there was a wider fashion around these years for such tracery. The precise date of the work in the aisles is unknown, but it was probably complete before Bishop John Winchester (1435–60) built his tomb in the north wall of the south chapel.

Another building operation in the north-east which must be considered here because of its similarities with the choir aisles of Elgin Cathedral is at the small cathedral of Fortrose, on the Black Isle.[79] This involved the addition of south aisle and chapel, which are now the only part of the cathedral to survive apart from the

FIGURE 1.37   Elgin Cathedral, the south flank.

thirteenth-century chapter house and sacristy block (see Figures 1.38 and 1.24a). The aisle was of two and a half bays with a porch, and probably with an altar in the eastern half bay; from the rougher masonry in its western parts, earlier fabric may have been incorporated. The two-bay chapel, to its east, is wider than the aisle, and may have been separated from it by a solid wall. Traditionally this addition to the cathedral is attributed to Euphemia, Countess of Ross, who died in 1395; arms which may have been those of her first husband, Sir Walter Leslie, who died in 1382, have been tentatively identified on one of the vaulting bosses.[80] However, the arms of Bishop John Bullock (1418–39) have also been identified, suggesting the work was only completed during his episcopate. If Lady Ross was indeed the instigator of the work, it is ironic that a building which shows links with Elgin should have been started by a woman whose second husband was that Earl of Buchan who had done his best to destroy Elgin Cathedral.

Despite the high quality of the work at Fortrose, it also illustrates the innate conservatism of the north-east at the turn of the fourteenth and fifteenth centuries since, in drawing ideas from Elgin, little importance was placed on the date of the details to be emulated. Thus the buttresses, with tall upper sections relieved by angle chamfers, and with gablets or half gablets capping all three faces, are similar to those of the 1270s campaign at Elgin. The tierceron vaulting was also inspired by the vaulting of the 1270s at Elgin, though this is less remarkable since such vaulting remained acceptable throughout the later Middle Ages. The clearest evidence for links with contemporary – as opposed to earlier – work at Elgin is seen in the four-light windows of the chapel's south flank, which had intersecting arcs containing cusped circlets, like those in the choir aisles there.

All of these parallels with Elgin are so close that it is conceivable the same master mason worked at both, and there are similarities between the mouldings around the

FIGURE 1.38   Fortrose Cathedral, the south chapel and aisle from the south-east.

windows at the two buildings to support this idea. If this is the case, Fortrose is of additional interest since the designing mason was less constrained by what was already there than at Elgin. As so often, his hand is best seen in the details, such as the chapel piscina. Equally handsome is the canopied tomb which forms an integral part of the chapel's east bay, suggesting the chapel was planned as a chantry for the person buried there. The tomb is set between short stretches of dwarf wall, on which are raised the arcade responds of this bay (see Figure 1.39). The canopy of the tomb has a broad triangular gable, carried by a two-centred segmental arch which demonstrates a subtle interplay between shafted orders on the outer faces, and inner orders which die into the jambs of the arch. The design is markedly sturdy, but the contrast between the plain massing of the overall forms and the delicacy of the arch mouldings is well handled.

A third building which falls to be considered with this group is the church of St Duthac (or Duthus) at Tain, where a heavy restoration in 1877 – which renewed much of the external stonework – has unfortunately created doubts on the authenticity of some of its details (see Figure 1.40 and 5.1b). It has been stated by some writers that the church was built by William Earl of Ross – the father of Countess Euphemia – who died in 1372.[81] It is possible this could have a basis of truth, though on analogy with Elgin and Fortrose a slightly later date is preferable. A date of around 1390 may be indicated by a bequest from Sir James Douglas of Dalkeith for material for vestments,[82] suggesting the structure was nearly complete and ready for furnishings.

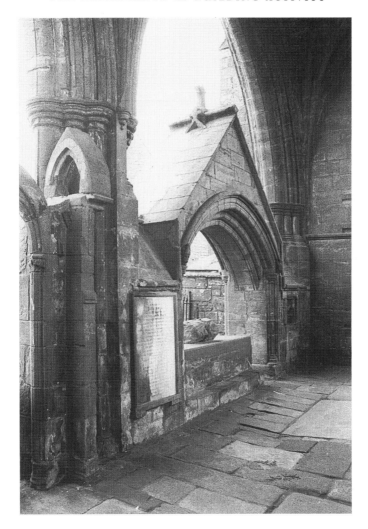

FIGURE 1.39   Fortrose Cathedral, the tomb canopy in the east bay of the south chapel.

There is also a tradition that the church was burnt by rebellious Highlanders in 1427,[83] but this could refer to one of the two other medieval churches in the town, one of which is immediately to the south of the church under discussion, and the other in the valley to its north. The church eventually became collegiate in 1487, on the instigation of James III, but it seems this was the formalisation of an established situation.[84]

Like so many lesser-scale churches of its date, St Duthac's is a rectangular aisle-less structure; it is divided into four bays by buttresses of a similar form to those at Elgin and Fortrose, and the two-stage chamfered base course is also like that at Fortrose. The south, east and west walls have windows of three, four or five lights. The majority of these have tracery of simple intersecting form, while that to the south of the high altar has circlets within the arcs, as at Elgin and Fortrose. The more elaborate tracery of the five-light east window has been particularly heavily renewed, but its division

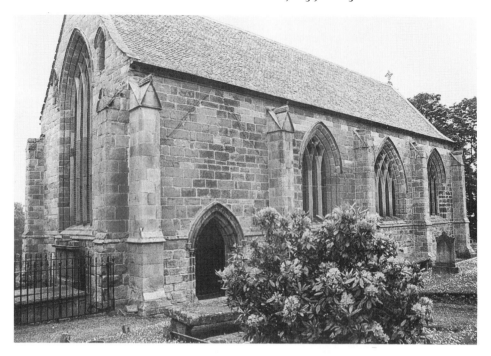

FIGURE 1.40   Tain Collegiate Church, from the south-west.

into groupings of 2–1–2 is basically the same as that of the east window of the chapel at Fortrose, and also as at Fortrose the circlet at the head of the window is subdivided into six triangular or trifoliate forms. The moulded details of Tain are no longer entirely reliable but, without being identical with any of those at Fortrose, they do show something of the same spirit.

Considering the similarities between the repaired Elgin choir aisles, the south aisle and chapel at Fortrose, and the church at Tain there seems good reason to think that – at the least – the designers of the three must have been aware of each other's work. Beyond this, there could be a case for arguing that the three churches had a common designer.

CHANGING PATTERNS OF PATRONAGE

From all of this it can be seen that there was a strong revival of church building during the last quarter of the fourteenth century. There is no space here for discussion of all of the projects initiated and, in any case, several are best dealt with below, since they represented only the start of protracted campaigns. Nevertheless, to round off the picture, a number of other operations dating from this period must be mentioned here. At Arbroath, for example, a major fire of 1380 caused such damage that the monks had to be accommodated elsewhere. Repairs were soon in hand, however, and by 1394–5 a contract was signed for the lead-work on the choir roof.[85]

At the Cistercian abbey of Sweetheart that ubiquitous patron, the third Earl of Douglas, became involved to such an extent that a charter of 1381 described him as the founder and reformer of the house, and in 1388 he was making yet further benefactions.[86] It has been suggested by some writers that one of his contributions could have been the adaptation of the great west window, involving the blocking of the lower part of the field of tracery and the replacement of the main lights by three smaller windows. But, considering the quality of work usually found in the building projects of Earl Archibald, it is improbable he would have sponsored such an ungainly modification, and it is more likely that – if anything – it was the window underlying those later alterations which was the earl's contribution. The surviving tracery at the window head, with a central rose as the main element, could be happily at home in a later fourteenth-century bracket, and would accord with other indications that the church started in the 1270s was only then being completed. Perhaps the later changes are more likely to have followed lightning damage which is referred to in the Vatican Registers for 1397.[87]

The closest parallel for the secondary partial infilling of that window is at the Valliscaulian priory church of Pluscarden, in Moray, where the large windows of the late thirteenth-century choir were contracted at some stage (see Figure 1.41). At Pluscarden it has been postulated that this was necessitated by unrecorded depredations of the Earl of Buchan – the natural scapegoat in that area – and the buildings are said to have been out of repair in 1398.[88] However, the necessary works of repair were long postponed, because in the 1450s it was said that nearly sixty years of neglect had led to a state of pending collapse.[89]

As at Pluscarden, repairs to religious houses could sometimes be postponed or drawn out, suggesting that, once the initial fervour of monastic life had passed, it was becoming less easy to attract the beneficence of patrons. This was perhaps the case at the Premonstratensian abbey of Dryburgh, where Richard II's attack of 1385 had almost as devastating consequences as at Melrose (see Figure 3.6). Robert III helped

FIGURE 1.41   Pluscarden Priory, before the restoration of the choir.

by diverting some of the endowments from the decayed Cistercian nunnery of Berwick-on-Tweed,[90] and there were further benefactions from the fourth Earl of Douglas. But rebuilding was slow, and there are clues in the positioning of doors in the rebuilt south nave wall towards the cloister, and from a fragment of westward-facing base course embedded in that wall, that the canons at one stage thought of reducing the length of the church.

The difficulties at Dryburgh and Pluscarden are partly symptomatic of a shift in lay patronage of the church. By its nature, monastic life involves a tension between the fervour underlying the original ideal on the one hand, and the inherent frailty of human nature on the other; in some ways the intensity of religious aspiration in the twelfth-century monastic revival had carried the seeds of its own decline. In the hope of gaining spiritual advantage from their assistance of the religious life, patrons had flocked to support the monks and canons who were making such efforts to shun the snares of the world. Yet those benefactions helped to push the highest levels of austerity and spirituality beyond the reach of the recipients. This, in its turn, left patrons disenchanted with the easier life they saw in the monastic houses.

Even so, the church was not losing its hold on men's minds. Nor – at a more practical level – was it losing its ability to attract their money, though that money was increasingly invested in other forms of spiritual life. There was a lean period for all of the orders in the second half of the fourteenth century when there were virtually no new foundations for either the older orders of monks and canons, or for the mendicant friars. When a steady trickle of new foundations did at last begin to gather momentum after 1400, except for the Perth Charterhouse and a few houses of nuns, all of the fresh patronage of the religious orders was directed towards the friars, with their active mission to the people. Especially favoured were the Observant Franciscans, who represented yet another promising reform. Nevertheless, the religious orders were never again to attract the levels of new support there had been at an earlier period.

The disenchantment which followed from the realisation that organised religious life tended to fall short of its highest aspirations was balanced by an increase in more personal forms of devotion; this was a change that found expression throughout later medieval Europe as a whole.[91] Religion was increasingly a matter of actively sorting out one's own salvation, and not simply of relying on the prayers of cloistered communities. In architectural terms one consequence was that the places where potential patrons themselves worshipped were more likely to be the recipients of their beneficence. This was a leading factor behind the increased energy put into building parish churches, collegiate churches and family chapels in the later Middle Ages. Nevertheless, we should minimise neither the wealth of the religious houses, nor the powers of patronage they continued to wield, and we shall see that many of them continued to build up to the eve of the Reformation. This is also true of the cathedral bodies. It is hoped, however, that by separate discussion of the various categories of building types in the remainder of this book it will be easier to appreciate the impact of this changed balance of patronage in the fifteenth and early sixteenth centuries.

PART TWO

From the Early Fifteenth to the Mid-Sixteenth Century

CHAPTER TWO

The Cathedral Churches

SOME SMALL-SCALE BUILDING OPERATIONS

By the later Middle Ages most dioceses had adequate cathedral churches of twelfth- or thirteenth-century construction, with the latter century having been a particularly productive period. They also had the advantage that, unlike some of the great monastic churches, they were set well back from the Border and escaped injury in the wars with England. On the face of it there was thus little reason for any major rebuilding. Nevertheless, it demonstrates the continuing vitality of the dioceses that two cathedrals – at Aberdeen and Dunkeld – were substantially late medieval creations; while at others, including St Andrews, Elgin and Glasgow, advantage was taken of structural catastrophes to instigate large-scale rebuilding. Beyond that, though the cathedrals probably no longer set the architectural pace, most of them have some work from the period that concerns us here.

Reference has been made to the north tower of Brechin; to the start of repairs after the 1390 burning of Elgin; to the aisle and chapel added to Fortrose; and to the western towers of Glasgow. Further attention must be given to some of those cathedrals in this chapter. Brechin, for instance, has a four-light west window filled with richly curvilinear tracery. With its pair of sub-arches defined by ogee curves and its complex pattern of interlocking dagger forms, this window has its closest parallel on the north side of the presbytery at Melrose Abbey (see Figure 2.1). A date for its insertion around the start of the fifteenth century is therefore most likely.

Among other smaller-scale operations were works at Whithorn and Kirkwall, the two cathedrals that had been – in differing ways – outside the orbit of the Scottish church for much of the Middle Ages. At the former, which – although within the kingdom of Scotland – came under the authority of the archbishops of York until as late as 1355, there is heraldic evidence of work for Bishop George Vaus (1482–1508) in a doorway that is a composite reconstruction of the 1630s.

At Kirkwall, which was under the archbishops of Trondheim until 1472 – by which time the crown rights in the Northern Isles had been transferred from Norway to Scotland – the process of construction started in 1137 was still under way.[1] The main requirement was to complete the western bays of the nave, and the upper parts of the west front. Internally the three-storeyed elevation was continued into the west bays with little modification; externally, however, the later work is marked by changes in the windows, buttresses, aisle wall-head corbel tables, and in the form

FIGURE 2.1   Brechin Cathedral, the west front before restoration.

of the remodelled doorway on the south side. This polygon-headed doorway is characteristic of the end of the Middle Ages, and tradition says it was the work of Bishop Robert Reid (1541–58). The one dispiriting aspect of the final phase of operations is the upper part of the west front, above the uniquely ambitious thirteenth-century triple portal; a central window with flabby intersecting tracery was its inadequate focus. This part has been attributed on heraldic grounds to Bishop Andrew (1477–c. 1506).

Minor works may also be seen at the cathedral of Dunblane,[2] where one or more of the three Chisholm bishops who ruled the diocese between 1487 and 1569 carried out various operations.[3] The arms of Chisholm are on both the parapet which caps the two storeys added to the mid-twelfth-century tower, and on the rebuilt parapet of the choir. An approximate date for one part of the work is indicated by royal gifts of drink-silver to the masons in 1501 and 1502. It must be conceded that these architectural operations amount to little more than tinkering around the edges of a building completed over two centuries earlier, and it is only when we look deeper into the activities of the Chisholms that we see it would be unfair to be dismissive. In a building requiring little more than care and maintenance it was natural that some patrons sought outlets other than new building for their beneficence. At Dunblane heraldry shows the Chisholms also provided the canopied choir stalls for the canons, six of which survive complete, while there are others without canopies (see Figure 2.2). William Chisholm also established the chapel of the Holy Blood and St Blaise in the western bays of the nave north aisle, where there are still two segmentally arched windows of distinctive form.

Clearly, at a time when church furnishings were becoming ever more magnificent, they could make as valuable a contribution to the setting of worship as the architecture itself. In assessing the contributions of later medieval patrons, then, it is important we make allowance for such gifts, despite their having left little physical evidence. Indeed, in many cases, including Scotland's greatest cathedrals at St Andrews and Glasgow, as well as those at Dunkeld and Aberdeen, we know that buildings and furnishings were planned as part of a unified approach.

FIGURE 2.2   Dunblane Cathedral, three of the canons' choir stalls.

ST ANDREWS CATHEDRAL

At St Andrews the work which followed the fire of 1378 and the collapse of the south transept in 1409 required several decades to complete. Apart from the reconstruction in the nave already discussed (see p. 35), the chief evidence for these operations is to be seen in alterations in the crossing area, and in the new window of the east gable, which replaced two of the three tiers of triple windows from the 1160s campaign (see Figure 2.3). This fragmentary evidence is enigmatic, but from written records we can appreciate that what we see was conditioned as much by liturgical as by structural considerations. Among the liturgical desiderata was a more spacious and elevated ritual area around the high altar, together with a longer choir for the stalls of the canons. It also seems a chapel was being formed for relics at the extreme east end, behind the high altar, though this may have been a remodelling of an existing arrangement.[4]

Bower, who had been a canon at the cathedral, says it was Prior James Haldenstone (1418–43) who remodelled the east gable,[5] and the position of the vast

FIGURE 2.3   St Andrews Cathedral, the east gable.

new three-light window was probably governed by the need for it to be visible above the relic chapel. Changes in the crossing area included the strengthening of the responds built in with the outer walls, to provide additional support for the partly reconstructed central tower. Additional bracing for the tower was also afforded by walls between the piers in the crossing area, though here the main intention was to enclose more completely the canons' choir and the altars which stood in front of the rood screen at its west end. Bower says it was Canon William Bower, vicar of Holy Trinity Parish Church between about 1410 and 1440, who paid for the rood screen and the altar above it, while the choir stalls were the gift of Prior James Bisset (1393–1416).[6] All of this indicates a major effort to provide fittings of appropriate splendour for Scotland's greatest cathedral as the structural work was nearing completion.

This effort should not be seen in isolation, however, but as part of a general movement throughout the European church towards a more lavish performance of the liturgy, in which architecture, furnishings, music and imagery all played their part. Hector Boece said it was in the reign of James I (1406–37) that this greater ceremony, together with new forms of music, reached Scotland,[7] and from surviving service books it seems that Scotland's prelates were increasingly looking to Europe rather than England for guidance.[8] Whereas the liturgical uses of Salisbury had earlier been thought to offer the best example for Scotland, it seems that churchmen were looking directly to Rome by the fifteenth century. By the end of the century, however, there was a further development, as national pride led to specifically Scottish variants being developed to meet the need for what James IV called 'our awin Scottis Use'.[9] Thus – albeit at the risk of gross over-simplification – it seems that liturgical developments were running in parallel with those in architecture, in the way that inspiration from mainland Europe rather than from England was being sought as the prelude to the emergence of a national synthesis.

GLASGOW CATHEDRAL

As the churches of the nation's leading prelates, it was in the cathedrals that there would have been the most ambitious liturgical furnishings, and the documentation points to a continuing drive to provide a fitting setting for worship within them. Indeed, one suspects that, once the shock of disaster had passed, structural catastrophe was not unwelcome because of the fresh opportunities it offered. At Glasgow, the cathedral of what was to be Scotland's second archdiocese, there were two main spurs to rebuilding. One was a continuing problem of structural failure because of the steep eastward fall of the site, and the vaulting bosses of the aisles and crypt show there were periodic repairs as late as the time of Archbishop James Beaton, who was translated to St Andrews in 1523. But the motive for the most extensive operations was a fire that followed a strike by lightning during the episcopate of Matthew Glendinning (1387–1408). It is specifically referred to in papal correspondence of September 1406,[10] in which it is said that the choir and bell tower were ruined and that the cathedral had lost its chapter house and vestry. Except for the last of those, which was above the treasury and no longer survives,[11] the architecture clearly reflects the extent of rebuilding, while heraldry helps to chart the progress of the work. The central tower was rebuilt by William Lauder (1408–25/6), whose arms are on its parapet, and the spire was completed by John Cameron (1426–46) (see Figure 2.5). Cameron also started repairs on the square two-storeyed chapter house at the north-east corner of the choir, since his arms are on the vault of the lower storey, along with those of James I, Queen Joan Beaufort and the fifth Earl of Douglas (who died in 1439). Cameron's work extended to the start of repairs on the upper chapter house, because his arms are on the fireplace inserted in it, although it was William Turnbull (1447–54) who completed it and placed his arms on the parapet. The existing roof within that parapet, however, is of the early seventeenth century.

In the new work at Glasgow we see how the mason was at pains to make his work sit sympathetically with what existed. Such respect for the work of predecessors was not new, but at Glasgow – as perhaps also at Elgin – we may be witnessing the further development of an almost 'antiquarian' approach to design. In parallel with the introduction of new ideas, the revival of earlier details was to become a significant strand in Scottish late Gothic, and one that was to be particularly strong in the west, as already suggested at Maybole (see p. 24).

The junction of old and new is best seen in the two storeys of the chapter house (see Figure 2.4). Externally, the most obvious change is in the form of the windows. At the lower level the old lancet windows were retained, albeit with some remodelled shaft bases. At the upper level the new windows are also single or paired openings, though their simpler mouldings and shallower arches framing lintels reveal their later date. Inside the chapter house, at the lower level the old vault was retained, but with some reconstruction that included new bosses. At the upper level the old vault was retained only in the small vestibule and adjoining area, and little attempt was made to match the new vault ribs with the old. That in itself is a significant indicator of architectural attitudes. Few would notice such relatively slight changes, and we are reminded that it is in the minor details that the individual approach of the mason is often most precisely identifiable, especially when his own contribution is being married in with earlier work. One other noteworthy change is in the design of the central pier, though here the change took place within the fifteenth-century campaign. Despite its new base having been designed for a bi-axially symmetrical pier, the pier itself was given an unusual asymmetrical sequence of hollows and engaged shafts.

The rebuilt central tower is an unbuttressed single-storeyed composition, with four equal-height window openings divided by transoms to each face (see Figure 2.5). (The two outer windows on each face were, in fact, wholly or partly blocked to give extra strength below the spire squinches.) This design may have set the pattern for towers elsewhere, as at Edinburgh St Giles and Haddington St Mary, each of which had triplets of equal-height openings to each face. The spire which capped this tower, however, was one of the most graceful ever to be raised in Scotland. At its base pinnacles emerge from broaches, and there are four levels of lucarnes, the upper three separated by crested bands. Unfortunately its lines are now slightly marred as a result of structural damage in 1739 or 1756.

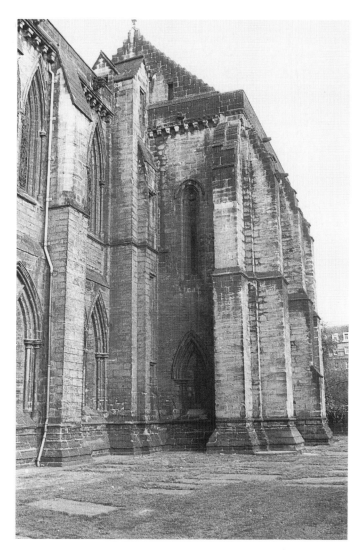

FIGURE 2.4   Glasgow Cathedral, the chapter house from the south.

Within the choir, there must have been a general reordering, culminating in papal permission being sought in 1420 for St Kentigern's relics to be placed in a shrine of gold or silver. [12] The process perhaps started in 1401, when Bishop Glendinning taxed the cathedral clergy to provide new vestments and ornaments, and the results are summarised in an *Inventory of the ornaments, reliques, jewels, vestments and books* of 1431–2. [13] It may have been at this period that the stone pulpitum was built, which survived the aftermath of the Reformation through providing a base for the wall built to separate the inner high kirk in the choir from the rest of the building. (see Figure 2.6). It has shallow blind arcading to each side of a three-centred arched doorway, and along its top is a traceried parapet punctuated by miniature buttresses supported

FIGURE 2.5   Glasgow Cathedral, the west elevation before the demolition of the west towers.

by carved figures of uncertain inconography. There also seems to have been a timber screen west of the crossing, the loft of which was reached from a doorway cut through the wall of the spiral stair at the north-east corner of the nave.[14]

FIGURE 2.6   Glasgow Cathedral, the pulpitum and the altar bases added in front of it.

At Glasgow the accumulation of furnishings was a progressive process, as is
evident from the growth in the number of side altars.[15] The diocese's first archbishop, Robert Blackadder (1483–1508), was a keen provider. He planned to be
buried within the crossing area, and left 300 merks in his will to complete works he
had started there.[16] These included the foundation in 1503 of an altar dedicated to
Our Lady of Pity, on one side of the pulpitum, and he re-established that dedicated
to the Name of Jesus on the other side.[17] The bases for these are still in place
and, despite their stereotyped figure carving, they are unique survivors which add
significantly to our understanding of church furnishings (see Figure 2.6). Also in his
time, the Dean and chapter in 1506 contracted with the wright Michael Waghorn
to have canopies constructed over the choir stalls, which were to be based on those
in the Chapel Royal at Stirling.[18] Blackadder's name is also traditionally associated
with the laterally projecting aisle off the south transept of Glasgow, of which only
the undercroft was ever completed. Close examination of the moulded details,
however, suggests the shell of the aisle was built by the mason who designed the
choir and its crypt in the mid-thirteenth century.[19] Only the tierceron vault, with
its rather chunky rib mouldings, appears to be of Blackadder's period, though this
did not inhibit him from applying his arms to other parts. The function of the aisle
is uncertain. Its closest analogies are with the incomplete later thirteenth-century
aisle on the south side of Iona Abbey,[20] and in both cases they were perhaps planned
in connection with the cult of the main saint venerated with the church. At Glasgow

the vaulting above the entrance to the aisle has a carving of Fergus, whose hearse St Kentigern is said to have followed from Carnock to Glasgow, and it may be that the aisle covered the area where Fergus was thought to be buried. Blackadder's completion of the crypt of the aisle was probably part of an attempt to revive interest in the Kentigern pilgrimage.[21]

Late medieval work at Glasgow extended to the two towers which projected from the west front, and which were demolished in 1846 and 1848 (see Figure 2.5).[22] The northern of the two was started during the later thirteenth-century building campaign on the nave, since it was noted during demolition that it blocked a window that had not yet been glazed.[23] Its superstructure, however, which had a belfry stage with pairs of lights and a squat lead-sheathed splay-foot spire, was rather later. This tower was used as the consistory house, or ecclesiastical court room. The southern tower was never raised to full height, and excavations in 1988 led to a tentative suggestion of a fifteenth-century date for its construction.[24] In support of this, a late source says it was Bishop Lauder who 'built the lower stepill at the west end of the cathedrall'[25] though drawings also suggest kinship with Cameron's work on the upper chapter house. One of these two towers may have been the source of the prophet figure corbels referred to in discussing the work of John Morow (see p. 48 and Figure 1.36).

ELGIN CATHEDRAL

At Elgin, reconstruction after the attacks of 1390 and 1402 continued over several decades.[26] Repairs to the eastern limb and central tower have already been discussed, and probably preceded operations on the nave, which are approximately dated by the arms of Bishop Columba Dunbar (1422–34) on the west gable. The fragmentary stumps of the piers show the four eastern bays of the nave had to be wholly or partly reconstructed, and there was extensive rebuilding of the outer nave aisles. It is not always clear, however, what is entirely fifteenth century, and what is partial reconstruction of thirteenth-century work. Thus, for example, the two surviving lateral gables of the outer south nave aisle embrace tracery which is certainly of the fifteenth century, though the diminutive intersecting arcading of the gable cornices could either be reused work of the thirteenth century or a late revival of thirteenth-century types (see Figure 2.7). On balance the latter seems more likely, because such lateral gables are probably best understood as one example of the influence of the renewed taste for such gables in the Netherlands, which was reflected in a number of other Scottish churches at this period, including some of the burgh churches (see Figure 6.2).

On the west front an inner skin was added to the doorway, and above it the gable wall was rebuilt, incorporating a large new window. The addition to the doorway has two arches carried on a trumeau; in the tympanum above the openings, with their framing bands of foliage, is a pair of angels censing a central vesica from which the figure is missing. The new window was of seven lights, with a rose as its centre-piece. Since the nave was timber-roofed, and probably had a curved wagon ceiling like that for which there is evidence on the inner face of the presbytery gable, the window

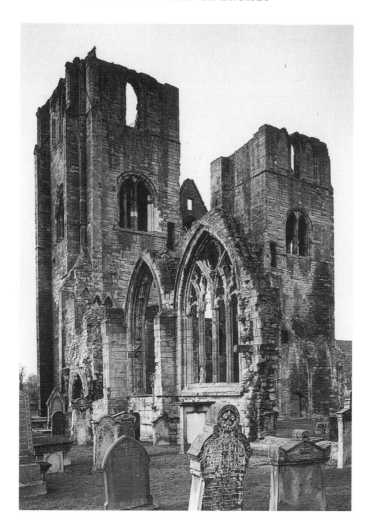

FIGURE 2.7   Elgin Cathedral, the nave from the south-east.

could be allowed to extend up into the gable itself. The upper part of the gable above the window was composed on two planes, with stepped sections to each side of a wall walk.

Apart from the second rebuilding of the central tower in 1506, one of the last major works at the cathedral was the remodelling of the octagonal chapter house, which had been first built after the fire of 1270 (see Figure 2.8). The patron of this operation was Bishop Andrew Stewart (1482–1501), whose arms are on the central pier which carries the vault. To provide additional support for that vault, the internal walls were thickened above decorative bands of foliage and the windows were reduced in size. It must be admitted that some of these windows – which have recently been restored – were rather ungainly in the inter-relationship of the individual forms, and are among the least successful aspects of the rebuilding of Elgin.

FIGURE 2.8   Elgin Cathedral, the interior of the chapter house.

Of the fixtures and furnishings within the cathedral, the most complete are the tombs in the eastern limb and transepts. One of the finest must have been that built into the arch from the north aisle into the presbytery, which had two gabled arches over the tomb itself, and a third over a doorway. Such a tomb was both a sepulchral monument and a handsome screen at an entrance to the presbytery. Another significant tomb is that of Bishop John Winchester (1435–69) in the chapel to the south of the presbytery, because of the evidence it affords for the activity of a local mason (see Figure 2.9). The basic design, with an arcaded tomb chest and a multiple-cusped ogee canopy flanked by tall pinnacles, follows the formula of many tombs of this period; but there are two at Fordyce – less than forty kilometres east of Elgin – that are so similar in both their basic design and moulded detail, that there is a strong case for their being by the same mason. Others, including at least one at Elgin, could also be his work.

FIGURE 2.9   Elgin Cathedral, the tomb of Bishop John Winchester.

For the less permanent furnishings we only have enigmatic clues, such as the way
the southern of the two massive responds separating the presbytery and choir has been
cut back, presumably for the canopy of the bishop's throne. Most tantalising of all is
the account of the destruction of the rood screen and loft in 1640, when they were
broken up for firewood by the minister and two local lairds.[27] Behind the loft there
was still a depiction of the crucifixion, against a background of stars, with a painting
of the last judgement towards the choir.

DUNKELD CATHEDRAL

According to Alexander Myln, whose account of the lives of its bishops is our chief
source of information on Dunkeld, the nave started by Bishop Cardeny in 1406 was
completed by Bishop Thomas Lauder and dedicated by him in 1464 (see Figures 1.24b
and 1.23).[28] Lauder also did much to enhance it, both with architectural additions and
furnishings. He added the porch over the main entrance for the lay folk, on the south

side of the nave, and on 13 April 1457 he started the square chapter house on the north side of the choir.[29] The latter probably also served as a sacristy, while its upper storey must have been a treasury.

Lauder's most important addition was the four-storeyed bell tower at the north-west corner of the nave, which he founded on 5 March 1469 (see Figure 2.10); it was completed by his successor, James Livingston. As first built, Dunkeld's nave had only a small stair tower attached to the west front, and the new tower added greatly to its architectural impact. In the most ambitious churches, including the abbeys of Arbroath, Dunfermline, Kilwinning and Holyrood and the cathedrals of Elgin, Glasgow and Aberdeen, the ideal was to have a pair of towers at the west end of the church, flanking the great entrance (see Figures 3.43, 2.7, 2.5 and 2.12). But such provision was expensive, and a single asymmetrically placed bell tower was also acceptable. At the abbeys of Lindores and Cambuskenneth there was a free-standing tower to the north of the church; elsewhere, as at Inchmahome Priory, the tower might be placed over the west bay of the north aisle. At Dunkeld the new tower was placed on the west side of the north aisle, so that it projected out from the west front, and in this it was like Brechin and Glasgow in their thirteenth-century states (though

CROSS SECTION

WEST ELEVATION

FIGURE 2.10 Dunkeld Cathedral, the west front.

Brechin also had its eleventh-century round tower to the south of the facade (see Figure 2.1)).

In adding his tower Lauder made other major changes to the west front. A narrow platform was built out over the west door, carried on arches, and above this most of the rest of the front was taken up by what must have been an exquisite six-light window. Only the stubs of its tracery now survive, but these are enough to show that it was closely similar to that in the south transeptal chapel of Linlithgow Parish Church (see Figure 6.11). The head of the window was taken up by an enormous spherical triangle containing three circlets and three bladder forms, each of which was filled by interlocking daggers and quatrefoils. This and the window at Linlithgow were the finest things of their kind in Scotland, and some similarities in their mouldings support the likelihood that they were the work of the same mason. More will be said about the possible identity of this mason in discussing Linlithgow (see p. 198).

Lauder also glazed all the windows of the nave, and gave furnishings and vestments for the services in the choir. He was particularly assiduous in enriching the high altar, providing a retable showing twenty-four miracles from the life of St Columba – the cathedral's patron saint – and he gave two columns capped by angels, which must have been the riddel posts from which hung the curtains on each side of the altar. Beyond this he paid for the canons' choir stalls. Another notable benefactor was Bishop George Brown (1483–1515).[30] The only survivor of his work is the remodelled window in the western bay of the south aisle, where he established a chapel dedicated to the Virgin. But he was active in obtaining yet more furnishings for his cathedral, including altarpieces and lecterns. It is a valuable indicator of artistic tastes in Scotland at this time that several of these furnishings – which were all destroyed at the Reformation – were imported from the Low Countries.

Whatever our losses from Dunkeld, however, at least through Myln we have an invaluable insight into the wealth of treasures which enhanced the setting of worship at what was, after all, a cathedral of only the middle rank. We have some additional reason to be grateful because the cathedral still contains some of the most complete mural paintings in Scotland. These are in the base of the tower, which was used as an ecclesiastical court room and was thus decorated with suitably judicial scenes, including the judgement of Solomon and the woman taken in adultery.

ABERDEEN CATHEDRAL

At Aberdeen, where the choir and much of the transepts are lost, we again have precise details of the course of construction in an account of the lives of its bishops. This was written by Hector Boece, the first principal of the nearby King's College.[31] Something of the early building history has already been given (see p. 24 and Figure 1.24c), but can be amplified here. The old church was demolished and a new choir built by Bishop Henry Chene (1282–1328). The second Alexander Kininmund (1355–80) started the nave, building the western towers and arcade piers to a height of 6 cubits (about 2.75 metres) (see Figures 1.24c, 2.11 and 2.12). Henry Lichton (1422–40) completed the internal walls of the nave and the two western towers, but left the central tower incomplete; he also built the north transept, dedicated to St John the Evangelist, in the north wall of which he placed his tomb. Ingram Lindsay's (1441–58) contribution was roofing and paving the nave. Thomas Spens (1457–80) gave furnishings and vestments, including the choir stalls, bishop's throne and many of the fixtures associated with the high altar. William Elphinstone (1483–1514) completed the central tower, which in 1511 he ordered to be modelled on that of St John's Church in Perth (see Figure 6.5).[32] He also covered the nave with lead and started rebuilding the eastern limb on a larger scale since that by Henry Chene was considered to be inadequate. The last major addition recorded by Boece was the heraldic ceiling over the nave, which was started by Gavin Dunbar (1518–32).[33]

In addition to what Boece tells us, we have some further pieces of evidence. We know that Elphinstone's work on the eastern arm and central tower extended into the transepts, since in his will he left money for the completion of the transept as well as the choir. It must also be remembered that Boece's account of the activities of successive bishops was written before the end of the Dunbar's episcopate, and as a result not all of his benefactions were listed; but we do know that he rebuilt the spires of the western towers. He perhaps also continued work on the transepts, since the memorial of Thomas French – or Franche, who died in 1530 – claimed he was the master mason of the south transept, and it was certainly complete in time for Dunbar's tomb to be built into its south wall.

Although slightly larger in floor area, the nave of Aberdeen as built by Bishops Kininmund and Lichton was less architecturally complex than Cardeny and Lauder's work at Dunkeld, and was of two rather than three storeys (see Figure 2.11). Internally the arcade of cylindrical piers carries simply moulded pointed arches, and the clearstorey has narrow single-light round-headed windows, with segmental rear-arches opening on to the wall passage. The two storeys follow largely independent rhythms, with no attempt to link them into a unified composition by articulation of the wall surfaces; there is even a difference of rhythm between the two sides at clearstorey level. The tendency towards simplification of detail must have been largely because of the general use of granite, a more intractable material than freestone. A modern change that has been particularly unfortunately in this cathedral is the stripping of the internal plaster to reveal the rubble walling; nevertheless, the impact of the interior remains one of impressive simplicity. Another cathedral which presented a comparable appearance was Dornoch, where Cordiner's view of the nave in 1776, before its restoration to a different design by William Burn in 1835–7, shows a similar arcade of cylindrical piers and simple clearstorey openings. This has prompted the suggestion that Dornoch's nave could also be of late medieval date, though Cordiner's view gives inadequate detail to be certain of this.[34]

Externally greater emphasis is given to the south than the north flank (see Figure 2.12). It has a two-storeyed porch over the main lay entrance, and two- and three-light intersecting-traceried windows rather than the much simpler windows of the north aisle. But the marshalling of bold masses, which is the external keynote, is seen most impressively in the west front. Above the round-arched doorway – with

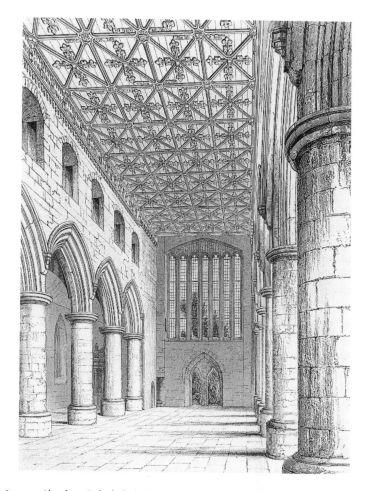

FIGURE 2.11   Aberdeen Cathedral, the interior of the nave looking westwards.

twin openings carried on a central trumeau – is a tight grouping of seven slender equal-height windows, which offer a disarmingly modern appearance. Even more striking is the pair of towers which flank the central part of the facade, and which rise only a little above the gable base of the nave roof. Pierced by narrow slit windows, and capped by machicolated parapets, they look more like a pair of tower-houses than ecclesiastical bell towers, and give an impression of scale beyond their size. Set behind the parapets are the spires added by Bishop Dunbar, which rise from square blocks and are the most robust splay-foot spires that could be imagined. Nevertheless, their detailing is busier than that of the towers, with embattled bands, multiple dummy lucarnes, and angle pinnacles rising from L-shaped sections of crenellated walls at the base of the splays.

Dunbar's other great contribution to his cathedral was the heraldic ceiling (see Figure 2.11). Rising above a deep cornice, its flat surface is divided by a grid of rectilinear and diagonal ribs, with foliage sprig bosses at the lesser intersections of the diagonal ribs, and heraldic shields at the major intersections of both diagonal and

FIGURE 2.12   Aberdeen Cathedral, the west front and south porch.

rectilinear ribs. The bosses show similarities with those of the wagon ceilings at King's College Chapel and the destroyed choir of St Nicholas' Church in Aberdeen (see Figures 5.21 and 6.19), both of which had been projects close to the heart of Bishop Elphinstone (see pp. 161 and 210). The latter ceiling – and probably the former as well – was the work of the wright John Fendour, who is also known to have been employed on the timberwork of the cathedral's central tower. The cathedral ceiling is recorded as the work of one John Winter[35] though it is not impossible that Winter is a misrepresentation of Fendour.

Apart from its artistic qualities, the ceiling reminds us of the intellectual activity centred on Aberdeen at the turn of the fifteenth and sixteenth centuries, in which Elphinstone, Boece and others played prominent parts.[36] Bishop Dunbar was the donor of the ceiling, but a guiding spirit behind its design was probably another protégé of Elphinstone's, Alexander Galloway; he was a cultivated patron of the arts and a canon of the cathedral, holding the prebendal stall of Kinkell.[37] One commentator has described the theme of the ceiling as 'a comprehensive illustrated lecture on the contemporary politics of Christendom about the year 1520'.[38] This lecture is embodied within the three rows of sixteen shields. The central row relates to the Scottish church under the leadership of the papacy; the southern row shows the Scottish aristocracy led by the king; the northern row depicts the monarchs of Christendom headed by the emperor. As a heraldically expressed summary of the national church, the Scottish state and Christendom it could hardly have been bettered. It also reminds us of how the Scottish church was becoming increasingly conscious of both its national and international roles, though the former was perhaps best epitomised in Elphinstone's compilation of the Aberdeen Breviary, as part of an attempt to establish forms of worship attuned to Scottish needs.

CHAPTER THREE

Monastic Architecture

T here were very few new foundations for any of the monastic – as opposed to the mendicant – orders in the period covered by this book. This was partly because Scotland already had sufficient monastic houses for a country of such limited wealth, and more simply were not needed. But it was also the case that monasticism was no longer seen to be driven by the zeal which had made it the power-house of church reform in the twelfth century, and benefactors increasingly chose to direct their munificence elsewhere.

Of all the indicators of declining fervour, it is in something as trivial as the culinary treats known as 'pittances' that we see most graphically those tendencies which made it difficult to pursue the highest ideals. There is nothing outrageous in the willingness of Melrose to accept Robert I's gift of an annual rent of £100 to provide a daily portion of rice made with milk of almonds,[1] and this is still strictly vegetarian fare. But, when we learn it is just the residue of that money which is to clothe fifteen poor men at Martinmas, we realise we have moved well away from an essentially self-denying spirit. Other indicators point the same way. The central aims of communal co-existence and personal poverty, for example, were threatened by a tendency for monks and canons to be allotted a 'portion' of their monastery's income. Indeed, they might even be prepared to stop their attendance at services if the portions were inadequate.[2] There is also evidence that monks might be allowed a higher degree of privacy and independence than had been the original intention. This may have involved only the subdivision of the dormitory by partitions. But in some cases the monks or canons had their own dwellings, as at Pittenweem, where in 1549 they had 'little houses in the priory garden', or perhaps at Melrose, where they certainly had private gardens.[3]

One telling development was the way many monasteries from the end of the fifteenth century were governed not by abbots who were members of their religious order, but by commendators. In the earlier stages of this development many commendators were simply non-monastic clerics, who professed as monks on their appointment. Later, however, it was regarded as unnecessary for the commendator to be a member of the order whose house he governed, thus creating a gulf between the community and its head. Many later commendators were royal appointees whose services to – or relationship with – the monarchy were rewarded with one or more religious houses; some were even under-age royal bastards. All observed the decencies by taking orders when appointed, if not already in holy orders; but in few cases was the spiritual welfare of their communities a matter of overriding concern.[4]

Of the few new monastic foundations at this period, the most significant was the Charterhouse in Perth, for the strict Carthusian order of hermit-monks, which was established by James I in 1429.[5] Nothing survives of this house, and the only architectural fragment about which we know anything was a porch tacked on to Perth parish church choir, which was finally destroyed around the end of the eighteenth century.[6] Apart from small foundations like that for the Augustinians at Oronsay, there were also a number of new nunneries. Three of these were for the orders of nuns attached to the Dominicans and Franciscans, and are therefore outside the remit of this chapter. The only new nunnery attached to an older order was the short-lived Cistercian house of St Evoca, in Kirkcudbrightshire, which has left no architectural trace.[7]

Based on these negative indicators it might be assumed the monasteries would not be architecturally active in the later Middle Ages, and it is true there was less building than there had been in the period of greatest expansion. Nevertheless, they remained major land-holding corporations, occupied by communities which probably still thought of themselves as a cultural élite, and which had continuing architectural needs. There was certainly notable rebuilding under way in the course of our period at Benedictine Dunfermline and Iona, at Cluniac Crossraguel and Paisley, at Tironensian Arbroath, at Cistercian Melrose, at Augustinian Inchcolm, Jedburgh, Pittenweem and St Andrews and at Premonstratensian Dryburgh. Beyond those, there are few monasteries of which we still have upstanding remains where there is not evidence of some significant late medieval rebuilding.

Some of this work was necessitated by accidental damage or through destruction during the wars with England. But much was simply in response to a wish for more fitting buildings, or because of changing requirements. Whatever the motivation, the sheer quantity of building shows the monasteries were still capable of sponsoring major architecture, and were hardly as moribund as the generally held picture of religious life at this time suggests. The life within the monasteries, and particularly in the larger ones, was different from what their founders had intended. But most were not demoralised, and at some houses efforts were even made to re-establish higher standards in the quality of the religious life and in intellectual standards. This is particularly clear in the activities of Abbots Chrystall and Myln at Kinloss and Cambuskenneth respectively,[8] and both James IV and James V took steps to encourage monastic reform, even though their expansion of commendation was linked with declining standards. On balance it is probably true to say that, although much was far from ideal in the last century of Scottish medieval monasticism, it was not always irredeemably so.

SOME LESSER OPERATIONS ON MONASTIC CHURCHES

As has been said, there are few monastic churches for which evidence survives where there were no late medieval alterations or additions, though in many cases the works were of a minor nature. At the other extreme, we know of at least five abbey churches that were substantially late medieval structures. Between those two poles there are about a dozen monastic churches where significant architectural changes were made, and those not already covered in the first chapter will be summarised briefly here before looking at the more ambitious operations.

At the preceptory church of Torphichen near Linlithgow, founded for the military order of Knights Hospitallers by David I, there was extensive remodelling of the transepts and crossing (see Figure 3.1).[9] An inscription on the north transept vaulting ribs says this work was sponsored by Sir Andrew Meldrum, who was preceptor around the 1430s. The scope of the work expanded while still in progress, because the habitable chambers above the transepts seem to be an afterthought from the way the south transept buttresses rise only to the height necessary for single-storey structures. Following the post-Reformation loss of the choir and the modification of the nave as a parish church, it is difficult to be certain how they related to the transepts, though the latter were the only areas known to have been vaulted. Their three bays of ridge-ribbed quadripartite vaulting, with a large bell hole to the crossing bay, now have a strikingly monumental appearance, as do the heavy responds inserted at the

FIGURE 3.1   Torphichen Preceptory Church, from the south east.

FIGURE 3.2   Torphichen Preceptory Church, the interior of transepts looking southwards.

crossing to support the existing tower (see Figure 3.2). The responds are of a type
which was to become widespread, with heavy filleted shafts and ogee mouldings to
the half-piers, and with upper cap and lower base mouldings cutting straight across
the faces at about forty-five degrees.

   A principal focus of the new work is a pair of three light windows, one in the south
transept gable wall, with the other in the east wall of the north transept because of the
presence of the claustral range to its north. These windows, with either two or three
quatrefoiled circlets in the tracery field, are early representatives of a revived taste for
mid-thirteenth-century geometrical designs. Usually the late date of such tracery is
betrayed by the half-unconscious use of some ogee curves, but at Torphichen it is only
the three-centred light heads with a central cusp in the south transept window which
point to a date later than the thirteenth century. Internally, below that south transept
window, is an ogee-headed tomb recess with an adjacent piscina, which shows that one
likely requirement behind the remodelling of the transepts was the formation of a
chantry or mortuary chapel. In this the chapels within the transepts are representative

of an emerging trend. Throughout the fifteenth century, and in all types of churches, we find growing numbers of laterally projecting aisles with burial recesses; these might be either full transepts, or chapels placed almost arbitrarily against a church's flank. Another example is the north transept of the Augustinian abbey of Jedburgh.[10]

Since its completion in the early thirteenth century, there had been little need for building at Jedburgh Abbey Church, and it was possibly English attacks in 1410 and 1416 that prompted remodelling of the north transept (see Figure 3.3). This involved removing the apse on its east face and lengthening the transept northwards; it also seems it was originally intended to place a barrel vault over it. The extended east wall was left blank so that altar retables could be placed against it, with light cast on them through two-light windows in the west wall. As in the south transept at Torphichen, the greatest architectural emphasis was reserved for the gable wall, which has a four-light window, with curvilinear tracery organised within two sub-arches, and also as at Torphichen there is a tomb recess below this window. Rather surprisingly, on the front of this tomb chest are the arms of Archbishop Blackadder of Glasgow who died in 1508; although Glasgow's bishops and archbishops took a close interest in what was one of the largest abbeys within their diocese, Blackadder's will shows he had intended to be buried at Glasgow if he had not died on pilgrimage. In any case, the aisle is earlier than his time, since arms above the north window are probably of Bishop William Turnbull (1447–54), and a date around then is supported by the window's similarity to one built at Melrose Abbey by Abbot Andrew Hunter (1441–71) (see p. 96).

FIGURE 3.3   Jedburgh Abbey, the north transept.

Turnbull went on to remodel the south choir chapel at Jedburgh, though it was later remodelled yet again, probably following a further English attack in 1464 (see Figure 3.4). The south piers of the crossing and the tower above them were also rebuilt soon after (see Figure 3.5). From their arms and initials we know this was done by Abbots John Hall (1478–84) and Thomas Cranston (1484–8), and heraldry at the wall-head shows the tower was completed in Archbishop Blackadder's time. In the heavily moulded shafts and the diagonally continuous cap and base mouldings of the new crossing piers we see a similar spirit as in the Torphichen transepts (see Figure 3.2). But Jedburgh has some puzzling features. From the south-east pier it can be seen it was intended to throw an intermediate arch across the south transept; but this idea was abandoned before the south-west crossing pier was built. Presumably also in the same campaign a semi-circular barrel vault was built over the south transept, below the clearstorey added in the later twelfth century. The clearstorey was thus blocked, possibly suggesting a failure of nerve that is also represented by the decision not to complete the higher barrel vault over the north transept. One other feature which may belong to this phase of works is a twelve-petal rose window in the reconstructed west gable of the nave, which is related to one in the west gable of the refectory at Dryburgh.

Jedburgh was to suffer again in the later phases of periodic warfare with England in 1523, 1544 and 1545. Probably after the earliest of these attacks the nave roofs were reconstructed to a lower pitch, those over the aisles cutting into the gallery openings in an ungainly way. After the later attacks the abbey retreated into an area within the crossing and transepts in the hope of better days that never came.

FIGURE 3.4 Jedburgh Abbey, the south choir chapel.

FIGURE 3.5   Jedburgh Abbey, the rebuilt south-east crossing pier.

Another of the Border abbeys that suffered in the wars with England was the Premonstratensian house of Dryburgh. Repairs after the English attack of 1322 may be identifiable in the north choir clearstorey, while damage caused by the English in 1385 – and the possibility that the canons had thought of making do with a shorter nave – has already been mentioned (see p. 55). There were further attacks in 1461, 1523, 1544 and 1545, though so little survives of the nave that it is difficult to be certain of the work they necessitated. Nevertheless, the west front and some pier fragments show there was rebuilding to a restrained two-storeyed design; the west doorway, with two bands of square flower in the hollows of three orders of continuous mouldings is the finest surviving feature (see Figure 3.6).

FIGURE 3.6   Dryburgh Abbey, the west doorway.

Damage from enemy action was not the only reason for rebuilding. At Dunfermline we know of various works during the later fourteenth and fifteenth centuries.[11] The purchase of stone from London for the shrine of St Margaret in 1368 shows there was then some refitting of her chapel at the east end of the church.[12] It is said that the outer north choir aisle, which was perhaps a Lady Chapel, was also of the fourteenth century; though the little we know of its large three- and four-light windows with cusped circlets could fit better in either the late thirteenth or the fifteenth centuries.[13] Other late medieval modifications in the nave included the cutting of a new western doorway from the cloister into the south aisle, and the progressive replacement of several twelfth-century windows by larger ones with intersecting tracery. The four-light window in the west front is a particularly poor exchange for the two tiers of Romanesque windows which were originally there (see Figure 3.7). Some of the new windows must have lit the altars which were being added through the nave, and were simply vehicles for stained glass. Some were perhaps paid for by the guild, the incorporation of merchants in the burgh, which had at least three altars under its patronage.

The greatest changes in Dunfermline's nave were at the west end of the north aisle, and were probably necessitated by structural difficulties (see Figure 3.7). In the upper parts of the north-west corner of the nave sympathetic round-arched openings at gallery and clearstorey level were reconstructed – though as now seen they may belong to a yet later rebuilding – but at arcade level a rather inappropriately busy pier of octofoil section replaced its cylindrical predecessor. At the same time, a porch was placed over the north doorway, which was the main lay entrance to the part used as a parish church. The porch has two bays of tierceron vaulting, while the arch opening into it has similar mouldings as the arcade pier. The work was carried out during the abbacy of Richard Bothwell (1446–82), whose arms are on the rebuilt vault, but it may have been supported by the Flesher's Incorporation, since arms with a bull's head are on the new pier. Work was also started on a new north-west tower, and the lower stage with its sexpartite vault is of this period. The upper stages, however, date from the late sixteenth century rebuilding by Queen Anne of Denmark's master of works, William Schaw.

FIGURE 3.7   Dunfermline Abbey, the interior of the nave looking towards the rebuilt north-west corner.

At Holyrood there are hints of late medieval work in the transepts and eastern limb and, as at Dunfermline, an outer choir aisle was added at some stage, though here on the south side. But so little survived the demolition of the damaged eastern parts in 1570 by Bishop Adam Bothwell of Orkney, who was commendator of the abbey, that there is little we can usefully say about them. What can still be seen are works by Abbots Crawford (1450–c.1483) and Bellenden (1484–1497), and those are in the nave.

The early thirteenth-century nave of Holyrood was one of the masterpieces of that period, and was unusual in having stone vaulting over the high spaces of the nave as well as the aisles.[14] However, the thrusts of that sexpartite vault created difficulties which may have been exacerbated by English attacks in 1322 and 1385. The earliest repairs and rebuilding after those attacks were perhaps in the eastern limb and transepts, and it was Abbot Crawford who eventually tackled the structural problems of the nave, and probably reconstructed much of the vaulting. To abut the vault, on the north side he more than doubled the projection of the buttresses, added pinnacles

FIGURE 3.8   Holyrood Abbey, the enlarged buttresses and the doorway on the north side of the nave.

and threw flyers across to the clearstorey (see Figure 3.8). On the south side the presence of the cloister called for more complicated measures, and there he built his buttresses against the cloister walk, necessitating two tiers of flyers up to the level of the clearstorey. Abbot Bellenden completed the work on the nave by obtaining lead for the roof.

Crawford also made a new doorway in the north aisle. This round-headed opening was flanked by pinnacles, surmounted by an ogee-arched hood moulding, and had pairs of tabernacles on each side of the arch. Unfortunately its detailing is rather two-dimensional, and the aisle window above it is uncomfortably off-centre. Inside the church there is a particularly interesting relic of Crawford's work: the screen at the entrance to the transept from the north aisle. Such furnishings are very rare, and it only survives here because it became part of the wall when what remained of the eastern parts was demolished in 1570. It has a central doorway, with Crawford's arms in a roundel on its lintel; flanking the door are blind arches, and above a cornice is an open triangular-headed arcade.

At a number of monastic houses there was more far-reaching late medieval rebuilding than at first appears. At the Valliscaulian priory of Ardchattan, on the shores of Loch Etive in Argyll, rebuilding embraced much of the church and some of the conventual buildings as well.[15] The clearest signs of this are in the eastern limb of the church, which was enlarged to a spacious rectangular plan with a northern sacristy. Only the lower walls remain, but the roll mouldings at its external angles indicate either a revival of earlier Irish-inspired ideas current in the area in the thirteenth century – and in evidence in the earlier work at Ardchattan itself – or a fresh infusion of Irish influence. In late medieval Argyll contacts with Ireland were often still easier than those across the mainland. Other moulded details, with simple repetition of filleted rolls and half hollows, support the idea that Ireland was a continuing source of influence. The most intriguing remaining feature of the new work is a round-arched recess in the south wall, near the site of the high altar (see Figure 3.9). Within its three blind arches are a piscina bowl and what may have been two credence shelves. But it is uncertain if the piscina and shelves are in their original positions; if not, the recess could originally have been intended as sedilia.

Ardchattan's sister Valliscaulian foundation of Beauly, in Inverness-shire,[16] also underwent extensive modifications; these may have followed claims in 1432 by the local landowner, Fraser of Lovat, that the buildings were decayed (see Figure 3.10).[17] His father is said to have built a timber bell-cote on the west gable, while Fraser himself added a chapel of the Holy Cross, of which there are traces against the north side of the nave. Another contributor was Prior Mackenzie, who died in 1479, and whose tomb is in the wall that cut off the south transeptal chapel from the monastic choir. It is possible the chapel was originally part of the east claustral range, but was absorbed into the church to create a cruciform plan in which it balanced the sacristy on the north.

The last works at Beauly date from the eve of the Reformation. By that stage it had passed through a difficult period, during which individuals who had plundered the priory were excommunicated by the Pope in 1506, and in 1510 it was decided the

FIGURE 3.9   Ardchattan Priory, the credence recess.

house should adopt the Cistercian rule. In 1531 the vigorous Robert Reid, who was already abbot of Cistercian Kinloss in Moray, and who was to become bishop of Orkney in 1541, became its head. He introduced a variety of reforms, following which Beauly was probably in better health than most other monasteries, and there may even have been an increase in the number of its monks.

Reid rebuilt the western part of the nave, including the west facade and the adjacent part of the north flank (see Figure 3.10). The former is of a satisfyingly simple design, with a central doorway surmounted by an image niche, and an echelon arrangement of three single-light windows below the steeply pointed gable. Reid's arms and initials are on the image niche. He probably also built the new doorway from the south transept into the cloister, since its details relate to those of the west doorway. Interestingly, there is a mason's mark at Beauly in the form of a heart with leg-like extensions, which is like others at the Earl's Palace at Birsay and at Noltland Castle. Both of those are in Orkney which suggests Reid could have taken masons from Beauly to Orkney when he became bishop, and that they worked for others after his death in 1558.

There may be relics of late medieval reconstruction at the Premonstratensian abbey of Tongland in Kirkcudbrightshire. The abbey had been founded in 1218, apparently taking over an existing church, and partly continued in use as a parish church after the Reformation until being replaced by a new building in 1813. Only parts of the west and north wall survive, and the sole feature is a doorway in the latter. On first sight that doorway, with two shafted orders and nailhead decoration around the caps,

FIGURE 3.10 Beauly Priory, the west front.

might be taken to date from the early thirteenth century. But closer inspection of the rather mechanically detailed mouldings suggests it is another example of revived twelfth- and thirteenth-century detail. Although it is dangerous to associate random architectural survivals with equally random documentary references, it is possible the doorway dates from after 1509, when James IV sought papal permission to grant the commendatorship of the abbey to the Bishop of Whithorn, citing as one reason the need to repair the ruinous buildings.[18]

Where late medieval architectural works were a luxury rather than a necessity, a favourite outlet was the construction of towers. The building of a rather utilitarian tower at Cross Kirk in Peebles was probably connected with the foundation of a Trinitarian priory there, within an existing church believed to house relics of the Holy Cross (see Figure 3.11).[19] There were probably Trinitarians there from about 1448, though they were under threat following accusations of mishandling the relics, and it was only in 1473–4 they were established on a fully conventual basis.[20] The western tower, which was probably built after then, is over 15 metres high, and contains five storeys, the lowest being a porch. The existence of fireplaces and window seats on some floors suggests it was habitable, perhaps by the official responsible for watching over the relics. A view of 1796 shows a corbelled parapet, behind which there could once have been a spire, though there was little other architectural embellishment.

So far as we know, most Scottish Cistercian houses continued to eschew lofty bell towers up to the end of the Middle Ages, though we know that at Kinloss a tower and spire were built by Abbot James Guthry (1467–82).[21] Ironically, the only tall Cistercian tower that has survived is at Culross, which is otherwise one of the best-preserved churches of early Cistercian plan in Britain. Culross had been founded by the Earl of Fife in about 1217, on the site of a community associated with St Serf. Despite its relatively late foundation, the church was laid out to the traditional

FIGURE 3.11   Peebles Cross Kirk, the west tower.

'Bernardine' plan, with a rectangular presbytery, a pair of chapels to each transept, and the choirs of the monks and lay brethren within the western limb, which was in this case aisle-less. The monks' choir, presbytery and transepts became the parish church in 1633 and, despite major losses in a restoration by William Stirling of 1824, which were partly reversed in a further restoration by Rowand Anderson of 1905, the medieval plan of those parts survives. The only major late medieval addition was the bell tower, which was raised not at the crossing of the main body of the church and transepts, but above the pulpitum and screen which separated the choirs of monks and lay brethren (see Figure 3.12). At the same time a lateral chapel was built out to

FIGURE 3.12 Culross Abbey, the tower from the west.

the north of the tower, though little of this has survived. An approximate date is supplied by the arms of Abbot Andrew Masoun (1498–1513) inside the tower's west wall.

To support the tower in this position the side walls at its base were thickened, and the way this was done had the advantage of ensuring the preservation of the early thirteenth-century screen. The two side doors at both floor and loft levels of that screen, however, had to be blocked, and a reused doorway was placed in the middle. The details of the tower were severely plain – though it now has an inappropriate modern parapet. The greatest emphasis is at the belfry stage, which has a single-light window on each face, with a more decorative traceried circular window above. Access between the floors of the tower is by a boldly expressed circular stair turret at the north-west angle. Internally, the lowest stage of the tower was covered by an octapartite vault which, like the sexpartite vault in Bothwell's tower at Dunfermline, reminds us of the renewed interest in earlier vault types at this period.

Where towers already existed there was the option of adding spires. A handsome example was raised above the slender eleventh- and twelfth century-tower at the centre of the small Augustinian priory church of Restenneth, in Angus (see Figure 3.13).[22] By the later fifteenth century that priory was seriously ailing and attempts were made to unite it with other religious establishments: with Jedburgh in 1476, with the Chapel Royal at Stirling in 1501 and 1507, and with St Andrews in 1508.[23] None of these was successful, but it is unlikely that the two canons who served the house could have provided the spire themselves, and credit is perhaps due to the lay folk who worshipped in the nave of the priory church. Constructed of finely cut ashlar, it is of graceful splay-foot form, with a single lucarne at the base of each main face.

One other spire which deserves mention is that once on the tower of St Rule's Church in St Andrews, which was lost several centuries ago, leaving only the added corbelled parapet. Its depiction on a sixteenth-century panoramic view of St Andrews suggests it was a timber structure sheathed in lead, and it is possible it was added when Prior John Hepburn (1482–1522) remodelled the ground storey of the tower. In the process he walled up the tower arches, leaving only narrow doorways – that in the east arch being polygonal-headed and having his arms above it. Hepburn was a prolific patron of architecture throughout St Andrews, and the mouldings at St Rule's Church are so similar to those at St Leonard's College Chapel that they may have been by the same mason.

THE CONTINUING WORK ON MELROSE ABBEY

The progress of the work started at Melrose in the 1380s, up to the early decades of the fifteenth century when the French-born mason John Morow was at work, has already been discussed (see p. 28). The third phase of the work can be linked with the change at clearstorey level from elaborately traceried windows to pairs of cusped single-light windows. These are introduced first in the upper part of the north transept west face, and then in the clearstorey of the monks' choir in the three eastern bays of the nave (see Figure 3.15). The change at this stage is also marked on the exterior of

FIGURE 3.13   Restenneth Priory, the central tower and spire.

the north aisle, where there is a sudden thinning of the wall after the first bay, and a
new design for the decorative wall arcading towards the cloister walk is introduced.
Instead of the deeply modelled and lavishly pinnacled and crocketed arcading of the
west face of the north transept and the first bay of the north aisle, the arcading is
reduced to a simpler and shallower trifoliate pattern, even the abbot's seat in the
fourth bay being only slightly enriched.

   Since this stage included the completion of the monks' choir, the arcades of which
belonged to the first campaign, it was presumably well advanced by 1441 when the
abbey went to law over the stalls they had ordered from Bruges (see Figure 3.16).
But it is clear that much remained for Abbot Andrew Hunter (c.1444–71) to
build, since his arms appear at several points. They are on the tierceron vault of
the south transept, on the buttress which rises above the first bay of the south nave

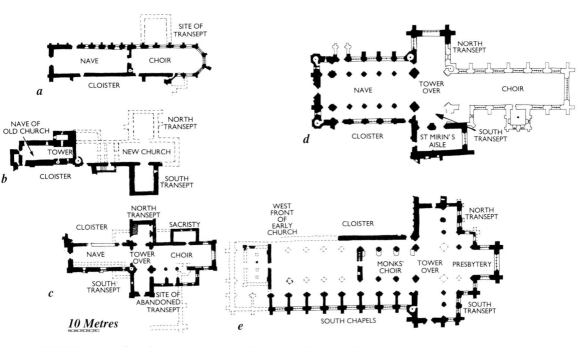

FIGURE 3.14   Plans of monastic churches: a. Crossraguel Abbey; b. Inchcolm Abbey; c. Iona Abbey; d. Paisley Abbey; e. Melrose Abbey.

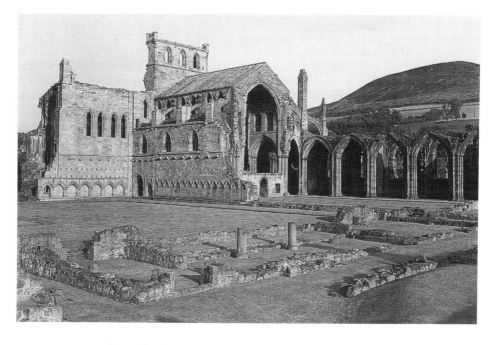

FIGURE 3.15   Melrose Abbey from the north-west.

aisle between the two ranks of flyers, and on the fifth buttress of the south aisle chapels. All of this suggests he was behind several important features of the later stages of work. He probably ordered the vaulting of the monks' choir which, like the transept vault, was of tierceron pattern (the present pointed barrel vault belongs to the early seventeenth-century parish church inserted there). He was presumably also responsible for the introduction of two new tracery types in the nave chapels. One of those is almost identical with the north transept window at Jedburgh, as already said (see p. 82); the other, used in three of the chapels, has triplets of spiralling daggers in a circlet, and is similar to a window in the nave of Linlithgow Church (see p. 199).

Hunter could also have been the provider of the four finest pieces of figure sculpture to have survived from the Scottish late Middle Ages: the figures of Sts Peter and Paul in the north transept, and those of the Virgin and child and of St Andrew in the upper buttresses along the south side of the monastic choir. The two former figures have well-characterised faces and heavy blanket-like folds of drapery, which offer a Scottish parallel for the figures produced under the direction of John Thirsk for the chantry chapel of Henry V in Westminster Abbey, of about 1441–50.[24] The pose and clothing of the other figures is more complex and more crisply executed, though the posture of the Virgin has, perhaps inevitably, a slightly stereotyped quality (see Figure 3.17).

After completing the monks' choir, work at Melrose slowed down dramatically, suggesting funds were less easy to find. There was apparently a pause before the sixth chapel was fitted out, since it has arms probably of Abbot Turnbull (1503–7) on the piscina. From the same phase are the arms and initials of James IV with the date 1505, on the eighth chapel buttress. However, aligned with that buttress are the remains of the west gable of the original church, showing that work progressed no further (see Figure 3.14e). Apart from the overwhelming costs of the work, conditions were no longer conducive to building activity within the community from the later fifteenth century onwards. There was a dissipating struggle over the abbacy between 1486 and 1507, and a further dispute in 1524.[25] After a relatively quiet period, in 1541 the abbey was granted in commendam to an illegitimate son of James V, who was already commendator of Kelso, and had so little interest in the life of the abbey that in 1555 the monks protested about his misappropriation of resources.[26] To add to the abbey's

FIGURE 3.16   Melrose Abbey, a carved capital in the monks' choir.

FIGURE 3.17   Melrose Abbey, the statue of the Virgin and Child in a buttress above the south aisle.

miseries, there was a devastating English attack in 1545. It was on these rocks that the stately – and incomplete – vessel of Melrose foundered.

THE NEW ABBEY CHURCH OF INCHCOLM

One of the most fascinating building campaigns in the course of the fifteenth century was that at the Augustinian abbey of Inchcolm, on its island in the Firth of Forth.[27] Because of its vulnerable position the abbey suffered grievously in the fourteenth century. In 1335 the *Scotichronicon* refers to an English attack; between about 1347 and 1355 a charter refers to manifold destruction by land and sea; another charter of about 1370 indicates the theft and destruction of the house's muniments; in 1385 an English attempt to destroy the church by setting fire to an outbuilding on the north side was miraculously thwarted by a change in the direction of the wind.[28]

The abbey's fortunes revived under the abbacy of Lawrence (1394–1417) and reached a high point when Walter Bower was abbot, between 1418 and 1449. Bower had been a canon of St Andrews, and was a notable scholar, extending the history of Scotland written by John of Fordoun to form the *Scotichronicon*. It seems likely it was under Laurence and Bower that both church and conventual buildings were almost completely rebuilt, in a way which indicates a slightly obsessive fear of fire. An unexpected feature of these works is that the existing nave and tower were retained but put to lesser uses, while a new church was built to their east, partly overlapping the site of the thirteenth-century choir (see Figures 3.14b and 3.18). Almost equally unexpected is the way the claustral ranges were rebuilt against the flank of the old church (see Figure 3.35).

Little survives of the new church apart from its cruciform plan and parts of the south transept, including the vault springing on its west side. It is generally assumed this transept was the Lady Chapel referred to as being constructed in 1402, under the direction of Prior Richard of Aberdour and Canon Thomas Crawford,[29] thus suggesting that the whole church was built in the early fifteenth century. We cannot be certain

FIGURE 3.18   Inchcolm Abbey, the site of the new church from the east, with the vault of its south transept to the left. The tower of the earlier church is in the background.

of this but, if it was, it must be one of the earliest examples of an approach to building that was to become characteristic of many churches of moderate scale in its combinations of rectangular spaces covered by tunnel-like vaults. In support of an early date it may be that the massively constructed walls and pointed barrel vaulting were partly inspired by castle construction, as at Dundonald and Threave, and it is likely that so robust an approach would be especially attractive at Inchcolm. A relatively early date, and some degree of inspiration by military architecture, is also suggested by the way the walls were initially unbuttressed.

The planning of the new church was conditioned by the peculiar needs at Inchcolm. Since the early thirteenth-century tower of the existing church was retained, a tower was not needed in the new one, and there was therefore no defined crossing. Also, since the island site probably meant few lay people ever came to worship, the part west of the transepts could be short, and was probably intended purely for the canons' choir, though the old choir was possibly briefly used as a nave. As a result the new church had proportions different from what was usual, approximating more to a Greek than to a Latin cross. The main body of the church was an undivided rectangle, with relatively narrow arches about half-way down opening into the transepts on each side, but with no transverse arches. East of the transepts was the presbytery, within the south wall of which a fragment of the sedilia survives. The rectangular transepts each had space for two altars. West of the canons' choir was a vestibule, into which a night stair from the dormitory eventually led. Further west still was the part of the old choir which may have been used as a nave for a while, but which was eventually converted into an open courtyard, with a spiral stair up to the first floor of the tower.

For structural reasons, the pointed barrel vaults covering the church sprang from a low level, and we know from later churches of this type – as at Queensferry or Dunglass – that the resultant appearance can now seem rather heavy (see Figure 5.28). But at Inchcolm the extensive surviving plasterwork reminds us that this appearance would have been diminished when the masonry of walls and vaults was still covered over. Unfortunately, however, the real weight remained, and in the north transept buttresses had to be added to withstand the thrusts of the vaulting.

PAISLEY ABBEY CHURCH

The Cluniac abbey of Paisley had been founded in about 1163 at Renfrew, and was moved to its present site some six years later. The existing abbey church is a complex architectural mixture dating variously from the late twelfth to the early twentieth centuries. The earliest work is the south-east doorway, while the south aisle wall of the nave and the west front, together with much of the south transeptal chapel, are substantially of the mid-thirteenth century (see Figure 3.14d). How much of this was ever completed we cannot know, but in 1307 there was an English attack, which necessitated extensive repairs. In 1389 Robert II made a gift to reglazing, suggesting that some phase of building was well advanced. It has been said above that the eastern bays of the north nave aisle are attributable to the mason John Morow, in the time of Abbot Lithgow (1384–1433) (see p. 47 and Figure 1.30). As part of the same operation work was probably also started on the nave arcades, since their bases are similar to those of the wall shafts in the Morow bays.

The majority of the nave, however, is attributable to Abbot Thomas Tervas (1445–59) (see Figure 3.19). It was said in 1444, in correspondence with Rome, that the church was collapsed and, even allowing for exaggeration, this shows much remained to be done.[30] In addition, the *Auchinleck Chronicle* says it was Tervas who built the nave 'frae the bricht stair up' – though we are uncertain where that stair was – and that he also roofed the nave and built part of the tower.[31] Work was probably nearing completion in 1455, when Tervas imported 'the statliest tabernacle [altarpiece] that was in al Shotland and the maist costlie'.[32]

Tervas's nave[33] is an impressive piece of architecture, but it must be conceded that it relies on a long-established formula for its three-storeyed elevations. Such conservatism was in part because of the limitations imposed by what was retained of earlier

FIGURE 3.19   Paisley Abbey, the interior of the nave looking westwards.

work: the bay rhythm was dictated by the aisle vaulting shafts, while the three-storey elevation was partly conditioned by the stubs of the thirteenth-century work at the west end. Nevertheless, on this last point Tervas's mason did put up some resistance, since the earlier western responds at triforium level indicate different proportions for the upper storeys than those we now see.

The three storeys of the elevation are carefully inter-related, with the transition from the single arch at arcade level to the paired arches at clearstorey level being eased by the way the segmental-arched triforium openings are subdivided into two parts. The main emphasis throughout is horizontal, with string courses marking the stages, though there are vertical wall shafts in the clearstorey. The emergent Scottish approach to design is emphasised in the caps of the octofoil arcade piers, which have upper mouldings continued in an unbroken line across each diagonal face. But the most striking feature of the design is the corbelling-out of the clearstorey walk-way around the stronger piers. This was perhaps partly through fear of weakening the main piers of masonry at this level, where the walls were already thinner than might have been wished. But such a conceit also shows an awareness of developments in the wider architectural world. Although it would be pretentious to see direct links with the approximately contemporary corbelled-out wall-walks in the aisles of St Lorenz at Nuremberg, or the walks at mid-height of the transept windows of Utrecht Cathedral, for example, it is worth remembering that such ideas were being explored over a wide area. Unfortunately, at Paisley the effect has been marred by the loss of the intended balustrade, leaving the corbels with a cumbersome appearance.

The last significant works at Paisley were in the transepts, and may have followed a fire in 1498. On the north transept are arms identified as of Abbot Shaw, who was appointed in 1499. It was therefore probably reconstructed by him, though the base courses show it was set out to its present plan at the same time as the adjacent north nave aisle, at the turn of the fourteenth century.

The narrow south transept and the chapel which opens on its south side are more complex. In its mid-thirteenth-century state the chapel was of the same east–west dimensions as the crossing, with two arches opening into it from the transept. It underwent remodelling about the same time as its northern counterpart, since we know it was fitted out as a chapel of St Mirin for James Crawford of Kilwynet in around 1499 (see Figure 3.20).[34] The chief changes involved may have been its eastward extension by one bay, the construction of a four-light eastern window, and the addition of a ribbed pointed barrel vault over it. Like the windows inserted at Torphichen (see Figure 3.2), the new window in St Mirin's chapel demonstrates a revival of mid-thirteenth-century geometrical types, although in this case the ogee curves within the sub-arches make clear the late date. In the ribbed barrel vault the decision to set out the ribs on a sexpartite pattern, with additional intersections above the arcade from the transept, shows the inherent versatility of such vaulting.

FIGURE 3.20   Paisley Abbey, St Mirin's Chapel.

CROSSRAGUEL ABBEY CHURCH

Scotland's other Cluniac foundation, Crossraguel in Ayrshire, also remodelled its church in the fifteenth century. Crossraguel was a far less wealthy house than Paisley, having an assessed income of £1,860 in 1561 as opposed to Paisley's princely £6,100. Nevertheless, it built a church which, although of small scale, was of high architectural quality. Nineteenth-century excavations showed that the original church had been an aisle-less cruciform structure. It had probably been started after a judgement of 1244 by the Bishop of Glasgow that Paisley should build an independent house here, with funds given for this purpose at a date around 1214 by Duncan, the future Earl of Carrick.[35] The main body of the church then built underlay all later developments, and parts of it survive in the walls of the nave.

The greatest change came when the eastern half of the church was rebuilt, and the transepts suppressed. In their new form the choir and presbytery consisted of a buttressed rectangle of five bays, with a three-sided eastern apse (see Figures 3.14a and 3.21). The precise date of these changes is not known, but it is likely they were carried out during the long abbacy of Colin, from 1460 to 1491. Father Richard Augustine Hay, writing in the early eighteenth century but thought to have had access to lost records, said that it had been Colin's first care to restore the abbey's buildings, and that he spent much time in superintending the work himself.[36] Although it is dangerous to place too much reliance on late sources, this date range is consistent with the architectural evidence, and particularly with the detailing of the eastern apse. More will be said about apses in discussing the collegiate and burgh churches, but it is almost certain that their introduction to Scottish churches represents another importation from the continent. They are perhaps most likely to have been introduced at the more cosmopolitan work carried out on St Salvator's College for Bishop Kennedy of St Andrews from 1450, and for Queen Mary of Guelders' Trinity College in Edinburgh of before 1460 (see Figures 5.19 and 5.36). Nevertheless, assuming that Crossraguel's apse was not one of the first of its kind, its sophistication suggests that its master mason was acquainted with work in the main centres; it should of course be remembered that Bishop Kennedy was a member of a prominent Ayrshire family, and that he could have offered architectural advice in this case.

Externally the eastern limb is divided into bays by two-stage buttresses, and the horizontal stratification is marked by a chamfered plinth course, a string course below the windows, and a wall-head cornice below a parapet. The windows have wide reveals, and stretch to take up the full space between the buttresses, string course and cornice. The external details are generally restrained, most of the mouldings being simple chamfers, except in the apse, where the enriched reveals of the windows around the altar have engaged shafts. Internally the detailing is more complex. The bays are defined by slender triplet wall shafts, rising from the floor in the presbytery, but only from the string below the windows in the choir to allow stalls to be placed against the wall.

Except around the apse, the internal window reveals are narrower than on the outside, leaving areas of wall to each side (see Figure 3.21). However, these areas were articulated by extending horizontal mouldings across from the wall shafts to the springing point of the window arches, above which the wall plane breaks forward. The most lavish detail is in the presbytery furnishings: the piscina and sedilia. The former has a three-centred arch with a crocketed ogee hood; the latter have four cusped arches, surmounted by finely detailed gablets separated by pinnacles. It is particularly regrettable that the window tracery has been lost since, in such a carefully considered structure, it would have told us much about the antecedents of its mason. (The horizontal transoms which now cross some of the windows at the level of the arch springing appear to be part of late alterations.)

It is unclear how the remodelling of the north and west faces of the nave fits into the sequence of works at the abbey, but perhaps the windows of the north nave wall belong to an attempt to make the nave sit more happily with the remodelled choir. One part of the nave which is more precisely datable is the first full window to the north-west of the screen wall between choir and nave, which lit the Lady Altar. Its remodelling was paid for by Egidia, Lady Row, a great benefactress of the abbey who lived at the nearby castle of Baltersan. Before her death in 1530 she ordered she was

FIGURE 3.21   Crossraguel Abbey, the interior of the choir apse.

to be buried here,[37] and the remains of her tomb formed part of an integrated composition with the window. The window is another example of the revived taste for geometrical tracery already noted at Torphichen and Paisley (see Figures 3.2 and 3.20), but it has the unusual motif of transoms at the level of the arch springing, each in the form of a shallow inverted letter V. It is closely related to a four-light window in the aisle which survives from the medieval parish church of Straiton, also in Ayrshire, and could be by the same mason.

THE ABBEY CHURCH OF IONA

Iona has the distinction of one of the longest histories of monastic life in Scotland (see Figures 3.14c and 3.22). From the arrival of St Columba in 563, despite Norse raids over nearly two centuries between 795 and 986, and allowing for the change to the Benedictine rule around 1203, the religious life continued for almost a millenium up to the time of the Reformation. Appropriately, for such an important foundation, the abbey church is also complete, even if that completeness is partly the result of restorations.[38] The first stage of restoration was between 1874 and 1876, when the eighth Duke of Argyll commissioned Rowand Anderson to consolidate the upstanding remains. Then, between 1902 and 1905, the eastern limb and transepts were restored by Thomas Ross and John Honeyman; the restoration of the nave, by Peter MacGregor Chalmers, followed between 1908 and 1910. In the eastern parts the work was closely conditioned by the surviving evidence, though the nave was less complete and the results are inevitably less authentic.

The church built after the introduction of Benedictine monasticism, in the early 1200s, was a cruciform structure, with short aisle-like vestibules in the re-entrant angles between nave and transepts for circulation. Pairs of chapels on the east side of the transepts were so shallow that they were little more than hollowings in the wall. Early in the thirteenth century the eastern limb was lengthened, with aisles down both sides for about two-thirds of its length; this new eastern limb also had a timber-covered crypt. Towards the end of that century a massive asymmetrical south transeptal aisle was started, but was never finished. The changes of concern here, however, are those datable to around the second half of the fifteenth century, when the line of the south side of the church was moved outwards, and the building was extensively remodelled throughout.

There is no documentation for the start of this operation, but it has been attributed to Abbot Dominic (1421–c. 1465), who attempted to make good the earlier mis-management of the abbey's finances by members of the MacKinnon clan.[39] There is certainly evidence that the abbey's affairs had been at a low ebb, and in 1428 a papal mandate stated the buildings were ruinous.[40] It is assumed that Dominic was in a position to start new building by the middle of the century. Like Ardchattan, Iona has as much of the feel of an Irish as of a Lowland Scottish building, and it is significant that a mason whose family was of Irish origin worked there. We know this because one of the carved pier capitals of the south choir arcade was signed by Donald Ó Brolchán, who must have been a member of a family from Donegal which had earlier established itself in the West Highlands.[41] Unfortunately, it is not clear

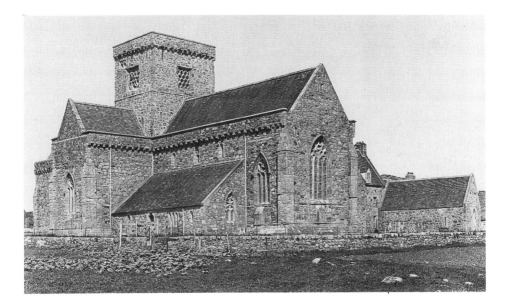

FIGURE 3.22   Iona Abbey from the south-east.

whether Ó Brolchán was claiming responsibility for the whole rebuilding or just the capitals.

Rebuilding probably started with the eastern limb, and included suppression of the crypt, reconstruction of the eastern bay of the presbytery, truncation of the north aisle to form a sacristy, and the rebuilding of the southern flank with the addition of an aisle that opened into the choir through three arches carried on cylindrical piers (see Figure 3.23). These changes involved some difficulties and inconsistencies. On the north side the two thirteenth-century arcade arches were retained, despite the lowering of the floor level into what had been the crypt, and a new door was slapped through what had been the crypt wall beneath the eastern of the two. However, this inconsistency would have been masked, since early views show the arches were partly blocked until being reopened in the restoration of 1902–5. On the opposite side of the choir, masonry tusks built into the south transept suggest the south choir aisle was to have been almost as wide as the choir itself, but was eventually built slightly narrower than intended. The quadrant arches carried on transverse spur walls which now divide the aisle into bays may indicate there was some difficulty in roofing the aisle.

The new eastern presbytery bay has large windows in all three faces to throw light on to the high altar. The use of spiralling dagger tracery in two of those windows (and also in the main south transept window) shows parallels with favoured types in the

FIGURE 3.23   Iona Abbey, the interior of the choir before restoration.

Lowlands; the basic design of the east window, for example, has similarities with windows in the nave of Elgin. But there is a chunkiness in the details which is unlike Lowland examples; though Irish parallels are equally hard to find, and this may represent what is quite simply a West Highland development. Rising a single storey above the roof-tops of the new crossing is a very solid tower, with unusual square belfry windows on three faces which look more like the sound holes of an East Anglian church tower than anything Scottish or Irish. These openings have tracery of spiralling daggers, reticulation or multiple quatrefoils. The closest Scottish analogies are the circular traceried openings in the towers of Culross Abbey and Linlithgow Church, and the intermediate level opening in the west face of Dundee Church tower (see Figures 3.12, 6.9 and 6.18).

THE CONVENTUAL BUILDINGS: GENERAL CONSIDERATIONS

The domestic buildings of monastic houses have survived less well than the churches; perversely, where they have survived well – as at Inchcolm (see Figure 3.26) and to a lesser extent at Oronsay (both Augustinian) – they are atypical. However, it has to be said that monastic planning tended to become less predictable in the later Middle Ages than it had been before. Although there has been little attempt to correlate the surviving documentation with the architectural evidence, this greater freedom of planning is a further indicator of a less rigid adherence to the original principles of monastic life.

It has been suggested above that the members of some houses came to enjoy a degree of privacy and independence, and this must have been reflected in architectural changes, even if we can do little more than speculate on the nature of these changes. At Holyrood (Augustinian), for example, by the time of James IV's marriage in 1503 the original canons' refectory may have become the great hall of the royal palace,[42] suggesting that communal life there was less strictly observed. This is perhaps some reflection of the stricture levelled at a number of English houses that the community had abandoned the refectory, presumably in favour of places where they could eat forbidden meats and delicacies.[43] At Holyrood there are references to a new refectory in 1564 (presumably built before the Reformation) which cannot have been in the customary position.[44] There may have been a related situation at Arbroath, where a description of 1517 says there were two refectories, one for everyday use and the other for feasts.

Another indicator of change is evident at Crossraguel (Cluniac), where the upper floor of the east claustral range was no longer set out as an unbroken dormitory hall in the form to which it was eventually completed (see Figures 3.24 and 3.25). Here we perhaps see a later echo of the problems identified at Scone (Augustinian) in 1365, where it was ordered that all canons must sleep within the dormitory, however late they returned, suggesting a growing preference for sleeping elsewhere within the precinct.[45] The same shift in attitudes could also be reflected in several abbeys where we find alterations to the upper floors of the east conventual ranges, as at Dryburgh (Premonstratensian) or Balmerino (Cistercian). These changes are generally assumed to be post-Reformation modifications to create residences for the later commendators;[46] but, while such assumptions may be correct, it is also possible that some represent pre-Reformation changes to meet modified needs.

In this connection, however, it must be admitted that we simply do not know the uses of many later monastic buildings of which traces remain, especially once we move away from the main nucleus around the cloister into the greater precinct. Documentation indicating their functions has seldom survived, and few Scottish monastic precincts have been even partly excavated with sophisticated modern techniques that might help to identify the full range of buildings and their uses.

At Crossraguel, where there are more extensive remains than usual for a late medieval monastic complex, there are buildings which starkly remind us of the difficulties of identification. Apart from the absence of an unbroken dormitory hall on the first floor of the east range already mentioned, it seems the refectory on the first floor of the south cloister range was also of relatively small scale in the fifteenth century (see Figure 3.25). Of course, for the eleven monks here around this time large communal spaces were not strictly necessary, but these changes could betoken more than just reduced needs. A particularly intriguing feature at Crossraguel is a series of small houses along the perimeter of the first courtyard of the precinct, to the south of the cloister. One writer has suggested these were houses for the holders of corrodies, that is individuals who had earned or paid for the right to live within the

FIGURE 3.24 Crossraguel Abbey, the east conventual range – containing the dormitory above the chapter house and sacristy – is on the left, and the choir of the church on the right.

monastic precinct, and to enjoy a monastic portion.[47] This is certainly possible; but it is also possible they were individual residences for the monks themselves, like the canons' little houses referred to at Pittenweem (Augustinian) in 1549, and this might explain why refectory and dormitory were relatively small.

FIGURE 3.25   Crossraguel Abbey, looking across the cloister to the east range. The refectory is on the right.

At Pittenweem itself, which became the permanent base of the Augustinian canons of the Isle of May around the early fourteenth century, there was much fifteenth- and sixteenth-century rebuilding.[48] Parts of those canons' houses may be incorporated in the courtyard of buildings south of the church, which is entered through a fifteenth-century gatehouse. A particularly interesting aspect of this courtyard is that it is completely detached from the parish church which was used by the canons for their conventual worship. Departures from normal planning were not uncommon at the smaller houses of the Augustinians, and were by no means confined to the later Middle Ages; but they were perhaps most common where the priory was attached to a pre-existing church. At Monymusk in Aberdeenshire, for example, where a community of Culdees was transformed into one of Augustinians before 1245, we have little

idea of where the conventual buildings were in relation to the church.[49] This readiness
to abandon convention by the Augustinians may also have been a factor in the
arrangement of buildings at Inchcolm.

The three ranges of buildings around the cloister to the south of the old church at
Inchcolm are still roofed, and represent the most complete conventual layout in
Scotland – though their date is problematic (see Figure 3.26). What is likely is that
they largely belong to the great period of renewal of the abbey's fortunes in the first
half of the fifteenth century under Abbots Laurence and Bower (see p. 97). Bower is
known to have fortified the abbey, and the fireproof vaulted reconstruction of the
monastic buildings was perhaps a part of that same process.[50] We also know that
construction works of some sort were under way in 1421, when a mason was among
those who survived the upsetting of a boat in a squall.[51] But none of this is sufficient
to date the new buildings with any certainty, particularly since there must have been
few periods when a mason was not required.

It might be argued that, because the buildings abut the old church, they must
predate the construction of the new church to its east. Against this, however, the
wish to retain the early thirteenth-century octagonal chapter house could have been
reason enough to keep the cloister in its earlier situation. But the strongest argument
for the conventual buildings post-dating construction of the new church is that the
nave and tower area of the old church themselves became the north cloister walk, by
which time the new church must have been in use. (A lean-to cloister walk was
eventually built against the south wall of the old church, but this was evidently a later
modification.)

If the relationship of the new buildings to the church is unorthodox at Inchcolm,
so is the way the ground floor of each range is given over to a cloister walk, in a
manner more frequently associated with English mendicant houses (see Figure 3.27).
These walks are covered by semicircular barrel vaults, and a similar vault was placed

FIGURE 3.26   Inchcolm Abbey, the claustral buildings from the south-west. The latrine block is on the
right.

FIGURE 3.27   Inchcolm Abbey, the south cloister walk.

within the nave and tower of the old church to create an almost complete circuit around the cloister. There are no precise parallels in Scotland for devoting the entire ground floor of the ranges to the cloister walks, though at the Augustinian houses of Jedburgh and Inchmahome in their final form some of the cloister walks were absorbed within the ranges. Opening on to the cloister garth from the walks are round-arched openings with seats in their embrasures.

The main rooms around Inchcolm's cloister are at first-floor level, where they are covered by pointed barrel vaults beneath stone-flagged roofs. How they were originally reached is now uncertain, since all of the staircases leading up to them seem to be later additions. In their arrangement, if not their appearance, these rooms follow the orthodox pattern. The dormitory was on the east side of the cloister (see Figure 3.28), and at its southern end was a latrine with a drain washed out by the sea, though that latrine had to be built out yet further after the drain had silted up. Unusually, a warming house – or perhaps it was some sort of dayroom – was provided against the east side of the dormitory, in a storey added above the octagonal chapter house. On the south of the cloister was the refectory, with a pulpit built out on an arch between buttresses (see Figure 3.26). The functions of the west range, and of the upper storey of the converted nave are uncertain, but they may have housed guest accommodation in their final state. Projecting eastwards at right angles from the extended reredorter

FIGURE 3.28   Inchcolm Abbey, the dormitory.

is a fourth range, also covered by barrel vaults at two levels. This was perhaps the abbot's lodging, since in this position lip service could be paid to the requirement for the abbot to live in common with his canons.

THE PLANNING OF THE CONVENTUAL BUILDINGS IN THE LATER MIDDLE AGES

As the most complete conventual complex, Inchcolm has been described in some detail, but we must now move on to consider the architectural treatment of some of the individual buildings which might be found within the precinct of a monastic house in the later Middle Ages. Space does not allow for full consideration of all of these, but it is important to mention some of the more important, if only to demonstrate how the religious houses were still major architectural patrons. It is perhaps worth stating that, where the limitations of site or water supply did not dictate otherwise the preferred situation for the main complex of buildings continued to be around a cloister against the south flank of the church, where they were not in its shade. Those buildings will be considered in a roughly clockwise fashion before looking at others elsewhere in the precinct.

Sacristies, where the vestments and vessels and some of the small movable furnishings required for the services were stored, were essentially an adjunct of the church. They could therefore either be next to the church in the east claustral range, or attached to some other part of the church's eastern limb. At Crossraguel, for example, the part of the east range adjoining the church – which included both the sacristy and the chapter house – was planned along with the new choir on the evidence of base course types, and was presumably also the work of Abbot Colin (1460–91). The sacristy was against the south wall of the choir, from which it was entered directly (see Figure 3.24). A noteworthy feature is its sexpartite vault, which is yet another example of the revival of such vaulting. However, it seems that the sacristy as built differs from what had first been planned, because on the north wall there are fragmentary shafts which do not relate to the existing vault; perhaps the original intention had been to have a slype here, a passage leading from the cloister to the area on its east side.

Two well-preserved monastic sacristies of a different type are at Arbroath (Tironensian) and Pluscarden (originally Valliscaulian, but by this stage Benedictine), both of which are divorced from the conventual ranges but against the church flank (see Figures 3.29 and 1.41). In each case the sacristy was on the ground floor, with a treasury for the storage of the most precious items on the floor above. Double-storeyed sacristy–treasury blocks were also built at other types of churches – as at Dunkeld Cathedral – and were not a purely monastic feature. The treasury could usually be reached by permanent stairs, but at Arbroath ladders were necessary. The

FIGURE 3.29   Arbroath Abbey, the sacristy and treasury on the south flank of the choir.

FIGURE 3.30   Crossraguel Abbey, the chapter house.

Arbroath sacristy bears the arms of Abbot Paniter (*c.*1411–49), although the architectural details might have been thought to suggest a later date. At Pluscarden the
sacristy vault has the arms of Dunbar, probably in reference to the prior of the house
between 1553 and 1560.

   Second in importance only to the church itself was the chapter house, where a
chapter from the monastic rule was read each day; it was also the setting for business
meetings and for the confession and correction of faults. A room of such importance,
prominently placed close to the church in the east claustral range, was a prime
candidate for rebuilding if funds were available. A number of later examples show
a return to square chambers with vaulting carried on a central pier, like the
thirteenth-century examples at Glasgow Cathedral (see Figure 2.4) and
Cambuskenneth Abbey. Largely complete examples of the type survive at Crossraguel (Cluniac) and Glenluce (Cistercian), and excavations have shown that the
third and final state of the chapter house at Jedburgh (Augustinian) was similar. The
example at Crossraguel is again part of the works attributed to Abbot Colin
(1460–91); however, it is likely to date from a late period in his abbacy, assuming
that his first efforts would have been expended on the church, and allowing for the
way there is evidence of a change of plan in the adjacent sacristy (see Figure 3.30).
The architecture of the Glenluce chapter house indicates a rather later date, but it
was probably inspired by that of Crossraguel, since the window tracery was strikingly
similar (see Figure 3.31).

FIGURE 3.31   Glenluce Abbey, the chapter house.

Balmerino (Cistercian) acquired a particularly handsome chapter house. As at the three already mentioned, it was a square chamber with a central pier to carry the vaulting – which was in this case of tierceron type. But here extra height was gained by placing it outside the body of the range, while the area within the range was treated as a lower vestibule (see Figure 3.32) – as had been done at St Andrews in the thirteenth and fourteenth centuries.

Other late medieval chapter houses which are still complete are at Inchmahome (Augustinian)(see Figure 3.33) and Iona (Benedictine). The former survived through serving as a mausoleum for Lord Kilpont after 1644, and is a simple barrel-vaulted chamber with stone benches. The latter, which is outside the body of the range, has arched seating recesses along its flanks and is also barrel vaulted. One other fragment requiring brief mention is at Kilwinning (Tironensian), where the entrance front is its main remnant. On first sight this front looks completely Romanesque, with a round-arched doorway symmetrically flanked by subdivided round-arched windows (see Figure 3.34). But by the time that Kilwinning was founded, probably at a date

FIGURE 3.32   Balmerino Abbey, the chapter house vestibule.

before 1189, its details would have been distinctly old-fashioned. Closer inspection
of the mouldings suggests it is more likely to be another example of the western
Scottish late medieval predilection for reviving earlier forms.

The refectory was the main building along the side of the cloister facing the church,
and was usually a large rectangular timber-roofed hall running parallel to the cloister
walk (the vogue for halls at right angles to the cloister, seen at several earlier Cistercian
houses, did not continue into the later Middle Ages). Of the refectories dating from
the late medieval period, reference has already been made to the examples at Inchcolm
and Crossraguel (see Figures 3.26 and 3.25), and it has been mentioned that the one
at Dryburgh (Premonstratensian) acquired a fine rose window. Many refectories were
at first-floor level – possibly in reference to the upper room in which the Last Supper
was eaten – though, since it was in some ways the equivalent of the hall in a private
residence, a first-floor situation must always have seemed appropriate. At Jedburgh
excavation indicated that the south cloister walk was slotted below the refectory
during later modifications, which also allowed the enlargement of the cloister garth.
There are unusually complete remains of the refectory at Ardchattan Priory
(Valliscaulian), where it was incorporated into a house for the commendators that is
still occupied.[52] Its most clearly identifiable feature is the pulpit, which has a screen
of two arches, and is covered by quadripartite vaulting. The original scissor-braced
timber roof also survives in part.

FIGURE 3.33   Inchmahome Priory, the chapter house before the restoration of the roof, with the choir of the church in the background.

FIGURE 3.34   Kilwinning Abbey, the chapter house entrance.

Cloister walks are a particularly vulnerable feature, since most had thin screen walls pierced by many openings and carrying timber lean-to roofs. In some cloisters the screen walls would have had traceried openings, as was probably intended at Melrose (Cistercian). The simple arched openings of Inchcolm might have represented the opposite extreme (see Figure 3.35), and most other cloisters would have been somewhere between the two. At Inchmahome there were two-light openings with stone benches in the embrasures, while Glenluce (Cistercian) eventually had a continuous arcade of narrow pointed arches (see Figure 3.36). At Oronsay (Augustinian) three of the four screen walls were rebuilt in an extraordinary fashion in the early sixteenth century, with triangular-headed openings formed in house-of-cards fashion by leaning one slab against another.[53] These arcades are much rebuilt, but incorporate two important inscriptions: one states that Canon Celestinus directed the work, while the other says that the work was carried out by the mason Mael-Sechlainn Ó Cuinn – who was clearly of Irish origin.

The uses of the range on the west side of the cloister varied. However, since it was the side that was nearest to the outer world, it generally housed those functions requiring regular contact with that world. The store-rooms for the provisions, which were the responsibility of the cellarer, were found here; but this side might also contain guest houses – as is thought to have been the case at the Augustinian houses of Holyrood and Inchcolm. At St Andrews, which was both an Augustinian priory and a cathedral, and where much of the range must have been rebuilt in the sixteenth

FIGURE 3.35   Inchcolm Abbey, the cloister looking towards the dormitory range. The large opening on the left was a later insertion at the time that a new walk was inserted within the existing cloister.

FIGURE 3.36 Glenluce Abbey, the reconstructed cloister arcades.

century, it possibly housed the consistory court – which belonged to the cathedral – as well as the residence of the sub-prior. In some cases this range was chosen to house the residence for the head of the community, the abbot or, towards the end of our period, perhaps for the commendator. At Inchaffray (Augustinian), for example, the west range as remodelled probably around the early sixteenth century has the domestic appearance that would accord with a commendator's residence.

The most impressive surviving example of an abbot's house associated with the west range is at Arbroath (Tironensian) (see Figure 3.37). As first built at the turn of the twelfth and thirteenth centuries the main element of the residence was a first-floor hall above a vaulted undercroft, which projected westwards from the south range at its junction with the west range. Around this nucleus a two-storeyed expansion above vaulted basements took place – in the early sixteenth century to judge from the architectural details. West of the hall, blocking lancet windows on that side, a new bed chamber was added, with what appears to have been a gallery beyond. On the north side of this extended range, where yet more original windows were blocked, a generously lit entrance corridor was added, originally reached by an external stair. Leading off the entrance corridor was a spiral stair, beyond which was a closet off the bed chamber. Latrines were placed where they were accessible from the entrance corridor and closet.

FIGURE 3.37   Arbroath Abbey, the abbot's house from the north. The original entrance was at
first-floor level at the left end of this view.

Presumably some of these extensions at Arbroath were carried out for the Beaton
family, the most ambitious ecclesiastical dynasty of late medieval Scotland, three
generations of which held the commendatorship of the abbey between 1517 and 1551.
The result of their work is one of the finest examples of purely domestic architecture
of the later Middle Ages. It is particularly instructive to see how such a house might
grow out from the claustral ranges, starting as little more than an appendage at one
corner, and then swelling into a major offshoot. After the Reformation it survived
while the ranges, which had given it birth but for which there was no longer any use,
were progressively destroyed. By the eighteenth century it was barely recognisable
as a product of the Middle Ages, and its medieval appearance was only restored in a
slightly heavy-handed restoration of the 1920s and 1930s.

Abbots' lodgings might also be to the south of the cloister, especially in Augustinian
communities. It has been suggested above that the range to the south-east of the
cloister at Inchcolm might have been planned for such use, while at Jedburgh the
abbot could have occupied the range parallel to the refectory. Similarly, at Holyrood
there was a group of buildings south of the cloister which survived into the seventeenth
century under the name of the Bishop's House, but which possibly originated as the
residence of the abbots.[54] It probably acquired its name after Bishop Bothwell of
Orkney was persuaded in 1568 to exchange the temporalities of his bishopric for those
of the abbacy of Holyrood.

Elsewhere abbots' or commendators' houses might be set towards the edge of the
main complex. At Dunfermline (Benedictine) recent investigations could suggest that

the building long known as the Abbot's House may indeed have been that, even if most of what is now seen is post-Reformation.[55] With a first-floor hall as its nucleus, this was a fine residence on the northern edge of the precinct, looking out towards the prosperous burgh which developed under the abbot's patronage. At Melrose (Cistercian) the commendator's house is also to the north of the site. As now seen, it is a restoration of a building of 1590, but its nucleus is an earlier structure – which perhaps had a hall and chamber on the first floor, and which could have been built for Abbot Andrew Hunter (c. 1444–71).[56] Hunter was certainly an avid builder and, apart from all the work he carried out on the abbey discussed above, he built an abbatial residence on the abbey's grange at Mauchline in Ayrshire (see Figure 3.38). Only the tower of this survives, and it is essentially a variant on the type of tower-house which formed the nucleus of most late medieval defensible residences. In this case the tower probably stood at the north-east corner of a larger courtyard complex. It may have housed the rooms of the abbot himself, and was almost certainly built by some of the masons who worked on the abbey, since its first-floor hall is impressively covered by two bays of quadripartite ribbed vaulting on which Hunter's arms are displayed.

FIGURE 3.38   Mauchline, Abbot Hunter's Tower.

There are some analogies for Mauchline in the abbot's house at Crossraguel (see Figure 3.39). This is a group of buildings of varying dates, around an irregular courtyard to the south of the abbey church choir. The earlier part probably contained a first-floor hall and chambers in a range running approximately east–west, with a kitchen block added at right angles to its eastern end. Behind the south-east angle of these ranges, a small four-storeyed tower-house is again likely to have contained the private rooms of the abbot. As first built, this tower was probably another example of the architectural patronage of Abbot Colin, because a mason's mark incised at several points – in the form of a cross rising from a star – is also found on the chapter house and sacristy of the east claustral range.[57]

FIGURE 3.39   Crossraguel Abbey, the tower of the abbot's residence.

At Kinloss (Cistercian) the abbot's residence was at the south end of the east conventual range, and as at Inchcolm may have been linked to the dormitory by the latrine block. It is a reconstruction of the time of Abbot Robert Reid (1528–53), whose arms were set above the entrance doorway at the base of a circular stair turret at its south-east corner. Reid was as energetic in his encouragement of high standards at Kinloss as had been his predecessor, Thomas Chrystall. Among his other projects was a fireproof library built in 1538. He was also a patron of art, and invited the painter Andrew Bairhum to decorate some of his rooms, though he may have come to regret this since Bairhum was a cantankerous individual.[58] Reid also built a new abbot's house at Beauly Priory in 1544, where he had become head in 1531, and he made additions to the bishop's palace in Kirkwall after he became bishop of Orkney in 1541 (see Figure 8.33). Clearly, even such an energetic promoter of monastic reform saw no inconsistency in housing himself in some style.

Abbot Alexander Myln, who was appointed to Cambuskenneth (Augustinian) in 1519, was another promoter of monastic reform who saw no reason to be housed inadequately. Major rebuilding called for a rededication of the church and other structures in 1521, and among these buildings could have been the new abbot's hall referred to in 1520.[59] It is possible the new hall was one of the buildings to the east of the abbey, on the banks of the River Forth.

Another building of which there are remains at one or two abbeys and priories is the guest house. It is possible that one survives within the suspiciously thick walls of a post-Reformation house to the west of the abbey at Melrose. The partly reconstructed range against the precinct wall west of the abbey church at Arbroath may also have served this purpose, though it is probably earlier than the period covered by this book. At St Andrews a new guest hall was built by Prior John Hepburn (1482–1522), and was known as the *Hospitium Novum*; from its rebuilt gateway it must have been a splendid building. But the most imposing example we have is that at Dunfermline, the scale of which suggests it was built mainly for the family of the abbey's founders, the royal house of Scotland (see Figure 3.40). Significantly, after the Reformation it was extended to form part of a palace for Queen Anne of Denmark. Its core, at the south-west angle of the abbey's outer courtyard, probably dates from a campaign patronised by Robert I in 1329, which also included the magnificent refectory block; but it was extended to the north-west and a number of details suggest this was done in the years around 1500. Unlike the basement of the original part of the range, which was initially covered by two aisles of ribbed quadripartite vaulting, the basement beneath this addition was at first unvaulted. It was later covered by barrel vaults, however, and it may have been at the same time that the first vaults in the main block basement were replaced by barrel vaults as part of an effort to reduce the strains on the outer walls – which soared vertiginously over the valley of the Tower Burn. The range was heightened shortly before the Reformation, the new top storey being lit by a series of delightful oriel windows; on the evidence of the arms of George Durie, which were placed on a representation of the annunciation on the soffit of one of those windows, this was carried out at some time after 1526.

FIGURE 3.40   Dunfermline Abbey, the interior of the guest house.

Both to increase the sense of isolation from the greater world, and to defend their possessions, the precincts of most monasteries were defined by strong walls through which access was controlled by gatehouses. Extents of these walls and of gatehouses remain at a number of sites, including Crossraguel, Coupar Angus, Pittenweem and Sweetheart. The most complete circuit is at St Andrews, where much of the wall enclosing the precinct of nearly twelve hectares stands to almost full height (see Figure 3.41). Along with the wall there are still no less than thirteen towers and four gateways. The approximate date for one of the earlier phases of wall construction may be indicated by the main archway into the precinct to the south-west of the cathedral; this gate, known as the Pends Yett, has decorative arcading above its arch rather like that of the west front of the cathedral, which post-dates the fire of 1378 (see Figure 3.42). But much of the present appearance of the wall dates from a heightening and strengthening operation by Prior John Hepburn – whose arms are displayed at many points. According to an enigmatic inscription on one of the towers, the work was completed by his nephew Patrick, who succeeded him as prior in 1522, before moving on to become bishop of Moray in 1538.

The precinct wall at Arbroath is less complete than at St Andrews, but the stretch that survives is impressive and presents a vivid picture of the power of a great monastery – and of its readiness to defend itself (see Figure 3.43). The wall runs westwards from the south-west tower of the abbey church, is punctuated by the main gate into the

FIGURE 3.41   St Andrews Cathedral Priory, the precinct wall.

precinct, and now terminates in a tower at the point where the wall turned southwards. It embodies work of several periods, including extensive remodelling in the fifteenth century, when machicolated parapets were added to the gatehouse and the tower, and the wall-head of the former was remodelled. Against the inner face of the wall were vaulted ranges, one of which housed the abbey's regality court. The angle tower, which had vaulted lower storeys, had comfortable chambers on some of its floors, presumably for one or more of the abbey's office holders.

    Both the west front of the monastic church and the great gatehouse tended to look on to the outer courtyard, a less formidably enclosed area than the main precinct. The resultant inter-relationship between the former, which was usually the church's frontispiece towards the world, and the latter, which was the chief entry into the precinct, could be developed to great architectural advantage – as at Dunfermline.[60] There, the fifteenth-century gatehouse was placed at a lower level than the church, between the existing refectory and guest house ranges, and had to have two full storeys above the entrance passage to rear its head in such distinguished company (see Figure 3.44). The intermediate storey above the entrance passage permitted access between the kitchen and the refectory block, while the upper storey had a single large vaulted chamber with a capacious fireplace.

    Whatever one may feel about the spiritual commitment of religious institutions that could present such an unashamedly secular – even apparently militaristic – face to the outside world, there can be no doubt about the powers of architectural patronage they continued to wield. The fifteenth and sixteenth centuries were not

FIGURE 3.42   St Andrews Cathedral Priory, the Pends Yett.

FIGURE 3.43   Arbroath Abbey, the precinct wall and the west front of the abbey church.

FIGURE 3.44 Dunfermline Abbey, the main gateway into the precinct, with the refectory on the right and the kitchen on the left.

generally a high point in the history of monasticism, and modern psychology may suggest the need to present such a bold face is evidence of awareness of inner failings; but, viewed as a crude measure of the ability to sponsor fine architecture, such buildings leave little doubt of the important role still played by many monasteries.

CHAPTER FOUR

The Architecture of the Friars

The urge to find a more completely apostolic or essentially missionary form of life was a recurring theme of medieval religion. With the enclosed monastic orders that ideal had proved unattainable, both because monasticism itself involved turning away from the world, and because the enclosed life almost inevitably necessitated the acceptance of endowments and the acquisition of property to support that life. But for some the ideal form of religious life continued to be one that was modelled on that of the disciples, involving a peripatetic mission and dependence on the alms the faithful chose to offer.

The rejection of property this involved was regarded with suspicion by the church hierarchy, since it carried an implied criticism of the wealth accumulated by the church, and also because it could lead to forms of individualism that might prove to be heretical. From the early thirteenth century, however, this ideal came closer to finding realisation than ever before, at a period when increased urbanisation in parts of Europe posed particular problems for the church. Towns fostered a looser social structure than rural estates, and offered fertile ground for religious dissent. There was thus a call for a mission to the urban masses, both to meet spiritual needs not adequately met by the existing parochial system, and to prevent the spread of heresy. It was in response to this that the mendicant (begging) orders – the friars – came into being, at a time when disenchantment with the established religious orders was also becoming more vocal.[1]

The two greatest of those orders, the Dominicans and Franciscans, emerged in Italy and Southern France simultaneously. After being regarded with alarm by the leaders of the church, and having to prove they were unlikely to encourage unacceptable extremes, they grew rapidly under the special protection of the papacy. The Dominicans, known as Black Friars from the colour of their cloak, or as Friars Preachers from their professed role, were formally instituted by St Dominic at Toulouse in 1215. Dominic had been an Augustinian canon, and took that rule as the basis for the religious observance of his friars. Under his leadership the order was organised with great efficiency, and with a particular view to fighting the heresy endemic in the area where it was founded. Special emphasis came to be placed on academic learning as a basis for countering error, and the order developed links with the universities; perhaps less fortunately, it also came to be identified with the Inquisition.

The Franciscans were known as Grey Friars, or as Friars Minor because of St Francis's emphasis on humility. They received papal approval the same year that Dominic's order was instituted, though St Francis never wished to found an order as such, and the consequent lack of basic organisation became a problem after his death in 1226. Rival factions soon emerged, partly because of the fundamental problem of the extent to which holding property could be justified. There was also conflict between those of its members who were priests and those who were laymen. Eventually the priests achieved supremacy and more systematic organisation was introduced, bringing them closer in spirit to the Dominicans. But there was always scope for conflict in the Franciscan ideal, because Francis's own vision of a loose brotherhood of spiritually driven like-minded souls was hardly applicable to an organisation which had spread across Christendom. In the later Middle Ages this conflict is seen in the emergence of a branch who wished to revert to a life closer to their founder's first intentions, and were known as Observants; the main stream of the order became known as Conventuals to emphasise the distinction.

Of the other mendicants the most prominent in Scotland were the Carmelites, known as the White Friars, who originated as groups of hermits in the Holy Land. The Trinitarians, although usually referred to as the Red Friars, were in fact not friars but canons who lived a life somewhat like that of the Augustinians.

Not unnaturally, the friars encountered opposition from the established monastic orders, since they attracted funds which might otherwise have gone to the monks. They were also opposed by some of the parochial clergy, whose parishioners were sometimes more drawn to the lively and well-informed preaching and spiritual guidance of the friars. But for some time to come the expansion of the friars was almost as remarkable as had been the spread of the Cistercians in the twelfth century, and they clearly met a need. According to the *Melrose Chronicle*, the two main orders of friars had reached Scotland in the 1230s: the Dominicans in 1230 and the Franciscans in 1231. The first certain foundation for the Carmelites was on the outskirts of Perth, at Tullilum, in 1262. The Observant branch of the Franciscans probably reached Scotland around 1463, when they were introduced to Edinburgh by Queen Mary of Guelders.[2]

Although the greatest number of foundations for the Dominicans and the Conventual Franciscans had taken place in the thirteenth century, they enjoyed fresh popularity from the later fourteenth century onwards; this meant both that there were considerable new late medieval foundations and that existing houses received fresh endowments. Beyond that, all nine foundations for the Observant Franciscans were, of course, of the fifteenth or early sixteenth centuries, and there were some late foundations for the Carmelites. Mention must also additionally be made here of the distinguished house of Dominican nuns at Sciennes in Edinburgh, and of those for Franciscan nuns at Aberdour and Dundee, all of which were founded in the late fifteenth or early sixteenth centuries.

AN OVERVIEW OF THE ARCHITECTURE OF THE MENDICANTS

Allowing for all late medieval foundations to have started new buildings, and for several of the older foundations to have commissioned some rebuilding, the friars must have been responsible for a significant proportion of the architectural patronage of the later Middle Ages. Unfortunately, however, the friaries have survived less well than the monasteries, for two main reasons. Since mendicancy was an urban movement, most friaries were accessible to the masses when inflamed by the reformers' oratory; they were also prime candidates for rapid post-Reformation redevelopment, particularly since they had no parochial function to justify retention of their churches. Beyond that, it is possible the reformers saw the more educated friars as posing a threat to their programme of reform, and were particularly anxious to remove them. Certainly the friaries in Dundee and Perth were to be attacked as early as 1543, and the Beggars' Summons in 1559 took the friaries as its specific target. But, whatever the reasons, our knowledge of the range of mendicant architecture is limited.

Before looking at the buildings of the friaries in greater detail, it will be useful to summarise what survives or is known of them from other sources. Of the sixteen Dominican houses, a chapel of the church at St Andrews, the church given to the order at St Monans and a single pier of the house at Inverness survive; additionally, we know of their church at Glasgow from engravings of the university. From the eight Conventual Franciscan houses we still have what may have been the guest house at Inverkeithing and a possible fragment of the church at Kirkcudbright. We are more fortunate with the nine Observant Franciscan friaries, because the church at Elgin survives in restored state, the plan of the complex at Jedburgh has been largely recovered through excavation, and fragments of window tracery have been excavated at Ayr.[3] The finest survival of this order, however, was the church at Aberdeen, which was destroyed only as late as 1902. The Carmelites had eleven houses, and the chancel, crossing and transeptal aisle of the church at Queensferry survive complete; apart from this, the lower walls of the church at Luffness are still to be seen, and the plans of Aberdeen, Linlithgow and Perth have been partly excavated. Nothing is known of the buildings of the three houses of nuns attached to the Dominicans and Franciscans.

So far as can be assessed on this limited evidence, the mendicant orders in Scotland preferred to set out their domestic buildings on a relatively conventional plan, with three ranges of buildings around a square cloister against one of the church flanks. But fitting into cramped urban sites must often have imposed compromise, particularly since the church had to be placed where public access was most convenient, and the domestic buildings where they were best sheltered from the noise of the street. This also meant that not all friary churches were correctly orientated, as at the Franciscan house at Aberdeen.

The most complete claustral plans so far recovered are of the Observant Franciscans at Jedburgh and the Carmelites at Linlithgow, where the arrangements seem to have been orthodox in having the refectory facing the church across the cloister, and

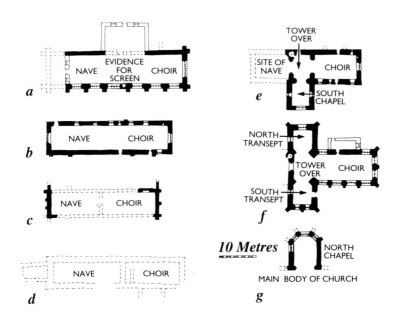

FIGURE 4.1 Plans of friary churches: a. Aberdeen Observant Franciscan Friary (demolished);
b. Elgin Observant Franciscan Friary; c. Luffness Carmelite Friary; d. Linlithgow Carmelite Friary;
e. Queensferry Carmelite Friary; f. St Monans Dominican Friary; g. St Andrews Dominican Friary.

a chapter house in the east range.[4] At the Observant Franciscan houses of Jedburgh
and Aberdeen the cloisters were on the north of the church, and there were also
northern cloisters at the Carmelite houses of Queensferry and Luffness. But the
Carmelite houses at Aberdeen, Linlithgow and Perth, the Observant Franciscan
houses at Elgin and the Dominican house at St Andrews apparently all had cloisters
to the south. There is little evidence for the form of cloister walks, other than at
Jedburgh, where, with one possible exception, they seem to have been lean-to
corridors of the usual type. Apart from that one walk at Jedburgh, it does not appear
that the practice of the English friars of placing some of the cloister walks within the
body of the ranges was followed in Scotland – although this was done at some Scottish
Augustinian houses.

The most imposing mendicant building that we have, other than a church, is what
is thought to be the guest house of the Conventual Franciscan house at Inverkeithing
(see Figure 4.2).[5] The friary there was in existence by 1384, and the guest house may
be of that period. However, it was so extensively modified when converted to secular
uses after the Reformation, and was so heavily restored in the 1930s by the Office of
Works, that it is difficult to be certain of its date. It evidently occupied the west side
of the cloister, and has a vaulted basement incorporating a transe leading through
to the cloister. The guest hall on the first floor is now approached by a reconstructed forestair; there is a composite lower double-pile block of uncertain use to
its south.

FIGURE 4.2   Inverkeithing Franciscan Friary, the guest house.

CHURCHES OF THE MENDICANTS KNOWN THROUGH EXCAVATION OR RECORDS

With the exception of St Monans – which was not first built for the Dominicans – Queensferry and St Andrews, most of the known mendicant churches had basically rectangular plans (see Figure 4.1). In this they were like a majority of Scottish churches, though it has been pointed out that the Carmelite priory of Hulne in Northumberland had a similar plan, so it is possible there was also some element of external influence.[6] Nevertheless, despite the simplicity of planning, from evidence found at Aberdeen and Linlithgow it is clear that even a rectangular plan might be the result of more than one building operation, and Linlithgow also had some sort of western annexe. Within the framework of such a simple plan, there might be structural subdivisions.

At Linlithgow the structural complexity is presumably because the founder, Sir James Douglas of Dalkeith, gave an existing chapel to the friars in 1401,[7] and this has been tentatively identified as underlying the nave of their church (see Figure 4.1d). Between choir and nave, Linlithgow had a double wall pierced by arches, the western of the two possibly having been the east wall of the original chapel. This double division may have formed a walk-way, a passage between the cloister and outer world that is often found in English mendicant churches at this point.[8] It was, however, usual for the walk-way to be aligned with the eastern cloister walk, which was not the case at Linlithgow. There are indications of a double wall in the same position at the Carmelite church of Luffness, but there it probably represented a pulpitum rather than an enclosed walk-way (see Figure 4.1c). Ironically, the closest Scottish analogy for an English walk-way arrangement is the only surviving part of the rectangular church of the Trinitarians at Dunbar (see Figure 4.3),[9] despite the Trinitarians not being strictly definable as friars. This part of the church at Dunbar was retained through being converted into a dovecot after the Reformation, but it retains much evidence for its original form; the way arches span the cross walls and support a small

FIGURE 4.3   Dunbar Trinitarian Church, the surviving fragment of the crossing.

central tower is presumably inspired by English prototypes, such as those surviving at King's Lynn in Norfolk or Richmond in Yorkshire.

There could have been another example of a walk-way at Glasgow if the view of the university in Slezer's *Theatrum Scotiae* of 1693 can be trusted.[10] The friary of the Glasgow Dominicans was closely connected with the university and, after the Reformation, it was given to the university in 1563. It was extensively remodelled after a fire in 1668 and was eventually demolished in 1870, but it was its earlier state that was depicted by Slezer. His view shows a square two-storeyed tower capped by a spire rising from the middle of a rectangular aisle-less church and, if accurate, such an arrangement would perhaps have been best supported as at Dunbar.

Elsewhere, the mendicants were probably happy enough with a lightly framed lead-sheathed timber bell-cote on the roof, as shown at Aberdeen Observantine friary on Gordon's map of 1661.[11] That church was an admirable demonstration of the way an unaugmented rectangular building could be a structure of considerable architectural finesse.[12] It was seven bays long, and measured about 35 by 8.4 metres. Along the south flank, which faced the outer world, were well-proportioned buttresses, and there were four-light windows in each bay, rising from a continuous string course (see Figure 4.4). The most complex window was that in the east wall, which was of seven lights of intersecting tracery arranged in three interpenetrating groups, and with shallow ogee curves cut into the transom which crossed the window at the base of the arch. We know from the south nave aisle at Aberdeen Cathedral, and from the north transept of Aberdeen St Nicholas, that intersecting tracery was greatly favoured

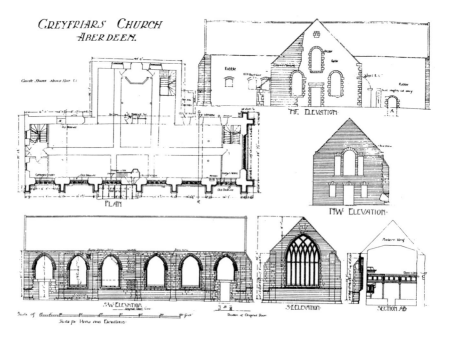

FIGURE 4.4   Aberdeen Observant Franciscan Friary, survey drawings made at the time of its demolition.

in the granite city. But this was unquestionably the most ambitious window of its kind of which we know in Scotland, and a similar sureness of touch was shown in the moulded details of doors and windows.

As at Linlithgow, the Aberdeen friary church had a more complex structural history than appeared from its rectangular plan (see Figure 4.1a). The friary itself began to take shape in the 1460s, and there were buildings ready for use by 1471 which presumably included a church. In its final form, however, the church was the product of a co-operative effort between Canon Alexander Galloway and Bishop Gavin Dunbar, whom we have already encountered in the heraldic ceiling of Aberdeen Cathedral (see p. 76, and Figure 2.11). We know this because – under 5 and 6 October – the obituary of the friary says Galloway built it at the expense of Dunbar,[13] and Dunbar's arms were displayed above one of the nave windows. The church was presumably finished by Dunbar's death in 1532 since his successor, William Stewart, turned his attention to the friary infirmary.

After the Reformation, the preservation of the church was ensured by its being used as the chapel of the college founded by the Earl Marischal on the site of the friary. In 1768 it was modified by the removal of its western bay and the addition of an aisle on the north side, resulting in a characteristically Scottish T-plan. In 1902, however, it was demolished and only the east window was retained for insertion into the new church – despite the fact that the college's architect, Marshall Mackenzie, prepared a scheme which retained the chapel in restored form.

Evidence revealed during demolition showed the division between friars' choir and nave would have been a timber screen, rather than the solid walls of a walk-way.[14] The arrangement of the screen would have been similar to that existing in a number of collegiate churches and, as with the planning, we again see that Scottish friars tended to adopt native usages rather than develop specific architectural solutions. The main evidence for the screen was a pair of blocked windows and an associated piscina in the south flank, west of the third window from the east. These small windows were set one above the other, and corresponding to them on the north side were traces of a spiral stair. This disposition of windows is similar to that at Foulis Easter and Innerpeffray (see pp. 153 and 157, and Figures 5.11 and 5.17), for example, where they were placed to light the altars associated with the chancel screen and the loft above it; the stair would have given access to that loft. It is tempting to suspect that the altars below the loft were those dedicated to the Virgin and St John the Baptist, reflecting of the figures on the rood above. We know two of the altars in the church had those dedications, and we also know the latter was founded by Alexander Galloway.

THE FRIARY CHURCHES AT ELGIN, QUEENSFERRY, ST MONANS AND ST ANDREWS

The church built for the Observant Franciscans at Elgin shared many features of its sister foundation at Aberdeen, albeit on a lesser scale (see Figures 4.1b and 4.5).[15] This friary was formally established by 1494–5, but may have existed for some time before then.[16] After the Reformation the architectural life of its church was extended through use as a court house, as a meeting place for the trades of Elgin, and for

Episcopalian worship. As a result, despite eventual loss of its roof, the walls were tolerably intact in 1896 when the Marquess of Bute had it restored as the Convent of Mercy, to the designs of John Kinross. Kinross's restoration was more creative than might have been ideal, but generally he respected the archaeological evidence, and some impression of the likely arrangement of the chancel screen and its altars can be gained from his work. It is likely, however, that the loft above the screen would have extended below the sill of the upper window, and that the nave altars would have been enclosed by other screens.

Kinross also restored the Carmelite church at Queensferry, which had been founded by James Dundas of Dundas in 1440 (see Figures 4.1e and 4.6).[17] Like Elgin, Queensferry survived because various uses were found for it after the Reformation. Between 1583 and 1635 it served as a place of worship and a school, and for many years it was the burial place of the Dundas family. But by the nineteenth century it was rapidly declining, and around the central decades of that century its nave was destroyed. Fortunately, in 1889, Bishop John Dowden of Edinburgh – a notable historian of the Scottish medieval church – persuaded the dean and chapter of his cathedral to have it restored for Episcopalian worship.

It has been suggested above that the church at Queensferry is different from the other mendicant churches of which we know, though it is still an essentially Scottish building.[18] It was set out to a T-shaped plan with three arms around the squat central tower, the southern arm being an asymmetrical transeptal aisle on the side away from the cloister. There was a well-established tradition of asymmetrical chapel aisles in

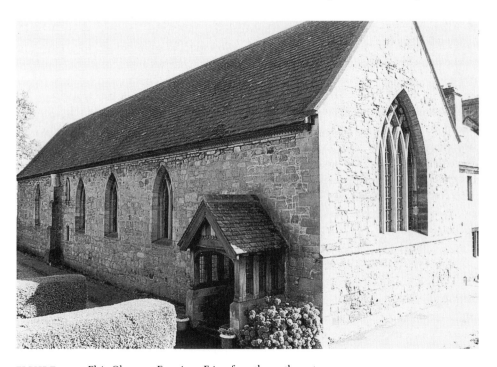

FIGURE 4.5   Elgin Observant Franciscan Friary from the north-west.

FIGURE 4.6   South Queensferry Carmelite Friary from the south-east.

Scotland, and it seems likely it was that native tradition which lay behind the
Queensferry aisle, rather than the influence of the preaching transepts of some Irish
mendicant houses.[19] The Scottishness of Queensferry is further apparent in the barrel
vaults over chancel and tower – which are pointed in the chancel and round in the
tower – and by the low arches carried on heavy responds which separate the
compartments.

   As with so much Scottish late medieval architecture of modest scale, the impression
given by the architecture of Queensferry is of sturdily modelled masses of masonry
rather than of delicacy, with little wish to articulate those masses. The stonework
itself, however, would originally have appeared less ponderous than now through
being rendered over both internally and externally, and it would thus have provided
a more unified background for a number of well-contrived details. The eastern
elevation is particularly pleasing. Its main window, with three simply arched lights,
is below a pair of lancets flanking an image niche in the gable, and there are corbels
for a bell-cote at the apex. The ogee-headed lights of the lintelled windows in aisle
and nave, and the triplet of round arches to the sedilia also provide well-judged relief
to the plain walls and vaults. An intriguing feature of the interior is the series of corbels
along the flanks of the chancel, which look as if intended for an entresol floor. But
such a floor would have made the presbytery and choir areas oppressively low; is it
more likely they were to carry a decorative timber ceiling within the curve of the
vault?

   The church at St Monans is not strictly a mendicant structure, being an adaptation
of an existing building for the Dominicans, and it is uncertain how far the friary was

ever viable since it never had more than two inmates. The original church had been built by David II between 1362 and 1370, in thanksgiving to St Monan for his recovery from an arrow wound;[20] it was only in 1471 that James III re-established it as a friary, apparently as part of an effort to have Scotland recognised as a separate Dominican province (see Figures 4.1f and 4.7).[21] Understanding of the building's architectural development has been blurred by a long history of later modifications. Its adoption as a parish church in 1649 probably involved many changes, and there were restorations by William Burn in 1826–8; by Peter MacGregor Chalmers in 1899; and by Ian Lindsay in 1955.

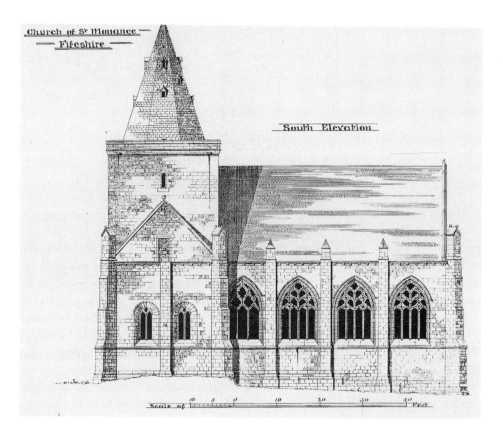

FIGURE 4.7   St Monans Church, the south elevation.

It was planned as an aisle-less cruciform structure, with a central tower and a sacristy on the north side of the choir. There is now no external trace of a nave, though internally there is a narrow arch on the west side of the crossing, showing that one was intended.[22] The basic structure is likely to be largely of 1362–70. But the rather loosely organised loop forms of most of the southern choir windows are probably of around 1471; beyond this – since the windows on both sides of the choir have the same mouldings – it seems the reticulated tracery on the north side, and a single window of the same type on the south, also belong to the adaptation for the

Dominicans. The biggest question mark is over the vaulting of the choir, which has miniature intermediate intersections creating a pseudo-sexpartite appearance (see Figure 4.8). The vaulting shafts are related to the crossing responds, and are likely to be original; but it must be a possibility that the vault itself is a later insertion. It would perhaps be more at home in the context of the late revival of sexpartite vaulting represented also in the sacristy at Crossraguel and the towers at Dunfermline Abbey and, Linlithgow and Stirling parish churches.

FIGURE 4.8   St Monans Church, the interior of the choir looking eastwards.

It has been emphasised that the mendicant churches so far considered are essentially Scottish buildings, with few obvious concessions to any specialised needs of the friars. There is nothing here of the vast preaching halls of the greater houses of the English and continental friars, for example. In the fragmentary remains of the Dominican church at St Andrews, however, we find signs of more cosmopolitan attitudes (see Figures 4.1g and 4.9). The Dominicans may have come to St Andrews shortly before 1464, when the university was beginning to expand. But they were given fresh life in 1516, when it was decided that money left by Bishop Elphinstone of Aberdeen should be devoted to a new house here, and the work was carried out under the direction of his executor, Dean George Hepburn of Dunkeld,[23] whose arms are on a vaulting boss. The only part of the friary to survive is the polygonal chapel which projected from its north side, and which could be linked with obtaining permission to encroach on to the street in 1525.[24]

In some respects this chapel is very Scottish. Its covering by a pointed barrel vault with a surface application of ribs imitating quadripartite vaulting is certainly Scottish, as is the blank east wall to accommodate a high retable behind the altar. Other features were relatively new to the Scottish architectural vocabulary, however, and some may even have been introduced directly to St Andrews from the Continent rather than from examples closer to home. While the polygonal plan of the side chapel, for example, had Scottish precedents at Ladykirk in Berwickshire and Arbuthnott in Kincardineshire (see pp. 224 and 227, and Figures 7.8 and 7.11), it was an idea of ultimately continental origin. Occasional examples of laterally projecting polygonal chapels or transepts are to be found throughout Europe, and include such diverse variants as Windsor in England, Annaberg in Saxony and Florence in Tuscany. But examples are particularly common in the Low Countries – as at churches in Delft, Zaltbommel and Leiden – and because it seems that inspiration from the Low Countries was a factor in the design of other features at St Andrews, it may also have been a factor behind the plan.

Netherlandish inspiration is seen particularly in the window tracery which, although restored by the Office of Works in 1913, is essentially authentic, and is

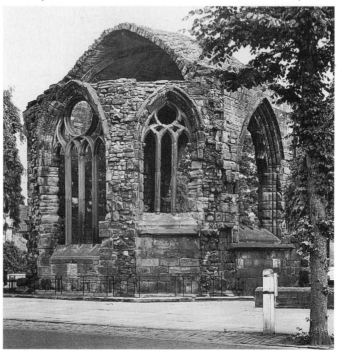

FIGURE 4.9   St Andrews Dominican Friary, the north chapel from the north-west.

composed of uncusped loop-like forms. Tracery of this type was used in several Scottish churches of the first half of the sixteenth century – including Tullibardine and Midcalder (see Figures 7.3 and 7.10) – but the type had almost certainly originated in the Low Countries, where the frequent use of brick for window tracery encouraged simplification of design. Examples close to the types at St Andrews may be seen in late fifteenth-century work at the churches of Kapelle and Kloetinge in the county of Zeeland, and there are more elaborate variants at the Dominican friary in The Hague, for example, of about 1500. The likelihood that the St Andrews tracery was inspired by examples in the Low Countries is strengthened by the known links with that area. John Adamson, the head of the Scottish Dominican province, took a close interest in his order's new house at St Andrews, and we know that his appointment in 1510 was made after delegates of the Dominican Congregation of Holland had carried out a reforming visitation of the Scottish province.[25] Taking account of this it is possible that St Andrews was one place where such tracery was directly imported into Scotland from the Netherlands and, if so, it is also possible the apsidal plan of the chapel was inspired by examples in the Netherlands.

The work at St Andrews suggests that a friary, as part of what was still an essentially international network, might occasionally be the channel for the importation of architectural ideas. Beyond that, in some aspects of planning – such as the walk-ways between choir and nave – solutions which had been worked out for the English friars might also be followed. However, on the basis of the scant evidence we have, it seems that by the later Middle Ages the friars tended to allow their master masons to build in the way in which they were most accustomed. Thus it is generally true to say that most buildings raised for what was one of the most important patronage groups in later medieval Scotland are Scottish first and mendicant second. Although this must be partly a consequence of the constraints imposed by the relative poverty of the Scottish mendicant houses, it is also a pointer to the increasing coherence of architectural attitudes in Scotland.

CHAPTER FIVE

Rural and Academic Collegiate Churches

Colleges were corporations of clerics – known variously as chaplains, canons or prebendaries – under the leadership of a provost or dean and, as such, they were not dissimilar from the chapters of clergy who served as the permanent staff of secular cathedrals.[1] In England and Wales some colleges claimed to trace their origins back to soon after the introduction of Christianity to these islands; some, such as Beverley in Yorkshire, grew to be enormously wealthy bodies with churches as big as many cathedrals. But in Scotland most colleges were more modest establishments, and the earliest were probably those of St Mary on the Rock at St Andrews and Abernethy. The former was founded around 1250, as an attempt to give the successors of the Culdees continued corporate existence.[2] The latter, founded in about 1328–31, also had its origins in a house of Culdees, though they had already been succeeded for about fifty years by a priory of Augustinian canons.[3] These two are probably the only Scottish colleges which approximate in type to the earliest English foundations. All the rest are late medieval creations founded to meet the craving for perpetual prayers for the souls of their founders and their families, as already outlined in discussing those of Carnwath, Lincluden, Maybole and Tain (see pp. 30, 46, 24 and 52).

One of the attractions of colleges for founders was their relative cheapness by comparison with monasteries. The smallest – like that at Maybole – had as few as three priests, and were essentially enlarged chantry chapels. The largest – such as the Chapel Royal in Stirling Castle, which was under the leadership of the Bishop of Galloway – might have as many as twenty-eight priests, assisted by half a dozen or more singing clerks or choristers. Thus, although a founder had to be rich enough to provide endowments to pay for prayers through all time to come, within certain limits collegiate foundations could be tailored to meet his particular requirements and resources.

Purpose-built structures were not essential for a new college, but most patrons chose to provide an appropriate architectural setting for their foundations, particularly since they were usually also family burial places. Domestic accommodation was also needed for the clergy though, except at Lincluden and possibly also at Seton, we know little about what was built for this. At the least, as a setting for the collegiate services, a small chapel was built either adjoining the founder's parish church or in its churchyard, though it need be no larger than the family aisles added against Airth or Borthwick Parish Churches (see pp. 230 and 229, and Figure 7.13). More ambitiously, the founder partly or wholly rebuilt his local church; sometimes this started as the addition of a more splendid choir but then extended to reconstruction of the whole building, especially if more priests were added to the original comple- ment. But not all colleges were founded within parish churches: one was established in a suppressed nunnery, some in chapels close to the main residence of their founder, and others may have had completely new buildings.

The colleges which were housed most grandly were those within the parish churches of the greater burghs – as at Edinburgh, Haddington and Stirling – which will be discussed in the following chapter. In them, however, we find a complex range of functions approaching more closely those of the cathedrals. Nevertheless, several rural colleges founded by great landholders had highly ambitious churches – so ambitious, indeed, that they were frequently never finished as intended. In some areas there may have been rivalry between families, driving them to build as grandly as possible, which may account for the concentration of fine collegiate churches in the Lothians.

For the founders it was sufficient that the priests within their colleges were praying for their souls, and thus hopefully ensuring their salvation. The pattern of these prayers was based on the canonical hours recited daily in all monastic houses, though possibly with even greater emphasis on the mass as the commemoration of Christ's redemptive act. But, because the church also emphasised the importance of good works as a path to salvation, many colleges carried out charitable functions. Lincluden, for example, had the hospital of Holywood for twenty-four poor bedes- men associated with it. Most also had a song school, which gave a rudimentary education to the choristers. Other colleges were attached to the newly emerging universities, and provided endowments for the teachers and in some cases the students as well. It is, of course, colleges of this type that are now best remembered, and the modern understanding of a college is of a place of learning and education, rather than of a group of priests. Unlike most other colleges, which were founded by laymen, these latter colleges were usually founded by senior ecclesiastics, because education was still the responsibility of the church.

The vast majority of collegiate foundations were in the Lowlands, with the greatest concentration in the central belt around the Forth-Clyde Valley. A thinner scattering spread northwards up the eastern coastal strip, with Tain in Easter Ross as the northernmost, and there were outlyers in the south-west at Maybole and Lincluden. The only college in the Western Highlands was on its eastern edge at Kilmun, the tower of which still survives.[4] But Kilmun was exceptional, being founded in 1441 by Sir Duncan Campbell – the ancestor of the Dukes of Argyll – whose plans for his family required a foot in both the Highlands and the Lowlands. Otherwise the concentration of colleges to the south and east of the Highland line is even more striking than that of the monasteries.

Of about fifty collegiate churches founded in Scotland, many continued in use after the Reformation as parish churches, family burial places or university chapels, and over thirty have come down to us at least in part. Their relatively high survival rate, together with their fine architectural qualities, means they are of a similar level of importance for the understanding of late Gothic architecture as are the great burgh churches. Those which remained in use were inevitably stripped of their chantry functions, but in some cases the associated ancillary functions survived. Thus, Trinity College in Edinburgh still provides money for pensioners even after the destruction of both church and hospital, while the educational functions of the colleges at St Andrews, Glasgow and Aberdeen continue, despite the loss of some of those chapels.

COLLEGES HOUSED IN ADDITIONS TO EXISTING CHURCHES

The simplest architectural provision for a college was an aisle attached to an existing church, though this was presumably adequate only when the college was small, and the clergy would probably expect to use other parts of the church when necessary. Sometimes the college grew from small beginnings, with a simple chantry becoming a college. At Seton in East Lothian, for example – where most of the church was eventually rebuilt on a large scale – the germ of the college was a chapel built against the south flank in the 1430s by Lady Katherine Seton, after the death of her husband. This chapel survived the building of the new collegiate choir around the 1470s, and was only demolished on the eve of the Reformation when a south transept was built on its site. Its foundations were rediscovered in excavations carried out around 1948 (see Figure 5.1n).[5]

At Methven, in Perthshire, the college probably started within a rectangular aisle off the north side of the church (see Figure 5.2). It was founded by Walter, Earl of Atholl, in 1433 and was augmented on at least two occasions, so that eventually there were about ten prebendaries, together with five chaplains and four choristers.[6] The small aisle would not have been sufficient for the college in its final form, and we must suppose it used other parts of the church as well. The aisle was presumably preserved after the rest of the church was demolished in 1783 simply because of its continued use as a burial place. (The Edinburgh Architectural Association published a plan of the church as a cruciform structure, but it is unclear if this was more than inspired guesswork.[7]) The main feature of the aisle is a three-light window with reticulated tracery in the north gable wall, which would certainly fit with a date around the time of the foundation of 1433. The upper parts of that wall, however, with coped crowsteps and a rather block-like tabernacle head, might date from rebuilding when the college was augmented in 1510 and 1516.

An aisle of similar scale as at Methven was added to Guthrie Church in Angus, presumably for the college founded by Sir Alexander Guthrie in about 1479 (see Figure 5.3).[8] There, some building may have been carried out earlier, since the papal permission for the college said that Sir Alexander's father, Sir David, had already enlarged the church. Although the rest of the church was pulled down in 1826, a drawing of 1814 shows how the aisle was attached to the south flank of the nave, and was thus towards the western end of the church. Part of the aisle's painted wagon

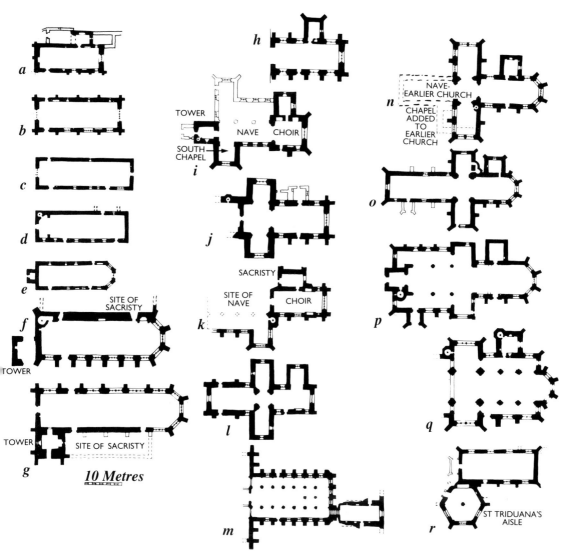

FIGURE 5.1   Plans of collegiate churches: a. Maybole; b. Tain; c. Foulis Easter; d. Innerpeffray;
e. Castle Semple; f. St Andrews, St Salvator; g. Aberdeen, King's; h. Bothwell; i. Corstorphine;
j. Crichton; k. Lincluden; l. Dunglass; m. Roslin; n. Seton; o. Biggar; p. Dalkeith; q. Edinburgh, Trinity;
r. Restalrig.

ceiling is preserved in the National Museum of Scotland. It had the crucifixion on its
east side, and the last judgement on the west, and is a reminder of how even a relatively
simple building might be richly finished inside (see Figure 5.4). The surface of the
ceiling was divided into panels by widely spaced parallel ribs and a ridge rib. The roof
to which it was attached remains in place, and shows how the curved profile was
achieved by placing formers at the junctions with the rafters of the ashlar struts and
collars; it also has the sawn place-marks for the correct assembly of the timbers.
Guthrie never became a large college, and probably had no more than five

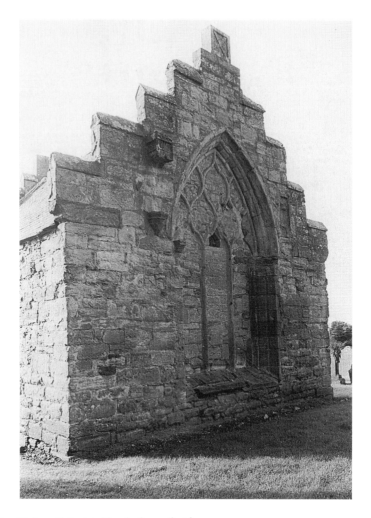

FIGURE 5.2   Methven Collegiate Church, the north aisle.

prebendaries. Two of these were additions of the early sixteenth century, when there may have been some remodelling of the chapel. The south window in particular – a rectangular opening with two mullions – certainly looks late, and the drawing of 1814 shows similar windows had been inserted in the church.

By far the most extraordinary collegiate aisle is at Restalrig, to the south-east of Edinburgh (see Figures 5.1r and 5.5).[9] It is a hexagon, originally of two storeys, against the south side of the western bay of the rectangular parish church and on first sight has something of the appearance of a polygonal chapter house. James III took a close interest in it, and for some time it was designated as a Chapel Royal; the earliest known reference to it is in 1477, when he founded an altar in the upper chapel, though in 1486–7 payments were still being recorded in the Exchequer Rolls for roofing.[10] Papal permission for the foundation was eventually received in 1487.[11] The lower aisle was dedicated to St Tradwell or Triduana, who is said to have reached Scotland

FIGURE 5.3   Guthrie Collegiate Church, the south aisle.

FIGURE 5.4   Guthrie Collegiate Church, the painted ceiling, showing part of the Last Judgement scene.

in the company of St Rule. She came to be associated with healing of the eyes after sending her own, impaled on a thorn, to King Nechtan, after he had offered her a compliment on them. The floor of this lower chapel is below the level of the water table, and it is possible the rising water was fed into a cistern in a recess within the north wall where those with afflictions could bathe their eyes. There also used to be a well nearby with a superstructure which was a miniature version of the Restalrig chapel; it was removed to Holyrood Park in 1859, where it is known as St Margaret's well.[12] The shape of both of these structures is significant, since hexagons were often chosen for conduit buildings, well-houses and other structures connected with water.

Excavations around the parish church of Restalrig in 1962–3 found evidence of late medieval operations which would have greatly enlarged it, but which were never completed[13] – perhaps because, after the death of James III, James IV became more interested in his new Chapel Royal at Stirling. Against the north-east face of the hexagon was found a wall respond, suggesting an aisle was planned along the south flank of the nave. It seems it was also intended to extend the church eastwards, because

FIGURE 5.5   Restalrig Collegiate Church, the chapel of St Triduana.

part of a major pier or respond was found against the north-east angle of the church. Another find was the footing of a rectangular offshoot against the north wall of the church, which could have been either a chapel or a sacristy. The entire complex was abandoned for worship at the Reformation, although the lower storey of the hexagonal chapel continued in use for burials, eventually being restored by Thomas Ross in 1907.

On its three southward-facing sides the surviving lower storey has windows with three cusped lights reaching up to the head of the three-centred arches. Internally it has vaulting rising from a central pier with six filleted shafts. The vault ribs which spring from the pier continue across as ridge ribs, meeting the walls above the apices of the windows, while the ribs that spring from the wall shafts extend in a straight line across the ridge before meeting those that spring from the next wall rib but one. From the surviving rib fragments, the vault over the upper chapel seems not to have required a central pier.

At Cullen, in Banffshire, a similar position was chosen as at Guthrie for the collegiate aisle founded in 1543 (see Figure 5.6).[14] The church itself was a two-cell structure, and the new aisle was built out from the centre of the south side of the nave. (The corresponding north aisle was only added very much later.) This college was a combination of a private foundation and of the type of foundation established in some burgh churches, since its patrons were Alexander Ogilvie of Findlater, Alexander Dick (Archdeacon of Glasgow), John Duff of Muldavit, the community of Cullen and the parishioners of the church. But the lead was probably taken by Ogilvie who, on heraldic evidence, apparently also remodelled the choir before his death in 1554. His tomb was

FIGURE 5.6   Cullen Church, the south collegiate aisle is to the left.

placed in the north wall of the choir, with relief carvings of himself and his wife in the spandrels to either side of the large multi-cusped ogee tomb arch, and with his own armoured effigy on the chest. To the right of the tomb is a sacrament house, on which two angels hold aloft the monstrance for the consecrated host. With such lavish reconstruction of the choir around the same time that the aisle was built, it is likely that the college of seven or eight prebendaries and two choristers used both parts.

The difficulty of determining which parts of a church might have been used by a college is also a problem at Corstorphine, on the western outskirts of Edinburgh (see Figures 5.1i and 5.7).[15] In a way analogous with Seton, the college was foreshadowed in a chapel founded by Sir Adam Forrester before his death in 1405, and in 1425/6 three more chaplainries were established within it; it was further augmented in 1429 and an inscription within the church ascribes the foundation of the college to that year.[16] Yet more additions were made by Sir John Forrester before 1436, though it was probably not until after 1444 that the full complement was reached.[17] The first chapel was said to have been in the cemetery beside the church, and from this it is sometimes assumed that the original church was on the north side of the surviving medieval parts. Unfortunately those northern parts of the church were replaced by an aisle in 1646 (around which time the western porch was probably also built), and there was further rebuilding of them by William Burn in 1828, and by George Henderson in 1903, all of which has greatly confused the evidence.

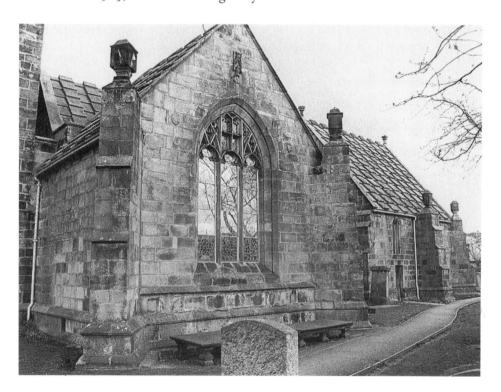

FIGURE 5.7   Corstorphine Collegiate Church, the south aisle is on the left and the choir on the right.

The surviving medieval elements at Corstorphine consist of an approximately square choir flanked by a rectangular northern sacristy; the walls of the choir overlap those of the narrower nave, which has a rectangular lateral aisle off the western end of its south flank, and a west tower. As already indicated, the original form of the north aisle is no longer certain, but the fact that the choir and the western tower are aligned with each other suggests that this was always the principal axis, and that anything to its north was of lesser importance. From the way the walls of the choir overlap those of the nave it seems it must have been a later addition; nevertheless, since choir, nave, south-western aisle and tower have a continuous base course beneath them, they must all have been remodelled to a unified scheme at some stage.

Taking account of all this, the most likely interpretation may be that Sir Adam's chapel in the cemetery was on the site of the lateral aisle on the south side of the nave; it may be added that the tomb below the south window is traditionally said to be his. However, the chapel must have been remodelled as part of the scheme which also involved remodelling the existing nave and adding a new choir. These works were possibly carried out around 1425–9, when chaplainries were added and the college was founded. Such a date would be consistent with the Perpendicular tracery of the south chapel, which is of a type related to tracery at Carnwath Collegiate Church of around 1424. In support of this interpretation, the choir contains the tombs of the Sir John who founded the college in 1429 and who died in 1440 in the position usually given to the founder; it also contains the tomb of his son – another Sir John – who augmented the college and died in about 1454 (see Figure 5.8). The former tomb has

FIGURE 5.8   Corstorphine Collegiate Church, the Forrester tombs in the north wall of the choir.

a three-centred arch, and the latter an angular two-centred arch; each contains the effigies of both husband and wife on tomb chests emblazoned with their heraldry.

Architecturally the staccato grouping and low-spreading lines of the church are highly attractive. Choir, nave, south aisle and tower are all constructed of excellent ashlar, with widely projecting buttresses to support the barrel vaulting over the choir and aisle. (The vaulting over the nave is a modern addition). The tower rises only a single storey above the nave and has a squat spire with crenellated bands and miniature lucarnes, and with pinnacles at the corners. Within the choir the concentration of tombs and liturgical furnishings, although bereft of their original colouring, remind us of the greater enrichment of this area. An especially intriguing internal feature is the barrel vault over the south aisle, which had ribs set out to a lozenge pattern, rather than to the usual cross-ribbed pattern; even lip service to the original structural function of the ribs was abandoned here. The combination of such a clearly Scottish vault with a window that is one of the few in Scotland to be of pronouncedly English Perpendicular type reminds us of the complexities of the developing architectural thought at this time.

At Corstorphine the choir would have been the setting for the main services of the college (though chantry masses would presumably be celebrated in Sir Adam's aisle), and at several other colleges it was the choir that was the main part to be rebuilt. For the college founded at Bothwell in 1397–8 by the third Earl of Douglas, for example, a rectangular choir of four bays with a sacristy on its north flank was added to the

FIGURE 5.9 (*left*)   Bothwell Collegiate Church, the exterior of the choir.
FIGURE 5.10 (*right*)   Bothwell Collegiate Church, the interior of the choir.

parish church not far from its founder's castle (see Figures 5.1h and 5.9).[18] It was attached to what must have been an unusually magnificent aisled Romanesque nave, of which only a few carved capitals survive. The relics of that nave were replaced by David Hamilton in 1833, while the choir was restored by Rowand Anderson in 1898.

Most of the window tracery in Bothwell's choir is of this last restoration, though the structural shell is largely as first built. The walls are of ashlar, strengthened by deep single-stage buttresses, and with a well-proportioned base course, a string course below the windows and a wall-head cornice. Internally there is a pointed barrel vault with parallel ribs connected by a ridge rib (see Figure 5.10). This vault springs from a relatively high level, and there is thus nothing of the sense of ponderous weight sometimes found in Scottish barrel-vaulted churches. Works patronised by Earl Archibald were always designed with considerable finesse, as can be seen in the sacristy doorway, which has two shafted orders, separated by a hollow, supporting the three-centred arch. It has been suggested there are parallels between this doorway and one inserted into the south wall of Haakon's Hall at the royal residence of Bergen in Norway, and that it thus provides evidence for architectural links between Scotland and Norway;[19] but, since the Bergen doorway is the finer of the two, it is more likely the similarity is a result of shared debts to continental prototypes.

COLLEGIATE CHURCHES BUILT TO A BASICALLY RECTANGULAR PLAN

As is to be expected at a period when so many churches were aisle-less rectangles, a number of collegiate churches were also of this plan. A good example is at Foulis Easter, to the north-west of Dundee (see Figures 5.1c and 5.11). There had been a church here since at least the mid-twelfth century, but inscriptions show it was rebuilt in 1452 and 1453.[20] This college was the project of Andrew Lord Gray,[21] though it may not have been finally constituted until the early sixteenth century, in the time of Patrick Lord Gray. As rebuilt by Andrew, it was an unbuttressed timber-roofed rectangle of about 27 by 8.5 metres and, though much internally dates from a restoration of 1889 by T. S. Robertson, the basic structure is largely authentic. The main lay entrance was through a south doorway surmounted by an enriched ogee hood-mould, but there was also a smaller entrance in the north wall and a priests' doorway on the south side of the chancel. Most of the windows were in the south and west walls, two of which are traceried: that to the south of the altar having three-light intersecting tracery, and that in the west wall having four lights grouped in two sub-arches containing simple dagger forms.

Internally there is unequalled evidence for the furnishings and fixtures of a rural collegiate church, which show more clearly than at any other how such building might be fitted out to create a lavish setting for the liturgy. As at the Franciscan churches of Aberdeen and Elgin (see pp. 134 and 135), the choir and nave were separated by a timber chancel screen and a loft. The loft was carried on corbels in the side walls, and there were low-level windows to north and south lighting the nave altars in front of the screen, with a single upper window on the south side lighting the loft. Supplementing the evidence of corbels and windows are the timber doors of the screen itself, now

FIGURE 5.11   Foulis Easter Collegiate Church, the exterior from the south-west.

FIGURE 5.12   Foulis Easter Collegiate Church, the doors of the choir screen.

reset in a modern screen towards the west end of the church (see Figure 5.12). These doors have simplified linenfold lower panels, open-work traceried panels at the intermediate stage, and an open top stage subdivided by miniature buttresses.

The most remarkable survival associated with the screen is part of the crucifixion painting which rose above it, which is the most extensive piece of Scottish medieval panel painting to have come down to us (see Figure 5.13). It is additionally interesting since the edge line of the painting indicates the profile of the original ceiling, which must have been rather like the wagon ceiling at Guthrie; the style of the painting has also been related to that at Guthrie. This extraordinary painting survived despite orders being given between 1612 and 1616 for it to be obliterated; fortunately the obliteration was superficial, and soon after 1746 it was rediscovered. Other paintings surviving here are an elongated panel bearing the figures of Christ with apostles and saints, and a panel showing Christ as the *Salvator Mundi*. The former possibly came from the front of the loft, and the latter perhaps from an altarpiece.[22] While the quality of these paintings should not be overstated, they are probably a guide to the type of paintings that would have been most frequently found in our later medieval churches, and they bring to life the descriptions of the paintings that were destroyed at Elgin Cathedral (see p. 71).

The *Salvator Mundi* theme was continued in the sacrament house, which has Christ in this role – flanked by angels holding the cross and the flagellation post – over the ogee-headed locker (see Figure 5.14).[23] Above these is carved the annunciation to the Virgin. One other fixture which must be mentioned is the font which, although badly damaged, is the finest of its kind in Scotland (see Figure 5.15).[24] Around its bowl are scenes from the passion and resurrection of Christ.

We must assume that similar furnishings existed elsewhere, as at the collegiate church of Innerpeffray in Perthshire, for example (see Figures 5.1d and 5.16).[25]

FIGURE 5.13   Foulis Easter Collegiate Church, the crucifixion painting from above the choir screen.

FIGURE 5.14   Foulis Easter Collegiate Church, the sacrament house.

FIGURE 5.15   Foulis Easter Collegiate Church, the bowl of the font.

There was a chapel for the Drummond family there from at least 1365, and it probably became collegiate by 1506–7 when John Lord Drummond established four further chaplainries.[26] It was specifically referred to as collegiate by 1542. The chapel survived structurally intact – apart from its northern sacristy – because it was used for burials after the Reformation, and later housed a library endowed by Lord Madertie in 1691. As at Foulis Easter, the rectangular interior was divided by a timber chancel screen and loft: the corbels for the loft remain, as does the low window on the south which lit the nave altars; the upper window for the loft apparently rose into the roof as some form of dormer (see Figure 5.16). Innerpeffray also has a second internal division in the form of a semicircular arch near the west end, but the original arrangements were modified when a laird's loft was inserted at a later date.

One other collegiate chapel now of this simple plan type is that of the academic college of St Leonard in St Andrews, a building with a very chequered history (see Figure 5.18).[27] It may have started its life in the twelfth century as part of a hospital, but by the early fifteenth century it also served parochial and academic functions. In 1512 Archbishop Stewart and Prior Hepburn established a college here for the education of Augustinian novices, after which the existing rectangular chapel was extended eastwards and a sacristy built against its north side. At the same time a tower was inserted within the western bays, and a two-storeyed porch was built against the south wall.

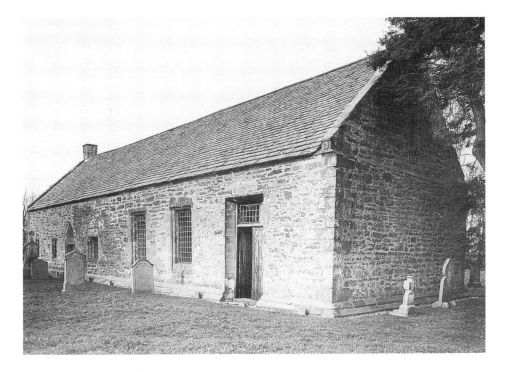

FIGURE 5.16   Innerpeffray Collegiate Church, from the south-east.

FIGURE 5.17   Innerpeffray Collegiate Church, interior looking eastwards.

FIGURE 5.18   St Andrews, St Leonard's Collegiate Chapel, from the south-west.

After the Reformation, from 1578, St Leonard's was used as a parish church as well as a college chapel, and in 1727 its tower was heightened and a spire added. In 1761, however, it was abandoned and the tower demolished, and in 1853 the Principal of United College created a make-shift west front when he ran his carriage drive through the site of the west bay. The chapel's fortunes revived in 1910 when what remained was reroofed and the windows glazed, and between 1948 and 1952 it was restored for worship. As a result of all these changes, though what we now see bears little resemblance to the medieval chapel, its rectangular mullioned windows do at least give something of its original flavour.

COLLEGIATE CHURCHES WITH APSED RECTANGULAR PLANS

Although a rectangular plan gives axial sense to a space, it does not provide a particular focus for the high altar. Those patrons or masons who knew continental architecture, however, would have been aware that most European churches terminated in a polygonal apse, either at the extreme east end of the building, or with a surrounding aisle and chapels beyond. Semicircular apses had in fact been common in Britain in the eleventh and twelfth centuries, as at Dalmeny, but had gone out of fashion around the middle of the latter century. On the Continent, however, apses had remained the norm, though after the earlier twelfth century they were usually polygonal. In some Scottish churches apses began to be introduced from around the mid-fifteenth century onwards, and an example has already been discussed at Crossraguel Abbey (see p. 102), but we cannot be certain when they were first introduced, or as a result of what influences. It might be argued the idea came from England, since some apses were built there in the fourteenth and fifteenth centuries – as at Lichfield Cathedral or at St Michael in Coventry. But English apses were exceptional by this period and, in any case, at a time when Scotland was still tending not to seek English guidance, it is unlikely that an unrepresentative group should have been so influential. On balance, it is more likely it was one of Scotland's better-travelled patrons who brought the idea from the Continent, and a likely candidate is Bishop James Kennedy of St Andrews, who founded the academic college of St Salvator there.[28]

The university of St Andrews had started life in the early fifteenth century, but was hardly thriving by the mid-century. In establishing the college of St Salvator in 1450, Bishop Kennedy was bringing new life by providing for additional teachers and students. Having left St Andrews as a student, Kennedy had graduated from Louvain in the Low Countries, but he also knew France, Burgundy and Italy as well as much beyond them.[29] So much is clear from debts to the constitutions of the universities of Paris, Oxford and Prague in those of his own college. His cosmopolitan approach for his new foundation is even more attractively illustrated by the exquisite ceremonial mace which was made for it. This was cast for Kennedy in 1461 by Jean Mayelle, the Parisian goldsmith of the French dauphin, at a time when we know from the queen's gift of drink-silver to the masons that construction of the college was still under way.[30]

Regrettably we have little more than the shell of Kennedy's college chapel, the stone vaulting having been removed in 1773, the window tracery having been replaced in restorations of 1861–2 and 1929–31, together with the wall-head parapet and pinnacles. Nevertheless, the plan and walls survive, and in them we have what may be the first Scottish example of a late medieval aisle-less church terminating in a three-sided apse (see Figures 5.1f and 5.19). Kennedy would have seen many examples of such chapels used for both private and academic foundations in the course of his travels through Europe, though it is tempting to speculate that the immediate inspiration would have been one of the examples which served the University of Paris, such as that of Cluny College which is still known from illustrations.[31]

St Salvator's chapel is of seven bays, apart from the apse, and the main public entrance was in the second bay from the west on the south side, where it is covered by a shallow porch between the buttresses. This porch has a ribbed barrel vault, and the main vault over the chapel is likely to have been of the same type: as might be expected, despite the likelihood of exotic influences on aspects of the design, there is much that is fundamentally Scottish. On the north of the chapel was a sacristy. The cloister around which the college buildings were grouped was also on the north, and one arch of its arcading survives in rebuilt form at the boundary gate opposite the south doorway. The main entrance to the precinct was through a gateway at the base of the tower at the south-western corner of the nave; its broached spire

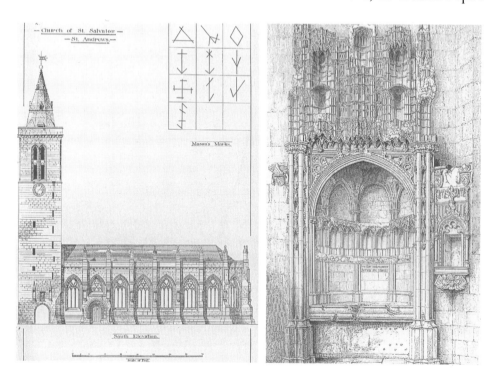

FIGURE 5.19 (*left*) St Andrews, St Salvator's Collegiate Chapel, the south elevation.
FIGURE 5.20 (*right*) St Andrews, St Salvator's Collegiate Chapel, the tomb of Bishop Kennedy and the sacrament house.

post-dates the siege of the castle of 1546–7, when artillery was mounted on the tower head.

The presbytery probably occupied the apse and the eastern bay, with the choir in no more than the two bays to the west of that, since there is a tomb recess on the north side of the fourth bay. But the choir must soon have been extended westwards and thus obscured that tomb, as is also the case in the modern arrangement. The finest internal feature is Kennedy's own tomb, in the traditional founder's position on the north side of the presbytery area; it was presumably ready for his burial in 1465 (see Figure 5.20). It is a strongly vertical composition, having a tall arch flanked by responds composed of thin shafts alternating with tiers of miniature tabernacles. Above this arch is a confection of tabernacle work showing a fascinating interplay between the inner and outer planes. The deep polygonal recess within the main arch, which was vaulted, had a band of tabernacle work at mid-height; the tabernacles at each end have miniature flights of steps leading tantalisingly to imagined spaces beyond in a way partly reminiscent of some of the details of Mayelles's mace. East of the tomb is a sacrament house, with a pair of angels carrying a monstrance below the locker.

Kennedy's chapel, with its innovative apsidal plan, would have been of seminal influence, and must have been a principal source of inspiration for the chapel which Bishop William Elphinstone built for his new King's College in Aberdeen (see Figure 5.1g).[32] That college was being planned by 1497, when Elphinstone bought gunpowder, carts and wheelbarrows from the Conservator of Scottish Privileges in the Netherlands, Andrew Halyburton.[33] The start of building is given by an inscription on the west front as 2 April 1500, though this may have been an idealised date, since it has analogies with the date of Solomon's founding of the temple.[34] Construction was rapidly pushed forward, since the date 1504 is inscribed on a tower buttress, and by 1506 a contract for the leading of the roof was agreed with the English plumber John Burwel (or Burnel).[35] The chapel was ready for dedication in 1509, though the tower and crown steeple may have been incomplete.

The aisle-less apsed plan of the chapel, with a tower at the south-west angle, is so like that of St Salvator's that there can be little doubt that one influenced the other. King's chapel, however, is longer and more slender, and of six bays rather than the seven narrower bays of St Salvator's. Some differences also resulted from the relationship between building and site and, since it was the west rather than the south front that faced the street at Aberdeen, the tower was aligned with the west front, while the two-storeyed sacristy range ran behind the tower along the south flank. Although probably planned from the start, the sacristy was built by Bishop William Stewart (1532–45) and had a chequered history – being dismantled and re-erected in 1725, and finally destroyed around 1772. By comparison, at St Salvator's the sacristy block was on the north, towards the cloister; but the arrangement of its doors – each opening out of the chapel – suggests that at both buildings the sacristy extended along much of the chapel.

King's chapel has a shallow timber wagon ceiling with a pattern of ribs in imitation of quadripartite vaulting (see Figure 5.21). A very similar ceiling had been started in 1495 over the choir of the parish church of St Nicholas in Aberdeen, another building in which Elphinstone took a keen interest (see p. 210 and Figure 6.19).[36] The example at St Nicholas' was constructed by the local wright John Fendour, and it must be likely he was also involved in that at King's. These ceilings present an interesting problem in cross-fertilisation of ideas. Timber wagon ceilings had a long history in Scotland: they were built over the nave and choir of Glasgow Cathedral, presumably in the thirteenth century, and there is evidence of another at Elgin after the fire of 1390. But those were steeply pitched. Nearer in date and closer in profile to the Aberdeen examples were ceilings at the collegiate churches of Foulis Easter and Guthrie, although with parallel ribs in one case at least. The idea for the configuration of ribs at the Aberdeen churches could have come from the many Scottish stone barrel vaults decorated with cross ribs, particularly since the difference of material would have been less evident when both vaults and ceilings were painted, and we must remember that the St Salvator's vault was probably of this type. But it is possible other influences were also at work. The widely sprigged bosses at the intersections of the Aberdeen ceilings – which were also found on Bishop Dunbar's heraldic ceiling at Aberdeen Cathedral (see Figure 2.11) – could show awareness of Netherlandish prototypes, because related bosses decorate the timber vault placed over the hall in the town hall at Bruges, the work of Jean de Valenciennes in 1402. It must also be remembered that ribbed timber ceilings were very common in the Low Countries, though they tended to be more steeply pitched than those in Scotland, and more often had ribs set in a parallel rather than diagonally crossed pattern.

On this basis the Aberdeen ceilings might show the impact of an admixture of ideas, and we shall probably never determine which were uppermost in the minds of Elphinstone and his craftsmen. It could be argued that the ceilings were part of a Scottish development, with no influence from the Low Countries. But we must not underestimate Scotland's involvement in the wider European intellectual and artistic exchange of ideas, and Netherlandish influences were almost certainly a factor in the design of another feature at King's: the window tracery. In most of the windows the predominant feature is a massive vertical mullion, rising up to the window apex, with loose combinations of forms on each side (see Figure 5.22). Though it was never common, the central mullion can be paralleled in several European countries, including France and England, but the heaviness of the examples at King's is best reflected in examples in the Low Countries, and this is also true of the loose tracery combinations. Parallels have been drawn by one writer with windows in St Jacques at Liège,[37] though those are later than Aberdeen, and a more telling comparison may be made with a window in the Domproosten Chapel off the south transept in Utrecht Cathedral, datable to around 1497, the year when Elphinstone was beginning to gather his materials. It must also be remembered that Elphinstone had been in the Low Countries on a diplomatic mission in 1495,[38] and that he maintained contacts with the area through his purchase of materials from Halyburton. The likelihood of Netherlandish influences in the window design is thus quite strong.

Externally, the chapel is dominated by the crown steeple on the tower at the south-west corner, but in the design of this part it was English influences that ultimately underlay the idea (see Figure 5.22).[39] Crown steeples represent one of the greatest flights of fantasy ever attempted by Scottish masons, and were also designed for the burgh churches of Dundee, Edinburgh, Linlithgow and Haddington. However, only those of Aberdeen and Edinburgh survive, and they are both now partly seventeenth-century reconstructions: Aberdeen's in 1634, and Edinburgh's in 1648 (see Figure 6.2). We do not know how extensively Aberdeen's was then remodelled. It is, however, still capped by an imperial crown, as was described by Hector Boece,[40] and since that crown is similar to one on the fountain at Linlithgow Palace, of around the 1530s (see Figure 10.4), it seems likely generally to replicate the original. Of the crown steeples known to have been built, Edinburgh's was the most complex. It had flyers from the faces of the tower as well as at the angles, and the details of the wall-heads at both Haddington and Dundee suggest they were similarly planned for eight flyers (see Figures 6.7 and 6.18). Only Aberdeen and Linlithgow had flyers at the angles alone.

Crown steeples must be understood as part of the late medieval vogue for handling stone in a way which seems to defy the material's nature. An earlier stage in the development of the idea is seen in towers with octagonal superstructures linked to the angles of the towers by flying buttresses – at places as far apart as Lowick in Northamptonshire, and St Ouen at Rouen in Normandy. In some cases the sense of lightness was taken even further, as with the spire rising through an octagon at Patrington in Yorkshire, or in the stone lattice-work of St Maclou at Rouen or at Notre Dame de l'Épine near Châlons-sur-Marne. But it seems it was English masons who took the step of cutting the connection between the tower and central super-structure, leaving it supported only by the flying buttresses. The crown steeple at Newcastle dates from around the 1470s and, on present evidence, it is likely to have been Newcastle that inspired the Scottish examples. Such renewed debts to England, as also with the employment of an English plumber on the roof at King's, remind us of the uneasy *rapprochement* which developed with England following the long truce of 1464; those links were strongest around the time of James IV's marriage to Margaret, the daughter of Henry VII, in 1503. The additional flyers and the accretions of pinnacles on the crown steeples north of the Border, however, show a marked Scotticisation of the original idea, and suggest that English ideas were no longer to be copied as closely as was once the case.

The finest internal features of the chapel are the carved choir stalls and screen, which represent the most impressive ensemble of woodwork we still have, despite an excessive restoration in 1823 and their movement westwards in the 1870s (see Figure 5.23). It seems that Scotland did not aspire to the elaborate essays in fretted tabernacle work of the best English canopied stalls, though the King's canopies show remarkable inventiveness in their openwork tracery designs. Like the few surviving canopy fronts from St Nicholas' church, which were commissioned from John Fendour in 1507, the canopies are divided into bays by miniature buttresses, within each of which is a multi-cusped and crocketed ogee arch against a screen of tracery. However, whereas the St Nicholas' canopies are single-tiered and the tracery is a restrained sequence of paired lights below quatrefoils, the wright at King's has carved inventively flamboyant forms, and there is also an upper tier of smaller panels. Even

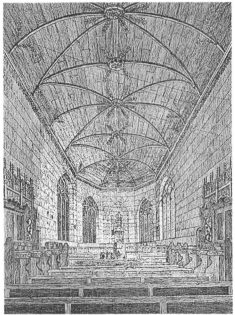

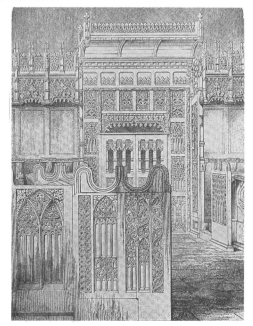

FIGURE 5.21 (*above, left*)   Aberdeen,
King's College Chapel, the interior as it was
between restorations of 1823 and 1891.
FIGURE 5.22 (*above, right*)   King's College
Chapel, the west front.
FIGURE 5.23 (*right*)   King's College
Chapel, the stalls and screen.

greater inventiveness was shown in the blind tracery of the bench ends and in the panels surrounding the doorway of the rood screen.

The relative ease of working wood allowed greater virtuosity than was usual in masonry carving, and we cannot assume that their complexity means the King's stalls are not of local production, particularly since Fendour carved a more restrained version of the same type of canopy for St Nicholas' Church. The closest local analogies for the woodwork at King's are in the Deacon Convenor's chair at Trinity Hall in Aberdeen, which could conceivably be made up from discarded woodwork from either King's chapel or St Nicholas' Church.

The plan of King's and St Salvator's was presumably as suitable for secular as for academic colleges, and it was certainly used for the choir which was the first stage of the rebuilding of Seton Church (see Figure 5.38). So far as we know, however, the only secular collegiate church that closely followed the type established at St Andrews – albeit on a smaller scale – was at Castle Semple in Renfrewshire,[41] which was founded in 1504 by John Lord Semple (see Figures 5.1e and 5.24).[42] That church appears to be a remodelling of an existing building, and was probably finished before its founder fell at Flodden in 1513. It is an aisle-less rectangle with a three-sided eastern apse and a tiny western tower; there was no division into bays either by consistent rhythm of windows or by buttresses, though the apse has three-quarter rolls marking its angles. Internally the choir and nave were originally separated by a timber screen and loft, the corbels of which have survived. The main internal focus is now Lord Semple's tomb, on the north side of the presbytery (see Figure 5.25). It

FIGURE 5.24   Castle Semple Collegiate Church, from the south-east.

FIGURE 5.25   Castle Semple Collegiate Church, the tomb of Lord Semple.

is a rather unresolved design, with a flat arch supported by two half-arches, and a top panel filled with a flaccid super-arch and low-relief foliage carving. Its architectural illiteracy is reflected in the two-light windows of the apse and choir, those in the south flank of the choir being ultimately – if rather confusedly – inspired by English Perpendicular types.

COLLEGIATE CHURCHES BUILT TO CRUCIFORM PLANS

The beau idéal for churches of any pretensions continued to be a cross-shaped plan, presumably both because of the symbolism and for the convenience of the additional altar space. A number of collegiate churches were cruciform, even if this was often only achieved through a process of progressive accretion. Such a process of accretion certainly seems to have lain behind the final state of one of the oldest collegiate foundations, that of Dunbar in East Lothian, if reliance can be placed on a plan made before its complete reconstruction in 1819–21. This shows a heavily buttressed choir, transepts, and a nave with a single north aisle and a western tower.[43]

The most eccentric cruciform collegiate church – largely because it is the one that has preserved least of its original fabric – is at Yester, or Bothans, in East Lothian (see Figure 5.26).[44] The college was founded in 1421 by the co-lords Sir William Hay, Thomas Boyd, Eustace de Maxwell and Dougald McDowall, and construction was probably started around then; additional chaplainries were founded in 1447 and

1535.[45] The evidence for the medieval form of the building has been confused by two phases of post-Reformation reconstruction. The church is now of a compressed cross plan, with rectangular transeptal chapels, a short choir, and a nave of less than a metre in length, all of which have pointed barrel vaults; of these only the transepts still reflect their original dimensions. Much of the church was remodelled in 1635, the date inscribed on the east window. Excavations have shown the choir was originally considerably longer,[46] and the collapse of part of the masonry recasing of the choir and transepts has revealed that some of the original windows were larger than those now seen. The nave was probably largely demolished when a new church was built in the village in 1710, after which what remained of the old building was used as a mausoleum. Across the truncated stump of the nave a charming rococo Gothic screen front was constructed in 1753, possibly by John Adam, who was working on the adjacent house.[47]

It thus seems that Yester once had a more conventional Latin cross plan, with pointed barrel vaulting throughout. The vaulting of nave and choir was probably continuous; as at Inchcolm there were no transverse arches to define a crossing, though there is now a classical arch at the entrance to the choir. The transepts are entered through low semicircular arches, below the vault springings of the main spaces, suggesting that the problems of placing pointed barrel vaults over lateral areas without leaving them spatially isolated had not yet been adequately resolved.

FIGURE 5.26   Yester Collegiate Church, from the south-east. The truncated choir is on the right and the south transept on the left.

Nevertheless, at a number of churches we begin to feel that compartmentalisation of spaces was an effect that was positively sought. This was possibly the case at another cruciform East Lothian collegiate church, at Dunglass,[48] though here the church acquired its more complicated plan only secondarily (see Figures 5.1l and 5.27). There was a chapel here by 1423, when Alexander Home provided additional endowments, and by 1448–9 it was being referred to as a college. Papal confirmation of the foundation by Sir Alexander Home came in 1451. Eventually there may have been about thirteen prebendaries.[49]

As first started, the church had only a choir, nave and an offshoot to the north of the choir, which possibly served as both a sacristy and a tomb chapel. The choir was narrower and shorter than the nave, and there was a low chancel arch between them. All the spaces were covered by pointed barrel vaulting (see Figure 5.28). This first phase of works could have been started as early as the time of Alexander's endowments of 1423, since the choir windows are similar to those in the flank of Carnwath collegiate aisle of about 1424, albeit with segmental rather than flat heads. But other details suggest the work was still under way around the date of the college's foundation in the 1440s, and variants on such windows were built over several decades. There are examples at South Queensferry Carmelite church of about 1440, a church which shows a similar taste for compartmentalisation of spaces by means of low arches, and we are thus reminded that attempting to date buildings on stylistic criteria can be difficult at this period. Among the details of Dunglass, the fine foliage carving on the capitals of the chancel arch and on the choir sedilia both seem more likely to be closer to the 1440s than the 1420s (see Figure 5.29).

It cannot have been long after the 1440s, however, that it was decided to add transeptal chapels to the west of the chancel arch, and to slot a tower into the east end of the nave. The dimensions of the tower were generated by the width of the chancel arch rather than the width of any of the spaces around the proposed tower, and consequently its western piers impinge significantly on the internal spaces. To accommodate the roofs of the nave and transepts to the walls of the tower various adjustments had to be made and, as with the junction of the transepts and central space at Yester, one is left sensing that masons might be nonplussed by the consequences of their planning once it came to the upper parts (see Figure 5.27).

Another Lothian collegiate church where the tower may be a secondary intrusion is at Crichton (see Figures 5.1j and 5.30). This college was founded in 1449 by William, Lord Crichton,[50] a member of a previously relatively minor family who rose to power by taking advantage of the vacuum created through the persecution of other families by James I and II. Crichton also made major additions to his nearby castle (see p. 268). Only the choir, transeptal chapels and central tower of the church survive, and those were crudely adapted in about 1729, and then restored by Hardy and Wight in 1898. It is usually assumed the nave was never built, though it is equally possible that an earlier nave was demolished after the Reformation; the sacristy on the north side of the choir was also demolished. As at Dunglass, oddities of planning must result from additions to the original plan but, whereas at Dunglass the tower seems too small for the transepts, at Crichton it is the transepts that are too small for the tower.

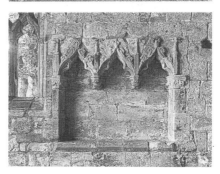

FIGURE 5.27 (*top*)   Dunglass Collegiate Church, from the north-east.
FIGURE 5.28 (*middle*)   Dunglass Collegiate Church, the interior of the choir looking westwards.
FIGURE 5.29 (*bottom*)   Dunglass Collegiate Church, the sedilia.

FIGURE 5.30   Crichton Collegiate Church, from the south-east.

At Crichton it seems likely the barrel-vaulted choir was an addition for the college to the existing parish church. Later, but probably while work continued on the evidence of the base courses, it was decided to add the barrel-vaulted transeptal chapels on each flank, possibly incorporating existing buttresses in the masonry of their east walls. In doing this no attempt was made to give the chapels a uniform size, suggesting there was no need to create a full crossing because there was still no tower. The tower was thus one of the last additions to the church, and it extends considerably further west than either of the transepts. It was clearly initially intended to be higher than built, since it now rises only a single compressed storey above the flanking roofs. Rather oddly, its stair turret is in an added section of wall well to its west, perhaps to set it clear of a chancel screen. Despite the inconsistencies resulting from this piecemeal development, efforts were made to achieve homogeneity, especially in the way the masonry of the transepts was married into the choir. Much of the work is of a high standard, the mouldings of the windows and doorway on the south flank of the choir being especially well detailed.

The central decades of the fifteenth century were a particularly productive phase for collegiate churches, and to this period belong the two most ambitious foundations outside those in the parish churches of the greater burghs or James IV's Chapel Royal at Stirling. These were at Roslin in Midlothian and Trinity College in Edinburgh, the former of which was founded by one of the great magnates, while the other was a royal foundation. Unfortunately, both were so ambitious that they were never more than half completed, and the latter is now only a distorted reconstruction.

The founder of Roslin was William Sinclair, Earl of Orkney and Caithness, who succeeded Lord Crichton as Chancellor in 1454, and who – like Lord Crichton – was a beneficiary of the eclipse and fall of the Black Douglas family.[51] The church, which was built close to Sinclair's chief Lowland castle, was referred to as being collegiate by 1456, and papal confirmation was received in 1477 (see Figure 5.31).[52] But according to Father Richard Augustine Hay, writing in about 1700 (the same writer referred to in connection with Crossraguel, see p. 103), Earl William had laid the foundation stone of the chapel as early as 1446. This may be correct, since references in additions to the *Scotichronicon* indicate work was in progress by about 1447.[53] A cryptic inscription on the cornice of the north clearstorey, however, appears to give a date of 1450, though such discrepancies are easily accounted for in the vagaries of medieval building operations.

Hay seems also to have had access to lost documents for his description of part of the design process. In this he says that Sinclair – although presumably the master mason – 'first caused the draughts to be drawn upon Eastland boords and made the carpenters to carve them according to the draughts theron, and then gave them for patterns to the masons that they might therby cut the like in stone'.[54] Such a precise account of the stages in producing the templates for cutting individual stones is likely to have had a basis in authoritative sources. Roslin is additionally informative on medieval design methods because of some scratched drawings on the walls of a lower chamber to the east of the chapel. These are for a cusped arch, related to those in the eastern ambulatory of the chapel, and for a crocketed and finialled pinnacle. They appear to be a mason's working drawings, and it seems the walls must have served a similar purpose to the tracing floors at York and Wells Cathedrals, even if it is difficult to imagine how vertical surfaces could have been used in this way.[55]

Work at Roslin stopped after the east wall of the transepts had been built. This was perhaps linked with Sinclair's difficulties from the later 1460s, as James III established his hold on Orkney and Shetland following the pledging of the Norwegian crown rights in the islands against the dowry of his queen, Margaret of Denmark. Despite compensation including the castle of Ravenscraig and other lands, Earl William's resignation of the earldom of Orkney to the crown must have caused real financial problems.[56] If completed, however, the church would probably have been larger than that of any other rural collegiate foundation. The choir was five bays long, with an aisle on each side, and with an eastern ambulatory opening on to a row of four chapels (see Figure 5.1m). At the west end of the choir were to have been transepts projecting two bays beyond the aisles, with a crossing area apparently as wide as the combined central space and aisles of the choir. Nineteenth-century excavations, supported by recent further investigations,[57] have suggested that foundations were laid for an aisled nave of a similar length as the eastern limb, ending in a narrow western tower, giving a total length approaching 56.5 metres. To the south-east of the choir, and at a lower level, is a large barrel-vaulted chamber, usually called a sacristy, though its planning may indicate other uses including, perhaps, a hall for the college's prebendaries.

Within the incomplete crossing and transepts are important remains of the liturgical fixtures, though they are now partly obscured by the vestry added by Andrew Kerr in 1880 (see Figure 5.32). Dividing the choir from the transepts was a substantial screen wall, the lower part of which was pierced by three doorways from the main space and the flanking aisles, the central doorway having an adjacent holy water stoup. Above that doorway was an arch rising almost the full height of the choir and flanked on each side by an image corbel. Within each transept a single chapel would have occupied the full two bays defined by the external buttresses. The seating for the altars is indicated by the absence of wall facing, some distance above which are corbels to support retables – which explains why these walls were windowless. South of each altar was a piscina recess, and in the south transept there was a sacrament house on the opposite side of the altar.

The plan of Roslin choir – with its straight ambulatory – is a reduced version of that of Glasgow Cathedral from the mid-thirteenth century, and was possibly employed previously at the Cistercian abbey of Newbattle in Midlothian. It is a type developed in England in the twelfth century, but particularly favoured by the Cistercians as a means of providing additional chapels without architectural ostentation. The vaulting at Roslin also has parallels with twelfth-century Cistercian usages, in the combination of a longitudinal barrel vault over the main space, and lower transverse pointed barrel vaults over each aisle bay (see Figures 5.33). But there the parallels end because, whereas the Cistercians cultivated architectural austerity, Sinclair's goal was apparently a building more lavishly enriched than anything previously produced within the British Isles.

The cost of Roslin must have been prodigious, because of the way all architectural features are enriched. Externally this is best seen in the carving around the window heads, and in the pinnacles at the aisle wall-head. The main pinnacles, from which extend the flyers to abut the main vault, are themselves supported by smaller pinnacles with smaller flyers. Internally, there is a plethora of foliage carving on the capitals, there are tabernacles in the window embrasures, and foliage or figurative carving on the transverse flat arches below the vault springings; there is even carving on the surfaces of the vaults (see Figure 5.33). But the most lavish treatment is in the eastern ambulatory and chapels. The quadripartite vaulting of the latter has cusping along the ribs, with pendants projecting improbably outwards above the springings. Most enriched of all is the so-called 'apprentice pillar' between the first and second chapels from the south, which has spiralled bands of foliage wrapped around its bundled miniature shafts (see Figure 5.34). Yet, despite the staggering quantity of decoration, the quality of the individual elements is not always as high as might be expected. It is repetition and multiplication that create the overwhelming impression.

Parallels for such excesses of enrichment have been sought in Spain by some writers, though this is probably unnecessary, because many buildings further north – and more likely to be known to Sinclair – showed a kindred taste for superabundant richness. Parts of France, for example, showed a strong preference for a plethora of decoration around these years – as in many churches of Normandy. Seeing works like the west porch of St Maclou at Rouen, or the west front of Caudebec-en-Caux – both

FIGURE 5.31 (*above*) Roslin Collegiate Church, the south flank of the choir.
FIGURE 5.32 (*below*) Roslin Collegiate Church, the crossing area before the addition of the vestry.

FIGURE 5.33 (*left*)   Roslin Collegiate Church, looking eastwards down the north choir aisle.
FIGURE 5.34 (*right*)   Roslin Collegiate Church, the 'apprentice pillar'.

started around the second quarter of the fifteenth century – could certainly have encouraged a desire for lavish sculptural effects. Moving on to specific details, there was a vogue for spiral decoration on piers like the 'apprentice pillar' throughout Europe, including French examples at St Croix in Provins (south-east of Paris), and at St Severin in Paris. This is not to suggest specific parallels with such churches, and indeed some are later than Roslin, but it could have been the same underlying trend which found expression at both them and Roslin. In all these cases, the effect is achieved by the multiplication of detail, though it is the local architectural repertoire that provides those details.

Roslin is not a typical Scottish late Gothic building, though its exotic glamour did at certain critical stages threaten to throw off balance the beginnings of the study of Scottish architectural history. By comparison with Roslin, Trinity College Church in Edinburgh must have seemed the epitome of the coolly sophisticated (see Figure 5.35).[58] It was founded in 1460 by the queen dowager, Mary of Guelders, following James II's death at the siege of Roxburgh, though it was possibly planned at an earlier stage.[59] Construction was pushed rapidly ahead during Mary's lifetime, under the direction of John Halkerston as master of works, and records indicate expenditure of about £1,000 on the church and associated hospital. But work languished after her death in 1463, and it was never completed, despite additions to the complement of the college in 1502 and efforts by James V to obtain indulgences for those who would assist the work in 1531.[60] After the Reformation, ownership of the college passed to the burgh, and in 1584 the church became parochial, continuing in use until the 1840s. By 1844 the hospital buildings had been removed for the new railway, and in 1848 the church followed, as the culmination of a lengthy *cause célèbre*. The intention was to rebuild immediately on an adjacent site, but this did not happen until 1872, by which time some of the original masonry had been lost.[61] As eventually rebuilt, the central space of the choir, stripped of its aisles, became the top element of a T-plan church, the main body of which was itself demolished in 1964. We are therefore left with a displaced reconstruction which only partly reflects its founder's intentions.

The choir was originally of three aisled bays and a five-sided apse (see Figure 5.1q). On the north was a two-storeyed sacristy and treasury block, and there was a shallow arched porch between a buttress and the south transept wall, rather like those already seen at St Salvator's and Roslin. The transepts were probably laid out with the choir, the northern one being of slightly greater projection. But the recorded details of the transepts show they were completed much later, and this is borne out by the fact that James V's request for indulgences referred to only the choir as complete. The nave was also to have had aisles, but there is no evidence that any of it was built.

Internally the choir was of a two-storeyed design divided horizontally by a string course a little way above the arch apices, and the clearstorey stage was only slightly less tall than the arcades (see Figure 5.36). The arcade piers, which have three-quarter shafts separated by diagonal faces, were of a similar section as those in the choir of Linlithgow Church, and they also showed similarities with those used throughout Haddington Church (see pp. 201 and 195, and Figure 6.6). However, the problems encountered in those churches through the necessity of placing the clearstorey windows above the sloping aisle roofs, and thus uncomfortably high, seem to have been overcome in the Edinburgh church by extending the internal clearstorey window openings downwards below a transom. The choir and apse had tierceron vaulting carried on triplet wall shafts rising from corbels set between the arcade arches. At the angles of the apse the shafts rose from that same level, leaving space for image corbels below. Little is known of the window tracery of the choir, though some of the aisle windows had a single mullion and transom, as in the windows which were to be built around 1545 at Biggar (see Figure 5.41). This may indicate they were inserted when James V was attempting to revive the project in 1531. The transept windows were almost certainly of that period, having uncusped loop tracery similar to that at Midcalder Church of about 1542 (see p. 227).

There is much about Trinity College Church that is characteristic of the mid-fifteenth-century Scottish architecture. Even the tierceron vaulting, although unusual for a collegiate church, is what might be expected in a particularly prestigious building – as in the choir of St Giles' Church in Edinburgh and the transepts and nave of Melrose Abbey. But there was also a sureness of touch in the proportions and inter-relationship of parts of Trinity that is sometimes lacking in Scottish works of the period, and the linkage between apse and choir was especially well handled. This is presumably because the queen dowager could pay for the best. Yet, considering that she was the niece of the Duke of Burgundy, as well as a daughter of the Duke of Guelders, is it possible that some of the polish of the design was because Mary had imported

FIGURE 5.35 (*above*)   Edinburgh Trinity
Collegiate Church, from the south-west.
FIGURE 5.36 (*right*)   Edinburgh Trinity
Collegiate Church, the interior of the choir
looking eastwards.

Burgundian masons to help achieve what she wanted? If we compare Trinity Church with a Burgundian church of similar plan and scale – such as Ambierle, which was started in about 1440 – it does not seem unreasonable to suspect that the approach underlying the latter has also influenced the former. There can be no certainty, but when we consider the outstanding quality of the altarpiece that was later painted for the church by Hugo van der Goes, between about 1473 and 1478, it becomes even easier to see this building as the focus of a cosmopolitan interchange of ideas.

Moving back to churches of slightly less ambitious scale, in the later fifteenth and earlier sixteenth centuries one particular cruciform plan type was used for a number of collegiate foundations, albeit sometimes as the result of an extended architectural development. In this type the aisle-less choir terminates in a three-sided apse, and usually has a sacristy on its north side, while the transepts are frequently of wide projection. From descriptions and early views it is possible one of the first was that founded at Hamilton by James, Lord Hamilton, in 1450–1. This church was largely destroyed when the new one was built in 1733. Only the family burial place in what may have been the sacristy survived, until a mausoleum was built on a new site in 1852 (see Figure 5.37). The details of the church are uncertain, though an engraving made by Grose during demolition shows that there was an apsidal termination. The transepts and nave may have been destroyed as early as the late seventeenth century if Slezer's view of the town is to be trusted.

At Seton, in East Lothian, the apsed cruciform plan was only achieved in several

FIGURE 5.37   Hamilton Collegiate Church, in the course of demolition.

stages,[62] a process documented by Sir Richard Maitland of Lethington in his *Genealogie* of the family of 1561 (see Figures 5.1n and 5.38).[63] The rectangular parish church had already had a chapel added to it by Lady Katherine Seton in the 1430s, but the main process of enlargement was started by the first Lord Seton, who died in about 1478. He began to build the choir and sacristy, and vaulted the eastern parts of the former. He also attempted to found the college in 1470, but was thwarted by the Pope's death. Papal authorisation was eventually received by the second Lord Seton in 1492,[64] and he completed the choir vaulting and built the residences of the prebendaries before his death in about 1508. These residences may be represented by the fragmentary structures to the south-west of the church. The third Lord Seton, who fell at Flodden in 1513, roofed, paved, glazed and furnished the choir.

The third lord's widow, Lady Janet, built the transepts and central tower, and provided more vestments and furnishings. The northern of her transepts was under construction by 1540, but the southern one – which necessitated the demolition of Lady Katherine's chapel – was probably started after the church had been sacked by the Earl of Hertford in May 1544. It was perhaps then intended to rebuild the nave, but the incomplete state of the spire suggests work came to an untimely halt at the Reformation. The church remained in use until united with Tranent in 1580, though seventy years later there was an abortive proposal to make it again parochial. In 1715 it was desecrated by the Edinburgh militia because of the Jacobite sympathies of the Earl of Winton, the descendant of the Lords Seton; after many years of lying derelict in 1878 it was restored as a burial place for the Earls of Wemyss by Maitland Wardrop.

The choir was of three bays, with a three-sided apse (see Figure 5.39). It was evidently intended to be a self-contained addition to the existing church, the side walls of which it overlapped, and an angled buttress at its north-west corner shows that nothing new west of it was contemplated. The design of the choir is one of the best illustrations of the Scottish idiom that had been emerging since the earlier years of the century. On the pointed barrel vault, the quadripartite-patterned ribs were confined to the presbytery area, reminding us that their function was aesthetic rather than structural. The two-and three-light window tracery was also characteristic, with two curved daggers surmounted in the three-light versions by a third vertical dagger. Similar windows had been – or were to be – used in the burgh churches of Haddington, Linlithgow and Stirling, as well as at Paisley Abbey. But the high aspirations of Lord Seton for his new college shine through all the details: the image corbels at the internal angles of the apse show an awareness of Trinity College Church in Edinburgh (see Figure 5.36), while the miniature architectural detailing of the piscina is notably refined.

In her two-bay transepts, Lady Janet followed the architectural lead of the choir, though the massive sub-arches of the windows in the gable ends may reflect Netherlandish influence. (The debt to the Netherlands was to be continued in the bell which her grandson had made there in 1577.) The 1544 attack by the Earl of Hertford, involved the theft of bells and organs, and prompted Lady Janet to be an active provider of furnishings; in this we see graphically the high place that a family's collegiate church had in its affections. Among her many gifts were costly vestments of damask, silk and

FIGURE 5.38 (*above*)   Seton Collegiate
Church, from the south-east.
FIGURE 5.39 (*right*)   Seton Collegiate
Church, the interior of the choir looking
eastwards.

velvet, a silver crucifix, monstrance and chalice, and hangings for the altar.

A church which was partly modelled on Seton was that at Dalkeith, in Midlothian (see Figures 5.1p and 5.40).[65] Six chaplains were endowed in the chapel here by Sir James Douglas in 1406, and this provided a basis for the college. In 1467 the church also became parochial, and there were further endowments of the college by the Douglas Earls of Morton in 1475–7 and 1503.[66] By the end of the Middle Ages the church had an aisled nave of four bays with a south porch, and the eastern bay of each aisle projected out as a transeptal chapel. A western tower was only added very much later, possibly in about 1762. The choir was very similar to that of Seton, having three bays and an apse covered by ribbed pointed barrel vaulting, and with a sacristy in the middle bay on the north side. But close inspection shows the choir is later than at Seton. This is most evident in the window tracery which, while basically like that of one of the types at Seton, is devoid of cusping, resulting in loop-like forms which are unlikely to date from before the augmentations of 1503.

Of the choir only the western bay remains in use, because it was absorbed into the parish church in about 1590, and the vaulting over the rest of the choir eventually collapsed in about 1770. The restoration of the nave by David Bryce in 1855 was to have extended to the choir but, since Bryce left little medieval work in the nave untouched, we should perhaps be grateful that economy led to its exclusion.

The most seemingly homogeneous of the cruciform apsed collegiate churches is

FIGURE 5.40   Dalkeith Church, the south flank of the choir.

the one started last of all, at Biggar in Lanarkshire (see Figures 5.10 and 5.41).[67] It was founded in 1545–6 by Malcolm, Lord Fleming, Chamberlain to both James V and Mary, though the idea had been first put forward six years earlier.[68] The college had nine prebendaries and four choristers, and there was an associated hospital for six bedesmen. The eastern parts of the new church were given a plan like that of Seton, with three bays and an eastern apse to the choir, a northern sacristy, and transepts of two bays each. The nave, however, was probably not rebuilt, since Grose's view of 1789 shows it used to be architecturally less ambitious than the rest, suggesting it survived from an earlier church. But, during restoration by David Bryce in 1869–71, the nave was also divided by buttresses into three bays, giving it a superficial similarity to the rest of the building. Bryce's own preferred option had been to abandon the church altogether and to build a new one elsewhere, suggesting that he was not in sympathy with it. As part of his work he covered the internal moulded stonework with cement and lined the walls with lath and plaster, though much of this was reversed in a later restoration of 1935.

The choir and transepts are strikingly simple in their detailing. The most complex mouldings are on the south transept doorway, which is of two orders, each consisting of a pair of rolls, one order being continuous around the opening and the other carried on corbels. In a similar spirit, the responds of the crossing arches, which have been extensively renewed, are plain semi-octagons. The windows are enclosed within rectangular frames and have minimal tracery. The most elaborate are those in the east face of the apse and the transept ends, where all three lights reach up to the main arch and there is a transom at the arch springing; the other windows have just a central mullion and a transom at the arch springing. Although the overall design of Biggar is still essentially in the medieval tradition, it gives a greater sense than any other church of the period that it represents the latter end of a tradition of design.

FIGURE 5.41   Biggar Collegiate Church.

CHAPTER SIX

The Greater Burgh Churches

THE SCOTTISH BURGHS AND THEIR CHURCHES

The greater burgh churches and the collegiate churches together represent the most impressive artistic contribution that Scotland made to the later Middle Ages. There is in fact some evidence that the burghs were entering a period of recession at the very time they were beginning to be most active in building their churches; and yet there can be little doubt that the magnificent structures raised by several represented an extraordinary expression of confidence in their own long-term future.[1]

In considering an aspect of the architectural history of the burghs it must be stressed that medieval Scotland was an essentially rural society, and that only a small proportion of the population dwelt in the burghs. Nevertheless, there had been urban groupings from an early period and, in giving impetus to the process of formally denoting some of them as burghs in the second quarter of the twelfth century, David I afforded them privileges in the hope of fostering trade to the economic benefit of the nation as a whole. Naturally enough, many early burghs were centres of royal administration – such as Berwick, Dunfermline, Edinburgh, Perth, Roxburgh and Stirling, and to a lesser extent Haddington, Linlithgow, Peebles and Rutherglen. They were thus obvious foci for trade with the surrounding hinterland, or even with the Continent through their dependent ports, and there were already Flemish burgesses at Berwick, Perth and St Andrews during David's reign. But foundation as a burgh carried no guarantee of success, and the continued existence of many burghs was precarious – as for example an early royal burgh at Dunfermline. The loss of the major burghs of Berwick and Roxburgh to the English in the course of the Wars of Independence must also have had wider economic consequences for a time. However, other burghs, including Haddington and St Andrews, came to benefit when much of the trade of the captured burghs was diverted through them.

By 1350 the four greatest burghs were considered by Bruges – which was well placed to assess such matters – to be Aberdeen, Dundee, Edinburgh and Perth, and the long-term future of all of these was well assured. But already by this time Edinburgh, with its port at Leith, was showing signs of the growth which was soon to eclipse all other burghs. It only had some four hundred houses in 1400, and yet by the 1440s it was handling 57 per cent of the all-important wool trade.

Our understanding of the relative importance of the burghs becomes clearer with the information generated from the levying of customs duties and taxation. Alexander III began to raise duties on exports in the later thirteenth century, and it was the customs which were to be particularly exploited to raise the ransom for David II after his release in 1357 – even though much of what was raised was applied to his own ends. Records show that the greatest wealth was increasingly concentrated in the east coast burghs, especially in the counties around the Forth basin and estuary, and it is in these areas that many of the best churches were to be built. However, these records also indicate a decline in trade from the later fourteenth century onwards, despite periods of improved conditions around the 1370s and 1420s. This picture is not entirely straightforward, because merchants were beginning to rely less on foreign boats for exporting their goods from the mid-fourteenth century, and were both using their own ships more frequently and sailing from more ports. They were probably also becoming more efficient in finding ways of avoiding payment. But, beyond that, it is possible there was something of a shift from trade towards the crafts around this period, the income from which would not be so identifiable in the usual indicators of wealth. Nevertheless, the pointers to some degree of economic decline over much of the later Middle Ages are undeniable, with significant improvements coming only after the Reformation.

Despite such signs of decline, several factors were favourable to major rebuilding projects at some of the burgh churches. One of these was the way that much of the wealth of the burghs had come to be concentrated in the hands of a small number of individuals. Already by the thirteenth century there were groups of merchant burgesses who formed themselves into privileged guilds at Aberdeen, Berwick, Dundee, Elgin, Perth and Stirling. A tendency for the burghs originally to concentrate on exporting raw materials rather than finished goods had strengthened the hand of the merchants at the expense of the craftsmen, and by the fourteenth century about nineteen burghs had such merchant guilds. These guilds wielded considerable powers of patronage, and since it was they who had most contact with Scotland's trading partners – and were most likely to know the churches that were going up in those areas – they were well placed to encourage the import of architectural ideas from them if they so wished.

Another factor of importance was the way that most Scottish burghs were single parishes until after the Reformation, with the possible exception of Edinburgh, where there were parishes centred on both St Giles' and St Cuthbert's. The parochial system in Scotland had been largely a creation *de novo* of the twelfth and thirteenth centuries,[2] with nothing of the way that many of the older English towns were broken up into very large numbers of parishes. Consequently, at a time when lay folk were increasingly looking for more personal ways of expressing their faith, the most obvious focus in the burghs was its single most important church.

It should be said that, so far as we know, the Scottish laity was little influenced by the more extreme forms of late medieval religious fervour. The Beguines, who found fertile soil in Cologne, and the Religious Brethren of Deventer in the Low Countries seem to have had little reflection in Scotland.[3] Neither is there much evidence for Scottish mystics who articulated the deep spiritual yearnings of such as Thomas à

Kempis, although Kempis was certainly an influence on one Scottish writer.[4] But there is no doubt that the shortcomings of earlier religious endeavours, as represented by the regular and to a lesser extent the mendicant orders, created as much disillusionment in Scotland as elsewhere in Europe. There was also some element of anti-clericalism.[5] Yet the need to find assurance of salvation, through the commemoration in the mass of Christ's Passion, was stronger than ever, though it was the local churches rather than the great religious institutions that increasingly benefited. To accommodate these masses large numbers of additional altars, served by attendant priests, were founded within the parish churches and chapels by individuals, by families, or by merchant and craft guilds.[6]

Supplementing purely religious motives, by the later fourteenth century growing civic pride – as well as interburghal rivalry – was also seeking a more tangible outlet. After the Reformation, construction of prominent tolbooths met this need, and even in the later Middle Ages a number were being built, though few have survived later rebuilding.[7] In general, however, it was the parish churches that were the obvious foci for civic pride and the natural setting for much of the ceremonial which gave corporate expression to the life of the communities. Yet rebuilding these churches was not without difficulty. Beyond the need to find funds for those parts for which the burgh was directly responsible, in most cases there was the obstacle that the church was appropriated to some distant religious institution, with which went responsibility for the fabric of the eastern limb. Unfortunately, the appropriating bodies did not generally share the enthusiasm of the burghs for costly rebuilding.

This in itself, however, allows us to see how important was their church to many burghs, because in several cases – including Aberdeen, Dundee, Haddington, Linlithgow, Perth, St Andrews and Stirling – the burgesses themselves assumed the chief responsibility for rebuilding the chancel. In doing this the way was cleared for rebuilding to a unified scheme, though it could be many years before work was completed – and in some cases the undertaking was so overambitious that it never was completed. Partly as a result of such arrangements with the appropriating body some churches, like Haddington and Linlithgow, have a strikingly homogeneous appearance, despite some differences of detail between the parts. At others, like Edinburgh, growth was so protracted that the result was a complex admixture of elements, although even there we might find a single underlying approach to aspects of the design.

When complete, the burgh churches came to outrival in scale and architectural sophistication some of the smaller cathedrals. With such buildings at the heart of their civic life the burgesses also began to expect forms of service and ceremonial closer to those of the cathedrals, as a suitably dignified expression of that civic life. As a result, at several burgh churches there were attempts to organise and augment the growing numbers of clergy – amongst whom were both the parish priest and those who served the various side altars – into collegiate bodies analogous to those established by some of the greater magnates. Abortive attempts to do this were made as early as 1419 at Edinburgh, and in the 1430s at Linlithgow and St Andrews. Eventually colleges of priests were successfully established at Aberdeen, Edinburgh, Haddington, Peebles and Stirling.[8] But even where this was not formally achieved, we must assume that the great burgh churches were the setting for services in which colour, music and even scent came together on an opulent scale to meet the need for spiritual satisfaction and communal identity. Interestingly, the first definite reference we have to a church organ in Scotland is for the burgh church of St Nicholas at Aberdeen, in 1437.[9]

EDINBURGH ST GILES

Appropriately, for the burgh which was assuming pre-eminence from the mid-fourteenth century onwards, Edinburgh's parish church became one of the largest in Scotland (see Figures 6.1c and 6.2).[10] Both the burgh and parish may have been first formally recognised as such in the time of David I, though there was probably a

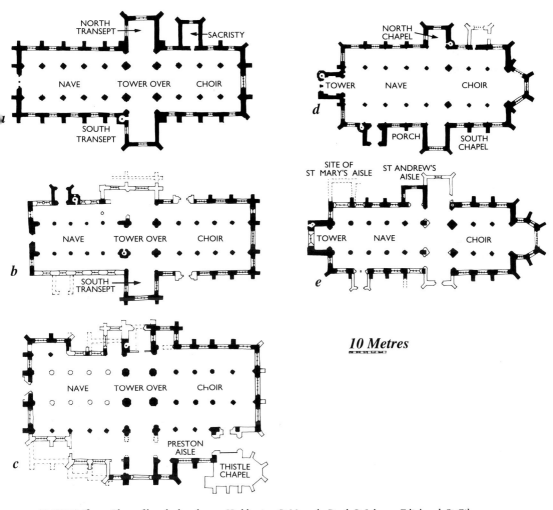

FIGURE 6.1   Plans of burgh churches: a. Haddington St Mary; b. Perth St John; c. Edinburgh St Giles; d. Linlithgow St Michael; e. Stirling Holy Rude.

settlement here for long before that.[11] An elaborately carved twelfth-century doorway survived on the north side of the church until 1796, amply illustrating the architectural ambitions for the church even as first built. Much of the late medieval appearance of the church, however, was the result of a series of additions around the original core, which eventually gave the church a uniquely complex external appearance.

Before discussing the late medieval expansion of St Giles' it is probably best to consider briefly the post-Reformation changes to it, since these had major implications for the medieval fabric. Like all of the burgh churches, it was periodically adapted and subdivided for changes in use and worship in the centuries after the Reformation. Similarly, they were all later restored as appreciation of their architectural qualities re-emerged in the nineteenth and twentieth centuries, though some of the earlier restorations might be more damaging than the original post-Reformation changes. This is particularly the case at Edinburgh where, between 1829 and 1833, William Burn amputated some of the peripheral parts in order to create façades that were more nearly symmetrical. He also encased the whole structure in a skin of uniformly large blocks of polished ashlar, so that the only original feature to remain externally visible was the central tower and its superstructure. We must respect the attempt to give St Giles' greater architectural presence, at a time when its setting was being improved by the removal of the buildings which had previously hemmed it in, and when a handsome square was being formed to its south by Robert Reid's new façades to the Law Courts. Nevertheless, the architectural development of the building has been made harder to understand as a result.

Further restoration was directed by William Hay between 1871 and 1884, when the internal cross walls which divided the building into three separate churches were removed, and more convincing details were applied to the nave arcades and west front. The last major addition to the church was Sir Robert Lorimer's chapel for the Knights of the Thistle of 1909–11, following the abandonment of proposals to restore Holyrood Abbey for this purpose. Taking account of these late changes, we must now return to consider the medieval fabric.

Before 1400 the core around which the late medieval additions were made had already developed into an aisled nave of five bays, an aisled choir possibly also of as much as five bays, transepts which probably projected no further than the line of the aisles, and a central tower. It is uncertain just when the church had reached this state, since the nave arcades were completely rebuilt and the clearstorey above it heightened in the nineteenth century, and the chief remaining evidence is provided by the octagonal piers of the choir arcades. These piers have bases of water-holding section, which might indicate a thirteenth-century date; however, detailed analysis suggests they more probably belong to a revival of such bases of the fourteenth century. (Other examples of this revival from the earlier part of that century can be seen in the undercroft of the Dunfermline Abbey refectory and at the chapter house at St Andrews, while from the later part of the century they are seen in part of Melrose.)

Whatever its date, however, the core of the church must have been in place by 1385, when it was set on fire by the army of Richard II, since signs of burning were noted during the late nineteenth-century restoration. It has already been said that the cross-ribbed pointed barrel vaulting over the western bays of the choir aisles probably belongs to repairs after that disaster (see p. 34 and Figure 1.21). There is similar vaulting over the inner part of the south transept, below the later clearstoreys, which probably indicates the level and form of the vault placed over the choir at this time. It also corresponds in height with the crossing vault, so that at this stage of its history it seems the main spaces in the choir and transepts were covered by vaults that were little higher than those over the choir aisles. This reminds us that, although few other parish churches had such extensive stone vaulting, it was probably not uncommon to have main spaces and aisles of similar height – as was also later the case at Cupar and perhaps in the nave of Perth. The extent of the transept vault at St Giles' is also of interest, since its north-south length is only about two-thirds of the width of the adjacent south choir aisle. This suggests that, although the choir aisles were probably widened as part of the post-1385 operations – the south aisle being made wider than that on the north – the transept depth corresponded to narrower nave aisles.

The first stage in widening the nave was under way soon afterwards, however, because on 29 November 1387 agreement was reached with the masons John Primrose (Prymros), John of Scone and John Squire (Skuyer or Squyer) to build five chapels on the south side of the nave.[12] Under this agreement the vaulting of the chapels was to be copied from that over St Stephen's altar on the north side of Holyrood Abbey Church, and four of the chapels were to have three-light windows of an agreed pattern. The total cost was to be 600 marks. Regrettably, these chapels – which were presumably in the form of a widened aisle – were almost certainly subsumed within the later extensions, and it is doubtful if anything of them is now identifiable. Later extensions came with great rapidity, and in the process the cross-shaped plan of the nucleus was almost lost. Externally, efforts were made to give some of the added chapels prominence by capping them with lateral gables and, as has been suggested for the outer nave chapels of Elgin Cathedral, this could be a reflection of the widespread fashion for such gables in the Low Countries (see Figure 6.2).

Among the more important additions were the following. The chapel of St John was added to the north-east of the north transept by not later than 1395.[13] The Albany aisle was placed against the north side of the two western bays of the nave, and the arms of the fourth Earl of Douglas on the capitals shows it was built after his succession in 1400. Work could have been in progress on the tower in 1416, when the *Scotichronicon* felt it was worthy of remark that storks had nested on it,[14] though it is unlikely to have been before the end of the century that the crown steeple was added. One of the most important changes to the building came when the presbytery was rebuilt with slightly longer bays and more lavishly enriched arcades, and over the whole eastern limb was added a clearstorey and tierceron vault. Excavation in 1981 suggested this change involved only minimal eastward extension;[15] it can be dated around the 1450s, since the heraldry of the rebuilt pier capitals refers to James II, Queen Mary of Guelders, Prince James and Bishop Kennedy of St Andrews among others. Soon after, the decision was taken to add the tierceron-vaulted Preston aisle

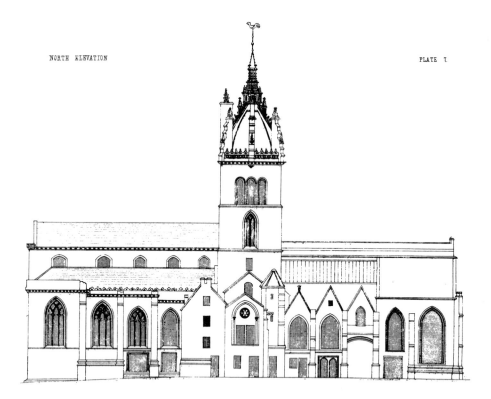

FIGURE 6.2   Edinburgh St Giles, the north flank before the restoration of 1829–33.

as an outer south choir aisle in 1454–5, in gratitude to Sir William Preston of Gourton, who had given the church an arm bone of its patron saint; it was to be finished within seven years.[16] Permission was given to build the Chepman aisle, off the west bay of the Preston aisle, in 1507, and it was dedicated in 1513.[17] The two-bay aisle of the Holy Blood, completed in 1518, was added to the south of the nave's outer south aisle, between a porch and the south transept.[18]

An attempt to establish a college of priests within the expanding church was made before June 1419, and there was another unsuccessful petition in December 1423. It was a petition supported by James III in 1466 – after the crown had resumed patronage of the church – that finally received papal consent in 1468–9. Eventually the college had perhaps as many as eighteen prebendaries, beneath whom were many chaplains serving the altars within the church;[19] these altars may finally have approached fifty in number.

As a result of all these accretions, St Giles' was ultimately as much as six aisles across in places. Yet, despite the wide date range of the additions, there was an attempt to give them internal unity by using a similar architectural vocabulary throughout. Thus the basic form of the arcade piers and arches used in the Albany aisle was copied with surprisingly little modification in the outer south aisle of the nave, in the remodelled presbytery, in the Preston aisle and perhaps originally in the Holy Blood aisle. These piers are of basically octofoil section, but between the shafts are spurs which were perhaps intended to register as the arrises of an octagonal core, so as to reflect the pier type of the choir and nave arcades. In most cases the main shafts are filleted and the diagonal shafts keeled, though in the Albany aisle the diagonal shafts are also filleted. The bases of these shafts have filleted rolls at two levels, although with some variety in the additional enrichment. The capitals invariably have octagonal abaci, with smaller individual caps above the shafts; the greatest enrichment is to the bells of the individual caps, but in some cases there are also foliate bands between the two levels into which the caps were divided. In the arches the main feature is a filleted roll flanked by hollows, though in all cases apart from the Albany aisle there is also an additional outer order of a quarter round and a fillet.

Octofoil piers had been, of course, common since the later twelfth century, and had already seen revived use in the late fourteenth-century work at Fortrose Cathedral and Melrose Abbey (see Figures 1.20 and 1.39). Parallels for subordinate elements between the shafts can be seen in the chapter house at Glenluce Abbey (see Figure 3.31) and in a fragment from Coupar Angus Abbey. But the uniformity of approach over so long a period in the design of details at St Giles' shows that internal unity of appearance was a major goal – even if the stately elegance of the new clearstorey over the eastern limb must have given that part visual pre-eminence. The relative internal uniformity of detailing, however, makes it additionally surprising that there was so little attempt at external homogeneity; perhaps this was because the exterior was always so hemmed in by other buildings.

The destruction of window tracery without record has been a major loss at St Giles'. Apart from simple intersecting tracery shown in early views of the choir aisles, two windows for which we have partial evidence of tracery are those in the Holy Blood aisle, west of the south transept. These had boldly looped forms related to the types seen at the Blackfriars Church in St Andrews, and this is consistent with the chapel's completion date of 1518.

Externally the church is dominated by its crown steeple, which is all the more striking because of the simplicity of the unbuttressed belfry stage of the tower which supports it, with three simply cusped lights to each face (see Figure 6.2). As already said for Scotland's other surviving medieval crown steeple at Aberdeen (see p. 162 and Figure 5.22), the Edinburgh example is one of the most delightful fruits of the briefly renewed architectural contact with England in the early sixteenth century, though the end result could be regarded as nothing other than Scottish. Regrettably, we do not know how closely John Mylne's reconstruction of 1684 perpetuated the original forms.

PERTH ST JOHN[20]

At Perth, as at Edinburgh, both the burgh and parish were first formally recognised as such by David I. Also as at Edinburgh, the church was prominently placed at the centre of the burgh; only the castle, at the northern end of the main urban axis of Kirkgate and Skinnergate, can have rivalled it as an architectural focus.[21] The decision to rebuild the church completely was probably taken in about 1440, and the importance of the church to the burgesses is shown by the way they decided to rebuild the choir first (see Figures 6.3 and 6.1b). The choir was in fact the responsibility of Dunfermline Abbey, the church having been granted to that abbey as early as 1128; but in 1440 it was agreed the burgh would rebuild the chancel if Dunfermline would forgo a proportion of the teinds, together with the fees for burials in the choir, over six years.[22] The choir must have been substantially complete by 1448, when an altar dedicated to St John the Evangelist was founded to the north of the high altar.

Operations would then have moved on to the transepts and nave and, although there may have been a delay while more funds were gathered, royal contributions of 18s. and 11s.6d. in 1489 and 1496 suggest work was again in progress.[23] Royal interest is also suggested by the involvement of a master mason much in demand for the king's works, because in 1496 Walter Merlioun was paid £20 for the work he had carried out between Martinmas and Whitsunday.[24] Merlioun was a member of a distinguished family of master masons, and in the same year he was at Perth he was working on the king's residence at Stirling Castle (see Figure 10.13). He was also to be involved in the royal works at Dunbar Castle in 1499, for which he received a life pension, and in the works at Holyrood Palace of around 1500. Other members of the Merlioun family worked at Falkland Palace in the 1530s, at Queen Mary of Guelders' castle of Ravenscraig in the 1460s, and possibly also at Holyrood Palace in the 1530s (see Figures 10.19, 9.2 and 10.18).

Completion of the central tower and spire were possibly postponed while the main effort was concentrated on the nave, but they were finished before 1511, when Bishop Elphinstone cited them as the model for his new tower at Aberdeen.[25] They may even have been finished around 1506, when the bell called John the Baptist was cast at Mechelen in Brabant. Five other bells for St John's were to be cast at Mechelen in 1526. From all this we can appreciate that a major extended effort was made to create a church of the highest calibre at Perth. There are indications, however, that work on the nave ground to an untimely halt before it was completed (see Figure 6.5); it is therefore particularly unfortunate that, as at St Giles', the architectural development of the church is partly clouded by post-Reformation losses and restorations, which may be briefly listed here.

In about 1598 the western part of the nave was divided off to form a separate Outer Church, and the Middle Church was eventually formed in the transepts and eastern part of the nave in the 1770s, possibly as the result of a decision taken as early as 1715. But the greatest damage was suffered in the earlier nineteenth century. Soon after 1817 the upper storey of the north porch – known as the Halkerston Tower – was dismantled, and in 1823 the north transept was truncated to allow road widening. Also in the 1820s, the architect James Gillespie Graham carried out major restoration of the choir, transepts and eastern bays of the nave. At that time the stonework of the choir was cut back, window tracery was renewed to modified forms, and the external mouldings of the windows were remodelled in cement. As part of the same operation, choir porches were added and parapets were placed around the wall-heads, which embraced the dormers already provided to light the galleries. In the eastern bays of the nave the most disastrous change was the replacement of the original windows on the north side as part of an abortive attempt to give the Middle Church a clearstorey above flanking aisles. Much of the evidence for the later fifteenth-century nave was destroyed in the process. More conservative repairs were carried out in the 1890s, to the designs of Andrew Heiton, who gave back to the choir something of its original appearance.

The last major restoration – which also involved the removal of the internal divisions – was carried out by Sir Robert Lorimer between 1923 and 1926, as a memorial to the dead of the Great War. Doubtlessly by then much work was required both to introduce greater structural stability, and to give a noble church a greater sense of the architectural coherence intended by its medieval designers. Nevertheless, it seems that Lorimer sometimes preferred to ignore the evidence for the original architectural forms in pursuing his own aesthetic goals, and the nave is now essentially a work of Lorimer rather than of Merlioun and his contemporaries.

Following all these changes, it is the choir that most nearly reflects the intentions of its original builders (see Figures 6.3 and 6.4). It is an aisled rectangle of five bays; lighting the central space is a clearstorey with two-light windows on the north and single lights on the south side. The arcades are carried by octofoil piers, with heavy filleted shafts to the main axes and smaller keeled shafts on the diagonal axes. In the three western bays the arcade arches are of three orders of segmental hollows, but in the two eastern bays emphasis was given to the siting of the high altar by richer mouldings. Further emphasis is given by the decorated band on the east pier of the south arcade, which commemorates the contribution to the work of John Fullar and his wife Mariota. The choir aisle windows were all heavily renewed in the 1820s, but probably still largely reflect their original designs. Some are of reticulated or intersecting designs, while others have spiralling daggers as the main motif, all of which are variants on types common in fifteenth-century Scotland. Above the choir the open-timber roof has been heavily renewed but incorporates original work. The principal tie-beams are supported by corbelled wall posts and braces, and between the tie-beams and collars are cross-braces and king posts.

Despite all modifications, the choir thus still gives a fair impression of what was intended for it; but the further west we go in the church the less this is the case. The transepts have been extensively modified, the northern one being almost completely modern. The greatest internal interest of this area is now the tower piers, which are of massive quatrefoil plan, with spurs between the filleted shafts. The south-western pier is even more massive than the others, because it contains the stair to the loft above the chancel screen and to the tower. The corbels which supported the loft also survive on the western piers. The tower carried by the piers is – as usual – unbuttressed, and has two patterns of narrow two-light windows. The lead-sheathed timber spire is of splay-foot form – the type most preferred in Scotland.

The best evidence for the late fifteenth-century design of the nave is in depictions of 1775 in *The Chronicle of Perth*, and of 1806 in *Memorabilia of Perth* (see Figure 6.5).[26] On the south side the former shows a spreading structure with low aisle walls, no clearstorey to the central space, and with a much altered two-storeyed porch towards

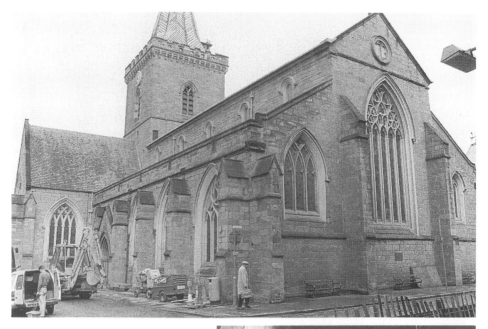

FIGURE 6.3 (*above*)   Perth St John, from
the south-east.
FIGURE 6.4 (*right*)   Perth St John, the
interior of the choir looking eastwards.

its west end. On the north side we see something very different in the view of 1806. This shows enormously tall aisle windows, capped by elaborate hood moulds, the finials of which reached up to a traceried parapet; the bays were marked by buttresses decorated with tabernacles and apparently intended to be capped by pinnacles. It also shows a western offshoot from the transept, and a richly detailed two-storeyed porch with an elaborate cusped arch to the upper floor, some of the details of which could be reminiscent of roughly contemporary royal works at Linlithgow Palace (see Figure 10.4).

Taking account of the presence of the mason Walter Merlioun here in 1496, what we probably see in these depictions is the tantalisingly sketchy evidence for a remarkably grand rebuilding of the nave. From the scale of the aisle windows it appears to have been conceived as a hall-church – that is with equal-height central space and aisles. The pictorial evidence also suggests that work was started with recasing of the north flank; but, beyond that, it perhaps indicates that the scale had proved too demanding and it was consequently never finished. It is a tragedy for our understanding of late Gothic architecture in Scotland that we know so little of the details of this scheme and that no serious attempt can be made to consider the sources of inspiration which may have lain behind it. However, although we have seen from the earlier state of the choir of Edinburgh St Giles that hall-churches were not unknown in Scotland, it could also be a possibility that the hall naves that were becoming increasingly common in the maritime provinces of the northern Netherlands from the later fifteenth century were an influence on the design of Perth's nave.

FIGURE 6.5   Perth St John, the nave from the north-west before modern restorations.

Much of the abortive late medieval attempt at rebuilding the nave recorded in these drawings was swept away in the 1820s by Gillespie Graham and later restored in a more seemly manner by Lorimer. Lorimer also largely rebuilt the nave arcades, and as a result it is no longer clear if they are part of the church which was being replaced in 1496 or if they were the result of a cost-paring operation after the scheme of the 1490s had been abandoned as unattainable. The only feature of the nave which still gives some idea of the ambitions entertained for it in the late fifteenth century is the tierceron vault above the ground-floor stage of the north porch.

HADDINGTON ST MARY[27]

Again, as with Edinburgh and Perth, the recognition as such of both the burgh and parish of Haddington is first documented in the time of David I. The earliest reference to the parish is its grant by that king to the cathedral priory of St Andrews in about 1139, and the chief evidence for the date of the late medieval rebuilding of the church is an agreement of 1462 with the prior of St Andrews over the costs involved.[28] By this the prior made an annual contribution of £100 towards the choir over five years, suggesting – doubtlessly over-optimistically – that was the expected period of construction. Nevertheless, the church must have been finished well before a college was eventually established within it in about 1540,[29] the last part to be completed probably being the central tower.

As rebuilt, Haddington was one of the most architecturally homogeneous of all the burgh churches, even though some details of the nave suggest it was only finished several decades after the chancel (see Figures 6.1a and 6.7). Haddington was also one of the most ambitious of the burgh churches, being designed for vaults over the high central spaces of the choir and transepts – that over the south transept being of tierceron type – as well as over the aisles flanking choir and nave. Considering the scale of the work, it is noteworthy that the Exchequer Rolls for the likely period of construction suggest Haddington's exports – through its port at Aberlady – were declining. After an increase from over £125 in 1454 to over £302 in 1474, there was a decline to £226 in 1476 and to £159 in 1479.[30] Perhaps optimism encouraged by the rise between 1454 and 1474 led the burgesses to undertake more than was wise.

There is the inevitable tally of later architectural set-backs, the greatest of which was the loss of roofs and vaults over the choir and transepts, probably in 1548 when the town was besieged by English forces (see Figure 6.6). Those parts were left derelict for over four hundred years but, despite the resultant weathering, this did mean it escaped later modification. The nave, on the other hand, was modified. To create more space for galleries, in 1811 its arcades and aisle walls were heightened, and the aisle vaults removed; at the same time plaster vaults were placed throughout the nave, heavy pinnacles were built above the aisle buttresses and some of the aisle window tracery may have been renewed in simplified form. This work was carried out by James Burn, apparently to designs by Archibald Elliot. Later in the century, in 1877, the east window of the ruined choir was filled with tracery copied from Iona, and in 1892 the nave galleries were removed. More recently, the choir and transepts were restored in 1971–3 by Ian Lindsay and Partners, when fibreglass replica vaults were installed.

The eastern limb is of four aisled bays, with a sacristy on its north side that was later converted into a burial aisle for the Maitland family. Separating the choir from an aisled nave of five bays are aisle-less single bay transepts. All of this was probably set out in a single operation, though the building sequence appears to have been choir first, next the transepts and then the nave, with the choir setting the pattern for the general design of the whole church. Internally the elevations were divided into two approximately equal-height storeys separated by a string course, and with the bay divisions marked by vaulting shafts carried on the abaci of the arcade piers (see Figure 6.6). In all of this there are echoes of Trinity Collegiate Church in Edinburgh (see Figure 5.36), though some critics have seen the proportions of the arcade piers as a little over-squat, and the clearstorey windows as rather uncomfortably pushed up into the vaulting. The piers have three-quarter shafts in the cardinal directions, separated by broad diagonal faces. In this they show parallels with the piers in the choirs of Linlithgow Parish Church and of Edinburgh Trinity College Church, though in both those cases the shafts are filleted; there may also be more local parallels with Dunglass and Seton in the arch profiles.

FIGURE 6.6   Haddington St Mary, the interior of the choir before restoration.

The choir aisles have two-light windows, with single cusped figures at their head, while the clearstorey has two-light windows, each with a pair of curved daggers. Similar tracery was used in the nave clearstorey as in that of the choir. The windows in the nave aisles, however, are more complex than in the choir, being of three lights with pairs of curved daggers surmounted by a third. All of these types were widely current at this time. The transepts have windows only in the west and gable walls in order to accommodate and throw light on altarpieces against the east wall, as in the north transept at Jedburgh.

The largest window is that in the west front: this six-light composition has a permutation of two units similar to those in the nave aisles, with two further curved daggers in the space between the sub-arches which contain them (see Figure 6.7). The sub-arches are of interest for their slightly ungainly over-massive construction. Similarly massive sub-arches are to be found in a number of windows elsewhere, including examples at Seton Collegiate Church, the parish churches of Stirling and Dundee, and perhaps also in a window known from early views at St Giles in Edinburgh. But it is unlikely that this detail originated in Scotland. It is found very widely in the Low Countries which, as with uncusped loop tracery, could be a result of the frequent use of brick for the window tracery there; it is possible it was from that area that the idea was brought to Scotland.

Taking the sub-arches as a starting-point, it may not be fanciful to see a degree of Netherlandish inspiration behind the design of the front as a whole. The way in which the gable of the front is set back behind a (heavily restored) arcaded parapet is decidedly un-Scottish, but has many parallels in the Netherlands. Even the setting of the great window within wide masonry margins and its relationship with the entrance doorway beneath it could indicate a fresh infusion of ideas on façade design, possibly from a building in the tradition represented by the transept façades at Dordrecht. Such comparison must not be carried too far, but in a burgh which gained much of its wealth from trade with the Low Countries, it is not unlikely that fresh ideas would have been found there. In support of this it should be said that the relationship between the doorway and window finds its closest Scottish counterpart in the tower of St Mary in Dundee and, as we shall see, the design of that tower was heavily influenced by models in the Low Countries (see p. 209 and Figure 6.18).

Any Netherlandish inspiration in the underlying design of Haddington's façade, however, was modified by Scottish usages in the construction and detailing. This is not to minimise the quality of the work which, in some of the foliage carving of the west doorway capitals, for example, is unusually high (see Figure 6.8). Rising above the rather schematic seaweed trails or mechanical square leaves which tended to be the norm, this foliage is closely ribbed, and the three parts of each leaf are themselves divided into three further parts terminating in tight volutes. The nearest local parallels for it are perhaps with the northern capitals of the chancel arch at Dunglass.

As so often, the last part of the church to be finished was probably the central tower (see Figure 6.7). While showing parallels with other towers in its rather cubical mass

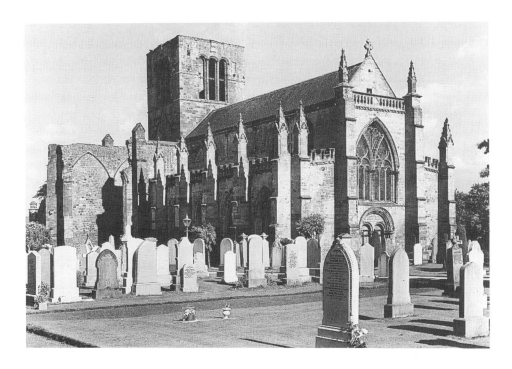

FIGURE 6.7 (*above*) Haddington St
Mary from the north-west, before the
restoration of the transepts.
FIGURE 6.8 (*right*) Haddington St
Mary, the carved capitals of the west
doorway.

and simple grouping of triplets of lights, it was more highly decorated than usual,
perhaps suggesting an effort to surpass the tower of Edinburgh. It is enriched by
tabernacles on each face, to each side of the window heads, and is divided at
mid-height by a string course. The latter is carried across the windows as lattice
transoms, which may show parallels with the intersecting arches which form the
transoms of the east window bay in the great hall at Stirling Castle. If this tower had
ever been capped by the eight-ribbed crown steeple that was clearly destined for it
from the corbelled-out projections in the middle of each face, it might have been the
finest central feature of any Scottish church.

LINLITHGOW ST MICHAEL[31]

Yet again, it is to David I that the formal establishment of the settlement of Linlithgow as a burgh and parish appear to be attributable and, as at Haddington, it was to St Andrews Cathedral Priory that he granted the church. The spur to late medieval rebuilding here is often said to have been a fire which devastated both church and nearby royal palace in 1424. Yet it is not certain how extensively damaged the church was at that time, since there is a reference to the queen of James I worshipping in it in 1429. A proposal by James I to found a college here in 1430 also seems inconsistent with its having then being in ruin,[32] and all the evidence for its reconstruction is from rather later in the century.

That evidence can be summarised as follows. The nave must have been substantially complete by 1489, when the mason John French (Frenssh) was buried in its north aisle. The tower was presumably nearing completion by 1490, when the bell known as Blessed Mary was cast. Thoughts had moved on to the choir by 1497, when it was agreed that the prior of St Andrews would make an annual payment if the priory was relieved of expenses of upkeep.[33] A royal gift of 9s. to the master mason of the 'the Queir of Linlithqw' in the Treasurer's accounts for 1506 suggests work was still in progress on that part.[34] It is said the timber roof of the choir was paid for by Bishop Crichton of Dunkeld (1526–44), who had earlier been vicar of the parish, and that his arms were on the roof before the insertion of the plaster vault in 1812. The choir was close to completion by 1532, when an agreement on the form of its wall-head was signed with the master mason Thomas French, son of the previously mentioned John.[35] In addition to all this there is the comparative evidence of some of the architectural details. The extraordinary tracery of the south transept window, for example, had as its only close counterpart the west window at Dunkeld, which was probably started along with the north-west tower there by Bishop Lauder in about 1469 (see p. 72 and Figures 6.11 and 2.10). Less precise comparisons can be made for other details, but together they all point to the main building effort starting well into the second half of the fifteenth century, and continuing into the 1530s.

After the Reformation St Michael's history is similar to that of the other burgh churches in that it was first adapted for changed requirements, was restored with excessive exuberance in the early nineteenth century, only to be restored more judiciously later in that century. At first only the choir was used for reformed worship, and in 1656 a cross wall was constructed to enclose it. In 1660 the parish moved into the nave, moving back into the choir again in 1812. At that latter date major changes were made by the omnipresent James Gillespie Graham, including the removal of the chancel arch and the construction of plaster vaults over the main spaces. About nine years later the crown steeple on the west tower was removed as unsafe. The period of more scholarly restoration began with the painstaking reconstruction of the south transept window by the mason William Roberts in 1840. But the main campaign was that directed by John Honeyman and John Keppie in 1894–6, when the chancel arch and sacristy were rebuilt, though the plaster vaults of nave and chancel were tactfully retained. The most recent addition has been Geoffrey Clarke's aluminium crown steeple in 1964.

By comparison with Haddington, Linlithgow has a strongly horizontal appearance, though the western crown steeple and the pinnacles intended for some of the buttresses would have compensated for this (see Figures 6.1d and 6.9). Despite differences between nave and choir in the details of arcades, windows and internal elevations, there is almost as strong a sense of architectural unity at Linlithgow as at Haddington. The external base courses are of a uniform type throughout, suggesting the church was set out and built to a single plan. Nevertheless, the western tower must have been an afterthought because of the uncomfortable way it joins up with the west end of the nave on the north side, and from the absence of bond on the south. One is left wondering if a central tower was the original intention, but the great width of the central space of the choir and nave, and the absence of any defined crossing make this unlikely.

The nave is of five bays, with a two-storeyed south porch, the upper floor of which has an oriel window similar to that which used to be above the porch at Edinburgh St Giles. There are transeptal chapels flanking the east bay of the nave, which only rise to the height of the aisles, and there is no acknowledgement of them in the arcades. Internally the nave has an elevation of three storeys which, as in the nave at Paisley Abbey, seems rather old-fashioned for so late a date (see Figures 6.10 and 3.19). The three storeys are without parallel in any of the burgh churches as existing, though it is possible something similar was intended for Stirling Parish Church in the final stages of rebuilding there (see Figure 6.15). The nave piers are of octofoil section, with fillets in the cardinal directions, and are thus similar to those in the nave at Paisley Abbey and in Abbot Bothwell's work at Dunfermline (see Figures 3.19 and 3.7) – although rather better proportioned than the latter. Decorating some of the diagonal shafts are shields, which were presumably painted with the arms of bene-factors. String courses mark the stages of the elevation, and in the upper storeys wall shafts divide the bays, but throughout there is a sense of the predominance of the wall planes. This sense is enhanced by the wide splays or casement-like mouldings which lead into the deeply recessed two-light triforium openings and clearstorey windows.

The window tracery of the nave aisles and transeptal chapels is an especially attractive feature (see Figures 6.9, 6.10 and 6.11). The two main types in the aisles have spiralling daggers or groupings of two spherical triangles and a dagger, and present a rather prismatic appearance for which there is no precise reflection elsewhere. Of the other windows, that in the south aisle to the west of the transeptal chapel is very like a window in Bishop Stewart's remodelled chapter house at Elgin of the end of the fifteenth century (see Figure 2.8); the way its head cuts into the wall-head parapet suggests it was a secondary insertion.

The finest window of this first phase of building is, of course, that of the south transeptal chapel, which has three circlets and three bladder shapes, all infilled with interlocking quatrefoils and curved daggers (see Figure 6.11). As has been said, apart from the treatment of the light heads, this tracery must be almost identical with that of the missing west window at Dunkeld Cathedral, and there are no other Scottish windows which approach it in richness of effect. Its rather French Flamboyant

FIGURE 6.9 (*above*)   Linlithgow St Michael, the south flank.
FIGURE 6.10 (*below*)   Linlithgow St Michael, the interior of the nave looking westwards.

appearance tempts one to wonder if it was the work of the master mason John French, who was buried in the north aisle of the church in 1489, and to suspect that he was of the French extraction that his name suggests. He was the first of three generations of master masons employed in royal works at Linlithgow and Falkland Palaces in the later fifteenth and earlier sixteenth centuries, his son being later involved in the completion of the choir. This possibility cannot be pressed too far, but it is worth noting that there are a number of churches in south-eastern France with windows which have tracery with circlets containing interlocking daggers. These include the cathedrals of Lyons and Vienne and the church of St Antoine-en-Viennois. Is it possible that John was brought over for the royal works, and that his son and grandson remained after his death?

The tower, although small in scale, has attractive details, such as the west doorway, with its trumeau continued up through the glazed tympanum, and hollowed out to contain an image tabernacle. The window above this doorway has tracery with simple combinations of vertical lights. Like some windows in the chancel and apse, this shows the new English influences that were reaching Scotland again around the time of James IV's marriage to Margaret Tudor in 1503. In other respects the tower displays parallels with that at Culross Abbey (see p. 92), especially in the single-light belfry windows and the traceried circlets above them on the south and west faces, and in the strongly expressed stair turret at the north-west corner.

The choir is of three bays, with an eastern apse rising only as high as the aisles (see Figure 6.12); the sacristy on the north side is modern, but is on the site of the original. The agreement with St Andrews in 1497, together with the contract for the wall-head of 1532, indicate an operation of about thirty-five years. The choir design continues many themes of the nave, but there are also several changes. Externally there is a deeper parapet above the clearstorey, the tracery is of later types, and the buttresses project more deeply. Internally the triforium stage is abandoned and there is a change of pier type, though the use of the nave pier type for the western responds of the choir arcades confirms that the nave was earlier. The new pier type has filleted rolls to the main axes, separated by diagonal faces. As said in discussing Haddington, this is like what had already been used at Trinity College Church in Edinburgh, and is related to the type used at Haddington. One of the two main tracery designs in the choir, with two inward-directed curved daggers capped by a smaller dagger, is also like that in the nave aisles of Haddington.

The most attractive feature of the interior is the culmination of the vista in the three-sided apse. Except at Trinity College Church in Edinburgh, Scottish masons had considerable difficulty in linking eastern apses with aisled buildings. At Linlithgow, however, the transition is relatively smooth; could this also be owing to the presence of a mason of French ancestry? Inside the apse the site of the altar is marked by the higher sill level of the east window; as also in the transeptal chapels, the siting of the altars in the flanking aisle chapels is shown by the blank east walls.

FIGURE 6.11 (*right*)   Linlithgow St
Michael, the south transept window.
FIGURE 6.12 (*below*)   Linlithgow St
Michael, the choir from the south-east.

STIRLING HOLY RUDE[36]

Stirling had a favourite royal castle from at least the early twelfth century, so it is hardly surprising that, as with all the other burgh churches so far discussed, it appears to be to David I that credit is due for formally establishing both burgh and parish. As at Perth, the church was granted to David's re-established abbey of Dunfermline, with which agreement was reached in the early sixteenth century on the rebuilding of the choir, once the nave had been completed.

As at Linlithgow, it has been suggested that the incentive for rebuilding Stirling was a fire, which is referred to in the Exchequer Rolls for 1414 when a royal donation was made to work in progress.[37] There are also references to the fire in the Chamberlain's accounts for 1413–14. However, if work was started then, all other evidence suggests the main effort on the nave was concentrated around the third quarter of the fifteenth century. In view of this it was probably the sacking of the burgh following James II's murder of the eighth Earl of Douglas in 1452 which created the occasion for complete rebuilding. The earliest dating evidence within the fabric is the arms of the burgess Adam Cosour and his wife on a vault boss in the south nave aisle. They were prominent benefactors of the church, who first appear in burgh records in 1446; they founded altars in the south aisle in 1471 and 1473, suggesting the nave was essentially complete by then.[38] In 1484 Cosour is also known to have built St Mary's aisle, against the north flank of the nave, apparently replacing an earlier chapel of that dedication mentioned ten years previously.[39]

The start of work on the choir is marked by an agreement of 1507 with Abbot James Beaton of Dunfermline, by which the burgh undertook to build the choir in conformity with the nave (though, rather curiously, the Treasurer's accounts also refer to a dedication in June of that year).[40] In exchange the abbey made a donation of £200 along with an annual payment of 40s., and agreed to provide all necessary ornaments for the high altar. In 1523, timber was being purchased, possibly for the roof, although in 1529 a mason named John Coutts (Couttis) was said to be still at work on the church.[41] Heraldry in the south choir aisle, apparently of Robert Bruce of Airth, also supports work being under way around this period, since Bruce became a burgess in 1520. In fact the choir was probably never finished as intended, and it seems that further schemes for other parts of the church also foundered. These included the construction of a central tower and transepts and the heightening of the nave. But work perhaps reached as far as it would be taken by the 1540s, because at some date before 1546 a college of priests was founded.[42]

Holy Rude's post-Reformation history followed a familiar course, with a cross wall being built to divide it into two parts in 1656. The east and west parts received their first major restorations in 1803 and 1818 respectively; the former being carried out by James Miller, and the latter by James Gillespie Graham. In the course of his work Gillespie Graham blocked the west doorway, deepening the window above it, and removed the porch and two of the three chantry aisles which are known to have flanked the nave; he also inserted his usual plaster vaults. There was further work on the choir in 1869 by James Collie. A more thoughtful restoration of the nave was carried out by Thomas Ross in 1911–14, during which he re-exposed the open-timber roof. The whole church was restored throughout in 1936–40, by a second architect named James Miller. In the course of this the wall dividing the church was removed, a replacement south porch was built, and a crossing and transepts were formed at the junction of the nave and choir. The church thus at last achieved a form of completeness.

The nave, of five aisled bays, has stocky cylindrical arcade piers for most of its length, but a pair of more complex piers to the eastern bay (see Figures 6.1e and 6.13). The arcade arches have two simple orders of broad chamfers. Windows with cusped intersecting tracery light the aisles, the vaults over which were modified during construction. The clearstorey stage is relatively tall internally, being slightly more than half the height of the lower stage. Like that in the choir at Perth, and possibly that in the nave at Edinburgh, it is different on the two sides. In this case it has round-arched windows only on its south side, with internal reveals of similar section as the arcade arches. A string course separates the stages internally, from which short wall shafts rise to the wall posts and arched braces beneath alternate tie-beams of the roof. The aisle roofs have been altered more than once, but on the south side the clearstorey remains externally evident, whereas the corresponding blank wall on the north side is largely hidden behind the roof (see Figure 6.14).

The complex piers at the east end of the nave were perhaps intended to emphasise the siting of the main nave altars. They differ markedly: that on the north having filleted shafts in the main directions, separated by quarter hollows; that on the south also having filleted shafts to the main faces, but flanked by small rolls, and with recessed filleted shafts on the diagonal faces. The mouldings of this south-east pier are essentially the same as those of the arch responds of the demolished St Mary's aisle off the west bay of the north aisle which, as already said, was founded in 1484 (see Figure 6.14). This similarity suggests the nave was started at the west end, presumably clear of any existing structures, and that the eastern parts were thus last to be built. It also suggests that at least one of the chapel aisles was added within the continuing programme on the nave very soon after its east end had been completed, and this is borne out by the way the same base course was used for the chapel as for the nave. The aisle dedicated to St Andrew – which was added at the east end of the north aisle by Matthew Forestar – must also have come soon after the completion of the nave since, like St Mary's aisle, it has the same base course as the adjacent nave aisle.

On the basis of the building sequence this suggests, the west tower was one of the first parts started (see Figure 6.17). In plan it is longer on its north–south than on its east–west axis, but is by no means alone in Scotland in being of oblong plan. The doorway through the west wall of the tower is now blocked, and its original form largely lost, though the bases and lower jambs have been re-exposed. Internally the tower opens into the nave through an arch rising the full height of the central space (see Figure 6.13); its lower storey has a sexpartite vault with an extra intersection in one quarter for the stair turret.

In the second phase of operations, starting with the agreement on the choir of 1507, and culminating in the formation of a college in about 1546, there were grand ideas

FIGURE 6.13 (*right*) Stirling Holy Rude, the interior of the nave looking westwards.

FIGURE 6.14 (*below*) Stirling Holy Rude, the nave from the north-west. The site of St Mary's aisle is in the foreground, and St Andrew's aisle is against the transept.

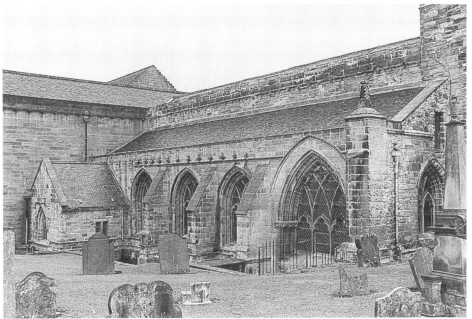

for remodelling the whole building which proved to be only partly attainable (see Figures 6.15 and 6.16). The new choir was to be separated from the nave by transepts, with a second tower over the crossing. Such a pair of axial towers would have been unique in late medieval Scotland, so far as we know, though there was a twelfth-century precedent at Kelso Abbey. It was also intended to heighten the main body of the nave, since a higher roof moulding was built into the east face of the second phase of the west tower, with doorways at the level of a heightened wall-walk. This shows that a new clearstorey was to have been added to the nave, and the old one presumably converted into a form of triforium. But, as with the transept and central tower, these schemes proved unattainable.

The elements of this grand scheme which were at least partly completed were those for the choir and the western tower. The new choir is of three bays, terminating in a large and rather awkwardly vaulted eastern apse which slightly overlaps the flanking aisles (see Figures 6.15 and 6.16). The arcades are carried on piers of eight filleted shafts, and have arches which differ on the two sides. These arches spring from caps with three tiers of diagonally continuous mouldings, which carry the Scottish taste for such caps – seen earlier at Torphichen, Jedburgh and elsewhere – as far as it could easily be taken (see Figures 3.2 and 3.5). In both the vaulted aisles and the apse the windows have standard late Gothic tracery types, with inward-leaning curved daggers, or with spiralling daggers in circlets; but the east window has simplified English-inspired Perpendicular tracery.

The tracery at Stirling thus shows a similar range of types as in the choir of Linlithgow. But internally it may have been the earlier nave of Linlithgow that was the greatest influence, because it seems a related three-storeyed elevation was initially intended. Although there is now a clearstorey directly above the arcade, before the aisle roofs were flattened in 1869 the windows at this level opened into the roof spaces, and were therefore part of what was in essence a triforium stage. With such an arrangement it is possible that a clearstorey was intended to rise above it. Three full storeys would have given the choir externally an extremely imposing appearance and, even allowing for a heightened three-storeyed nave, it would have been considerably taller than that. We can only speculate why these schemes were never finished, but the high costs together with the difficult sloping site, could both have been factors.

The most successful feature of the latest phase of work is perhaps the superstructure of the west tower (see Figure 6.17). Because of the laterally elongated plan of the lower stages, the two top stages were corbelled out to east and west, while to north and south they were contracted and walk-ways created. The three-dimensional geometry of the tower is further complicated by a square stair turret at the north-west angle, which continues the main plane of the lower stages and is capped by a pinnacled spirelet. Squinches across the internal angles of the top storey show the tower was intended to have a spire, and one is known to have existed before the nineteenth-century restorations. Even without its spire, there is no tower quite like this in Scotland; nevertheless, the wall-walks along two faces at three-quarter height could show some influence from the telescoped tower at Dundee (see p. 209).

FIGURE 6.15 (*right*)   Stirling Holy
Rude, the interior of the choir looking
eastwards.
FIGURE 6.16 (*below*)   Stirling Holy
Rude, the north flank of the choir.

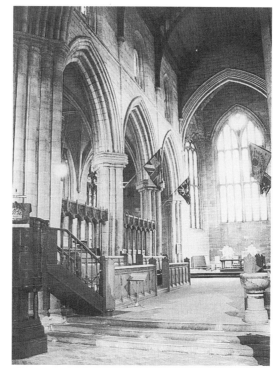

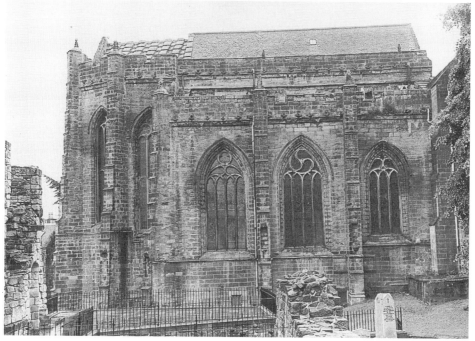

FIGURE 6.17   Stirling Holy Rude, the west tower.

THE OTHER BURGH CHURCHES

Edinburgh, Perth, Haddington, Linlithgow and Stirling are the best preserved of the greater burgh churches. But others survive in more fragmentary state, or are known about from records, and must be taken into account if we are to understand the architectural range of this group of buildings.

The most impressive relic of any of these other churches is the 46.5-metre-high tower of St Mary's Church at Dundee (see Figure 6.18).[43] The church had been founded by David, Earl of Huntingdon, in the 1190s, and was immediately granted to Lindores Abbey. Agreement was reached with Lindores over the rebuilding of the choir in 1442–3, the burgh accepting responsibility for the work in return for an annual payment of 5 merks from the abbey.[44] The choir may have been nearing completion by 1461, when lead was obtained to cover it, and work then probably moved on to the nave and tower. The latter was itself presumably nearly complete by 1495, when a bell was donated. It seems unlikely, however, that the eight-ribbed crown steeple anticipated in the design of the top parapet was ever built. The chief alterations to the tower are the cap-house built in 1570, and the upward extension of the stair turret by John Mylne in 1644. The church now adjoining the tower dates from two operations designed by William Burn between 1842 and 1847, at a time

FIGURE 6.18   Dundee St Mary, the west tower.

when it was divided into two separate churches. Sir Gilbert Scott restored the tower in 1870, and in a more recent campaign there was an unfortunate scraping-back of stone surfaces.

In discussing Haddington it was said that there are similarities between the west door and window there and those at Dundee, though Dundee is the more elaborate of the two (see Figure 6.7). At both, the arches and capitals of the round-headed doorways are enriched by foliage trails, and there is a division into two round-arched openings by a trumeau; the six-light windows which sit closely above the doorways at the two churches are each divided into two parts by massive sub-arches, between which is a pair of curved daggers – albeit with tracery of differing complexity within the sub-arches. In all of this the similarities are significantly close and suggest similar sources of inspiration, but above this point the Dundee tower naturally develops differently. Counting the doorway and the great window as part of a single tall stage, which is flanked at the angles by buttresses capped by pinnacles and miniature flyers, there are four further stages. The top two stages are set back telescope-like within the lower walls, and there is a traceried and pinnacled parapet running around the walk-way thus formed.

The most striking feature of this tower is its telescoped form and, in a burgh which enjoyed extensive trade with the Low Countries, there can be little doubt this was an idea derived from the northern states of the Netherlands, where there are several towers of related form. The earliest was that of Utrecht Cathedral, which was built largely between 1321 and 1382, but it was probably one of the later examples – which were also on a more accessible scale – that immediately inspired Dundee. The example at Amersfoort, which was under way by 1471, is certainly a little closer in scale, though there is a rather closer kinship with parochial examples such as Amerongen and Culemborg. Nevertheless, as might be expected, the net result at Dundee could be nothing other than Scottish. What we presumably see here is not a Netherlandish mason designing the work, but a Scottish mason or patron drawing inspiration from something he had seen and admired, yet had only partly understood since it belonged within an alien tradition. Nevertheless, even allowing for the changes resulting from such a process, it is worth noting how many of the details could have been inspired by the Netherlandish prototypes in addition to the basic telescoped form. These include the traceried and pinnacled parapet, the triplet of windows on the first stage of the superstructure above the parapet, and the massive sub-arches of the main west window. The pair of round-arched doorways within a semicircular containing arch also has Netherlandish parallels, such as the west entrance of St Lebuinus' Church at Deventer.

Another burgh church which possibly owed something to inspiration from the Low Countries was St Nicholas at Aberdeen, which was already a large cruciform structure with an aisled nave by the later twelfth century.[45] Except for the crypt below the apse and parts of the transept, what we now see is the result of post-Reformation rebuilding: the nave having been designed by James Gibbs in 1755, and the choir by Archibald Simpson in 1835, with later rebuilding after 1874. However, a view of the late medieval choir before reconstruction shows it to have had cylindrical piers to the arcades and a ribbed timber wagon ceiling over the choir and its eastern apse (see Figure 6.19). The master mason from 1483 was one John Gray, but much of the quality of the interior was due to the design of the timber work.

The ceiling was closely similar to that over King's College Chapel in Aberdeen, which has been discussed above (see p. 161 and Figure 5.21). The wright in charge of the timber work at St Nicholas' was John Fendour, who was also responsible for the timber of the cathedral's central tower as well as being involved in the sale of materials to the royal building operations.[46] He received payment 'for the making of the ruff and tymmir of the queyr' at St Nicholas in April 1495, but it must have taken some time to complete since inscriptions on the north cornice have the dates 1510 and 1515. By then Fendour had also undertaken to carve thirty-four choir stalls in December 1507,[47] in anticipation of the foundation of a college of priests. Fragments of those stalls survive in the National Museum of Scotland, together with smaller fragments from the roof itself. A college was eventually formally established in 1540, though the clergy attached to the church were already following regulations given them by Bishop Lindsay (1441–58), with new regulations being drawn up in 1519.[48]

Two inter-related churches which must be mentioned at this stage are at St

FIGURE 6.19   Aberdeen St Nicholas, the interior of the choir looking eastwards before the rebuilding of 1835.

Andrews and Cupar. At St Andrews the parish church was granted to the priory in about 1163, when it stood within the priory precinct to the east of the cathedral, perhaps on the site of one of the churches of the important early religious settlement of Kinrimund. The late medieval rebuilding of the church was a particular project of the family of Lindsay of the Byres.[49] In 1411 it was formally transferred to a site at the heart of the burgh, on land granted by Sir William Lindsay in November 1410, and by 1433 his son, Sir John, was unsuccessfully petitioning the Pope to found a college within it.[50] Building probably started immediately after the transfer. Prior James Bisset played an active part in the operation, presumably concentrating his efforts on the choir, although in 1494 Prior Hepburn signed an agreement which handed over to the burgh the priory's responsibility for that part, in return for an annual payment of 6 merks.[51]

Little of the medieval fabric of Holy Trinity Church at St Andrews survives, because its outer walls were largely rebuilt by Robert Balfour in 1798–1800, only to be enthusiastically restored by Peter MacGregor Chalmers in 1907–9. The chief identifiable features are the tower at the north-west corner of the nave (see Figure 6.20), and parts of the arcade piers. The latter are cylindrical, with more complex caps and bases in the choir than in the nave – although this difference may be the result of restoration. The tower is a plain unbuttressed structure, which continues the plane of the west front, with a rectangular stair turret at its north-western angle. It is capped by a squat spire with a single tier of lucarnes, set behind a plain corbelled parapet; as a counterpoise to the spire the stair turret has a cap-house surmounted by a spirelet.

Like St Andrews, St Michael at Cupar was built on a new site in the early fifteenth century, and it was also appropriated to the priory of St Andrews.[52] It is said to have been built in 1415[53] by the same Prior Bisset who was involved at St Andrews. By analogy with what happened elsewhere, however, the priory's main concern would have been the choir, and there is evidence of the burgesses playing their part at a date before 1429.[54] All that remains of the medieval church is the rectangular tower, above the west bay of the north aisle, and a short stretch of the north arcade, from which we can see there was no clearstorey (see Figure 6.21). The surviving section of the arcade has one cylindrical column and an unusual hexagonal one at the south-east angle of the tower. A similarly angular approach to design is seen in the lowest window of the tower's west face, where the slit opening has a lozenge-shaped head. The tower was presumably complete before 1485, which is the date on one of the recast bells. The original belfry stage of the tower had a single lancet in each face, but in 1620 the minister, William Scott, capped this stage by another and by a splay-foot spire behind a balustraded parapet. The church was superseded in 1785 by a more compact structure on the site of the choir to the designs of Hay Bell.

All the burgh churches so far considered are in the east of Scotland or the Forth Valley, presumably because it was those areas which were financially best able to undertake major rebuilding of their churches in the later Middle Ages. Nevertheless, we know of a number of building operations in other burghs which deserve brief mention. At David I's burgh of Rutherglen, where a large aisled Romanesque church was built possibly even before its grant to Paisley by William the Lion, the unique

FIGURE 6.20   St Andrews Holy Trinity, the north and west elevations of the north-west tower.

eastern tower is at least partly late medieval.[55] At Peebles – yet another of David's burghs – where only the tower remains, there were additions including a chapel dedicated to the Virgin founded by John Geddes of Rachan before 1427.[56] This was perhaps the projection from the asymmetrical north aisle shown on early plans, but we know nothing of its architecture.

At Elgin, a burgh of David I's where there was a parish church from at least the time that William the Lion granted it to the nearby cathedral in the late twelfth century, the present building was designed by Archibald Simpson in 1827. In 1621 its medieval predecessor had been divided into two churches by a cross wall, and in 1700 its transepts were demolished. However, early views show it to have been a cruciform building with a central tower and an aisled nave, the latter apparently

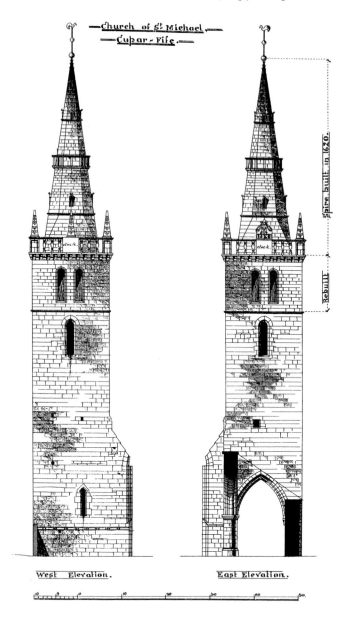

FIGURE 6.21   Cupar St Michael, the west and east elevations of the north-west tower.

without a clearstorey. Parts of this structure were of later medieval date, including
the central tower, with what was perhaps a stone-flagged roof above a barrel vault.
    One final building to be mentioned here is St John's parish church at Ayr, a burgh
which had been accorded royal status between 1203 and 1206.[57] Only its tower now
stands complete, and that has suffered drastic changes in 1778 and heavy restoration
in 1913–14. However, excavations in 1891 and 1985 showed the church was an aisled
cruciform structure and, though the dates of the constituent parts are uncertain, the

one surviving arcade base is of the later twelfth century. The tower, which has four storeys above a vaulted ground-floor stage, is partly late medieval — though it incorporates two late twelfth-century windows at the lower levels of the wall it shared with the nave. The tower has a corbelled parapet with rounds at the corners, giving it the defensible air of several other fifteenth-century church towers, such as Dysart (see p. 232). Also as at Dysart, there are fireplaces on the upper floors, though it is unclear what function these rooms were intended to meet.

In considering these last churches we have moved away from the splendours of the unified architectural conceptions which gave us Haddington and Linlithgow. In the cases of St Andrews and Cupar this is simply because we have lost the greater part of the buildings, and what remains suggests the scope of the original conceptions once approached those of the churches considered earlier in this chapter. In the cases of Ayr, Peebles and Rutherglen, however, we must assume either that the burghs did not have the same aspirations for their churches as their east coast counterparts, or — and this is more likely — that they could not muster the resources to attempt such projects.

CHAPTER SEVEN

Parish Churches and Chapels

THE PROBLEMS OF LOW SURVIVAL RATES

By comparison with the collegiate and burgh churches, the parish churches and chapels have not survived well; though a high proportion remained in use for some time after the Reformation, most were eventually superseded. In some cases they were so completely remodelled that their medieval forms were lost or rendered unrecognisable, but many others were replaced by completely new buildings either on the same site or elsewhere.[1] In the latter case the original church often survives as a ruin, and it is not uncommon to see the abandoned shell of a medieval church sharing the same churchyard with a later one, as at Kinfauns in Perthshire; in some cases, however, the new church was a short distance away, as at Muthill, also in Perthshire (see Figure 7.15). Sometimes, when a new church was on the same site as its predecessor, it was smaller or set slightly aside, leaving part of the old building standing – as at the Fife church of Kinghorn. But it was more usual in such cases for all traces of the original church to be completely lost to sight, as at Morebattle in Roxburghshire, where excavation has traced foundations west of a church that is now substantially of 1757.

A majority of Scottish churches and chapels were structurally undivided rectangles, and adapted well to the earlier needs of reformed worship. Indeed, for long they were the churches with the best chance of survival, albeit with the main internal focus shifted from an altar at the east end to a pulpit at the centre of the south wall. Well into the early nineteenth century many rural churches were still built to a rectangular plan and, where a rectangular post-medieval church is known to occupy the site of an earlier building, it could be possible that church at least partly incorporates medieval fabric. This may be the case at Dalton in Dumfriesshire, for example, where the church was rebuilt on an old site in 1704; but Dalton had a similar subsequent history to many other churches, being itself replaced by a completely new building on an adjacent site, in 1895.

In retrospect it seems rather perverse that, although the simplest churches were most likely to survive in the centuries following the Reformation, changing preferences often led to the replacement of such simple buildings in due course. By the earlier nineteenth century explicitly medieval architectural detail was returning to favour, as interest in the architecture of the period re-emerged. However, for a while it was the superficial appearance that was valued more than the substance, and at

Dalgety in Fife a rectangular church (surrounded by a remarkable array of post-Reformation aisles) was replaced in 1830 by a more regularly 'Gothic' church designed by James Gillespie Graham. A further reason for losses was to be the Disruption of 1843, which depleted many congregations, and may have encouraged the reduction of some churches.[2]

From the later decades of the nineteenth century, however, the loss of medieval work became less acceptable. A strong influence in this was the Aberdeen (later the Scottish) Ecclesiological Society,[3] which encouraged a more scholarly interest in the architecture and liturgy of the Middle Ages. But even this could have disadvantages and some churches, including Fowlis Wester in Perthshire, were rather excessively restored. More recently, the continuing streamlining of congregations – which has inevitably followed the welcome union of the Established and United Free Churches in 1929 – can still cause the abandonment of churches – such as that of Dunning in Perthshire.

Because of all these losses, surprisingly few medieval churches have remained in use, though many have at least survived either wholly or partly as ruins. The main single reason for their preservation after going out of use has been their conversion into burial enclosures or mausolea. One part which often survived was the choir, because ownership of that part passed from the parson or appropriating institution to the laird after the Reformation. As a result, while the church was in use, lairds frequently placed their pews or lofts here, with burial vaults below and, if the church was later abandoned for worship, this part was likely to continue in use for burials out of family piety – as at the Perthshire parish church of Auchterarder.

In other cases families had burial rights in aisles built on to the flanks of churches, and this was especially important when, after the Reformation, burial was discouraged within the main body of the church. Sometimes these had originated as medieval chantry chapels where prayers were offered for the soul of their founder. This was the case with the aisle of the Lindsay family at the old church of Edzell, for example, which was probably built around the 1540s by the ninth Earl of Crawford, who was also architecturally active at the nearby castle. But similar aisles continued to be built after the Reformation – albeit without chantry functions – as at Uphall in West Lothian and it can sometimes be difficult to tell whether they are of medieval or post-Reformation origin. However, in cases where a family had a continuing interest in them, such aisles were likely to survive even if the rest of the church was abandoned. Sometimes a whole disused church might be retained because of its use for burials, as at the chapel of Tullibardine in Perthshire, within which a burial vault was created for the Dukes of Atholl (see Figures 7.3 and 7.4). Alternatively the roof might be removed but parts of the walls maintained as a burial enclosure, as was done at Dysart in Fife, for the Sinclair family (see Figure 7.16).

Even allowing for those churches which survive at least partly as ruins, however, it is sadly the case that we have insufficient evidence for an adequate idea of the architectural range of the lesser churches in the later Middle Ages, or of the ways that existing churches might be adapted to meet modified needs in the century before the Reformation.

CHURCHES LARGELY OF LATE MEDIEVAL DATE

One of the largest parish churches to be rebuilt entirely in the later Middle Ages was at South Leith,[4] which was originally a chapel within the parish of Restalrig. It was under construction in 1487 and 1503, when the Treasurer's Accounts record royal gifts,[5] but we know little about the finished building because hardly any of the original fabric has survived. The eastern parts were destroyed by the English in the mid-sixteenth century, and the rest was largely rebuilt by Thomas Hamilton in 1848. Nevertheless, early views show that the nave had an aisle along each side, and there appear to have been transepts. Although the existing nave has the same basic plan as the original, virtually the only authentic elements are the semi-octagonal responds of the west crossing piers and the west window – which is now rebuilt in St Conan's Church on Loch Awe.[6]

Churches of the scale of South Leith were exceptional outside the great burghs and, although we shall consider other churches of complex plan in this chapter, simple rectangular churches continued to meet the needs of a majority of both parish churches and chapels. The small Perthshire church of Grandtully, although extended westwards in 1636 when a painted ceiling was also inserted, is a relatively complete example of the type. It was built in 1533 as a chapel for the township of Pitcairn, because the parish church was six miles away at Dull,[7] and its founder was Alexander Stewart, whose castle was below the hillside on which the church stood. As first built it was a rectangle of 15.25 by 6.75 metres, with all its windows and doorways on the south side.

A rectangular plan was not in itself a sign of poverty, or of parsimony, as has already been seen at the collegiate church of Foulis Easter (see p. 153). Another church which

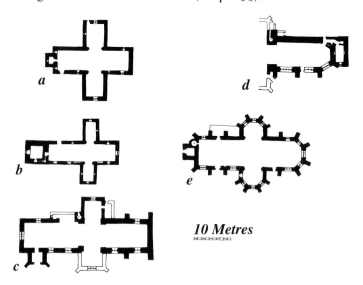

FIGURE 7.1   Plans of some of the more architecturally ambitious parish churches and chapels: a. Tullibardine; b. Rodel; c. Whitekirk; d. Midcalder; e. Ladykirk.

was a setting for some rich furnishings was that of the parish of Kinkell in Aberdeenshire. This was the prebendal church of Canon Alexander Galloway of Aberdeen Cathedral, the trusted adviser to Bishops Elphinstone and Dunbar, and who was closely involved in the liturgical revival represented by the Aberdeen Breviary.[8] There had been a church at Kinkell from at least the fourteenth century, when it belonged to the Hospitallers of Temple, and in 1420 it was granted to Aberdeen Cathedral.[9] The remains of the church of 23.75 by 7 metres, which – like Grandtully – had no openings in the north wall, could be of any date, but Galloway clearly did much to beautify it. In the north wall he built an unusual sacrament house which, with its combination of textual and carved panels took on a cross-shaped pattern (see Figure 7.2). It bears his initials and the date 1524. West of it he placed a carving of the crucifixion, which has his initials and the date 1525.[10] He also provided a font, which is now in St John's Episcopal Church in Aberdeen.[11] The panels along its sides have the sacred monogram, a crowned 'M' for the Virgin, shields with the wounds of Christ, and his own initials.

Considering all these additions by Galloway to his prebendal church, it was possibly he who inserted the traceried east window, the northern reveal of which is all that survives. He was perhaps also active at some of the six chapels associated with Kinkell church: at Drumblade, Dyce, Kemnay, Kinnellar, Kintore and Skene. Certainly at the small rectangular chapel of Dyce he provided yet another sacrament house, the surviving fragment of which is inscribed with his initials and the date 1544.[12]

A rectangular plan underlies many churches which eventually assumed a more complex form, though the care taken to present architectural unity often means the original plan is difficult to detect. At the chapel of the ancestors of the Murray Dukes of Atholl, at Tullibardine in Perthshire, close to the site of their castle, there is a tradition the building was erected by Sir David Murray, who died in 1452.[13] This is supported by the prominent display of the arms of himself and his parents on the chapel walls. From the scale of his benefactions it seems likely Sir David intended to

FIGURE 7.2   Kinkell Church, sacrament house.

found a college, although any such plans never reached fruition, even though his son added another priest to the establishment in 1455.[14]

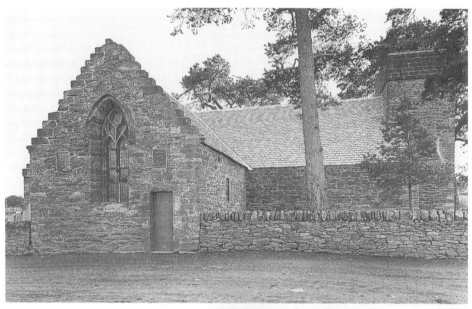

FIGURE 7.3 (*above*)   Tullibardine
Chapel, the exterior from the north.
FIGURE 7.4 (*right*)   Tullibardine
Chapel, the interior looking eastwards.

However, much of the cross-shaped chapel looks considerably later than the 1450s (see Figures 7.1a, 7.3 and 7.4). The transepts have tracery with uncusped loop forms which would be out of place before the early sixteenth century, and the heavy filleted roll mouldings and simplified imposts of the south doorway are also of late type. Confirmation of a late date is afforded by heraldry on the south transept gable, which evidently relates to the marriage shortly before 1500 of Sir Andrew Murray – a younger son of the family – and Margaret Barclay. (They were to be the ancestors of the Earls of Mansfield, and built the tower-house at Balvaird Castle, see p. 257 and Figure 8.17.) What therefore seems likely is that Sir David had built a church which was augmented about fifty years later by Sir Andrew, who added transeptal chapels and a small western tower, thus creating a Greek-cross plan not dissimilar from that of Inchcolm. Although the church passed out of use for services at the Reformation, except for occasional illicit acts of worship, its use for burials ensured its preservation. It still has much of its original open-timber roof, which is of characteristic late medieval type. Collars connect the rafters at the upper level, and at the wall-head on each side is a triangle formed by sole-pieces and vertical wall posts; longitudinal wind bracing is provided by the sarking boards.

A similar architectural development may be suspected at other cruciform churches, including St Clement at Rodel, near the southern tip of Harris, though restorations after a fire in 1784, and in 1873 have confused the evidence there.[15] The rectangular main body of the church has lower and slightly asymmetrical transeptal chapels towards the eastern end, while the western tower has flanks that continue the line of the side walls of the nave (see Figures 7.1b and 7.5). Details such as the rough base course which runs along only one part of the south wall suggest the church was built in more than one phase, and the tower must have required at least three campaigns. Its lowest storey, being built on a higher ledge of rock, is reached by dog-legged flights of stairs within the wall thickness. That storey has plain quoins, while the two upper storeys have angle-rolls above a stepped string course, with a change of masonry between these two upper storeys which is additionally marked by projecting heads. However, the surprisingly improper carvings which decorate the tower tend to draw most eyes away from such minutiae.

Internally the mouldings of the transept arches are unexpectedly sophisticated; these and the east window must have been ultimately inspired by Iona. But the finest individual feature of Rodel is the tomb of Alexander MacLeod, in the south wall of the choir, and it seems likely it was he who gave the church its final cruciform plan (see Figure 7.6). Although MacLeod was not to die until about 1546, an inscription shows he prepared his tomb as early as 1528[16] The arch which frames the tomb recess has voussoirs depicting the apostles, the evangelists and the Trinity, while the tympanum within the arch shows a mixture of the sacred and the secular. At the centre is the Virgin and Child flanked by St Clement and another unidentified bishop saint, with angels above, and the weighing of souls below. Around these are what appear to be Alexander's castle and his galley, and there is a hunting scene depicted in fascinatingly full details along the bottom, which perhaps represents Alexander's own idea of heaven. On the tomb chest is his armoured effigy, clasping a two-handed sword. In an area that was not otherwise remarkable either for major ecclesiastical architecture or for mural monuments, Rodel and its tomb offer an outstanding testimony to the potential within the West Highland repertoire.

A church at the opposite corner of the kingdom which similarly eventually assumed a cruciform plan is at Whitekirk in East Lothian (see Figures 7.1c and 7.7).[17] The

FIGURE 7.5 (*above*)   Rodel Church, the south flank.
FIGURE 7.6 (*right*)   Rodel Church, the tomb of Alexander MacLeod.

parish was probably founded during the reign of David I, in whose time the church was granted to Holyrood.[18] By the fourteenth century a nearby well was attracting pilgrims through its miraculous powers, and their offerings may be reflected in the relatively grand scale of the church. The most memorable of those pilgrims was the Italian humanist scholar, Aeneas Silvius Piccolomini, who later became Pope Pius II. He walked to the church barefoot through the snow in thanks for having been spared from shipwreck in 1435, and was consequently permanently disabled by rheumatism.[19]

Interpretation of the sequence of building has been made difficult by modern rebuilding and restoration. The south transept was reconstructed in 1832, and a family pew thrown out on the north side of the nave at the same time; after a fire in 1914 the whole building was extensively restored and re-medievalised by Sir Robert Lorimer. Of the original building, the choir, a buttressed rectangle covered by a pointed barrel vault, is said to have been built by Adam Hepburn of Hailes in 1439.

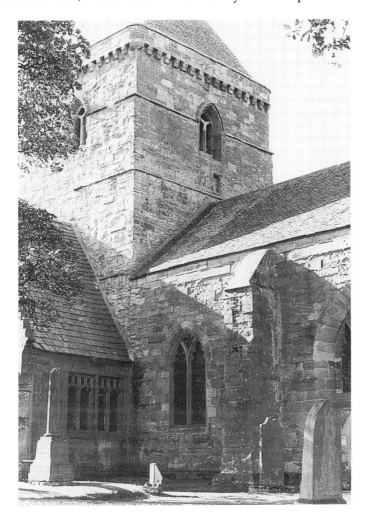

FIGURE 7.7   Whitekirk Church, the choir, south transept and tower from the south-east.

The structure would accord well with such a date, though arms above the circular window in the east gable – identified as those of Abbot Crawford of Holyrood (1460–83) – add an element of uncertainty. The date of the central tower, north transept and nave are unknown, though it seems that the nave could predate the choir. The final medieval addition was probably the south porch. It has pinnacled angle buttresses with tabernacles facing in towards the doorway. Internally the porch has a pointed barrel vault with a surface application of ribs in a sexpartite pattern.

If all these churches took on a cruciform shape as a result of a complex architectural development, others were rebuilt in this way to a single plan; the best surviving example of such unified rebuilding is at Ladykirk, also known as Kirk of Steill, in Berwickshire (see Figures 7.1e, 7.8 and 7.9).[20] There was apparently a church at Upsetlington, the name of the parish of Ladykirk, by the time of the papal taxation of about 1287. Rebuilding was in progress from about 1500, with the involvement of the mason Nicholas Jackson, on the evidence of contributions from James IV.[21] The only significant part of the existing structure which does not date from that operation is the western tower, which was built in 1741 – supposedly by William Adam – at a time of general restoration. There was a further restoration in 1861.

The main body of Ladykirk has a three-sided apse at the east end and a tower at the west end; about half-way down each side is an apsidal transeptal chapel. Internally both main body and transepts are covered by pointed barrel vaults; these have widely spaced parallel ribs, except at the groining of the apsidal vaults where the ribs are arranged radially. Externally the bay rhythm is strongly defined by buttresses, which have simple pinnacles above the wall-head cornice. As usual over pointed barrel vaulting, the roofs are of stone flags. The windows have two-or three-centred arches, within which the light-heads all reach up to the arches, except in the east window, which has intersecting tracery. In general there is a striking fluency in the handling of the parts which is not always found in apsed churches, though there is a slight clumsiness in the way the chapel roofs stop against gables above the flanks of the main body instead of extending back to the main roof.

Ladykirk is perhaps the best instance of a new wave of interest in building churches with apsidal terminations in the years around 1500. At Culross in Fife, excavations in 1926 revealed that the small chapel of St Kentigern there also had an apse as the culmination of its rectangular plan. It was probably rebuilt by Archbishop Blackadder (1483–1508) of Glasgow, as part of his effort to regenerate the cult of his cathedral's patron saint, since it was at Culross that legend said Kentigern had been brought up by St Serf. Blackadder's interest in the chapel was to be continued up to his death, and he left £10 to it in his will.[22]

There would almost certainly have been other apsidal churches – some of them vaulted – which are now lost. Views of the chapel of St Nicholas' Hospital in Glasgow, for example, which was founded in 1464, appear to show a small apsed building with the low-set windows associated with barrel vaulting.[23] But, apart from Ladykirk the most architecturally ambitious of the smaller apsed churches about which we know anything was the parish church of Midcalder, in West Lothian.[24] Quite apart from its high architectural merits, this building has added interest because of the survival

FIGURE 7.8 (*above*) Ladykirk Church,
the south flank.
FIGURE 7.9 (*right*) Ladykirk Church,
the interior looking eastwards.

of a bond for its completion, and which is invaluable for its information on an interested patron's part in the process of building, although in fact the conditions of the bond were only partly carried out.

There was a church at Midcalder when the Earl of Fife attempted to grant it to Dunfermline in the 1150s, and Bishop Bernham of St Andrews carried out one of his many dedications here in 1242.[25] Nothing remains of any earlier buildings, however, because the site was cleared for the new building planned in the first half of the sixteenth century by its parson, Master Peter Sandilands, a younger son of the landholder. The church now consists of a two-bay choir terminating in a three-sided eastern apse, with a rectangular sacristy above a burial vault against the east wall (see Figures 7.1d and 7.10). At the west end is now a transept built by Brown and Wardrop in 1863, but a nave was originally planned, with a steeple over the rood loft, and with a porch covering the main entrance. Most unusually, there was to have been a lean-to cloister walk on the north side of the choir, the roof corbels of which survive.

From the bond of 1542, by which Master Peter provided funds for his nephew and great-nephew – Sir James and John Sandilands – to complete the church to his plan, it seems little more had then been carried out than the start of work on the sacristy and the laying-out of the choir walls. Before work eventually came to a halt – possibly because Sir James had by then allied himself with the reforming party – the walls of the sacristy and choir were complete and roofed, though the vault that was intended for the choir was never built. According to the bond the vault was to be copied from that over St Anthony's aisle of St Giles' Church in Edinburgh – that is the outer part of the south transept there. The area cited is now covered by a plaster vault, but at

FIGURE 7.10   Midcalder Church, the interior looking eastwards before the restoration of 1863.

least the vault springings at Midcalder were built, and show that it was to be of tierceron pattern rather than the more usual pointed barrel form. It was itself eventually completed in plaster during the operations of 1863.

Those parts of Midcalder which were built were finished to the highest standards, with walls of excellent ashlar, and an abundance of heraldic decoration. The window tracery is of uncusped looped forms related to windows at St Andrews Blackfriars chapel and in the transeptal chapels of Tullibardine (See Figures 4.9 and 7.3), though some of the combinations are more complex than at those churches. As at St Andrews, the windows must owe something to influence from the Low Countries, and we do know that – like growing numbers of Scotland's landed families – members of Master Peter's immediate family were sufficiently well travelled to have seen buildings on the Continent. In 1526 Sir James Sandilands himself went to Rome in penance for a murder, for example, while his son John was a student at Paris.[26] Both could have travelled through the Low Countries to reach their destinations, and it must be assumed that Master Peter had similar opportunities to travel.

LATE MEDIEVAL ADDITIONS TO EXISTING CHURCHES

One other eastern apse which might be late medieval is at Terregles Church in Kirkcudbrightshire. Because the date 1585 was inscribed on its cornice, this apse is assumed to be post-medieval, and to have been started by the fourth Lord Herries before his death in 1583.[27] The Herries family were notable Catholic recusants, and this could explain the use of an essentially medieval feature in the rebuilding of their parish church. But, since there had been a church on the site from at least the later thirteenth century,[28] is it possible that Lord Herries was remodelling an existing feature, and that the date refers to that rather than to the original construction? Although the pronounced angle rolls of the apse point to a relatively late date of construction, there are related rolls at Castle Semple of about 1504 (see p. 164).

As at Ladykirk, and as discussed previously at Blackfriars' church in St Andrews (see p. 140), apses need not be confined to the eastern ends of choirs, but could also be used for lateral chapels. The only case we know of a single apsidal aisle being added to the flank of an existing parish church, however, is at Arbuthnott in Kincardineshire.[29] There was a church at Arbuthnott by 1242, when Bishop Bernham carried out one of his dedications,[30] and the existing choir of the basically two-cell parish church was probably standing then. The aisle-less nave may be a reconstruction of the early sixteenth century, though it is now largely a renewal after a fire in 1890. The patron of the striking apsidal chapel which projects from the side of the choir was Sir Robert Arbuthnott – the landholder – who died in 1506, and who did much to beautify his church (see Figure 7.11).[31] Arrangements for the endowment of the chapel, dedicated to the Virgin, were completed in the year before his death. Among his other projects was the provision of a series of service books including a missal, a psalter and a book of hours. These were partly executed by the vicar, James Sibbald, and, apart from some higher quality miniatures by a different hand, were decorated in an endearingly amateurish style.[32]

FIGURE 7.11 (*above*)   Arbuthnott Church,
the south aisle from the south-east.
FIGURE 7.12 (*right*)   Arbuthnott Church, the
tabernacle on the south-east buttress of the south aisle.

There is nothing amateur about the architecture of the two-storeyed aisle, however, which is constructed of carefully laid ashlar and has tall buttresses capped by pinnacles at the angles. The chapel itself has long single-light arched windows in each face, except behind the site of the altar in the east wall, where there is a smaller rectangular window. The buttresses are decorated with tabernacles, that at the south-east angle having a corbel with a version of the *arma Christi* (see Figure 7.12).[33] Internally the chapel has a plain barrel vault, above which is a timber-roofed priest's room.

Arbuthnott was exceptional among parish churches for the quality of its lateral aisle; such aisles were becoming increasingly common, but were usually rectangular and less architecturally enriched. That which perhaps most closely approaches Arbuthnott in quality is against the south flank of Borthwick Parish Church (see Figure 7.13),[34] and was probably built by the first Lord Borthwick who erected the nearby castle after 1430 (see p.258 and Figures 8.19 and 8.20). The aisle was heavily restored in the 1860s, at the time that the adjacent church was largely rebuilt, but much of its original quality is apparent in the decorated cornice and excellent ashlar masonry. It is of rectangular plan, with buttresses to support the barrel vault. The windows — containing modern tracery — are predictably confined to the west and south walls,

FIGURE 7.13   Borthwick Church, the south aisle.

and there is a tomb recess below the south window. Internally, the original arrangement has been confused by the placing of a largely modern tomb structure against the
east wall, which now contains the excellent effigies thought to represent Lord and
Lady Borthwick.

Related aisles survive at many other churches, as at Glamis in Angus, where it may
have been the widow of the first Lord Glamis who built a chapel on the south side of
the church before her own death in 1484. It probably originally opened from the choir
through the wide arch in its north wall, and is covered by a two-bay cross-ribbed
barrel vault. Dynastic aspirations are frequently discernible in the way that the
landowners who built such family aisles were often the same individuals who were
building or enlarging the family's main residence, as seems also to have been the case
here.

However, family piety was as common among prelates as among secular landholders. It may be assumed that the chapel of St Mary, which Archbishop Blackadder of
Glasgow added to the parish church at Edrom in Berwickshire in 1499–50,[35] would
have been of similar architectural pretensions as those at Borthwick and Glamis. His
family originated at Blackadder within Edrom parish and he is unlikely to have stinted
himself; indeed, it was still in his mind when he left £10 to it in his will in 1508.[36]
Unfortunately the only recognisable details are the buttresses, one of which bears his
arms, initials and archiepiscopal cross.

More typical of the lateral aisles added to parish churches was that of the Bruce of
Stenhouse and Airth family, at the ruined church of Airth.[37] It was built against the
south flank of the church by Alexander Bruce at a date between about 1450 and 1487,
and was a simpler version of that at Borthwick, having no buttresses since it was
unvaulted. It is of rectangular plan, being longer on its north-south than its east-west
axis, and has windows only in its west and south walls, with a tomb recess below the
latter. The sadly eroded effigy within this recess is a unique representation of a female
figure beneath a drawn-back shroud. Apart from the effigy, an image tabernacle in
the east wall, the scale of the window arches, and the excellent masonry are all
indicative of the efforts made in constructing such a family burial place – which
presumably also housed a chantry for the offering of soul masses.

In Scottish usage the word 'aisle' is applicable to lateral projections that can vary
in size from the Blackadder aisle at Glasgow Cathedral to the smaller aisles we have
just discussed. But it can also be applied in the more widely accepted sense to a space
running alongside the main body of a church and separated from it by an arcade, as
at South Leith. In parish churches outside the greater burghs the former type of aisle
was probably more common, though there are many churches which have aisles along
part or all of their length, and several were added in the later Middle Ages.

At Alyth in Perthshire a three-arch arcade, carried on octagonal piers, survived the
demolition which followed the construction of the new church in 1839. It appears to
have been part of an added north aisle, and was spared destruction through being
deemed to be 'Saxon', presumably because of its round arches.[38] Another arcade was
demolished, however, suggesting that the aisles had been added in architecturally
distinct styles in separate operations. A similar additive process took place at the

Angus church of St Vigeans, on the strikingly motte-shaped mound that was presumably the location of the early community for which the many surviving fine early stones were carved.[39] As now seen this church owes much to a restoration by Sir Robert Rowand Anderson in 1871, but a case has been made that the south aisle, with its octagonal piers, was built shortly before a dedication of 1485 (see Figure 7.14).[40]

As can be seen from Alyth and St Vigeans, some churches must have had an unbalanced appearance for much of their existence. But elsewhere a pair of aisles may have formed a single addition. At Muthill in Perthshire, for example, the two nave aisles were probably added simultaneously to a church which had a twelfth-century western tower as its earliest part (see Figure 7.15). There is a tradition that this enlargement was carried out for Michael Ochiltree, who was dean of Dunblane from about 1419 to 1429, and then bishop until 1446.[41] Certainly the church had been granted to the bishops of Dunblane by the early thirteenth century,[42] and the aisle windows may have been inspired by windows on the north side of the choir at Dunblane, although the attribution to Ochiltree cannot be substantiated positively. The arcade arches develop directly from low octagonal columns without capitals, and the nave had a steeply pitched roof which swept across both central space and aisles.

FIGURE 7.14   St Vigeans Church, from the south-west.

FIGURE 7.15   Muthill Church, from the south-east.

Muthill, like South Leith, thus had no clearstorey windows above the arcade arches, and was therefore distantly related to the hall-church type; in some other churches, though there was similarly no clearstorey, a low wall might rise above the flanking aisle roofs to support a separate roof over the central space. This was the case at the large Fife church of Dysart,[43] but there a number of small windows were later cut to light the galleries installed after the Reformation. Dysart was replaced by a new church in 1802 and much has since been lost; indeed, a road overlies the site of its north aisle. But the surviving fabric, together with a survey of 1778, shows it was an impressive church in its final form.

Set on the coastal fringe of Fife, it is within one of the wealthier parts of medieval Scotland, where there was a tradition of large aisled parish churches – including nearby Kirkcaldy and Kinghorn as well as St Andrews, Cupar and Crail further north. Dysart had a nave of six bays and a choir of two wider bays, with aisles extending all the way up to the east end; the arcade piers were variously cylindrical, oval or T-shaped. From changes in the details of the piers and levels of arch springings, together with a diagonally staggered break in the masonry coursing at the junction of the tower and west front, it is clear the church is not a single-phase structure, though the relative chronology of its parts is uncertain. The main focus is an eight-storeyed tower of rectangular plan, which projects southwards from the south-west bay of the nave; there is a single-storey barrel-vaulted porch in the re-entrant angle between itself and the south aisle (see Figure 7.16).

Considering its moulded details, the unusual array of inverted key-hole shot-holes in the two lower storeys and the grey ashlar masonry, the idea that this tower was planned in tandem with Ravenscraig Castle for coastal defence is not implausible (see Figure 9.2).[44] That castle was started for Queen Mary of Guelders, in 1460, and a date not long after that is reasonable for the tower. The two lower storeys – those with shot-holes – are vaulted, and the only link between them is through a hatch. From the first floor there is a spiral stair, which rises into a crow-stepped cap-house behind the corbelled parapet. The main roof runs at right angles to the cap-house, and the resultant solid geometry might be more at home on a tower-house than on a church tower; this domestic appearance is reinforced by the chimney from the fireplace within the garret storey. Apart from the upper windows, in the form of a single lancet to each face rising through two storeys, all of the other windows are of simple rectangular shape.

Many other churches in all parts of Scotland received additions at this period, especially where there was an interested landholder. We may suspect that in some such cases, as already suggested at Tullibardine, there was also an intention to found a college of priests, even if this was never accomplished. At Rothesay, on the Isle of Bute, for example, it was probably around the mid-fifteenth century that the choir of the parish church of St Mary was rebuilt, and canopied tombs of the Stewart family were prominently placed in the flanking walls.[45] Looking beyond such buildings, one would like to know more about the original context of effigies that survive in churches

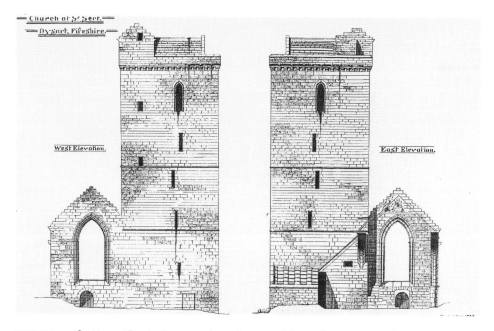

FIGURE 7.16   Dysart Church, the west and east elevations of the south-west tower and west front.

as far apart as Renfrew, Cupar or Ceres (Fife), since the setting of such memorials elsewhere suggests they may have been housed within a new or refurbished part of the structure. Unfortunately, however, although the remains of the smaller late medieval churches are of great value in supplementing information from the more fully represented burgh and collegiate churches, the losses mean we can understand little more than general architectural trends, in the design and planning.

CHAPTER EIGHT

Castles and Domestic Architecture

THE HISTORICAL BACKGROUND[1]

In most parts of Scotland, castles – or residences with some of the external trappings of defensibility – are a more prominent feature of the landscape than are medieval churches. This is partly because they continued to be built into the seventeenth century while, additionally, a higher proportion of them were being occupied later than might be expected in other parts of Europe. But there probably always were considerably more fortified houses than ecclesiastical buildings, and it is not simply the accidents of survival which have left us with so many. This has been regarded as supporting an image of later medieval and early modern Scotland as a country plagued by chronic unrest, in which all men of substance had to be prepared to defend themselves. The monarchy and magnates have been seen as striving with each other for supremacy; both the magnates and lesser landholders have been visualised as being constantly at each other's throats; and there has been a picture of endemic warfare with England on the southern Border and of uneasy confrontation with the Highlanders to the north and west. There is, of course, an element of truth in all of this.

It is certainly true that Scotland did not have its difficulties to seek in this period. Two kings, James I and James III, were murdered – in 1437 and 1488 respectively; two others, James II and James IV, died on the battlefield in 1460 and 1513. Perhaps even worse in an age when the lack of an effective monarch could be highly destabilising, there were long periods of royal absence or of minority. James I was imprisoned in England from 1406 to 1424, and all of the monarchs who followed him were minors when they succeeded to the throne: James II was six in 1437, James III was eight in 1460, James IV was fifteen in 1488, James V was one in 1513 and Mary was only a few days old in 1542.

As evidence of conflict between the crown and the nobility it is also true that at least two of those kings conducted what appear to have been ruthless campaigns against certain of the magnate families. At the time of James I's return from England in 1424 there were fifteen earldoms and one dukedom; but of those, only eight earldoms remained by the time of his murder in 1437, and only four of those were still with the original families. Significantly, James's main efforts seem to have been concentrated against members of his own Stewart family. However, this allowed other families to rise to even greater power. Among these the most spectacular success was that enjoyed by the already-powerful Black Douglas family, particularly after the reunification of the family's estates through the marriage of the future eighth earl with the Fair Maid of Galloway. It was against them that James II in his turn concentrated his greatest efforts, killing the eighth Earl of Douglas with his own hands in 1452, and confiscating the estates and titles of the ninth earl three years later. James III was so erratic in his dealings with his greater subjects that it is difficult to perceive any consistent attitude towards the magnates on his part, although it was two of the earls who led the rising which resulted in his death at Sauchieburn in 1488, suggesting – at the least – that his relationship with them was not all it might have been.

Moving on to another area of difficulty, English attacks and occupation of Scottish land were a continuing problem for the southern parts of the kingdom and, although there was less of the concentrated warfare that had characterised parts of the fourteenth century, there were still lengthy periods of hostility. Even while James I remained in English captivity, there were attacks on the towns of Berwick and Roxburgh in 1417, the English occupation of which was such a thorn in the Scottish flesh, though it was not to be until 1460 and 1461 that they were recaptured or surrendered to the Scots. Needless to say, every advantage was taken by the Scots of the opportunities offered by the English civil wars in the 1450s and 1460s, and Henry VI was afforded Scottish asylum until the signing of the long truce with Edward IV in 1464. Relationships again deteriorated in the last decades of the century, only to be restored around the time of the marriage of James IV and Margaret Tudor in 1503. The period after James's death at the battle of Flodden in 1513 was a particularly dangerous phase in Anglo-Scottish relations, and the situation was exploited by France in its own interests, first in trying to maintain peace with England between 1515 and 1517, and then in endeavouring to reopen hostilities between 1521 and 1524.

The snub to England represented by James V's failure to meet Henry VIII at York in 1541, followed by the disastrous Scottish defeat at Solway Moss and the king's death in 1542, opened a new phase of hostilities which was exacerbated by Henry's wish that Scotland should follow England in rejecting papal authority. The 'rough wooing' of Scotland in 1544, by which Henry tried to force the Scots to agree to the marriage of the young Queen Mary to Prince Edward under the terms of the Treaty of Greenwich, saw the devastation of much of the Borders and Lothian. There was further harrying and occupation of those same areas in 1547, when the English claimed to be endeavouring to liberate the Scots from the papal domination represented by the French-oriented policies of Mary of Guise and the recently murdered Cardinal Beaton.

These represented some of the most politically significant events in cross-Border affairs, but for those who lived on either side of the Border smaller-scale hostilities were a fact of life. This encouraged those with the means to defend themselves to do this as best they could, and there is a wider range of defensible house types in the Border areas than anywhere else. Sometimes castles in this area were built with royal encouragement. In 1481, for example, there was an ordinance for the defence against the English of castles near the Borders or on the coast,[2] and there was a further ordinance of 1535 which directed holders of land of a rental of over £100 to have fortified enclosures.[3] By contrast, however, in 1528 castle building in the Borders was prohibited without the consent of the King and Council.[4] An element of royal policy may also underlie some of the licenses granted for the building of castles, such as that of 1491 for the fortifying of Inchgarvie in the Forth, which was specifically referred to as providing protection against English and Danish pirates.[5] On the whole, however, castle building in these most vulnerable areas was apparently subject to few controls and was largely at the discretion of the individual landholder.

From all of the above there can be little doubt that late medieval Scotland was something less than a haven of peace and harmony. Nevertheless, it is now coming to be realised that unrest in Scotland at this time may have been little worse than in other countries. If it is the episodes of conflict between kings and magnates that are best remembered, it must also be recalled that the underlying loyalty of the nobility was sufficient to maintain the same dynasty on the throne throughout – and well beyond – the period covered by this book, despite the recurring dangers of royal minorities. It is also evident that most of the kings felt able to trust the majority of the magnates as their natural advisers – and as their deputies in outlying parts of the Kingdom – and were anxious to refill their ranks when they were depleted for any reason. Beyond this, it appears to be the case that many Scots saw real improvements in their lives. A growing concern for more even-handed government and justice, for example, is to be seen in such as James I's act of 1428, which endeavoured to give the lesser landholders a place in parliament,[6] and again in James V's efforts to set up a college of justice in 1532.[7] In addition, the architectural evidence indicates steadily improving standards of comfort and domestic convenience – although, of course, this particular evidence only relates to a small proportion of the population.

It must also be said that, while there were often cogent reasons for those who had possessions worth defending to make architectural provision for that defence, it is coming to be appreciated that there might be less alarming reasons for the belligerent appearance of the majority of residences dating from this period. For many patrons castles were built not simply to create a defensible shell for the owner's household, but also to present beholders with a clear statement of the standing, power and lineage of that owner. It is also worth remembering that, as artillery became increasingly effective as a siege weapon, very few could hope – or wish – to enclose themselves with the forms of defence that were being slowly developed against it. Indeed, the trappings of a symbolically defensive appearance may well have become more desirable as the reality of defensibility against major attack declined, and as late as 1632 Sir Robert Kerr said it was battlements that distinguished a castle from a pele.[8] That is not to say that a castle built by one landholder would not be defensible from the small-scale attack of another, for example. But such a castle would have had little hope against the siege weapons of the king or one of the greatest magnates and – like the plumage of some exotic bird – the appearance of aggression might be emphasised as the substance waned.

Changes in the way land was held may also have contributed to the late medieval increase of the construction of castles or houses of castellated appearance. Among the most important factors was the growing tendency of the crown to grant its lands as feu-holdings rather than as short-term tenancies, particularly after an act of 1503, since this gave much greater security of tenure.[9] The new feu-holders were evidently among those who saw the advantages of providing themselves with stone-built castles as an expression of their more secure status. It has, in fact, been argued that a greater sense of security and settled conditions were more likely to have encouraged the major investment represented by building a fortified residence than was the uncertainty of chronic disorder.[10] Seen in this light, the majority of licenses to build castles – which can only have been granted for a minority of the total number erected – could be indicators of a particular wish to obtain royal confirmation of the rights of the builder to his lands rather than as evidence of a state of emergency. Similarly, the way in which some castle builders chose to resign their lands to the king, only to have them regranted soon afterwards, may be interpreted as the sign of a desire to have possession of their holding formally confirmed in advance of the long-term investment represented by building operations.

The range of late medieval domestic and defensive architecture is varied. At the upper end of the scale great courtyard castles, with high walls and extensive ranges of accommodation, continued to be modified – or, less frequently, newly built – for the king and his greater magnates or prelates. These included such as Ballinbreich, Balvenie, Bothwell, Caerlaverock, Dirleton, Kildrummy, St Andrews, Spynie and Tantallon (see Figures 8.32, 1.8, 1.7, 1.11, 8.40, 8.9 and 1.10). Towards the end of the period a number of major fortifications aimed specifically at the problems of providing an effective defence by and from artillery were also engineered, and these will be dealt with in a separate chapter. At the same time, several splendid palaces were raised which not only delight us with their architectural extravagances, but also allow us an insight into the framework created for the complex etiquette and rituals of courtly life. The minimal defences provided around these palaces permit no doubt of the sense of security that Scotland's kings enjoyed within their own kingdom, while the high architectural qualities they display dispel any idea of Scotland being a cultural back-water. But by the later Middle Ages the great majority of residences for the magnates and lesser landholders had a tower-house as their nucleus, with a variety of other buildings disposed in one or more courtyards around them, depending on the wealth and standing of their builder.

A major interest of Scottish later medieval secular architecture lies in seeing how the planning of such tower-houses developed to meet increasingly sophisticated requirements (even if many of the more complex developments lie outside our period). It is also important to try to understand both how these towers were used and how their functions inter-related with those of the other buildings around them – of which a hall was usually the other important residential element. Those other buildings have more frequently been lost to sight but, at the risk of reading too much into the formal terminology employed, it is worth noting that licenses to build castles may indicate something of the likely range of structures. A good example of this is at Little Cumbrae, where in 1534 the license refers to a mansion with hall, chamber, kitchen, barn, byre and other offices; it could be of significance that it is not until a license of 1537 that permission is specifically given to build a tower, though there may be a number of reasons for this (see Figure 8.1e).[11] These are areas in which work is still actively in progress, however, and the outline offered in this chapter – which can consider only a small sample of the large numbers of tower-houses and other fortified houses that still survive – must be regarded as no more than provisional.

It should be said here that the way most castles at this period came to have a tower-house as their nucleus is not altogether the shift of emphasis that it might at first seem. It has been pointed out earlier – in looking at major castles such as Doune, Bothwell and Tantallon – that, by the later fourteenth century, the relationship between a tower-like lord's residence and an adjacent hall was not dissimilar from the relationship between tower-house and hall in a smaller castle (see pp. 14 and 15). It is therefore not surprising that the idea of providing a tower-house as the main unit of accommodation came to be found attractive at a number of even the greater castles. The idea may have been rendered more acceptable by the prestigious example of David's Tower as the core of the royal residence at Edinburgh Castle. Thus, at the castle of the bishops of Moray at Spynie, an enormous tower-house was added to the existing courtyard castle (see Figure 8.9).[12] Even at that mightiest of curtain wall castles, Kildrummy, the rectangular Elphinstone Tower was probably built to supplant the circular Snow Tower as the main residence.[13] Complementing this development, some castles planned with a tower-house as their main focus – such as Urquhart[14] – were provided with remarkably extensive courtyards entered through imposing gatehouses, so that the distinction between 'courtyard castles' and 'tower-house castles' loses much of any earlier significance.

TOWER-HOUSES AND FORTIFIED HOUSES OF RECTANGULAR PLAN

There is as yet no satisfactory chronology for the development of the tower-house in the fifteenth and earlier sixteenth centuries, although strides are being made towards this. Recent more systematic analysis of the documentary evidence for many sites on which tower-houses stand, in particular, has been of great value in showing that those sites have often been occupied for longer than had been thought.[15] (The temptation to assume that such documentation necessarily refers to the structures which happen to survive, however, has to be guarded against, unless the documentation is highly specific.) Where individual structures can now be dated more firmly, perhaps the greatest need is for more detailed regional studies to allow them to be placed within their wider architectural context.

In the Lowland areas, at least, the established view of the basic development of the tower-house type is probably still largely acceptable. The earlier examples are more frequently of simple plan, with only limited voiding of the relatively thick walls in order to create mural spaces; windows are usually relatively small and irregularly spaced; wall-head parapets are of slight projection from the wall face. The earlier tower-houses are also more likely to have their entrance above ground level. On all of these counts the rectangular towers at Balgonie, Castle Campbell and Crichton, for example, are likely to be relatively early (see Figures 8.27 and 8.2).

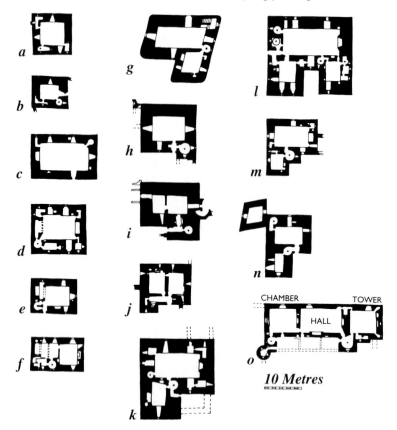

FIGURE 8.1   Plans of tower-houses: a. Moy (first floor); b. Breachacha (first floor); c. Threave (first floor);
d. Comlongan (first floor); e. Little Cumbrae (first floor); f. Saddell (first floor); g. Neidpath (entresol floor);
h. Rosyth (ground floor); i. Craigmillar (ground floor); j. Edzell (ground floor); k. Cessford (first floor);
l. Borthwick (first floor); m. Balvaird (first floor); n. Dundas (ground floor); o. Melgund (first floor).

As was said in discussing tower-houses of the later fourteenth century, under
normal circumstances such buildings were probably intended to hold little more than
the main core of living accommodation for the owner of the castle and his immediate
household (see p. 20). At ground-floor level provision was usually made for storage,
often with an entresol floor slotted below the barrel vault which generally covered
this level. On the first floor, above the vault, was the hall. This was the most 'public'
room of the owner's accommodation within the tower-house, but access to it was
probably increasingly limited at a period when there was a growing concern for
privacy; it must not be confused with the hall which was frequently built within the
courtyard and which was often more spacious. On the upper levels – including the
garret within the roof space – were bed chambers. In larger towers the upper floors
were frequently subdivided by timber partitions, either to provide more than one
chamber on each floor, or perhaps to create a lodging of inner and outer chamber for
the owner. Little original timber work has survived, but the roofs at Alloa in

FIGURE 8.2   Castle Campbell, the tower-house.

Clackmannanshire and Bardowie in Stirlingshire show that great efforts might be expended on those parts.

By the later fifteenth century, although the basic disposition outlined above continued, planning within the confines of rectangular towers was becoming more elaborate in the increasingly lavish provision of closets, corridors and stairs within the wall thickness. Architectural detailing was also tending to be more highly enriched, as is seen particularly in the treatment of the skyline. There, wall-head parapets might be carried on tiers of multiple corbelling, and be finished with carefully proportioned coping running around both the merlons and embrasures of the crenellation, while at the angles and mid-points rounded turret-like projections punctuate the progress of the parapet. The combination of such parapets with crow-stepped or coped gables, tall chimney stacks and eventually with pedimented dormer windows resulted in the type of silhouette that is so characteristic of late medieval and early modern secular work in Scotland, though the greatest achievements in this direction were to be outside our period, as at Elcho or Amisfield.

However, if the basic development sketched here is fundamentally acceptable, allowance must be made for the varying depth of patrons' purses, and for regional variations which resulted from a variety of economic, geological and social factors that are still only partly understood. As an illustration of this, a considerable proportion of the few tower-houses in the northern Highlands – such as Wick (see Figure 8.3), Forse, Dirlot and Braal – are as simple as they could possibly be, with no dressed stone to the doors and windows, and frequently without stone stairs, mural fireplaces or stone vaulting.[16] As a consequence, some of them have been dated to the twelfth or thirteenth centuries, though consideration of them as a local group suggests that their simplicity is more likely to be attributable to local preferences and to the difficulties of working the available materials. A later date for the group is supported by the way that Braal, for example, while being closely related to the other towers in its construction and simplicity, has the stairs and fireplaces which also relate it to late medieval tower-houses elsewhere in Scotland.

The tower-houses of the Western Highlands and Islands tended to be similarly rudimentary in their frequent absence of vaulting and mural fireplaces, though there

FIGURE 8.3   Castle of Old Wick.

were also identifiable local usages. These included a common preference for straight flights of mural stairs as well as – or instead of – spiral stairs, as at Kilchurn or Moy. This may have sprung partly from the intractability of many of the locally available building stones, from which the key-shaped stones required for a properly constructed spiral stair could not easily be cut. It must, however, also have been a matter of preference since Moy and Breachacha, for example, originally had straight flights between the lower storeys, but a narrow spiral flight between the upper floors (see Figures 8.1a and 8.1b). Occasionally Irish rather than Lowland Scottish influences can be detected, as at Dunollie near Oban, where the vaulting was evidently constructed on top of wicker-work mats rather than the short planks that were more usually placed over the centering. It is also worth noting that the castle depicted on the MacLeod tomb at Rodel has Irish stepped crenellations (see Figure 7.6).

On the Border, the continuing need to make some provision for the defence of personnel, livestock and possessions – which was a consequence both of periodic warfare and endemic cross-Border raiding – meant that defensible houses were desirable for a wider social spectrum than elsewhere. Thus, while the greater landholders tended to provide themselves with tower-houses comparable to those built elsewhere, towards the end of our period there was also a rather greater spread of lesser towers and of the smaller defensible houses known as bastles and pelehouses, some of which may have been built as a result of the act of 1535 (see p. 236).[17] The terminology is confusing since those two terms were probably originally interchangeable. Current usage in Scotland, however, tends to apply the term 'bastle' (or 'bastle-house') to substantial rectangular houses which may have a stair turret, and which usually have gables rising directly from the lower walls, without crenellated wall-walks at eaves level; they frequently have a vaulted basement. Pelehouses are usually smaller and rather barn-like houses, often with a forestair for access to the main level at first-floor height, above a basement where animals could be kept in emergency. The example at Mervinslaw is one of a group of such structures in the Roxburghshire parish of Southdean, which all appear to have been the work of the Oliver family.[18]

As might be expected, the spread of bastles and pelehouses tends to reflect the relative wealth of the areas in which they were built. It is a sign of the generally greater affluence of the Scottish than of the English Borders that pelehouses may have been more common in England, whereas it is the larger categories represented by tower-houses and bastles that were more widespread in Scotland. Within Scotland bastles appear to have had a more concentrated spread on the better agricultural lands. In 1544 the village of Lessuden, for example, was said to have no fewer than sixteen, though some of those were probably what we would now call pelehouses. Recent work has also identified a group of related structures extending up into Clydesdale, suggesting they were more widespread than was once assumed.[19] These latter examples appear to date chiefly to the years around 1600, but may perpetuate an earlier tradition.

On the basis of surviving evidence it seems that a rectangular plan remained most common for the full range of tower-house and fortified house types throughout all of the peripheral regions. But it is also true that a rectangular plan continued to be widely acceptable for major tower-houses in the Lowland areas up to the end of the Middle Ages and beyond. Considerable ingenuity was to be shown in developing new plan types that allowed greater flexibility of planning, and increasing numbers of tower-houses were to be of these more complex types. Nevertheless, a number of the finest fifteenth- and sixteenth-century tower-houses were still unaugmented rectangles, and towards the end of our period it may have been the case that some owners were already beginning to prefer the aesthetic qualities of a relatively symmetrical rectangular block.[20]

A particularly impressive rectangular tower-house is at Comlongan, in Dumfries-shire, of around the central decades of the fifteenth century (see Figures 8.1d and 8.4).[21] It was built for the Murrays of Cockpool, and later members of the family must have been grateful for its sturdy walls in the course of their long-running feud with Lord Maxwell, who was himself securely installed in Caerlaverock Castle. The basic arrangement is like that already seen in the tower-houses of the fourteenth century. The ground floor was embraced by a barrel vault, with provision for an entresol floor within the curve of the vault. At first-floor level was the hall, the main foci of which were a fine fireplace with shafted jambs, and an aumbry of decidedly ecclesiastical appearance, with a cusped arch flanked by pinnacles; it is possible that both fireplace and aumbry could be later insertions. Above the hall were two storeys of chambers, which were evidently subdivided by timber partitions on the evidence of the disposition of fireplaces and mural closets. The entrance was at ground-floor level, from which doors led either to the spiral stair which ran the full height of the tower, or into the rooms at that level; most visitors, of course, would ascend directly to the hall.

If Comlongan differs from its fourteenth-century predecessors in little of this, where it does differ is in the greater complexity of the additional provisions. There was a second stair running between the ground floor and the hall, presumably for discreet service access, and a small kitchen – which was largely taken up by the fireplace – was provided at the entrance end of the hall. However, the greatest advances are to be seen in the increased voiding of the wall thickness to provide supplementary spaces. Apart from the kitchen and second stair, there are no less than three small closets leading off the hall; from one of these there is access to a mural pit prison – though one wonders if such prisons did not spend more of their lives as strong rooms for the storage of family papers. The second floor had no less than five closets leading off the two chambers at this level.

At wall-head level of Comlongan there have been extensive alterations, and in its final stage there were open wall-walks behind crenellated parapets on only three sides, while on the fourth side was a narrow covered gallery. Similar wall-top galleries were eventually constructed at a number of other castles, including Bardowie in Stirlingshire and Neidpath (see Figure 1.14), where they are probably relatively late in date, and could have been provided as much for sheltered exercise as for defence. An additional interest of Comlongan is the well-preserved timber floor construction above the hall. Corbels carry wall plates down the long walls, which in turn support the principal

FIGURE 8.4 Comlongan Castle, from the north-west.

joists; those joists are themselves rebated for the secondary joists which carried the floor boards. Such construction reduced the risk of rotting at the beam-ends, but called for relatively sophisticated carpentry techniques.

The voiding of the core of the wall was taken even further at the Midlothian Castle of Elphinstone,[22] which was demolished in 1955 following damage from subsidence (see Figures 8.5 and 8.6). This tower was datable on heraldic grounds to around 1440, and was like Comlongan in a number of aspects – including the construction of a diminutive kitchen at one end of the hall and the subdivision of the upper floors. The provisions for access between the floors, however, were altogether more complex. A straight flight, covered by stepped vaults, created an imposing means of access from the entrance to the hall; from that level there were then two spiral stairs at diagonally opposite corners, as well as lesser stairs which were required to reach a number of intermediate levels. For anyone not acquainted with the interior, getting around it must have been a baffling process, though the main concern was presumably to allow separate access to the various lodgings and chambers.

FIGURE 8.5   Elphinstone Tower, before its demolition.

Perhaps the only tower-house which surpassed Elphinstone in complexity was Borthwick, which will be considered below along with tower-houses of more elaborate plan (see Figures 8.1l, 8.19 and 8.20). The possibility has been raised that a number of the same masons could have been involved at Comlongan, Elphinstone and Borthwick, and this may be supported by the existence of similar masons' marks at the first and last of those,[23] though this does not necessarily mean that the same master mason was responsible for the design of them all.

There is evidence in several parts of Scotland, however, that certain master masons were indeed responsible for groups of tower-houses. In Kirkcudbrightshire, it has been suggested that the same master designed the tower-houses of Cardoness, Garlies and Rusco, all of which date from the years around 1500 (see Figures 8.7 and 8.8).[24] There are particularly clear similarities of planning between Cardoness and what remains of Garlies, in the way that the entrance has a small guardroom to one side and the stair to the other, and additionally in the way the ground floor was divided into two unequal spaces. All three also have closely related fireplaces with triplet-shafted jambs. Among the other groups which have been recognised is one in Ayrshire that includes Little Cumbrae (referred to above in connection with licenses of 1524

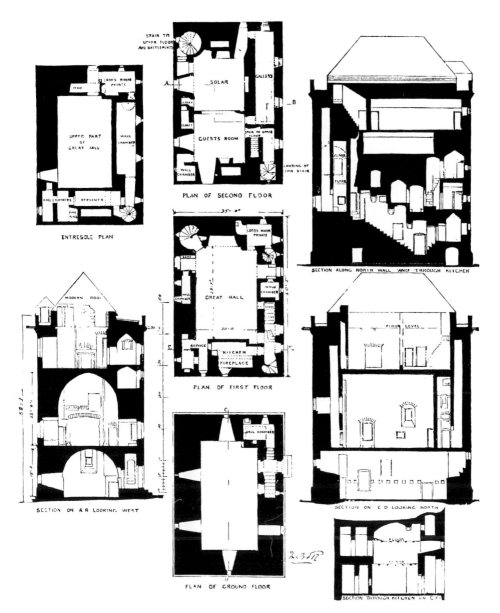

FIGURE 8.6 Elphinstone Tower, measured drawings showing the complexities of planning.

and 1537, see Figure 8.1e), Law, Fairlie and Skelmorlie.[25] Some members of this group have strikingly similar dimensions to each other, and all of them – like Comlongan – have a narrow kitchen at the entrance end of the hall. However, since they were all set within a few miles of each other near the mouth of the Firth of Clyde, it is by no means certain whether the similarities are attributable to the presence of the same master mason at each or whether, more simply, details of some were copied at others. Again, detailed local studies would help our understanding of the transfer of architectural ideas in such cases.

FIGURE 8.7 (*above*)   Cardoness Castle.
FIGURE 8.8 (*below*)   Cardoness Castle, the interior showing the first-floor hall and the subdivided chamber floor above it.

Tower-houses were by no means invariably the exclusive province of the lay landholders; two of the most impressive examples of rectangular plan type – at Spynie in Moray and Saddell in Kintyre – were built for bishops. That at Spynie, which seems to have been raised over the stump of an earlier circular tower at an angle of the curtain wall, may have been the largest ever built in Scotland (see Figure 8.9).[26] On heraldic evidence it is known to have been started by Bishop David Stewart (1462–76), and completed by his successor, William Tulloch (1477–82). It was later modified by Bishop Patrick Hepburn (1538–73), to whom are attributable the massive wide-mouthed gunholes in the lower walls. Above the vaulted two-compartment basement are five full storeys, which were embraced below the roof by a second barrel vault, and there would have been a garret in the roof space. The various floors were well supplied with mural closets, but especially so on the eastern side towards the

FIGURE 8.9   Spynie Castle, the tower-house.

courtyard, where the walls were reduced to two thin skins throughout most of their height in order to accommodate an unusually regular arrangement of closets. Unfortunately, the thin inner east wall and heavy vault at wall-head level proved to be a less than ideal combination.

The tower-house at Saddell was built after the estates of the Cistercian abbey of Saddell had been transferred to the bishopric of Argyll in 1507,[27] and the tower appears to have been finished by 1512, during the episcopate of David Hamilton (1497–1523). Around that time there was an abortive proposal that the cathedral of the diocese should be moved from Lismore to Saddell, which may have been a motive for the building of a new episcopal residence. Above a vaulted basement with an entresol the tower had three main floors and a garret, and there is a particular interest in the way those floors were planned.

Saddell is an unusually elongated tower-house because each floor was intended to be subdivided either by a stone cross wall below the vault or by timber partitions on the upper floors, although the planning details of the upper floors are no longer certain (see Figure 8.1f). To allow for separate access to the two parts of each floor, the spiral stair which interconnected the floors was placed not at a corner as was usual, but about a third of the length along one of the long walls, where it had to project into the internal spaces because of the relative thinness of the walls. The entrance opened directly on to this stair at entresol level. Thus, although the basic form of the tower was a simple rectangle, within that framework an ingenious arrangement was contrived which is not immediately evident externally. This must be understood as one aspect of a widening range of ingenuity in planning in the fifteenth and sixteenth centuries, a range that is to be seen even more obviously in some of the more complex plan-types developed for tower-houses.

DEVELOPMENTS ON THE TOWER-HOUSE THEME: MORE COMPLEX PLANS

With the exception of the circular example built around the mid-fifteenth century at Orchardton in Kirkcudbrightshire for a member of the Cairns family (see Figure 8.10),[28] the more complex tower-houses generally consisted of a rectangular core around which other elements might be grouped in a variety of combinations. It would be over-simplistic and misleading to identify a progressive evolution of increasingly complex plan types but, as already indicated (see p. 22), probably the earliest variant on the basic rectangle was the L-shaped plan. In this a smaller rectangular wing, or jamb, usually projected at the end of one of the longer sides of the main rectangle, and in the earlier versions one side of the wing was generally set flush with the side of the main block. Versions of this variant had been developed by the later fourteenth century, as at David's Tower in Edinburgh Castle and at Neidpath (see p. 22 and Figures 1.14 and 8.1g). A traditional explanation for the development of this plan type is that it allowed the entrance to the tower to be afforded the additional protection of fire either from the flanking wing or from the main body of the tower, depending on its position. In many cases the positioning of shot-holes suggests that this was a factor, though it is likely the greater versatility of planning which resulted

FIGURE 8.10   Orchadton Tower.

from breaking free of the straitjacket of a rectangular plan weighed just as heavily with patrons.

At its simplest the wing contained the main spiral stair of the tower. This was welcome, because a combination of a wish for more spacious stairs and a tendency for the wall thickness of tower-houses to be reduced meant that it was increasingly difficult to find space for the stair within a corner of the tower without impinging on the interior spaces to an unacceptable extent. At the later fifteenth-century Stewart family castle of Rosyth, in Fife, the narrow wing is of just sufficient projection to allow the stair a little extra breathing space (see Figures 8.1h and 8.11);[29] but it was usual in such cases for the stair to be more completely relegated to the wing. This was the case at another Fife castle, at Scotstarvit, which was first built for a member of the Inglis family at some date after the estates had been confirmed to them in 1487 (see Figure 8.12).[30] Even at far grander castles, such as Edzell in Angus, which was probably built in the early sixteenth century for Sir David Lindsay, the wing contained no more than the stair (See Figures 8.1j and 8.31).[31] But in many towers the wing instead contained additional chambers; in this situation there was scope for making them larger than mural closets within the main body of the tower, and they could also be set at different levels from the main rooms and given lower ceiling heights appropriate for their smaller size.

Neidpath had chambers rather than stairs in its wing, and this was to be the case with many later L-plan towers, as at Craigmillar on the southern outskirts of Edinburgh (See Figures 8.1i, 8.13 and 8.26e).[32] Within the wing there, at ground-floor level there is a short passage leading to the spiral stair at the end, while the entrance to the basement of the main block is to one side of that passage. However, at the upper levels the stair moves progressively sideways, leaving the wing largely free for chambers. The chamber off the first-floor hall was used as a kitchen for at least part of its life. The date of Craigmillar's tower-house is uncertain; but it was built after the estates had been granted in 1374 to the Preston family, since their arms are set above the entrance doorway, and construction around the earlier fifteenth century is most likely.

In reaction to earlier interpretations which saw defensibility as the leading factor in tower-house design, it is currently fashionable to minimise the importance of

FIGURE 8.11   Rosyth Castle.

FIGURE 8.12   Scotstarvit Tower.

defensive criteria, and they certainly cannot have been of such over-riding concern as was once thought. At the time that Craigmillar was built, however, defence was still a factor, since the tower was placed with its wing towards a steep drop. Thus, those who approached the castle were made to pass between its main block and the drop in order to reach the doorway at the base of the latter, and part of the access path was intersected by a gap in the rock which would have been crossed by a retractable timber bridge. Nevertheless, the planning of the internal domestic arrangements clearly received as much care as the defensive arrangements.

FIGURE 8.13   Craigmillar Castle, the tower-house from the south, with the later curtain wall to its right.

The range of ways in which the relationship between main block and wing could be handled is almost as great as the number of towers of L-plan type, and no more can be attempted here than to indicate some of the possible changes on the basic theme. One dated example is at Dundas,[33] near South Queensferry, where the castle was probably first built after the grant of a license to James Dundas of 1424, which specified, incidentally, that it was to be crenellated in the manner that was usual in the kingdom of Scotland (See Figure 8.14).[34] The entrance was directly into the main block, at the junction with the wing, and the stair up to the hall at first-floor level was at the junction of the two. Above that point, however, access was by a stair at another corner of the main block, emphasising the distinction between the hall and the more private upper chambers; this left the wing free for use as chambers, each of which was vaulted. Construction of the tower was probably largely complete by 1440, when the Dundas family turned its architectural attentions to the building of the nearby Carmelite friary at Queensferry as the other aspect of its territorial lordship (see p. 136 and Figure 4.6).

The planning of the splendid Borders tower-house of Cessford was even more complex, though there it is likely that earlier work was embodied (see Figures 8.1k and 8.15).[35] The estates were granted to Andrew Kerr in 1446, and the final state of the tower must post-date that, but it is possible it incorporates structures built when the lands were owned by the Sinclair family. There are two entrances, one into the ground-floor level of the main block, and the other at first-floor level of the wing; both lead by dog-legged passages on to the spiral stair at the junction of the two parts, which rises the full height of the building. A second spiral stair led from the first-floor hall in the main block to an upper chamber in the wing, even though this chamber was also accessible from the main stair. A remarkable feature of this tower is its enormously thick walls, which are even more massively constructed than some late artillery defences.

FIGURE 8.14   Dundas Castle.

FIGURE 8.15   Cessford Castle.

Another impressive late medieval L-plan tower is at Auchindoun, on a remote hillside in Banffshire.[36] It is traditionally said to have been built by Thomas Cochrane, the same favourite of James III to whom was attributed the great hall of Stirling Castle (see p. 304), and who was probably murdered at Lauder Bridge in 1482. Whether or not Cochrane was indeed responsible – and there must be real doubt about that – a date of before 1482 is certainly acceptable for what remains of the tower. Any idea of the prime function of the wing being to provide protective cover for the entrance here is contradicted by the way the main entrance was apparently in one of the end walls, as had earlier been the case at Neidpath. The arrangement of the stairs was also unusual at Auchindoun, since there were two of them – at the corners of the main block away from the jamb – though there was possibly also a mural service stair from ground- to first-floor levels.

What gives Auchindoun even greater architectural interest, is the covering of the hall and flanking chamber by quadripartite vaulting, that over the hall being ribbed

FIGURE 8.16   Auchindoun Castle, looking into the hall of the tower-house from its collapsed west end.

but that over the chamber being simply groined (See Figure 8.16). Rather curiously, at the angles of the hall vault there is a break above springing level marked by a horizontal string course, beyond which is a change in the arc of the ribs. One of the few Scottish parallels for this feature is in the choir vaults at St Andrews Cathedral as reconstructed after the fire of 1378, which also had a horizontal string above the springing – albeit without the change in curvature beyond that point. The vaulting must have made the hall an impressive space, for which there could have been few equals. The rib-vaulted hall of the tower-house at the monastic grange of Mauchline in Aryshire – built for Abbot Hunter of Melrose (1444–71) – offers one approximately contemporary parallel (see Figure 3.38); and the hall at Craigie in Ayrshire another.[37] But most other examples of such vaulting in a domestic context are either earlier – as at Tulliallan in Fife – or rather later – as at Balbegno in Kincardineshire and Towie Barclay and Delgaty in Aberdeenshire.[38] One of the few parallels for the groined vault over Auchindoun's chamber is the much more impressive vault over the hall at Alloa in Clackmannanshire, which is now largely hidden by later work.

The problem of providing adequately spacious circulation between the floors without impinging on the spaces within either the main block or the wing was solved particularly effectively at Balvaird Castle, near Glenfarg in Perthshire.[39] The heraldry above the entrance indicates this tower was built after the marriage of Sir Andrew Murray to the heiress of Balvaird, Margaret Barclay, which places it around 1500, and probably within the first quarter of the sixteenth century. At Balvaird the stair was housed in an extra projection within the re-entrant angle of the main block and wing, thus creating a stepped plan, and the entrance was placed at the base of this stair tower (see Figures 8.1m and 8.17). A tower of rather similar plan was built a few miles to the north-east of Balvaird at Creich for the Betoun family, possibly at a date before 1553. In devising such a plan the builders were only going one stage beyond a building like Glamis, in Angus, where the tower built for the widow of the first Lord Glamis – before 1484 – had the stair partly extruded into the angle. But at Balvaird and Creich there is a logic and spaciousness underlying the design which anticipates the more sophisticated planning of the later sixteenth century.

Balvaird is also remarkable for its completeness up to the wall-head, where there is a crenellated parapet with open rounds at the angles and mid-points, a cap-house over the stair like a miniature tower-house in its own right, and a full array of chimney stacks – all of which gives interest to the silhouette. There are also some handsome internal fittings, although – as at the Murray house at Comlongan, already discussed (see Figure 8.4) – the lack of fit between the various parts of the elaborately carved aumbry in the hall may point to its having been brought from elsewhere, possibly around the time that the adjacent gatehouse range was added in 1567. An ingenious feature is the water basin in the hall, the waste from which flushed the adjacent latrine.

Within the period that concerns us here, rectangular plans and variations on an L-plan were to be most common for tower-houses. But they were not the only ones. At Crookston, in Renfrewshire, within the earthworks of a twelfth-century castle, an extraordinary tower was built which had smaller tower-like wings at all four of its angles (see Figure 8.18).[40] Archaeological evidence shows it was constructed around

FIGURE 8.17   Balvaird Castle, the tower-house from the south-east.

1400, at the time that it was in the possession of the Stewarts of Darnley; they claimed kinship with the royal house, which may explain the elaboration of the design. In some ways this arrangement shows similarities on a more compact scale with Hermitage Castle in its final state (see p. 14 and Figure 1.9), and there may also be parallels with earlier towers in the English Borders – such as Dacre in Cumberland or Langley in Northumberland. But Crookston must have given the impression of a more unified design than any of those, and the calibre of the work is particularly high, especially as seen in the parallel-ribbed pointed barrel vaulting which covers the ground floor.

    Another 'one-off' tower-house forms the magnificent core of Borthwick Castle in Midlothian,[41] which was built following the grant of a license to the future Lord Borthwick in 1430.[42] (The same Lord Borthwick built a family aisle on the flank of the nearby parish church (see p. 229 and Figure 7.13), and as so often we see that a family church or chapel was as important an expression of status as a family castle.) At this tower-house there are two wings, projecting symmetrically from each end of the westward long face of the main core, resulting in a C-shaped plan (see Figures 8.11 and 8.19). Borthwick is an immensely powerful essay in tower design, with

FIGURE 8.18 Crookston Castle.

soaring walls capped by machicolations, and it is completely surrounded by a courtyard wall. If the design of any tower-house could be regarded as having been chiefly conditioned by military requirements it should be Borthwick. And yet, if so, why are the two wings placed on the same side of the tower, so that each negates any enfilading potential that the other might have had? By the same token, why is the entrance on the flank of the castle rather than between the wings? One is led to conclude that it was so important to overwhelm the beholder with the apparent might of the castle and its owner that purely strategic considerations were not allowed to detract from the architectural composition. Nevertheless, Borthwick would have been a hard nut to crack, with its thick walls and massively vaulted construction, while its small windows and first-floor entrance would also have made forced entry difficult.

Internally, the planning of Borthwick is a virtuoso performance, with a labyrinth of rooms at different levels in order to take advantage of the differing scales of the main block and wings (See Figure 8.19). Such complexities of planning hint at an equally complex ordering of the household it was designed for and, although we now know nothing of the details, this was certainly a time when we find expanding provision of lodgings in the major castles. Access between all of the various levels meant there were no less than five spiral stairs and one straight flight, but these were contrived so that only certain levels were interconnected by each. This would have

FIGURE 8.19 (*right*)   Borthwick Castle, the cross-section
through the main block and one of the wings.

FIGURE 8.20 (*below*)   Borthwick Castle, the hall.

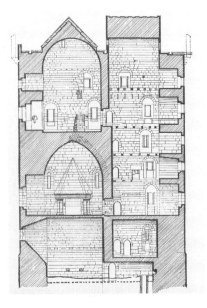

been mainly for convenience of access but it would also offer advantages for security. The finest internal space was the hall, which rose through two storeys and was covered by a pointed barrel vault; as was usual by this date, it had a great canopied fireplace in the end wall as the main focus (see Figure 8.20). Several of the other internal fittings had detailing that would not be out of place in a collegiate church, yet without the religious references of the aumbry at Balvaird. They include an arched aumbry in the hall, and a mural water basin within what must have been the screens passage at the entrance end of the hall.

Among other permutations on the tower-house theme is the cross-shaped massing of Denmylne in Fife,[43] which was possibly built after 1541, when it was formally granted to Patrick Balfour on condition that he built a hall here.[44] The cross plan results from the way the stair turret is placed towards the middle of one of the long sides, with a latrine projection corresponding to it on the other. This arrangement followed from the tower being divided into two chambers on each floor and, as at Saddell, it was decided that the stair should straddle the division to provide separate access to each. As will be evident from what has already been said, separate access to each chamber, and individual provision of a latrine and fireplace, were becoming more important as one aspect of a growing concern for the privacy and convenience of those fortunate enough to live in tower-houses.

Before closing this discussion of the range of planning to be found in late medieval tower-houses, brief reference must be made to a plan type in which wings were placed at diagonally opposite corners of the main block and thus created a Z-shaped arrangement. For those who wish to see military needs as dictating the design of tower-houses, the plan can be justified for the enfilading fire it permitted along all faces of the main block. This must have been a consideration behind the design of the forbidding but unfinished castle of Noltland in Orkney, which was built for Gilbert Balfour after he had acquired the estates in 1560, and before his forfeiture in 1571.[45] Balfour was described by Knox as a man with 'neither fear of God nor love of virtue', and his castle conveys that same impression, with its astonishing display of gunholes in the outer walls (see Figure 8.21). Even so, it did contain a magnificent stair in one of the wings, leading up to a spacious first-floor suite of rooms lit by large windows on the courtyard side. Most Z-plan castles were altogether more domestic in appearance than Noltland, however, and the convenience of having smaller chambers in the wings at each end of the main block, which could be separately reached by different staircases, must have been a great attraction.

The majority of Z-plan towers fall outside the period of this book, but one example which could be within it is at Colliston in Angus. It is dated by inscription to 1553, and bears the arms of John Guthrie, to whom the lands were conveyed by Cardinal Beaton in 1545.[46] Guthrie's wife, Isobel Ogilvie – incidentally – is said to have been an object of some interest to the cardinal, though there seems to be no support for this notion.[47] Despite major alterations in 1620, which gave the house a more monolithic massing than first intended, it can still be seen to have been characteristic of the type. At diagonally opposite corners of a rectangular main block were

FIGURE 8.21   Noltland Castle, the side towards the courtyard.

three-quarter round towers with square cap-houses carried on multiple corbelling.
The hall at first-floor level was reached by a spacious stair in one of the towers, above
which the upper chambers were reached by one or more smaller spiral stairs corbelled
out in the angle between main block and wings. The lower walls were pierced by
wide-mouthed gunholes showing that, although defence was not perhaps the main
factor, it was still a consideration.

SECONDARY AUGMENTATION OF TOWER-HOUSES

It has been said in discussing the earlier tower-houses that, under normal circumstances, they were probably not intended as more than the residential accommodation
for the immediate household of the owner or his representative. Yet, as ideas of
domestic comfort and privacy expanded, or as families grew in social consequence –
both of which led to a need for more complex provision of lodgings – some
tower-houses came to be deemed inadequate for that purpose. It is one of the
fascinations of the type to see how individual examples could be adapted to meet
changed needs over an extended period; indeed, behind the walls of many eighteenth-
and nineteenth-century country houses – from Dunrobin in the north-east to Culzean
in the south-west – a tower-house still forms the nucleus. Even within the later Middle
Ages and early modern periods, inventiveness was being shown in enlarging or
augmenting existing structures.

At its simplest this could be achieved by adding a wing. At Dundas, in West Lothian, a block was added to the L-plan castle built about 1424 at the corner where there was already a stair (see Figures 8.1n and 8.14).[48] It contained a kitchen at the level of the hall, and additional chambers at the upper levels. The entire wall-head is now finished by a machicolated parapet, which may have been constructed at the time of the wing's addition, and which gives unity to the whole building. A similar addition was made to the originally rectangular tower-house of Levan in Renfrewshire, with a more spacious stair being constructed at the junction of the two.[49] As at Dundas, architectural unity was given to the expanded structure by the construction of a wall-head parapet carried on an enriched corbel table. From such cases we see that considerable efforts might be made to give an enlarged tower an appearance of architectural homogeneity, and this means it is not always clear when an earlier building is embodied within an enlarged structure.

One of the most common ways of enlarging a tower-house, or of making a hall-house into a tower-house, was by heightening it, and the latter may have been the case at Aberdour in Fife. Several of the most striking examples of the heightening of a tower-house fall outside the period of this book, as at Spedlins in Dumfriesshire, Preston in East Lothian and Niddrie in West Lothian. However, there is a particularly intriguing case at the Bruce castle of Clackmannan, where the small fourteenth-century tower was not only heightened, but a second tower of greater height was added against it in the later fifteenth century (see Figure 8.22).[50] Again, architectural cohesion was attained by the construction of a machicolated parapet around the top of the whole structure. (Unfortunately, structural cohesion was less easily attained, and a great part of the masonry at the junction of the two sections fell as a result of modern subsidence, and has only recently been reconstructed.) Doubling-up of tower-houses – but without the heightening of the original structure – was also carried out elsewhere – as at Falside in East Lothian.[51]

In other cases one tower-house might be augmented by a second one. This was what was done at Huntingtower, on the outskirts of Perth, where it has been suggested the reason could have been that in 1480 the estates were divided between two legitimised sons of the first Lord Ruthven (see Figure 8.23).[52] There a gatehouse was heightened to create a rectangular tower-house, and a separate L-planned tower-house was built to its west; the two towers were later joined up in the seventeenth century. It may be added that within the eastern of the towers is some of the earliest painted decoration in any Scottish tower-house (see Figure 8.24). Elsewhere towers might be duplicated without such complications of inheritance, as at Cramalt in Selkirkshire, where excavation has shown there were two towers set in an almost arbitrary relationship with each other.[53] Macduff's Castle in Fife is another example of a castle which eventually had what were in essence two tower-houses, but there the towers were carefully linked into a unified composition by the gatehouse range that ran between them (see Figure 8.25).[54] In such a case the appearance may have shown similarities with a fourteenth-century courtyard castle of the type seen at St Andrews, in which there were towers at the angles with ranges extending between them.

FIGURE 8.22   Clackmannan Tower, before its partial collapse and subsequent rebuilding.

THE PLANNING OF COURTYARDS AND THE WIDER SETTING OF CASTLES

Tower-houses have tended to survive better than other buildings within a castle. This is because they were often more substantially constructed, and were less easily replaced than the associated structures as fashions and ideas of domestic comfort changed. However, we may assume that in residences of any pretensions the other accommodation would eventually have included at least a hall range. The function of this range in relation to the tower is not always clear. When it stood by itself it was perhaps intended as a grander and more public room than the smaller hall in the tower, which was essentially a part of the owner's private lodging. But it was often the main element in what seems to have been a lodging, with a chamber at one end and sometimes with a kitchen either at the other end or on a lower floor. In such cases the owner may have been providing himself with more spacious accommodation than

FIGURE 8.23 (*above*) Huntingtower, the
two tower-houses were later joined up and
provided with larger windows.

FIGURE 8.24 (*right*) Huntingtower, the
painted ceiling in the first-floor hall of the east
tower.

FIGURE 8.25   Macduff's Castle, the two tower-houses before the demolition of that on the east.

was possible within the tower, and which was also more convenient and imposing in being set out on one level.

In a number of cases it is possible construction of the hall range preceded that of the tower – as perhaps at Little Cumbrae, if the sequence of licenses is any reflection of the order of building.[55] Indeed, at some castles a tower-house may never have been intended, or may only have been added at a much later stage. Elsewhere the hall may have been roughly contemporary with the tower, as at the modest mid-fifteenth-century Pringle residence of Smailholm, in Roxburghshire. Excavations there have shown that the small courtyard on the rock summit contained a ground-floor hall and chamber in a range on one side, and a kitchen block on the other,[56] and it is likely that represented the usual variety of accommodation in a castle of such scale (see Figure 8.26a). But it seems probable that in most cases the hall was only added at a later stage. At Plean, in Stirlingshire, there is what must have been a spacious first-floor hall and chamber above a kitchen, built at right angles to a rather diminutive tower-house; this was probably a sixteenth-century addition to fifteenth-century tower.

One of the most impressive hall and chamber ranges to have survived within the same complex as a tower-house is at Dean Castle near Kilmarnock.[57] It was almost certainly built for the first Lord Boyd in the time of his brief period of high royal favour under James II and James III, and before his fall from power and execution in 1469. Above a ground floor – which, as at Plean, housed the kitchen and other offices

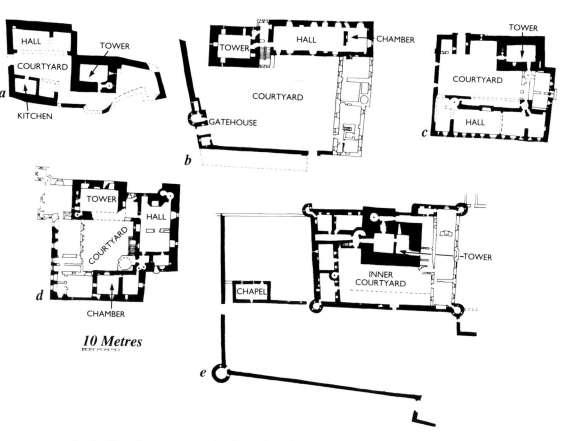

FIGURE 8.26 Plans of tower-houses within their wider architectural setting: a. Smailholm Castle; b. Balgonie Castle; c. Castle Campbell; d. Crichton Castle; e. Craigmillar Castle.

— was a large hall, with a chamber block at the end furthest away from the tower-house. It was restored by James Richardson for Lord Howard de Walden in 1933–7. A similar hall range was built at Balgonie Castle in Fife, adjacent to the earlier tower (see Figures 8.26b and 8.27).[58] There it can probably be linked with works being carried out in 1496 by Sir Robert Lundie, Lord High Treasurer of Scotland. Such very grand ranges could accommodate the most important visitors whom the owner was ever likely to receive, and they were the precursors of the 'state apartments' of the seventeenth century. Nevertheless, this does not preclude their being used by the owner under normal circumstances, since he would give up his own lodgings to one who was of higher social standing.

Another hall range built by a landholder who moved in the highest circles is at Castle Campbell in Clackmannanshire (see Figures 8.26c and 8.28).[59] There it is possible the designer was one of the royal masons, since the range is strikingly similar to James IV's own lodging in Stirling Castle, now known as the King's Old Building (see p. 315 and Figure 10.13). The hall, with chamber blocks at each end — one of which could have contained a kitchen — was raised on vaulted cellars, and

FIGURE 8.27   Balgonie Castle, the tower-house and adjacent hall range, with the later stair wing between them.

reached by a spiral stair capped by an octagonal superstructure and flanked by lean-to corridors. Since the King's lodging at Stirling was being completed by Walter Merlioun in 1496, the Castle Campbell hall range is likely to have been built by the second Earl of Argyll, who succeeded his father in 1493, and fell at Flodden in 1513.[60]

The scale of – and relationship between – tower-house, hall range and other structures varied, depending on the physical constraints of the site and its existing buildings, as well as the tastes and wealth of the patron. At Balgonie, the tower and hall range were grouped along one side of a very large courtyard which gives a sense of great openness, though there were other ranges round its perimeter, one of which survives in modified form. At Castle Campbell the tower and hall range face each other across a much smaller courtyard, which also had buildings along its other sides, and there must have been a greater sense of enclosure.

This is even more the case at Crichton Castle in Midlothian, where the same Lord

FIGURE 8.28   Castle Campbell, the stair tower of the hall and chamber range.

Crichton who founded the nearby collegiate church (see p. 168) built two ranges at right angles to each other for a hall and chambers to the south and west of his family's small tower-house (see Figures 8.26d and 8.29).[61] The result of this operation is a tightly planned and inward-looking mass of building, with walls capped by machico-lated parapets. Within this the courtyard is reduced to little more than a light-well, and it might almost be thought from the outside that the whole complex block had originally been roofed over. Yet, inside those walls, as might be expected in the residence of so powerful a patron, the accommodation was spacious and carefully detailed. A handsome forestair led up to the first-floor hall entrance, within which a large fireplace flanked by multiple-shafted jambs was the main emphasis. After the addition of the diamond-rusticated north range around 1585, the courtyard acquired something of the feel of the *cortile* of an Italian *palazzo*, though there may have been a little of this feeling even before then.

In some cases the tower and hall range were so closely inter-related that, despite their differing dates, they might appear to have belonged to a unified design, as perhaps at Balgonie. Hardly surprisingly, in due course castles were to be built in which they were indeed both part of a single design, and the earliest of those may have been at Melgund, in Angus.[62] The barony of North Melgund was acquired in 1543 by

FIGURE 8.29   Crichton Castle, the hall and chamber ranges on the west and north sides of the courtyard.

Cardinal David Beaton, and his mistress – Marion Ogilvy – lived there until her death in 1575.[63] The castle was started soon after Beaton's acquisition of the lands, and the arms of both the cardinal and his mistress are displayed on the structure. The main building is a block of over 31 metres in length, with what is essentially an L-plan tower at its western end (see Figures 8.10 and 8.30). The stair in the wing of that tower also served the adjacent hall, which was raised above a vaulted basement and had a chamber at its east end. A lean-to range ran along the hall and chamber on their northern side towards the courtyard, with a second stair at its eastern end. The principal rooms were, of course, at first-floor level, and from the position of the hall dais it seems the cardinal's own chambers were at the far end of the hall from the tower. The standard of workmanship throughout is very high, though the bundled-shaft jambs of the hall fireplace are perhaps more curious than beautiful.

    Many of the hall ranges discussed above must have presented a rather similar appearance to earlier free-standing hall-houses, such as those at Rait in Nairn and Morton in Dumfriesshire and there is probably far greater continuity between the two groups of structures than is generally appreciated. This similarity must have been

FIGURE 8.30   Melgund Castle, the south face.

even more marked in a series of hall and chamber ranges which, like some of those
earlier hall-houses, were given additional éclat by the provision of a three-quarter
round tower at one angle. There was probably such a range on the east side of the
courtyard at Huntly Castle in Aberdeenshire, where the even grander later building
is assumed to incorporate the 'new wark' built by the fourth Earl of Huntly.[64] That
range is thought to have been largely finished in time for the visit of Queen Mary of
Guise to Huntly in 1556, but it is now difficult to extricate the original structure from
the sumptuous remodelling for the first Marquis of Huntly, of around 1606. There
may have been a similar building at Edzell Castle, where the gatehouse range – with
a hall and chamber at first-floor level – was probably built in 1542 by the ninth Earl
of Crawford (see Figure 8.31).[65] It is unclear, however, whether the existing corner
tower was erected with that range, or with an even larger hall range added at right
angles to it in the later part of the sixteenth century.

     Within a castle, hall and chamber ranges could be largely independent structures,
and they are sometimes found as additions to older castles where a tower-house was
never built. At the stronghold of the Comyn family at Balvenie, the fourth Earl of
Atholl remodelled the buildings on the east side of the rectangular courtyard, and the
most imposing feature of this was a first-floor hall and chamber above the entrance
passage, with an inner chamber in a massive tower at the north-east angle (see Figure
8.32).[66] Work was started in about 1550, and was sufficiently complete by 1562 for
Mary Queen of Scots to be able to stay there. The lower walls of the range and tower

FIGURE 8.31 Edzell Castle, the entrance front. The tower-house is to the right of this view.

were amply supplied with wide-mouthed gunholes, and the potential for enfilading fire from the widely projecting tower must certainly have been a consideration; indeed, that tower has something of the character of a blockhouse (see p. 295). There were also heavy metal grilles on the windows and an outer line of defence to keep unwanted visitors at bay. Nevertheless, while not denying the defensive elements, the large outward-looking windows of the first floor, and the lavish architectural detail which includes what seems to have been a series of charming oriel windows at second-floor level, leave no doubt that the desire for architectural impact was of similar importance as the pursuit of defensibility.

There is something of the same feeling in the bishop's palace at Kirkwall in Orkney.[67] That residence was extensively remodelled by Bishop Robert Reid (1541–58), who had already raised fine houses for himself at the abbey of Kinloss and the priory of Beauly (see p. 123). As at Balvenie, the defensive capability of the stout walls and carefully positioned gunholes in the angle tower at Kirkwall must have been a comfort to a hard-pressed bishop at times of emergency;[68] but, again, the large windows and elegant detailing suggest that just as much comfort was derived from the high architectural qualities of the residence (see Figure 8.33). The possibly French-inspired *chemin-de-ronde* treatment of the wall-head, with a covered wall-walk encircling a cap-house, seems to have been particularly aimed at impressing the beholder with the cosmopolitan outlook of its occupant, who had studied at Paris and taken part in embassies abroad.

FIGURE 8.32 Balvenie Castle, the entrance front.

Space will not allow further discussion of the buildings that might be found within the courtyard of a tower-house, but there must be brief reference to the range of treatment of the enclosing walls. This varied according to the scale of the castle itself, but in general such walls were not particularly substantial except where the walls predate the tower-house itself – as at Lochleven in Fife or Spynie in Moray (see Figures 8.36 and 8.38). Nevertheless, there are cases where the enclosing walls were both high and strong, as at Roslin in Midlothian. The castle built there in the mid-fifteenth century, in the valley below the collegiate church, was on a scale that left no doubt of the importance of the Sinclair family which it housed.[69] On the east was a steep drop to the River North Esk, which meant the wall on that side need rise to no great height above the level of the courtyard, and it was there that a five-storeyed residential range was later added against the cliff face, between about 1597 and 1622. But to the west the site was overlooked from higher ground, and an unusually strong wall was constructed on that side as part of the fifteenth-century works, running from a tall gatehouse at the north end to a tower-house at the south. The drawings prepared to illustrate Father Hay's family history of the Sinclairs, written in about 1700, show the tower-house as circular and the curtain walls as being free of any courtyard buildings, though they are probably wrong on both scores.[70] However, they do illustrate the most remarkable feature of this wall, which is that it is corrugated by a sequence of tapered buttresses. Parallels with the buttressed walls at Caerphilly of the late thirteenth century, or with those at French fortified residences such as Farcheville of around the 1290s or the episcopal residence at Albi, show that the wall

FIGURE 8.33   Kirkwall, the tower of the bishop's palace.

is not unique, even if they cannot explain why such an unusual form should have been adopted in this particular case.

Other castles planned to have unusually large-scale courtyard walls include Rosyth,[71] where the stump projecting from the stair-wing of the tower-house shows that a wall of surprising proportions was planned (see Figure 8.11). It would probably have been of a similar scale as the wall of the rectangular enclosure wrapped around Craigmillar Castle in Midlothian, which has three-quarter round towers to reinforce its angles and a machicolated parapet at the wall-head (see Figures 8.26e and 8.34).[72] The wall at Craigmillar is traditionally said to have been dated by inscription to 1427, but a date after the middle of that century is far more likely from the inverted key-hole shot-holes in the towers. Apart from this wall, Craigmillar offers a particularly good illustration of how the castle of a major landholder might be progressively enveloped by a series of courtyards within which space could also be found for pleasure grounds and gardens. The main ranges of additional lodgings flanked the tower-house within the inner courtyard, but an outer courtyard was added in 1549, containing walled gardens, together with other buildings including a handsome little chapel. There is also a decorative fish-pond in the valley behind, which is shaped like a letter 'P' in reference to the Preston family who owned the castle; it must have been the centre-piece of an elaborate garden layout (see Figure 8.35).

FIGURE 8.34 (*above*)   Craigmillar Castle, the curtain wall.
FIGURE 8.35 (*below*)   Craigmillar Castle, the ornamental pond.

The circular towers at the corners of the curtain wall at Craigmillar belong within a long-established tradition in military architecture, and were to have parallels at several other fifteenth- and sixteenth-century castles. Two larger ones were built at angles of the earlier courtyard wall at Lochleven[73] around the 1540s, for example, one of which survives (see Figure 8.36). Apart from its function of enfilading the walls, the Lochleven tower had residential accommodation on its upper floors, the first and second floors forming a single lodging, with a separate chamber reached from the wall-walk above. The basement had a water intake from the loch and may have been used for storing water. Compared with the angle towers of a late thirteenth-century castle such as Kildrummy, or the far more purposeful artillery blockhouses that were to be built at St Andrews (see p. 295), such towers appear rather flimsy, but by this stage they were an important part of the imagery of any self-respecting piece of castellated architecture.

FIGURE 8.36   Lochleven Castle, the surviving angle tower added to the curtain wall.

A similar tower dominates one end of the entrance front of the curtain wall of another mid-fifteenth-century Midlothian castle, that of the Ramsay family at Dalhousie, where it is set close to the gatehouse (see Figure 8.37).[74] In the design of the gatehouse, which has turrets at the upper angles and provision for a drawbridge within an arched recess, there are echoes of the later fourteenth-century gatehouses at Dirleton and Tantallon (see pp. 13 and 16, and Figures 1.7 and 1.10). The relationship between the gate and the round angle tower is also comparable to the former. However, comparison reinforces the first impression that, while the defences at Dalhousie and Craigmillar would be of some use in the case of an attack by an offended neighbour, they were not designed as serious artillery defences. They were, like the angle towers at Balvenie and Edzell, part of the architectural vocabulary of a landholder who wished there to be no doubt about his right to surround himself with such trappings. The same is true of a number of other gatehouses of this period, including the rather endearing example at Spynie, which has polygonal projections for the wall-walk on top of the buttresses flanking the gate, and between which are machicolations (see Figure 8.38). It has been tentatively suggested that arms from the gateway at Spynie are those of Bishop John Winchester (1435–60) and, while there can be no certainty, the date range that suggests is certainly attractive.[75]

Everything suggests that, by the end of our period, domestic amenity was increasingly being allowed to dictate much of the layout and detailing of castles and defensible houses; but an essential basic measure of defensibility was retained, and it was still important to retain the outward symbols of aggression. The growing emphasis on domestic amenity is also apparent from the number of references to gardens at castles. Apart from those at Craigmillar already mentioned, few dating from the pre-Reformation period are still identifiable. However, since by the 1570s the fourth Earl of Morton could lay out the extensive terraced gardens at Aberdour,[76] it must clearly have had forerunners elsewhere. The monastic houses had cultivated plants over a long period, and this interest extended to the prelates from references such as that to the gardens and orchards of the bishop of Moray at Spynie in 1556.[77] Records of gardens of secular landholders – other than those of the king – are less frequent, but increase in numbers from the mid-fifteenth century. There was evidently a predecessor of the early seventeenth-century walled garden at Edzell, for example, and in the more sheltered parts of the kingdom there must have been many others.[78]

FIGURE 8.37   Dalhousie Castle, the entrance front.

FIGURE 8.38   Spynie Castle, the gatehouse.

SECULAR ARCHITECTURE IN THE BURGHS

Finally in this chapter, a little must be said about buildings in the burghs. The greatest architectural contribution of the later Middle Ages to the burghs was the series of parish churches built within the more wealthy of them. By comparison with those churches, unless the burgh also had a cathedral, an abbey or a major royal castle, other buildings must have paled into insignificance. It is true that by the very end of the Middle Ages some burghs were also beginning to provide themselves with tolbooths as the symbol of secular authority, and after the Reformation tolbooths sometimes became an even more potent symbol of civic pride than the churches.[79] But, with the exception of part of the tower at Crail, which could date from 1517, it is likely that most of those which remain are outside our period. Town defences may also have had a more important role in the later Middle Ages than previously, though few have survived. Initially, any boundary defences around most towns are likely to have been just the linked back walls or dykes of the houses on the perimeter. Exceptionally, Perth was said to have a mud wall by the 1330s, and in 1336 Edward III gave instructions to rebuild the walls in stone.[80] Something of the impressive form of the wall that was built there is known from Slezer's view of the burgh. Additionally, evidence for its line, its interval towers and ditch have been found through excavation;[81] sadly, the last relics of the wall were destroyed as recently as 1834.

In Edinburgh the King's Wall, first referred to in 1427, may have started as the sort of linked boundary wall referred to above, though by 1450 it was being constructed in more permanent form.[82] Parts of this wall running parallel to the High Street were excavated in 1973–5.[83] A more substantial wall was started in Edinburgh in 1514, perhaps because of the fright of Flodden, and significant parts – including some of its towers – survive. Apart from Edinburgh, the most impressive sections of stone-built town wall are those at Stirling and Peebles.[84] At Stirling the work was probably instigated in 1547 at the time of a threat of English invasion, and the work was directed by the master mason John Coutis. As well as stretches of wall, two towers survive, with rectangular wide-mouthed gunholes, though these could partly date from later works of 1574. At Peebles the wall dates from 1570.

Many of the burghs were at important river crossings. The building of bridges to help pilgrims, merchants and other travellers was regarded as a worthy act of charity, as is evident from Boece's account of the construction of a bridge over the Dee by Bishop William Elphinstone[85] – and such acts might attract handsome indulgences as an additional inducement. A number of fine late medieval bridges survive, though the dating of most of them is problematic, and they have all undergone extensive reconstruction on more than one occasion.[86] Elphinstone's bridge was only completed after his death, in 1529, and was widened in 1841; but its seven arches, each with a span of nearly 13.75 metres, are still enormously impressive. Of the other burgh bridges the best are those at Ayr of 1491 (with four arches of over 17.35 metres in span), at Dumfries of 1464 (with six arches, the largest being over 10.5 metres in span) and at Stirling (with four arches, the largest being over 17.5 metres in span) (see Figure 8.39). The last of these must have been particularly imposing when there were gatehouses at each end and over the middle pier. Other handsome later medieval bridges survive at Brechin, Haddington, Jedburgh and Musselburgh.

FIGURE 8.39   Stirling Bridge.

So far as we can now judge, the planning of houses built within the burghs could vary greatly. By the later Middle Ages the higher clergy had residences which paid little regard to whether they were in a rural or an urban setting. The castle of the bishops and archbishops of St Andrews as rebuilt by Bishop Traill in about 1400, for example, made few concessions to its urban situation (see Figure 1.11).[87] Even when Archbishop Hamilton rebuilt the entrance front after the siege of 1546–7 (a date which may have been 1555 was inscribed above the entrance), there was little that was specifically urban about it from what we can understand of the finished building (see Figure 8.40). Nevertheless, despite the complications of the need to incorporate earlier walls – which had probably been started by Cardinal Beaton – the end result was sumptuously palatial. Along the wall-head is evidence of an array of French-inspired dormer windows, flanking the main centre-piece above the gateway. Above an armorial panel, that central feature developed into a three-part design with a salient central section, which suggests that the dormer above it must have been of the triptych form seen at Azay-le-Rideau or Chambord.

The castle of the bishops and archbishops of Glasgow was a short way to the west

FIGURE 8.40   St Andrews Castle, the gateway of the entrance front as remodelled by Archbishop Hamilton.

of their cathedral, and its last upstanding fragments were only destroyed in 1789 (see Figure 8.43).[88] The main building was a tower-house, enclosed by a high towered curtain wall with an elaborately corbelled – and probably machicolated – wall-head. Of the various contributors to the castle, it seems that Bishop Cameron (1426–46) built the angle tower at the south-west corner, while Archbishop Beaton (1508–23) is assumed to have rebuilt the courtyard walls from the way his arms were said to have been carved on them. It may also have been those two bishops who built and enlarged the main tower, on which it is said Cameron's arms were displayed. The gatehouse – a large rectangular block with three-quarter towers at its outer angles – which was capped by a corbelled parapet, was decorated with the arms of Archbishop Dunbar (1523–47), which are now preserved in the cathedral.

Reference must also be made here to the episcopal residences at Dunblane and Dornoch. Much of the present appearance of the latter dates from a restoration of 1813, but it was evidently essentially like the defensible residence that any substantial landholder might have built, with a combination of a hall range and one or more chamber towers.[89] Of the former little survives but vaulted substructures.

A town house that was possibly built for one of the religious orders survived at Linlithgow until the later nineteenth century, and was one of the most fully recorded medieval houses from any of the burghs (see Figure 8.41).[90] Traditionally it is said it was built for the Knights Hospitallers of nearby Torphichen. It had a four-storeyed tower at a back corner of the site, with an adjoining hall and chamber block extending down towards a range which ran along the street frontage. An arched pend led through the latter to the small courtyard around which the buildings were grouped, and at the junction of the two ranges was a stair tower. This arrangement is similar to what we might expect in any house of a substantial landholder, the main concession to the urban setting being the tighter grouping of elements and the relatively small scale.

Of other houses built for churchmen, the best-preserved is the manse of the chantor, or precentor, of Elgin – usually known misleadingly as the Bishop's House (see Figure 8.42).[91] It is dated to 1557 – though it is likely to be a composite construction – and consisted of a main block containing a hall on its first floor, which was connected to a chamber block by a stair tower. Its details included what could have been an oriel window on the floor above the hall. Fragments of other prebendal manses also survive at Elgin, including that of the prebendary of Inverkeithny.[92] Additionally, we have early views of the manses of Unthank and Duffus, which were demolished in 1840, and together with the remains of the precentor's manse, they allow us at least a glimpse of the architectural splendours of the chanonries that grew up around the medieval cathedrals.

A little is also known about some of the manses associated with cathedrals elsewhere, and especially at Glasgow (see Figure 8.43).[93] The manse of the archdeacon there lived on in modified form for some years as a residence for the Duke of Montrose, while the manse of the prebendary of Renfrew survived into the later nineteenth century. The only one of Glasgow's manses still to remain, however, is that which may have housed the prebendary of Barlanark, and is usually known as

FIGURE 8.41   Linlithgow, the hall of the house traditionally said to have been built for the Hospitallers of Torphichen.

Provand's Lordship. It was probably originally built for the hospital of St Nicholas, by Bishop Durisdeer (1455–73). Part at the northern end is missing, but the pattern of the windows suggests it could have been divided into chambers and closets for the twelve old men for whom the hospital was founded. By what process the hospital became a prebendal manse, if indeed it did, is uncertain.

    All of these residences, however, were designed to meet special needs, and were not typical of the range of house-types that would have been most common within the burghs. Excavations in Aberdeen and Perth have shown that the majority of houses would have been of wattle or of timber, and conditions for most urban dwellers must have been squalid.[94] Nevertheless, by the end of the Middle Ages the wealthier burgesses were beginning to house themselves within a combination of stone and timber. A fifteenth-century drawing of the battle of Bannockburn seems to show the

FIGURE 8.42   Elgin, the manse probably built for the precentor.

houses of Stirling as two-storeyed timber-framed structures, with upper storeys jettied outwards.[95] A view of Edinburgh of 1544 shows a close concentration of two-storeyed houses with thatched or tiled roofs.[96] Both these drawings are schematic, and only limited reliance can be placed on them, though the information they provide is supplemented by some documentary evidence. In 1501, for example, a house in Niddrie's Wynd in Edinburgh was said to have a hall, chamber and work-house above two cellars.[97] This was perhaps a fairly standardised combination of elements for the house of a modestly wealthy burgess family, and another house is described as having hall, chamber, kitchen and lofts above three vaults.

Regrettably, no complete building has survived to show how such a house might have looked, and we have to rely on fragments in the house known as St John's, on South Street in St Andrews, or the so-called John Knox's House in Edinburgh's High Street.[98] We can, however, probably imagine many such houses as starting their life with a stone core two rooms in depth, set at right angles to the street, and possibly with a stair turret at some point. Above a ground floor, which may have been vaulted, would have been the main hall floor, with a garret in the roof space above. Timber galleries would often have been built out towards the street front, the upper storey being jettied out beyond the lower.

Moving higher up the social scale we find that landholders, like the prelates, often built town houses which differed little from their houses in the country;[99] indeed, in

FIGURE 8.43   Glasgow, the chanonry around the cathedral as it survived into the later seventeenth century. The bishop's castle is immediately to the west of the cathedral, and some of the manses of the prebendaries extend beyond it.

many cases any attempt to distinguish between a rural or an urban setting is meaningless. The tower-house built at Alloa in the late fifteenth century for the Lords Erskine, for example, now stands in relative isolation on the edge of the town, but before the gargantuan landscaping schemes of the seventeenth century it seems the town extended around its walls.[100] A similar relationship between castle and dependent township is illustrated by Paul and Thomas Sandby's views of Inverarary before the rebuilding of the ducal castle in the mid-eighteenth century,[101] and it is easy to understand Duke Archibald's wish to withdraw a little way from the bustling township around his walls.

The continuing importance of town houses is demonstrated at the Ayrshire town of Maybole, where both the laird of Blairquhan and the Earl of Cassillis seem to have had residences.[102] The former's residence is said to underlie the tolbooth; the latter's – which is perhaps the finest of all urban tower-houses – survives, and has as its best feature a delightful oriel at the top of the stair wing, from which the earl could look down on his burgh. With such a tower, however, we have moved well out of our present date range.

CHAPTER NINE

Artillery Fortification

CASTLES AND ARTILLERY: THE FIRST PHASE[1]

Artillery began to enter general use in Europe around the second quarter of the fourteenth century.[2] It was probably first deployed against the Scots by Edward III of England in 1327, and that same king used it at Berwick in 1333 and at Stirling in 1342.[3] The noise of guns being fired must have been a terrifying novelty, though for some time to come it is doubtful if they were of positive help in the prosecution of siege warfare. Indeed, for many years it may have been little less dangerous to stand behind a gun than to be in the line of fire. In England the growing significance of artillery only began to be reflected in the design of castles from around the last quarter of the fourteenth century, when shot-holes in the form of inverted key-holes – with sighting slits above the gunhole – were designed for a number of buildings. In Scotland, however, it was not until the central decades of the fifteenth century that such modifications started to be introduced.

A prime mover behind this change was James II who was himself killed when one of his own cannon burst at the siege of Roxburgh in 1460. Following in the footsteps of his father, who had acquired at least one Flemish bombard, he started to build up an arsenal from early in his reign, and by 1458 he had sufficient for it to be deemed expedient to appoint a master of the artillery.[4] As early as 1456 he had also asked some of his greater subjects to supply themselves with pieces of artillery, presumably in order to augment the royal artillery train in times of need. This could be a sign of the confidence he placed in his magnates though, equally, it could have been simply because artillery was not an established feudal due. By 1457 he was the owner of what was for long the most massive gun in the British Isles, when his uncle-in-law, Duke Philip the Good of Burgundy, sent him the bombard known as Mons Meg along with a sister gun.[5]

One of the first Scottish fortifications to be designed for artillery may have been a curtain wall at Threave Castle (see Figures 1.3 and 9.1a).[6] Until recently this was assumed to have been built either after James II had besieged the castle in 1455, during his vendetta against the Black Douglas family, or as part of repairs carried out by Lord Maxwell after 1513. Excavations between 1974 and 1978, however, showed the wall is more likely to have been built by the ninth Earl of Douglas shortly before the siege of 1455, and its construction could even have been one of the factors behind the charge of treason levelled against him in June that year. It was a right-angled structure wrapped around the two most vulnerable sides of the tower-house built by the third

earl (see p. 20), and had circular towers at the ends and the change in angle; the
gateway was at the middle of the eastern section.

In much of this it foreshadowed the inner curtain at Craigmillar (see Figure 8.34).
Unlike Craigmillar, however, the walls between the towers were relatively low and
were built with an external batter, in which they demonstrated a fuller appreciation
of the problems of resisting artillery shot. A squat profile and massive construction,
with angled faces to deflect shot, were to provide a more effective defence than walls
built high enough to thwart siege towers and scaling ladders. Another significant
feature of the curtain is the close concentration of firing apertures both in the straight
walls and the towers. Those in the walls are simple vertical slits. Those in the towers,

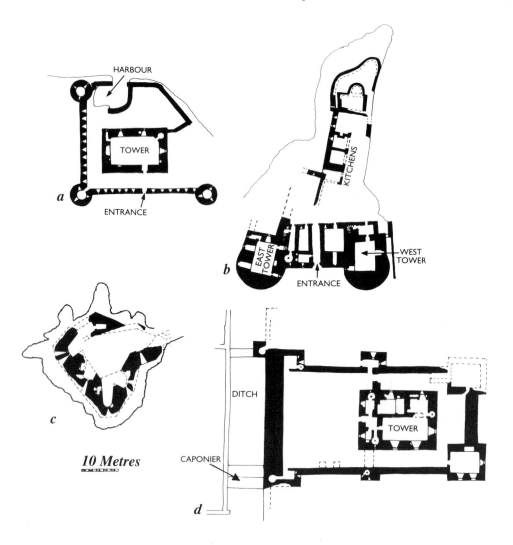

FIGURE 9.1   Plans of some fortifications designed for artillery: a. Threave Castle;
b. Ravenscraig Castle; c. Dunbar blockhouse; d. Craignethan Castle.

which are directed both along the faces of the flanking walls and diagonally out into the field, were intended for firearms; some were shaped like inverted key-holes, but others – with a circular aperture at top and bottom of the slit – have the appearance of a vertically-set dumb-bell.

James II's own interest in artillery fortification was demonstrated in the Fife castle of Ravenscraig (see Figures 9.1b and 9.2). He started to build this in the name of his queen, Mary of Guelders, in 1460, under the direction of the master mason Henry Merlioun.[7] It is a puzzling building. Although work continued after James's own death in 1460, it stopped with the death of the queen three years later, by when it cannot have been completed. Later, in 1470, the castle passed by exchange to William Sinclair Earl of Orkney, as part of James III's plans to win control of the Northern Isles through acquisition of the estates of the Norwegian earldom. The Sinclair family eventually completed Ravenscraig to a reduced design, and there is considerable difficulty in determining which parts are attributable to James II and which to the Sinclairs – a family whose members were also to show some interest in the growing potential of artillery as a means of supporting their own power struggles.

There was little that was obviously revolutionary in the overall design at Ravenscraig. The main building was a range behind a rock-cut ditch across the neck of a coastal promontory. At each end of the range are residential towers with

FIGURE 9.2   Ravenscraig Castle from the north-east.

three-quarter round fronts, and there is a central block containing the entrance between them. The western tower was planned rather like a standard tower-house – albeit with a rounded outer face – and was probably intended as the residence of the queen herself or of her constable. The eastern tower was similar, but the separate access to the chamber on each floor suggests they were planned to be occupied individually. Domestic buildings extended along the promontory behind this entrance range.

In its basic form Ravenscraig might thus be regarded as a compressed version of a castle like that at Tantallon (see p. 15 and Figure 1.10). What was particularly significant, however, was the great wall thickness in proportion to the size of the castle, with a particularly massive thickening in the rounded fronts of the two towers (although small closets were hollowed out of this mass in the western tower). There was also a carefully planned provision of inverted key-hole shot-holes to cover the approaches to the entrance and a postern gate at one of the flanks, and the wall-head of the west tower was eventually capped by solid weathered-back masonry rather than a wall-walk – even if a rather flimsy cap-house was inconsistently allowed to poke through this mass.

Certain parts of the building clearly represent the later completion by the Sinclairs rather than the original design. Thus, the wide-mouthed gunholes at the upper level of the central block – the wall of which was built thinner than originally intended on the evidence of tusking behind the inner face – are certainly no earlier than the 1520s. It is also clear that the eastern tower is both less deep and less tall than first intended, with make-shift crenellation at the wall-head, so that its completion to a reduced form must be attributable to the Sinclairs. It is possible, however, that even some of those parts which have been assumed to belong to the royal works are also attributable to the Sinclairs. On balance, therefore, it is probably safe to assume little more than that the underlying design and the lower parts of the main components represent James II's perception of the way castle-builders should provide for – and meet the threat of – artillery, at a time when that threat was still only partly understood.

ARTILLERY FORTIFICATIONS IN THE EARLY SIXTEENTH CENTURY

Except in such relatively specialised works, the threat and potential of artillery were slow to have an impact on Scottish castle design. Even when the implications of the improving technology were increasingly appreciated, around the early years of the sixteenth century, they usually evoked little more response than the provision of shot-holes for hand-held guns where once there might have been arrow slits. Thus, the gateway of James IV's forework at Stirling Castle, of about 1500, was given shot-holes of dumb-bell shape in its towers (see Figures 10.12 and 9.9), while some tower-houses began to have shot-holes of inverted key-hole shape in their basements – as at the Lindsay family's castle of Edzell.[8] The Stirling gate was in a class of its own, and it must be assumed that James IV was there more interested in having an aesthetically pleasing frontispiece to one of his favourite castles than in creating an impregnable line of defence. Intriguingly, the form of the shot-holes may itself be partly historicist rather than strictly defensive, since shot-holes of the same form are shown on a drawing of the castle which appears in the background of a fifteenth-century depiction of the battle of Bannockburn. Could it be that the earlier gate shown there was one of James II's experiments with fortifications suitable for the use of artillery?

Edzell, and its like, are a different matter (see Figure 8.31). Whether such limited response reveals ignorance that siege warfare was undergoing a fundamental change, or simply that the works necessary to fit it for defence by and from artillery would have been unacceptable, is uncertain. For most landholders, however, it is likely that the risk of major artillery attack was distinctly remote, since only the king and the greatest magnates could afford the artillery trains that would have posed a threat. In any case, even when great cannon were brought into play, the issue was not necessarily beyond doubt. Faced with a choice between making an expensive and domestically restricting major investment against a threat that was unlikely to materialise, on the one hand, or, taking modest precautions and striving for ever greater comfort, on the other, it is not surprising most landholders chose the latter.

It was near the Border with England that the construction of artillery defences came to be taken most seriously, and here the crown took the lead. In 1481 James III hastily took guns to Berwick in a vain effort to avert its capture by the English – and this implies a simultaneous effort to construct suitable defences on which they could be mounted. The earliest of such defences to have left any trace, however, date from the period when James IV's support of the claims of Perkin Warbeck against those of Henry VII necessitated some strengthening of the eastern marches. Since Berwick had been finally lost to England in 1482, it was Dunbar that received attention, and the fragmentary remains of the new gatehouse and forework built at the castle between 1496 and 1501 retain some of the inverted key-hole shot-holes then constructed.[9] Around the same time, between 1489 and 1496, the English captain of Berwick, Sir William Tyler, built the work there that came to be known as the Bulwark on the Sands at the southern tip of the town, which was apparently also intended to hold guns. But even in these works it is hard to see that there was more than a nod towards the threat of artillery, and it was only after Flodden, in 1513, that such defences came to be more systematically planned for the new weaponry.

To appreciate the change in attitudes we must look again at Dunbar.[10] Even before the arrival from France in May 1515 of the Duke of Albany as Governor of the kingdom – during the minority of James V – Dunbar had been chosen as his main Scottish base, perhaps because it was an easier port to reach than Leith for ships coming from France. Between 1515 and 1523 a great polygonal blockhouse was constructed there, set on an inaccessible promontory, and connected to the existing castle by a traverse wall containing a corridor (see Figure 9.1c). In this work the Scots were introduced for the first time to more up-to-date notions of what was appropriate for such artillery fortifications. It was almost certainly built under the supervision of the Sieur de la Bastie, a French military leader with engineering expertise; it is also possible that James V's French mason, Mogin Martin, was involved.

The walls of the blockhouse, which followed the lines of the promontory, were up to 6.5 metres thick, and were pierced by the latest kind of wide-mouthed gunholes, with a circular throat and an outwardly-flared oval embrasure that allowed guns to be pivoted. These appear to have been the first examples of such gunholes to have been built in Scotland, and were to be widely copied, albeit often on a much-reduced scale. On top of the walls was a massive parapet, behind which a second tier of guns could be mounted. Even if not in the vanguard of European military architecture, such a fortification introduced a new factor into Border warfare, and Lord Dacre advised Cardinal Wolsey that it was impregnable. The English responded with new works at Berwick between 1522 and 1523 – though, since that town was to remain continuously in English hands, its later fortification falls outside the remit of this book.

Where necessary, existing fortifications might also be effectively adapted to meet the English threat at this time, though the evidence for this has frequently not survived. At Cessford, for example, the castle was strengthened at the behest of the Warden of the East Marches – its owner – to such an extent that it almost defeated the efforts of the Earl of Surrey in 1523 (see Figure 8.15). Indeed, he confessed that, if the garrison had not surrendered, he doubted his artillery would have brought about a successful conclusion. The walls of the tower-house at Cessford are enormously thick (see p. 254), but that was not Surrey's problem; it was, rather, the earthwork *vawmures* that were raised in front of the castle.[11] This fairly minor operation at Cessford offers an important pointer to the growing importance of earthwork in fortification against artillery. Similarly, at Berwick – after Flodden – massive earthwork *countermures* were raised behind the decaying medieval walls of both town and castle, and detailed contemporary descriptions of this hasty strengthening give a clue to what was happening at several sites in Scotland regarded as under threat. It is worth noting that, even though the Cessford earthworks were clearly substantial, nothing remains of them today.

ARTILLERY: IN THE SECOND QUARTER OF THE SIXTEENTH CENTURY

The next phase in the history of Scottish artillery fortification opened in the years around 1530. A leading contribution at this time was made by Sir James Hamilton of Finnart, a larger-than-life figure who was the oldest of the first Earl of Arran's bastard sons. For over a decade he enjoyed James V's favour, and played a leading role in both affairs of state and in many of the king's building projects, until 1540, when that fickle monarch had him executed for reasons which remain unclear. The king's own interest in artillery fortifications was first shown at Tantallon, which he began to strengthen after he had wrested it from the pro-English Earl of Angus in 1528, following an abortive siege (see Figure 1.10).[12] However, the main campaign there may not have started until ten years later,[13] by which time James was also modifying some of his other castles.

Tantallon, with its high walls and prominent cliff-top site, had been designed in response to traditional medieval siege techniques, and had even defied James's own attempt to take it with artillery in 1528. But it was increasingly appreciated that masonry should be ever more massively constructed if it was to be equal to concentrated artillery fire, and so the king's efforts were aimed at reinforcement of the main line of defence. The eastern tower was strengthened by the insertion of stone vaults, and wide-mouthed gunholes were pierced through its walls. In the curtain wall itself some of the mural chambers were blocked, while a new wall-head parapet suitable for guns was constructed. But the greatest works were reserved for the central gate tower, where the relatively lightly constructed barbican was at least partly removed, and a massively built outer front was instead provided – with rounded corners to deflect shot, and a small doorway to minimse the weakness of this inherently weakest spot.

It is not known if Hamilton of Finnart was involved at Tantallon, though he certainly was at the royal castle of Blackness.[14] There, between 1534 and 1540, he was in charge of works at the castle which had been first built at a date before 1449; he was receiving payments for works up to the time of his execution, after which the parson of Dysart superintended the completion of operations until 1542. This work involved a massive reinforcement of the walls at the southern end of the courtyard, facing the main line of approach (see Figure 9.3). The layout of the existing curtain wall was taken as a starting-point, and this resulted in a plan rather like that of the blockhouse at Dunbar (see Figure 9.1c); also like Dunbar was the daunting array of wide-mouthed gunholes. There the resemblance stopped, however, because at Blackness the curtain walls were carried up even higher than before in order to

FIGURE 9.3   Blackness Castle, the heightened south end of the courtyard.

accommodate a hall on the upper floor. (It is of additional interest that, in doing this, the original mid-fifteenth-century crenellated parapet was preserved within its masonry, and is now one of the best-preserved examples of its type.)

Hamilton of Finnart's interest in artillery fortifications was not limited to the works he superintended for his royal master, and it is at his own castle of Craignethan that we see his ideas expressed most coherently.[15] Work was in progress there no later than 1532, by which time he had consolidated his holding,[16] though it may have been started some years before. It was set on a spur of high ground in a curve of the River Nethan at its junction with the Craignethan Burn. It originally consisted of a rectangular courtyard, containing a spacious residence with much of the appearance of a tower-house on the central east–west axis, towards the eastern end of the enclosure (see Figures 9.1d and 9.4). The courtyard was separated from the higher ground to the west by a deep ditch, on the far side of which was a much larger outer courtyard. The latter had probably been planned by Hamilton of Finnart from the start, but may only have been built after his death.

In building the rectangular tower-house, its designer was at pains to achieve relatively symmetrical façades. Despite its superficially conventional external appearance, with the customary wall-head wall-walk blossoming into open rounds at the angles, there is much about the tower that is out of the ordinary. Most unusual of all is its double-pile plan, with a lofty barrel-vaulted ground-floor hall occupying most of one side and interlocking with suites of rooms on the upper floors. The latter are reached by no fewer than three ingeniously contrived spiral stairs which allowed independent access to the various lodgings. It may be that the placing of the hall on the ground rather than the first floor was partly because the fall of the land to the east allowed a basement to be provided below the entrance floor, but was perhaps also because Hamilton did not wish to give his tower too high a profile.

The courtyard wall surrounding the tower was strengthened by six symmetrically set rectangular towers at its angles and at the mid-points of the longer walls. Between the two western towers, and extending down to revet the eastern face of the ditch, was constructed a massive five-metre-thick wall, which screened the tower-house on its most vulnerable side. Entrance to the courtyard was by a timber bridge across the ditch, and from there through a small gate in the west face of the tower at the mid-point of the north wall. The ditch was additionally protected by Craignethan's most advanced feature: a stone vaulted firing gallery known as a caponier, which must have been the first example of this device of Italian origin to have been built in Scotland (see Figure 9.5). In addition, needless to say, the towers and outer rampart were amply provided with wide-mouthed gunholes; those in the tower-house being placed just below the wall-head parapet, to allow the defenders to fire over the enclosing courtyard walls.

In all of this, Craignethan is a rather hybrid complex, displaying some conservative features alongside others that are unexpectedly advanced. As a piece of architecture, what is most striking about the castle is the underlying symmetry of the whole design. This must be a reflection of the more regular approach to design that Hamilton would have become aware of in the course of his travels in France, even if it would be hard

FIGURE 9.4   Craignethan Castle, the tower-house.

FIGURE 9.5   Craignethan Castle, the caponier in the ditch.

to find precise parallels since the vocabulary of the treatment at Craignethan is firmly Scottish. As a piece of military engineering, however, the most striking innovation was the caponier; although, with the exception of a firing gallery inside the spur added to cover the entrance of Blackness Castle in the reign of Mary, it probably had few immediate followers.

Other than Craignethan, the fortification with which Hamilton of Finnart is most likely to have been involved is another family castle, at Cadzow, on the outskirts of Hamilton, high on a rocky cliff above the Avon Water (see Figure 9.6).[17] The documentation relating to this castle is confusing, since Cadzow was the original name of Hamilton itself, and references to Cadzow Castle may relate to the Hamilton family's other castle in the valley. The architectural evidence is equally confusing, since in the eighteenth and nineteenth centuries the ruins of the abandoned castle were treated as a romantic ruin in the landscape of the 'ducal dog-kennel' of Châtelherault, within the High Park of Hamilton Palace. However, it seems that Cadzow must certainly have been under construction by around 1530 for the second Earl of Arran and, since that earl as a minor was under the guardianship of his half-brother, Hamilton of Finnart, there are good reasons for assuming that Hamilton had a part in its planning. It was probably completed by the earl himself between about 1542 and 1554.

So far as they can now be understood, the buildings of Cadzow were grouped within three courtyards, with rock-cut ditches around their sides away from the gorge. Two of these courtyards were set adjacent to each other along the cliff which forms the south bank of the Avon Water, with an outer court – now represented by very fragmentary remains – on their landward side. The western of the two courtyards towards the river had habitable ranges around its perimeter. These were within walls of modest thickness, which were nevertheless pierced by shot-holes – some of dumb-bell type. By comparison, the eastern courtyard has an altogether more purposefully aggressive air. It was of massive and low-set construction, and had on the landward side two three-quarter round towers of about 5.5 metres diameter; these towers had weathered-back wall-heads which invite comparison with that over the west tower at Ravenscraig (see Figures 9.6 and 9.2). Wide-mouthed gunholes enfilade the walls from the towers and point outwards into the field. Assuming that the low profile represents the original design, rather than landscaping for the Dukes of Hamilton in an attempt to make the castle a more sublime experience, Cadzow's eastern courtyard shows one of the most consistently thought-out artillery schemes produced so far for a Scottish patron.

Thus, while neither Craignethan nor Cadzow could be regarded as advanced works in European terms, it is clear that they could only have been produced for a patron who had a greater understanding of the requirements of artillery than was general in Scotland at that time. This understanding must have been gained partly in the course of his travels and military activities, and partly in the course of his supervision of works for his royal master. However, this should probably not tempt us into assuming that Hamilton of Finnart was himself ultimately responsible for the design of the various fortifications with which he was involved. He doubtlessly had a clear idea of the range

FIGURE 9.6   Cadzow Castle, one of the towers of the eastern courtyard.

of functions these buildings were designed to meet, and is likely to have had strong
views on how those functions might be met. Nevertheless, there is little to support
the idea of Hamilton of Finnart having been the single creative mind linking all of
these buildings, and we must probably conclude that his role was essentially that of a
strong-minded private patron and of an energetic superior master of works for his
monarch – a post to which he was eventually formally appointed in 1539.[18]

The round towers at Cadzow were probably intended to function as semi-inde-
pendent gun-towers, or blockhouses. We have already briefly considered the
blockhouse at Dunbar, which was of multangular form as a consequence of the
configuration of the site; but, like those at Cadzow, most Scottish blockhouses appear
to have been rounded. One of the earliest may have been the D-shaped example
known to have been built to protect the harbour at Aberdeen.[19] That tower could
have been planned as early as 1497, though construction probably only started in
1533, when the contract was drawn up with the masons Peter French and Saunders
Monypenny. It was finished in 1542. The arrangement of the blockhouses at Cadzow,
however – in which two strong towers are placed at each end of the main front of a
castle – was an extension of the tradition seen earlier at castles like Tantallon and
Ravenscraig. At the former it has already been said that there were adaptations for
artillery after the siege of 1528; but an even more formidable provision for artillery
along those same lines is to be seen at St Andrews Castle.

At St Andrews, probably in the time of Archbishop James Beaton (1521–39), blockhouses were placed at each end of the south front, where they are likely to have replaced square towers constructed in Bishop Traill's campaign of around 1400.[20] These blockhouses were much larger than the examples at Cadzow, having a diameter of over 16 metres, within walls that were about five metres thick. They must also have been considerably higher than those at Cadzow. Unfortunately, apart from a fragment of the inner wall of the western tower, they were completely destroyed by a combination of the artillery bombardment of 1547 that followed the murder of Cardinal Beaton, and of the rebuilding by Archbishop Hamilton after that. But enough survives to show that they had a careful disposition of wide-mouthed gunholes in their lower walls at least; these were directed both towards the outer world and towards the courtyard, showing that the towers could be held independently if need be.

From accounts of the cardinal's murder, it seems the blockhouses had residential accommodation within their upper floors, since the cardinal's own chamber was in the eastern of the two. It is also evident there must have been a wall-head platform and parapet, since Beaton's body was hung from the parapet of the eastern tower. In this the blockhouses were closer to Dunbar than to those at Cadzow, since the latter were capped by shallow cones of weathered-back masonry rather than by an open platform. We cannot be certain of the form of the parapet, though it may have been like the massive breastwork built at the wall-head of Tantallon Castle as part of the post-1528 works of strengthening (see Figure 1.10). A related parapet survives in a better state of preservation in the slightly unlikely setting of Carberry Tower in Midlothian, where it was possibly built after it had passed to Hugh Rigg in 1547.[21] There the crenellation has thick merlons which are pierced by wide-mouthed gunholes and finished off by weathered-back masonry; it is carried on a charming string course of winged angel-heads, rather like those on the palace at Stirling Castle (see Figure 10.24).

The loss of the St Andrews blockhouses in the siege of 1546–7 is regrettable, but that campaign has at least left us with one extraordinarily valuable relic. A report to the French ambassador in London of 10 November 1546 said the Earl of Arran was mining beneath the castle, and had almost reached the foot of the tower.[22] That mine was rediscovered while digging the foundations of a house in 1879, and it is now possible to walk through both the mine and the counter-mine which intercepted it (see Figure 9.7). There can be no more vivid evocation of the conditions of siege warfare than is sensed in the contrast between the spacious gallery of the mine and the tortured twistings of the counter-mine, where the diggers were guided by only the muffled sounds of the approaching miners.

The siting of the shafts of the counter-mine is also of interest for its clues to the extent of the castle by that time. The shaft which eventually intercepted the mine was started outside the main body of the castle, east of the old gatehouse, reminding us that there must already have been outworks to afford the counter-miners adequate protection to carry out their work. Two abandoned shafts are positioned within the masonry sandwich created by Bishop Traill's south-west curtain and the later addition built in front of it; this shows that the latter already partly existed before Archbishop Hamilton's rebuilding of the 1550s. This doubling-up of the south-west curtain must,

FIGURE 9.7   St Andrews Castle, the mine.

in fact, have compromised the effectiveness of the southern blockhouse very soon after it had been built, because of the way the new wall reduced its field of fire.

BASTIONED FORTIFICATIONS

In the buildings so far discussed in this chapter we see a very small number of the better-placed Scottish patrons – among whom the most important was the king – beginning to respond progressively more systematically to the threat and possibilities of artillery. The wide-mouthed gunholes of Dunbar and the caponier of Craignethan must have appeared especially innovative to contemporaries, and the former were soon to have a wide following. But we should not forget that, by that stage, as the culmination of a development stretching back to the mid-fifteenth century, the Italians had already perfected the angle bastion.[23] This was the element that was to provide the essential basis of artillery fortification up to at least the early nineteenth century and, until its introduction to Scotland, our artillery works have to be regarded as second-rate.

The first appearance of the bastion in Scotland was during the phase of the wars with England which opened with Scottish defeat at Pinkie in 1547. As part of their campaign, the English forces of occupation, led by the Duke of Somerset, speedily constructed a series of forts across the southern half of the country against the threat of the impending arrival of French forces.[24] They were designed and built chiefly under the guidance of the engineers Sir Richard Lee and Thomas Petit, though Italian engineers were also present in some cases – including Archangelo Arcano, Giovanni di Rossetti and Gian Tommaso Scala. There are highly informative contemporary 'platts' of most of the forts in the collection of the Duke of Rutland at Belvoir Castle, including those at Dunglass in East Lothian, at Lauder and Eyemouth in Berwickshire, at Roxburgh Castle, and at Broughty near Dundee.[25] There is also important physical evidence at Dunglass and Eyemouth, and one indistinct bastion of the Lauder fort protrudes from the present Thirlestane Castle, which extends over most of the 1540s site. There are also lesser fragments still to be seen at Roxburgh, on Inchcolm and at Fast Castle in Berwickshire. Regrettably, there are neither drawings nor physical remains of the largest-scale bastioned design which was that defending Haddington.

The earliest of these forts was probably at Eyemouth, where a massive single bastion was built across the neck of a coastal promontory (see Figure 9.8).[26] Set back behind the shelter of the projecting ends of the bastion – known as orillons – were flankers, or protected gun emplacements, and extending in front of the whole formation was a wide ditch. Small-scale excavations have recently confirmed the basic disposition indicated by the Belvoir plan. At Broughty the mainly earthwork fort was started in 1548 to the designs of Rossetti; it took the form of a square enclosure defended by bastions at the angles and with an associated base court.[27] Dunglass was built in the same year, and was also a roughly square enclosure with angle bastions adapted to the configuration of the site.[28] The most elaborate of this group of forts about which anything is known was at Lauder, the faces of which were defended by a complex sequence of bastions and demi-bastions.[29]

FIGURE 9.8   Eyemouth, an aerial view of the English fort.

However unwelcome the construction of such fortifications on Scottish soil was, they were to be an incentive to renewed efforts by the Scots themselves and their French allies, at Edinburgh, Stirling, Leith, Eyemouth and on the Forth island of Inchkeith. At the two former, great triangular bastion-like spurs with flanking defences were constructed in front of the main approach to these most important royal castles. At Edinburgh the spur has been completely destroyed and is now only known from somewhat impressionistic early views. It is, however, likely to have been the work for which payments were made to an Italian 'deviser' in the Treasurer's Accounts for 1547–8, and it has been suggested that the Italian concerned could have been Migiorino Ubaldini, who had been sent over by Henry II.[30]

At Stirling the new works are traditionally said to date from the period when the castle was garrisoned by French troops in 1559 (see Figure 9.9).[31] Plans of the castle made before the changes to the outer defences of 1708–14 show the mid-sixteenth-century fortifications to have consisted of a large angle-spur pointing south-eastwards, with an orillon demi-bastion – known as the French Spur – to its east; a smaller spur was built on the west side, flanking the main entrance. The presence of the arms of France on the angle of the demi-bastion supports the possibility that the work was carried out while the castle held a French garrison, and it is now appreciated that about half of those works still survive within the outer defences as remodelled in 1708–14. This was confirmed by excavation in 1977–8;[32] more recently, in 1992, parts of the approach road were identified in further excavations. In essence, the eastern face of the main spur stands virtually complete, together with the demi-bastion to its east, although the mouth of the latter was walled over in 1708–14 to allow the construction of two levels of embrasures. There is also possibly a fragment of the small western spur in the masonry of the early eighteenth-century casemates.

FIGURE 9.9   Stirling Castle, the artillery spur, with the forework and hall rising behind.

At Eyemouth a French work, consisting of a single demi-bastioned front cutting off a promontory just north of the English fort of 1547, survives as an earthwork. Small parts of the fortifications on Inchkeith also remain, despite orders having been given for their demolition in 1567. Between 1554 and 1559 work is known to have been in progress there under the superintendence of sir William Macdowell, the queen's master of works, though it is likely that the design had been provided by French or Italian engineers.[33] Because of the configuration of the island site the plan was an elongated one, with an irregular sequence of bastions and demi-bastions. The fort seems still to have been under construction at the time of a visit by Mary Queen of Scots in 1564, when a dated pediment with the royal arms was placed over one of the gateways; that pediment is now reset in the buildings of the lighthouse complex. At Leith nothing survives of the fortifications being constructed for the French by 1548, under the direction of Peter Strozzi, though the evidence of plans and descriptions indicates there were no less than eight bastioned fronts, and it is possible to reconstruct the basic form with the help of a map of the siege of 1560 – which survives at Petworth House in Sussex.[34]

With the taste that these operations must have given the Scots for thorough-going bastioned works, it might have been expected that Scotland was about to enter the mainstream of European artillery fortification. But, with the departure of the French and Italian engineers, the interest in first-rate fortifications also seems to have passed for a while. This is perhaps best demonstrated by the half-moon battery at Edinburgh Castle, which was wrapped around the remains of David's Tower after the siege of 1573, and which still presents the castle's most prominent face to the outside world. The problems of providing a high-level defence on an awkward site must not be minimised, and it is now seen without the outer defences which were once in front of it. Nevertheless, it is hard not to see it as a rather make-do-and-mend contrivance, and it was not to be until the Cromwellian defences of the mid-seventeenth century that Scotland again witnessed the construction of major bastioned artillery works.

CHAPTER TEN

The Royal Residences

S o far as secular architecture is concerned, the Middle Ages passed into the age of the Renaissance on a triumphant note with the construction of a series of magnificent royal residences. On the evidence of the surviving documentation – which is far from complete – the finest of these seem to have been largely the work of James IV and James V, and in them we find a swaggering architectural expression of the claims of the Scottish monarchy to a role on the wider European stage. But the earlier phases of the development which culminated in these high achievements had begun soon after the return of James I from English captivity in 1424, and it is likely James was partly inspired to house himself on a more expansive scale than his predecessors by what he had seen during his eighteen years in England.

The surviving accounts for the palaces dating from James I's reign – which may only partly represent the full range of his activities – make reference to various building projects, among which are works at Edinburgh and Stirling Castles.[1] These included a great chamber under construction at the former in 1434, which presumably adjoined the tower built by David II, and thus stood on the site of the later palace block.[2] It is conceivable that the vaults built to support it are among those beneath later buildings, and that some of its masonry could be embodied in the walls of the existing palace block, though this is less certain. There are also references to a vegetable garden, which offer a pleasingly domestic picture of parts of the castle.[3] Since it is not possible to identify positively any of James I's works either there or at Stirling, however, it is to Linlithgow that we must look to appreciate what might have been built for him.

There was a devastating fire at the royal residence of Linlithgow in the year of his return to Scotland (the same fire that is supposed to have destroyed the nearby church), and it was progressively rebuilt over the following century and more.[4] The palace eventually assumed the form of a quadrangular structure with towers rising above the four corners (see Figure 10.22). In this it shows parallels with the type seen from the later fourteenth century in northern England, at Bolton or Lumley. However, it took on this form coherently only in its final stages, by which time the greater emphasis placed on the central courtyard and the façades which looked on to it suggests the influence of French quadrangular palaces was also at work (see Figure 10.4). The difficulty we have in understanding Linlithgow is that, while there is considerable documentation for its building, and there is also evidence within the

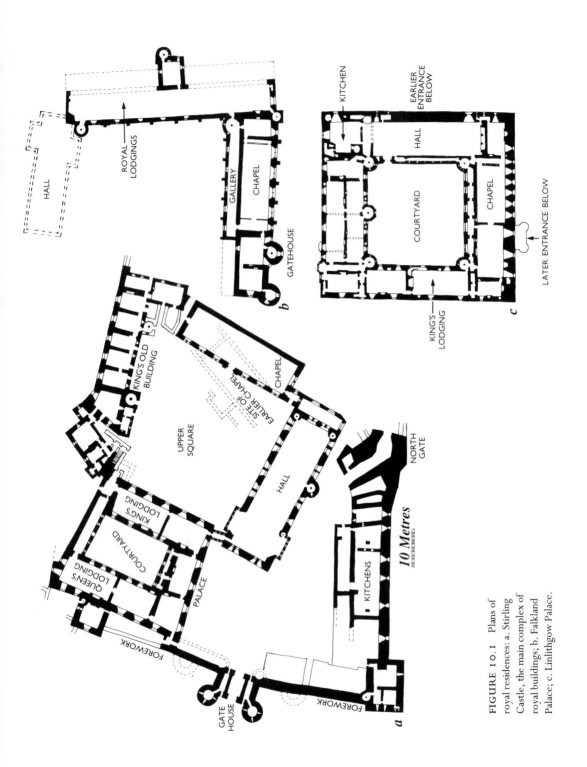

FIGURE 10.1 Plans of royal residences: a. Stirling Castle, the main complex of royal buildings; b. Falkland Palace; c. Linlithgow Palace.

fabric for the stages by which it was built, the documentation is both incomplete and largely unspecific; we therefore cannot be entirely certain of the scope of the operations at each stage. Nevertheless, we do know that the work carried out for James I was pressed ahead at considerable cost under the master of works, John de Waltoun, and enough was complete for the king to be able to stay there in 1428, though construction was to continue up to his death nine years later.[5]

What is probably attributable to this campaign is the main body of the east range, possibly with shorter sections extending back at the north and south ends that were eventually to form the beginnings of the ranges on those sides (see Figure 10.3). As modified later in the century, the east range contained the hall, with the kitchens to its north, and it is likely that this was also the arrangement in the time of James I, albeit in a rather different form. Thus there would have been a first-floor hall, with a kitchen block at one end and probably a chamber block at the other – a combination of elements with a long history in medieval domestic architecture, but deployed here on a particularly princely scale. Running through the middle of the ground floor was an entrance passage, access to which could presumably have been partly controlled from the hall above. Framing the archways at each end of this passage are elaborate sculptural compositions on the two façades, though these could date from one of the later phases of alterations to the range (see Figures 10.3 and 10.4).

During the reign of James II we know of little 'palatial' building, apart from minor repairs and small-scale works at Linlithgow and Stirling. This could have been because he was more interested in purely military architecture of the sort we see at Ravenscraig (see Figure 9.2). Nevertheless, in 1449 the Exchequer Rolls record a minor flurry of building activity at Holyrood, Stirling, Linlithgow and Falkland, presumably to get them ready for the reception of his new queen, Mary of Guelders.[6] There were also further works at Falkland, for example, in 1453 and 1454, and yet others there for the queen dowager in the years after his death. Nothing of these can now be identified with certainty, though this does not necessarily mean that they did not make a significant contribution to the development of the palaces.

Moving on to James III we come to a king whose reputation is at a low ebb. But, as is suggested by his reputed pleasure in the company of practitioners of the arts, he was perhaps more architecturally active than his father, and it must be remembered that his effective reign was considerably longer than those of his father or grandfather. There are references to works at a number of palaces, even if, again, little has survived in identifiable form. Nevertheless, these suggest his reputation for parsimony may be unfair, particularly since we know of his interest in church architecture – as best exemplified by his patronage of the collegiate church at Restalrig, his partial rebuilding of St Monans for the Dominicans, and his involvement in the pilgrimage church at Tain (see Figures 5.5, 4.7 and 1.40).

Of the royal castles, Lindsay of Pitscottie claimed Stirling was James III's favourite, and that he built the chapel royal and the hall there.[7] Against this, the former was not formally established as a collegiate corporation until his son's reign, while the hall is known to have been completed by his son (see Figure 10.14). Nevertheless, this does not mean that James III did not build a chapel within the castle, and we shall see that it seems unlikely James IV found the opportunity to rebuild the chapel for his collegiate foundation before his early death. Equally, while the tradition that the hall was designed by his reputed favourite, Thomas Cochrane, is probably unacceptable, this does not rule out the possibility that James III started the building operations. We certainly know from the documentation that in the 1460s he was building a gate in a structure known as the White Tower, as well as part of the wall,[8] which gives at least some basis of truth to the story of his architectural endeavours at Stirling.

At Linlithgow we are on firmer ground since records show that James III's master of works, Henry Livingston, spent over £500 between 1469 and 1471, around the time of the king's marriage to Margaret of Denmark.[9] This is likely to have involved extension of the royal quarters further into the south and west ranges, in areas where there was again extensive later remodelling.

THE WORKS OF JAMES IV AT LINLITHGOW, HOLYROOD AND FALKLAND

With the reign of James IV (1488–1513) palace building enters a better-documented phase.[10] This monarch saw his kingly role as extending beyond Scotland, and was more of a force to be reckoned with in European politics than his predecessors. It was perhaps as much his European interests as his support for the church – so far as that did not conflict with his other interests – that was recognised in Pope Alexander VI's gift of the rose and sceptre in 1494 and Pope Julius II's gift of the blessed hat and sword in 1507. For our purposes, a more important element in James's elevated view of kingship was that a monarch should be housed in an appropriate manner. Major works at Edinburgh, Falkland, Holyrood, Linlithgow and Stirling were consequently pushed forward to accomplish this aim, even though in many cases the sheer volume of work must make us suspect that he was continuing work initiated by his predecessors. All this new building was not, however, simply a matter of providing palaces of appropriate scale and convenience, it was also important that what might be termed the 'architectural iconography' of the buildings should be correct.

In this we see an aspect of James projecting himself as the Renaissance prince, and the well-known encomia of the Spanish ambassador, Don Pedro de Ayala, on his learning and personal qualities reflect this image.[11] Although much of what Ayala says has the ring of conventional praise, there is little doubt that Margaret of Denmark had ensured that James received an excellent education – in which such noted humanists as Archibald Whitelaw may have played a part. Nevertheless, in seeing James as partly a product of the new intellectual climate of the Renaissance, we must also remember that such learning was compatible with a romantic hankering after medieval ideals. Where appropriate, courtly elegance and chivalric aspirations were cultivated as assiduously by James as they were to be by François I of France and Henry VIII of England. This is graphically illustrated by the great Edinburgh tournament of 1508, in which there was a 'counterfuting of the round tabill of King Arthour'.[12] Such an attempt to recapture an idealised past is indicative of the attitudes of the time.

These were among the factors underlying the palace building on which James expended such vast sums. But any attempt to determine how far the results were medieval or to what extent they represented Renaissance thought at this transitional period can be little more than an academic discussion of categories. Judged by the simple criterion of whether a medieval or a classical vocabulary was employed for them, however, it has to be said that there is still very much in them that is essentially medieval in form.

At all the major palace-building projects with which James IV was involved the main buildings were planned relatively regularly – if not necessarily symmetrically – around a quadrangular courtyard, and in this he showed himself to be keeping step with tastes in France and England.[13] There must also be a suspicion that rivalry with his future father-in-law, Henry VII of England, encouraged him to undertake more building – and that on a grander scale – than he might otherwise have done. Here it should be remembered that, although some building was started soon after his accession, much of what is recorded in the accounts was towards the end of his reign. This may not be unrelated to the fact that, although the prudent Henry had attempted little palace building in the decade after he gained the crown in 1485, by the time his coffers had filled ten years later he was at work on Woodstock, Langley, Richmond, Greenwich, Woking and Hanworth.[14] Around this same period Louis XII and his court were also actively building, though the French crown was not itself to assume the leading architectural role until the accession of François I in 1515. Nevertheless, reports of Louis' own work at Blois, together with that of two cardinals of the church at Gaillon and Châteaudun, may have inspired James with an appreciation of palatial architecture as the setting for courtly life.

At Linlithgow James IV probably continued his father's work by extending the north, south and west ranges to complete the quadrangular plan (see Figure 10.1c). In doing this, the whole scale of the royal accommodation was expanded, and what had already been built must have been extensively remodelled to create a more coherently planned sequence. That sequence was again modified when James V carried out further works, and even more so when the north range had to be rebuilt for James VI, following its collapse in 1607; but the broad lines of planning are relatively clear. Work must have been restarted immediately after James's accession, following an inspection of the building in the first year of his reign[15] – suggesting that it was a continuation of an established programme of works – and it continued up to his death at Flodden in 1513. Among the master masons who worked for him were Nicholas Jackson – who was presumably the same mason who worked for him at Ladykirk Church – and Stephen Balty (or Bawtee), whose names enter the records in the earlier sixteenth century.[16]

In the east range, which was still the side from which the palace was entered, major modifications were carried out (see Figures 10.2 and 10.3). The main space in this part, the hall, may have been extended a short way southwards, and it was given greater nobility by a variety of other modifications. The main windows had probably always been in the form of a clearstorey, but they were reconstructed, with a wall passage on the side towards the courtyard to improve circulation. At the same time a large window – which may be that referred to in accounts of 1502–3[17] – was cut through the east wall to light the dais at the south end of the hall. To give emphasis to that dais a magnificent three-bay fireplace was constructed, the lintel of which was

FIGURE 10.2   Linlithgow Palace, the hall in the east range.

carried on small piers with foliate capitals, while above the lintel were corbels for statues in front of the sloping chimney breast. The dais was eventually afforded additional emphasis by a section of semi-circular barrel vaulting immediately above it. Although the main function of this vault was that of carrying part of the upper floor (and in this it could be a later insertion), it also acted as a canopy of honour, since the rest of the hall was covered by a timber roof at a higher level.

Remodelling of the east range was also aimed at making the entrance to the palace more imposing (see Figures 10.3 and 10.4). The chief element in this was the construction in front of the gate of a forework – known as the outer great bulwark – which may have incorporated a more utilitarian earlier attempt to buttress a structurally vulnerable corner of the palace where the ground fell towards the loch. In its final form this bulwark must have given a more castle-like appearance to the approaches. But, despite its drawbridge and array of towers, there can be little doubt it was intended as much to create the right impression on those who approached the castle, as to provide an outer line of defence. While it might have afforded some degree of added protection in an emergency, properly directed artillery would have made short work of it; however, to an educated courtier versed in knightly lore it would have been clear that this was the prelude to the castle of a champion of chivalry.

Behind the forework, the wall above the entrance gateway itself was enriched at

FIGURE 10.3 (*above*)   Linlithgow Palace, the east front. The remains of the outer great bulwark are to the right.

FIGURE 10.4 (*below*)   Linlithgow Palace, the courtyard. To the left is the inner gate of the east range; to the right are the corridors added against the inner face of the south range.

some stage by an elongated frame in which the slots for the drawbridge beams were set to either side of a heraldic panel containing the royal arms, all of which was surmounted by a suspended band of cusping. Flanking the panel was a pair of lofty image tabernacles. Although this French-inspired design could have been part of James I's work, it is perhaps more likely that it belonged to a later phase of enrichment, particularly since the new dais window had a similar band of suspended cusping. In this it also shows some similarities with the details of Louis XII's less overtly military entrance front at Blois. In favour of an earlier date, it might be argued that the complete tressure around the royal arms suggests that it predates changes to the royal arms introduced by an act of 1471.[18] However, the terms of that act were observed rather erratically, and James IV's arms at both King's Chapel Aberdeen, of 1504, and Melrose, of 1505, also have the full tressure. Above the inner gate was set an only slightly less elaborate scheme of carved decoration, with three tabernacles and three angels below a multi-cusped ogee hood mould (see Figure 10.4), a partial parallel for which was to be seen on the upper storey of the south porch of St John's Church at Perth – of the last decades of the century (see p. 193 and Figure 6.5).

Internally, remodelling extended from the east into the south and west ranges, where an imposing sequence of rooms was created in the royal lodging. This expansion of the royal accommodation created difficulties of circulation which were circumvented by the addition of corridors at all three levels along the courtyard side of the south range, though there may also have been earlier galleries here. Around the same time towers for spiral stairs were added at the angles of the courtyard (see Figure 10.4). From the courtyard side the new corridors are identifiable from the rather English-looking three- or four-light flat-headed windows. Behind the corridors, west of the dais end of the hall and probably on the site of the earlier royal chambers, James created a lofty chapel rising through two storeys (see Figure 10.5). It was lit by a tight progression of five tall round-headed windows in the south wall, an arrangement which – as in the west front of Aberdeen Cathedral or the towers of Edinburgh and Haddington – illustrates the Scottish taste for groupings of equal-height windows. Between the windows, internally, are image corbels carved with an angelic orchestra (see Figure 10.6). Timber for the chapel roof was being bought in 1492, and it was presumably finished by 1504, when there were payments for work on the organ.[19]

The king's own lodgings were mainly in the west range, though much of what is now there could date from the reign of James V (see Figure 10.7). The queen's lodging was either on the floor above or in the adjacent north range. The original designation of the rooms which made up the king's lodgings is no longer certain and, since this was a period when royal planning was tending to expand, the use of the rooms was probably modified more than once. But they perhaps originally functioned as a hall followed by an outer and inner chamber; at the very end of the sequence was a closet reached from a polygonal oriel window overlooking the loch to the north, from which there was also access to the gardens.

Even now that the palace is a roofless shell, it is easy to appreciate how the delightfully intimate rib-vaulted spaces of that oriel and closet offered a charming counterpoint to the imposing spaces of the main rooms of the lodging, and must have

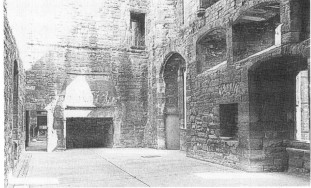

FIGURE 10.5 (*above*)   Linlithgow Palace, the chapel, looking eastwards towards the site of the altar.
FIGURE 10.6 (*left*)   Linlithgow Palace, one of the angel corbels between the windows of the chapel.
FIGURE 10.7 (*right*)   Linlithgow Palace, the hall of the king's apartment.

afforded the king a welcome refuge. Indeed, the sophistication of the spatial orches-
tration throughout the palace as remodelled for James IV shows an impressively subtle
sense of balance in which full consideration has been given to creating the correct
scale of ambience. Starting with the great 'public' space of the imposing hall – which
was approached by an external stair from the courtyard – the main 'parade' probably
by-passed the chapel and ante-chapel to reach the king's own hall. From there the
favoured few might have access to more private chambers, but only the king's most
intimate familiars would enter the miniature complexity of the closet. Those with

more regular rights of access would probably also avoid the outer rooms and approach the royal lodging by one of the corner stair turrets.

Building of a similarly palatial character was also carried out for James IV at Holyrood and Falkland; but at the former it has been almost completely destroyed, while at the latter much has been lost or overlaid by later work. At Holyrood the royal residence had a rather parasitic relationship with the Augustinian abbey founded by David I in 1128. As a royal foundation the abbey naturally expected to provide hospitality for successive kings, but this function became increasingly important in the later Middle Ages, and eventually survived the collapse of the abbey as a religious institution. It was within the abbey that Queen Joan Beaufort gave birth to the future James II, for example, and we have already seen how that king was carrying out work on the royal lodgings at the time of his marriage to Mary of Guelders. But even more was done for James IV, in the years before and after his marriage to Margaret Tudor in 1503.[20]

From a description of their wedding it is evident the royal residence had become a quadrangular structure on the west side of the cloister.[21] By this stage it is also possible it had absorbed the canons' refectory as a great hall, and may have taken over the west range of the cloister for some uncertain use.[22] The lodgings for king and queen – each of which consisted of a hall followed by a great and then an inner chamber – probably extended through the south and west ranges of the palace, while the chapel was in the north range, abutting the south-west tower of the abbey church. At some stage James added a tower to the palace, which was completed in 1505, possibly towards the southern end of the west range.[23] Views of the palace from an elevated position, by Gordon of Rothiemay and Hollar – before rebuilding in the 1670s – give some idea of the resulting layout, although much of the architectural detail shown by them dates from the time of James V. The only upstanding work which might date from this period is the flank of a demolished gatehouse on the west side of the abbey courtyard, which could be the gate recorded as being under construction in 1503.[24] It had tierceron vaulting over the passage, and three-quarter-round towers at the angles.

More of James IV's work survives at Falkland, though there also major rebuilding for James V transformed what had been built for his father.[25] Of the palace as built for those two kings the south range survives virtually complete, the east range partly as a shell, and the north range as inadequately excavated foundations (see Figure 10.1b). The barrel-vaulted lower storeys of both south and east ranges are almost certainly attributable to James IV. If the north range contained the hall, as may be suggested by its plan, it is likely the royal apartments were in the east range, as they certainly were to be for his son. In its final state the south range contained the chapel, and this may also have been the original arrangement, since the rather ecclesiastical buttresses of its south face – with tabernacles at the level of the chapel – are more likely to be attributable to the fourth than to the fifth James (see Figure 10.8).

THE WORKS OF JAMES IV AT EDINBURGH, STIRLING AND ROTHESAY

The two most important royal castles of the later Middle Ages were Edinburgh and Stirling, the dramatic volcanic rock sites of which were strikingly similar to each other.

FIGURE 10.8   Falkland Palace, the south range with the chapel on the second floor.

At both, the royal residential enclave developed around a square at the summit of the rock. In each case it seems James IV was chiefly responsible for the first of the truly palatial structures, though we cannot rule out that the basis for his achievement was laid by his predecessors.

At Edinburgh the core around which the palace grew, on the east side of the square, was probably the chamber built for James I in about 1434, adjoining David II's tower-house.[26] West of David's tower, the north side of the square was already fixed by St Mary's Church, which had been rebuilt as part of David II's works on the rock summit (the site of which is now occupied by the Scottish National War Memorial). Another element known to have been present by the mid-fifteenth century was a great hall, though its relationship to the other buildings is uncertain. The main works by James IV of which we know were the augmentation of the royal apartment where the palace now stands, and the construction of a new great hall on the south side of the square.[27]

In the case of the former, the building has been further augmented and reconstructed on a number of occasions, particularly at the time of James VI's homecoming of 1617, and the extent of the work of around 1500 is uncertain. The eastern half of the block, however, has the appearance of having been built as a lodging range, perhaps including a hall, a chamber and a closet. Two of the fireplaces within those rooms are of types that would be expected in high-quality work of around 1500, one having triplets of engaged filleted shafts with multiple-moulded capitals and flared bases (see Figure 10.9). The truncated relics of oriels which once looked eastwards from the range, and which have analogies with those in the north range at Linlithgow and in the guest house range at Dunfermline, might also be the work of James IV.

The grandest building raised for James IV at Edinburgh was certainly his great hall (see Figure 10.10). Having been used as both a barrack and a hospital for many years from the mid-seventeenth century onwards, with the consequent insertion of floors and partitions, it has undergone many changes. Its restoration in 1887–91, by Hippolyte Blanc, fortunately gave it back much of its original appearance, albeit at the cost of a slightly sterile antiquarian air, which induces a – partly unfair – sense of mistrust of much of the detail. Although many of the windows had to be rebuilt, some of the details of the roof restored, and the new entrance completely invented, it seems the work was carried out in as scholarly a manner as the information then available would allow.

To achieve a level platform for the hall on the south side of the square – in an area where the rock stepped down steeply and irregularly – James IV's masons had to build vaulted substructures, which in places were two storeys high. The hall itself is a rectangular structure of about 29 by 12.5 metres externally, with provision for a lean-to corridor along the side towards the courtyard. It was lit by large rectangular windows in the north and south faces, some with a single mullion and one or two transoms. While there is nothing specifically classical about such windows, their form could indicate that the hall's designer was looking to contemporary works in France – where such windows were as much a part of the vocabulary of the early Renaissance as they were of the later Middle Ages. Rather more precocious are some of the stone corbels supporting the roof wall posts, which are carved as sophisticatedly classical consoles. These consoles have prompted some writers to assume that the hall must be the work of James V but, since James IV's cypher is carved on them (see Figure 10.11), this is unlikely, particularly since payments for slating in 1511 appear to refer to the hall.[28]

The open-timber roof above these corbels had principal rafters of complex hammer-beam construction (see Figure 10.10). This, and its sister roof at Stirling, were the most ambitious roofs we know to have been built in Scotland since that over the hall at Darnaway Castle of the years around 1387 (see p. 11 and Figure 1.6). It seems likely that, in constructing a roof of this form, James IV was emulating the hammer-beam roofs over the halls of the English kings at Westminster and Eltham. Such complex open-timber roofs, including that later built over the hall at Hampton Court, were one of the particular glories of English late medieval architecture. Yet it must be said that the largely unmoulded square section timbers of Edinburgh – which are of slighter section than anything that might have been expected in England – have a slightly utilitarian appearance when compared with their likely models.

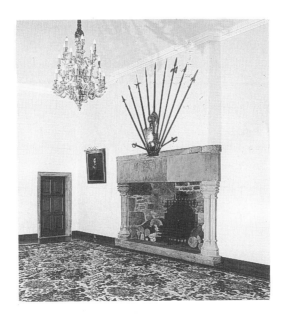

FIGURE 10.9 (*above*) Edinburgh Castle, the 'King's dining Room' in the palace block.
FIGURE 10.10 (*left*) Edinburgh Castle, the hall.
FIGURE 10.11 (*right*) Edinburgh Castle, a corbel in the hall bearing the cypher of James IV.

James IV's work at Stirling was even more far-reaching than that at Edinburgh.[29] As a sign of where his main interests lay, it was at Stirling that he established the Chapel Royal, a major foundation with at least nineteen canons and ten lesser canons under the leadership of the Bishop of Galloway as dean.[30] As at Edinburgh, the main elements to be ranged around the courtyard on the rock summit were the royal lodging, the great hall and a church or chapel. But at Stirling he was additionally concerned to create a grand outer face to the castle, though it may be that his not doing this at Edinburgh was because David II and Robert II had already constructed an impressive outer line there.

At Stirling the new outer face was a towered forework across the main axis of approach to the castle, along a line at least partly occupied by an earlier wall (see Figures 9.9 and 10.12). The work is known to have been in progress between about 1500 and 1510, with the masons John Yorkstoun and John Lockhart both having been involved.[31] The latter was particularly responsible for the tall gatehouse at the centre of this forework, which had three-quarter-round towers at all four angles, and a half-round tower a short way down the curtain wall on each side to create an imposing build-up of elements. Terminating the wall to east and west was a rectangular tower, while on the east side – where the rock was less steep – the curtain wall extended back from the tower as far as the existing north gate. The gate of the forework was reduced to about half its original height in the eighteenth and nineteenth centuries, and is now capped by inappropriate crenellation; the semi-circular towers flanking the gate are almost totally gone, and the eastern of the square terminal towers has been cut down to create a platform for artillery, probably at the time of the Revolution of 1689. Nevertheless, from a combination of what remains – especially at the western end, where the Prince's Tower and curtain wall stand complete – and from views taken before the destruction began, the nobility of the original design may still be understood.

James was clearly wanting more than a military defensive line, even though considerations of artillery did play at least some part in its design, as can be seen from the shot-holes of dumb-bell type in the gatehouse towers, and from the relatively thick curtain walls. But the elaborate grouping of the towers, the soaring proportions, and the French-inspired *chemin-de-ronde* treatment of the tops of the gatehouse towers – in which a walk-way passes around a conically roofed cap-house – are even more of an expression of chivalric aspirations than is his forework at Linlithgow. Indeed, they are perhaps closer to the spirit of French early fifteenth-century manuscript paintings than of modern artillery fortifications. If all of those elements can be seen as nostalgically medieval, it has also been pointed out that the triple entrance – with a pair of pedestrian gates flanking a central carriage-way – may have imperial connotations inspired by the triumphal arches of the classical past.[32] Seeing such complex imagery we cannot doubt that James was prepared to be as eclectic as need be in presenting an appropriate foretaste of one of the principal settings for his court.

At the top of the rock, James's new buildings were set out with the hall on the east side of the square, and the royal lodging at the highest point of the rock on the west side of the square (see Figure 10.1a) – where it could enjoy views over Flanders Moss towards the hills around Loch Lomond. The chapel – within which the collegiate foundation of the Chapel Royal was established in 1501 – was on the north side. There were also buildings on the south side, but these have been absorbed into the later palace, and they are no longer comprehensible. The main problem in understanding the layout of the square in the time of James IV, however, is the precise position of the chapel.

The existing chapel is that built by James VI in 1594 for the baptism of Prince Henry. However, its carefully planned position in relation to both the hall and royal lodging, allowing all their façades to be directed towards the square, is what might also have been expected in a chapel built for James IV. This could suggest that the chapel as now seen is in fact a remodelling by James VI of a predecessor built by James IV, and some inconsistencies in the masonry on the west and north sides might be interpreted as supporting this idea. Yet, against this possibility, foundations have been found of an older and more correctly orientated building which partly underlies the existing chapel, and which is on the same oblique alignment as the – largely rebuilt – north curtain wall of the castle's main enclosure. (It is also on the same axis as other earlier buildings traced through excavation, or still surviving.) The likelihood that these foundations were of the chapel in use during James IV's reign appears to be reinforced by the discovery of a drain on a similar alignment further east, since this overlies a vault itself inserted secondarily above the sunken passage running along the west face of the hall.[33] This would seem to indicate that the building represented by the foundations beneath the present chapel continued in use after the hall had been built for some considerable time.

If these foundations did belong to the chapel that housed James IV's collegiate foundation, however, it would have obscured the entrance to the hall, and this makes it unlikely to have been actually built by James IV, who was evidently so anxious to achieve architectural regularity. Perhaps the most reasonable explanation is simply that he never found the opportunity before his untimely death at the age of forty in 1513 to replace the chapel that was already there – and that had perhaps been built by his father – by one on an alignment more appropriate for his new square. This would also be consistent with indications implicit in proposals made in 1583 that the chapel should be moved to a position further back, presumably to a site close to that of the present structure; at that time it was also said to be in poor repair, suggesting it was a relatively old building.[34] It seems, however, that James IV must have made some stop-gap improvements to make the existing building more suitable for its enhanced use, since the Treasurer's accounts record work on the ceiling in 1494 and 1497, and there was also work on the altar in the latter year. In addition, the copying of the stalls at Glasgow Cathedral in 1506 suggests they were still new enough to excite interest.[35]

There is less uncertainty about James IV's own lodging, which almost definitely occupied the range known as the King's Old Building, along the west side of the square (see Figure 10.13). Since at least the eighteenth century this range has been adapted for military uses, and its northern end was rebuilt by R. W. Billings after a fire of 1855. But recent analysis and investigation have shown the building was originally a

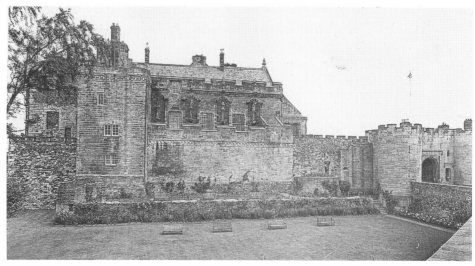

FIGURE 10.12 (*above*)   Stirling Castle, the western part of the forework. The truncated gatehouse is to the right and the Prince's Tower on the left.

FIGURE 10.13 (*below*)   Stirling Castle, the King's Old Building.

two-storeyed structure, with major rooms at first-floor level, above a ground floor planned as a series of barrel-vaulted compartments similar to those at Falkland.[36] The main rooms were reached by a wide spiral stair in a tower capped by a semi-octagonal superstructure. The lodging probably consisted of a hall and chamber, with smaller chambers or closets in a cross-range at one end, and with what may have been a kitchen at the other. The few moulded details that have been found are of a similar quality and date range as those of the great hall on the opposite side of the courtyard. In view of this, it is likely that this range is the 'King's House' for which there is in the Treasurer's Accounts for June 1496 a reference to a contract with the mason Walter Merlioun (Merlzioun) – the same mason who was also working on St John's Church in Perth in that year (see Figure 6.5).[37] The house seems to have been nearing completion in the same year.

Work on the hall had probably been initiated, or perhaps restarted, some years before then (see Figure 10.14). It was nearing completion when the Treasurer's Accounts recorded work on its wall-head in 1501, and there were payments to a plasterer in 1503.[38] Following James VI's succession to the English crown in 1603, and even more after the union of the kingdoms in 1707, little royal interest was taken in the hall, and in about 1800 – following the outbreak of war with France – it was subdivided to provide barrack rooms. It has only been since the castle ceased serving as a regimental depot in 1964 that it has been possible to remove these subdivisions. From the evidence found in the course of this operation, together with what can be learned from record drawings of the seventeenth, eighteenth and nineteenth centuries, the original forms of the hall are now understood with reasonable certainty.

It was larger than the hall at Edinburgh, having overall dimensions of about 42 by 14.25 metres. (In this it was only a fraction of the size of the great hall of the English kings at Westminster or that of the French kings in Paris, but a little larger than those at Windsor and Eltham.)[39] Because of the slope of the rock it was raised on a vaulted substructure, west of which – on the side towards the square – there was a sunken passage which was later vaulted over. The hall required five fireplaces: two in each long wall and one behind the dais at the south end. That dais was marked by a rectangular bay window on both sides, each of which rose the full height of the hall, and was capped by a deep arch that was ribbed to give the appearance of a vault (see Figure 10.15). The main lighting, however, was through paired rectangular windows in the upper half of the walls, which were set on the inner wall plane and embraced externally by outwardly-splayed segmentally arched openings. On the courtyard side of the hall, covering the main entrance and the sunken area on that side, was a pentice roof. Four stairways served the different levels of the hall, the basement and the wall-head parapet: two at the northern end, one in the centre of the east wall, and a fourth in the south-eastern bay. From a survey of 1719 the hall is known to have been covered by a hammer-beam roof closely related to – but not identical with – that over the hall at Edinburgh Castle.[40]

Free-standing halls are essentially medieval in conception, and even the planning of that at Stirling is more medieval in spirit than at Edinburgh – as is seen in the emphasis on the longitudinal axis of the hall through the added prominence given to the dais end by the projecting bays. In this it was like Edward IV's hall at Eltham of the later 1470s, and the hall at Falkland may have been similar. Additionally, whereas we have seen that Edinburgh had some classical details, nothing of the sort has been found at Stirling. On the two main façades of Stirling, for example, there were Gothic tabernacles between the windows, with elaborately Gothic canopies, and with angels on the corbels which might almost have been recruited from the same heavenly host as those in the chapel at Linlithgow Palace (see Figure 10.16). On the east side of the

FIGURE 10.14 (*above*)   Stirling Castle, the hall in course of restoration.
FIGURE 10.15 (*left*)   Stirling Castle, the western of the two bay windows which lit the dais end of the hall.
FIGURE 10.16 (*right*)   Stirling Castle, an angel corbel on the west face of the hall.

hall particular emphasis was given to the bay window, where there are ranks of small figures in miniature tabernacles on the main piers, and the medievalism of the design is further emphasised by the way in which those transoms were in the form of intersecting and overlapping arches. The mouldings throughout the hall are also essentially medieval combinations of filleted rolls and hollows.

By comparison with his contributions to Edinburgh and Stirling, James IV's work at Rothesay Castle was on a very much smaller scale;[41] nevertheless, both as a documented royal residence, and as evidence for his active response to the problems of the Western Isles, it is worth mentioning. Building was under way by 1512, with John and Huchone Cowper as master masons,[42] and it was eventually finished after 1541 by James V. The new work, known as the donjon, was a residential gatehouse tower on the north side of the circular enclosure, with a hall and chambers on the upper floors above the entrance passage (see Figure 10.17). Much of the architectural

FIGURE 10.17   Rothesay Castle, the donjon.

detail is lost, though there are traces of ribbed vaulting in one of the first-floor rooms. The rectangular two-storeyed chapel dedicated to St Michael, towards the east side of the courtyard, may also have been remodelled around the same time.

THE WORKS OF JAMES V AT HOLYROOD, FALKLAND, LINLITHGOW, EDINBURGH AND STIRLING

Considering the effort put into rebuilding the royal residences by James IV, it is astonishing that his son carried out works on a similar scale soon afterwards. In some cases this may have been because the accommodation provided by James IV was insufficient; at both Stirling and Edinburgh Castles, for example, it is hard to see that more than one new royal apartment had been built, which may mean the queen was housed within less modern buildings elsewhere at those castles. It is also likely that James V's imagination had been fired by the Renaissance palaces built for François I of France, and that aspects of his father's work must thus already have seemed old-fashioned. Here we must remember that in 1537 James married François' eldest daughter, Madeleine de Valois, and that when she died soon afterwards he married the daughter of the Duke of Guise, Marie de Guise-Lorraine. It was essential that these French princesses should be housed in their accustomed style if the prestige of the Scottish crown were to be upheld.

It must additionally be remembered that James had travelled in France before his marriage, when he apparently took with him Mogin Martin – a French mason already employed at Dunbar – perhaps to consider with him some of the architectural ideas that might be most appropriately followed up in Scotland. The intellectual and artistic life of the Stewart court embraced many who had been trained on the Continent, and foreign masons were no novelty in Scotland, but there do seem to have been more in the royal service around the second quarter of the sixteenth century than before.[43] Most of these masons were French – such as Nicholas Roy, who worked at Falkland, and John Roytell – but James's interests were not limited to France, and there were some from the Low Countries. These probably included Patrick Fleming, who worked at Holyrood, and Peter Flemishman, who worked on the chapel at Falkland (see Figure 10.8). As part of his effort to attract artists and craftsmen of suitable calibre, James even had his parents-in-law organised into recruiting suitable masons for him, and in 1539 the Duchess of Guise sent two, one of whom was probably Nicholas Roy.

Many of James V's buildings were designed with a self-consciously classical vocabulary, albeit with varying degrees of concession to Scottish tastes. This classicism is seen particularly coherently in the remodelling of his father's work at the palace of Falkland, and in the new palace block at Stirling Castle (see Figure 10.20 and 10.24). Nevertheless, there is still something of his father's medievalising romanticism in a number of his works, especially in the gateways at Linlithgow and in the towers at Holyrood and Falkland (see Figures 10.22, 10.23, 10.18 and 10.19).

One of the first major building operations carried out for James V was at Holyrood where, between 1528 and 1532, he constructed a tower at the north-west corner of his father's palace, probably to the designs of the master mason John Ayton (see Figure

10.18).[44] Originally approached by means of a drawbridge on its eastern side, this tower was a rectangular block with three-quarter-round towers probably at all four angles. Its basic design showed significant similarities with James IV's gatehouse at Stirling, especially in the *chemin-de-ronde* treatment of the wall-head (see Figure 9.9). But these same elements, combined with a rather keep-like overall appearance, could also be partly indebted to French prototypes, such as the donjon at Vincennes of the years around 1370.

   The tower contained two principal lodgings, the king's on the first and the queen's on the second, each with an outer and inner chamber; below them was a barrel-vaulted basement, and there was lesser accommodation in the third floor and garret. Stairways were constructed in the two eastern towers, and closets in the western towers, the latter leading off the inner chambers. Major alterations were made to the lodgings and to the windows in the 1670s, when the first-floor king's lodging was adapted as part of the new queen's apartment, and further alterations were made later. The best surviving pointer to the quality of the internal fittings provided for James V are the wooden ceilings in the second-floor lodging. In the outer chamber the ceiling is divided by ribs into rectangular panels, while in the inner chamber it is divided into interlocking lozenges and hexagons. (In both cases the ceilings were enriched at the time of the homecoming of James VI in 1617.)

   James V instigated further major works at Holyrood in 1535–6, shortly before his marriage.[45] At that time he remodelled the west range of his father's palace to create a suite of rooms that was probably intended to function as a spacious state apartment, supplementing the more circumscribed accommodation in the tower (see Figure 10.18). Among other changes carried out at the same time he moved the chapel from the north to the south range, and it was apparently intended to build a second tower as a pendant to that on the north. All of this work may have been executed to the designs of John Brownhill. Despite the complete reconstruction of the four courtyard

FIGURE 10.18   Holyrood Palace, the tower and entrance range as built by James V.

ranges in the 1670s, we know the appearance of the outer face of the west range from an engraving by Gordon of Rothiemay of 1649, and we also know the plan of the whole palace from a survey by John Mylne of 1663.[46] From these we can see there was a marked contrast between the character and scale of the rooms in the tower and those in the remodelled west range.

The tower, with its thick walls and relatively small windows, had presumably been intended to provide some limited degree of security within an otherwise inadequately defended monastic enclosure. By contrast, the walls of the west range had a closely set array of vast windows, lighting rooms which rose through the equivalent of almost two of the storeys in the tower. It was true that there were gun-holes in the basement storey of the new range, and the gateway into the courtyard was flanked by semi-circular tower-like bays. But the three large windows which opened up most of the upper walls of those semicircular bays would have made nonsense of any attempt to repel assailants, and the polygonal bays which project from the main face of the range further along to each side show that decorative effect was consulted more than defensibility.

These bays of rounded or polygonal plan, combined with large mullioned and transomed windows, decoratively crenellated wall-heads, and elaborate cupolas or spirelets, were all elements finding favour in several countries of northern Europe at this period. It is probably in English work, however, that the closest analogies are to be found, as in the queen's long gallery range at Hampton Court, which was being built for Henry VIII between 1533 and 1537.[47] In the entrance range at Holyrood, therefore, what we seem to see is James V declaring himself the equal of his English uncle. At Falkland, by contrast, we see in building operations carried out between 1537 and 1541 architecture in which James's French tastes are more evident.[48]

At Falkland there were two main elements to the work: the creation of a gatehouse, which may have incorporated earlier work, and the remodelling of the south and east ranges already built for James IV. Several masons were involved, but the master chiefly concerned with the gatehouse – which was finished in 1541 – was probably John Brownhill, who had already worked at Holyrood (see Figure 10.19). As is appropriate for a gatehouse, that at Falkland has an externally martial air, with an appearance very like that of the north-west tower at Holyrood in its three-quarter-round towers capped by *chemins-de-ronde* (see Figure 10.18). The adjacent façade of the south range remained largely as built by James IV, though its cornice and crenellated parapet were evidently rebuilt along with the gatehouse, and carved figures were added by Peter Flemishman.

Towards the courtyard side, however, the south and east ranges were given an altogether different, sophisticatedly classical, appearance. In the east range this simply involved a surface remodelling, which was dated by inscription to 1537. The main element in this was the division of the façade into bays by columns in front of pilasters at the principal level; these were carried on complex pilasters at ground-floor level, and capped by aedicules at second-floor level. The first floor was afforded further emphasis by carved portrait roundels set to either side of the window lintels. The south range was given essentially similar treatment, though there the work was less

FIGURE 10.19   Falkland Palace, the gatehouse.

superficial because it formed part of new galleries added in front of the chapel range (see Figure 10.20). The quality of both the conception and the execution was therefore less compromised by what was already there, and it is no exaggeration to see it as being the most advanced classical work to have been produced within the British Isles by its date.

There can thus be little doubt that these façades were the work of one or other of the French masons then working in Scotland. It has been argued that the remodelling of the east range may have been by Mogin Martin, but that the greater confidence shown in the south range was due to Nicholas Roy, who had come to Falkland by 1539.[49] It has also been convincingly suggested that parallels for these façades can be found in recent work for François I, such as Villers-Cotterets, which had been started in 1533.[50] In particular, the articulation into bays by pilasters at the lower level and columns at the upper level is significantly similar. Parallels for the use of portrait roundels are to be found in several French buildings, including the Hôtel d'Alluye in Blois, built for a minister of Louis XII before about 1508.[51]

Within the ranges, James V's modifications were equally extensive. The royal lodgings were in the east range, with galleries on the east face overlooking the gardens there; unfortunately that range is now gutted, and it is no longer clear if the two apartments were placed adjacent to each other or one above the other. In the south range, despite much of the chapel's present internal appearance deriving from a restoration by the Marquess of Bute in 1896, some of the original fittings still survive

FIGURE 10.20 (*above*)   Falkland Palace, the galleries on the courtyard side of the south range.
FIGURE 10.21 (*below*)   Falkland Palace, the chapel in the south range as restored by Lord Bute.

(see Figure 10.21). The ribbed timber ceiling was the work of the wright Richard Stewart, for which he was paid in 1539–41, though it was later enriched for the home-coming of Charles I in 1633. It is a more complex version of the ceilings in the tower at Holyrood, in this case with rectangles overlaid by a second pattern of elongated hexagons. Another fine feature of the chapel is the screen, with tall bobbin-turned balusters, which may also be the work of Stewart.

At Linlithgow James V's intervention was probably less than at Holyrood or Falkland, and yet the large sums spent show that he did much more than is now apparent. As early as 1526 he had appointed as keeper of the palace Sir James Hamilton of Finnart, whose contribution to artillery fortification has already been discussed (see p. 290).[52] Hamilton seems to have supervised the work when building started in earnest in March 1534.[53] The master mason was Thomas French, who had been at Holyrood and Falkland, and was already at work on the adjacent parish church. As already said, French was one of a dynasty of masons much involved in royal works, the first of whom may have been of French birth. Among James V's works we know he provided a new ceiling and altarpiece for the chapel, the former probably being similar to that at Falkland. Within the royal lodgings, the chief evidence for his changes is in his own outer chamber, since the fireplace there is related to those that were to be installed for him at Stirling Castle.

His most visible remaining contribution to Linlithgow, however, was the removal of the main entrance from the east to the south range (see Figure 10.22). In doing this he also remodelled the western end of the south range so that its façade was on a continuous plane. In cutting a new passage through the ground storey he constructed a small twin-towered gatehouse as the proscenium to it which, despite its wide-mouthed gunholes, was on an even smaller scale than his father's bulwark. Aligned with the new entrance, at the precinct wall, he constructed a second gate on a similar scale – albeit with octagonal rather than three-quarter-round towers (see Figure 10.23). Running along its crenellated parapet are panels with the arms of the four chivalric orders of which James was a member: the English Garter, the Scottish Thistle, the Burgundian Golden Fleece, and the French order of St Michael.

Within the central courtyard of the palace, what is perhaps the loveliest of James's additions was constructed: the octagonal fountain (see Figure 10.4). Arranged in three upwardly diminishing tiers of basins, which are connected by cusped and crocketed diminutive flying buttresses, the whole composition is capped by a miniature imperial crown. Like the gatehouses, this is an essentially Gothic composition and it is only the figures and the roundels containing heads which show something of the new influences of the Renaissance. It was restored from the original fragments in 1930.

James V was also active at the royal castles. His building works at Edinburgh, however, suggest that he was becoming less interested in it as a first-rate royal residence, presumably partly as a consequence of the greater relative importance of Holyrood as the main royal residence in the vicinity of what was now regarded as the national capital. Even under James III, Edinburgh Castle's importance as an arsenal and foundry may have made it less pleasant to live in, and by the time of James IV there seems to have been an artillery house on the opposite side of the main square

FIGURE 10.22 (*above*)   Linlithgow Palace, the south range remodelled as the entrance front.
FIGURE 10.23 (*below*)   Linlithgow Palace, the outer gateway.

from the palace. James V gave further impetus to this tendency to use the castle primarily as an artillery depot when he converted St Mary's Church, on the north side of the square, into a store for munitions. Other than that, his main activity was the construction of a register house in 1540–2 for the royal records;[54] this was evidently sited at one end of the great hall, although its precise position is no longer known with certainty.

In contrast to his comparative lack of interest in Edinburgh Castle, at Stirling Castle James V constructed his most impressively homogeneous essay in palatial architecture (see Figures 10.1a and 10.24).[55] As at Linlithgow, Sir James Hamilton of Finnart was in control of the work, and preparations were evidently under way as early as 1538, when Hamilton is said to have entered the castle.[56] In the following year there was a complex transaction by which he seems to have funded part of the work in exchange for grants of land. It was also in 1539 that he was appointed principal master of all royal works throughout the realm,[57] and he continued to control works at Stirling until his execution in 1540. After that, the work was supervised by sir James Nicholson, who had earlier been master of works at the castle from 1530. It is likely building was nearly complete in 1541, when the carver Robert Robertson was appointed principal overseer and master of all works concerning his craft at the castle.[58]

Hamilton of Finnart's involvement in so many building projects leaves no doubt of his profound interest in architecture, and he doubtlessly expected his views to count in much of what was done. It is, however, difficult to see convincing evidence of his having been the main hand behind their design, since there are such fundamental differences between them.[59] It seems more likely that, at Stirling as at Falkland, the design of the palace was drawn up by one of James V's French masons, but it must have been radically modified in execution, and the end result defies categorisation to a greater extent than any other of James V's palaces. If we have to identify a contribution by Hamilton, it is probably in this modified implementation of an initial design.

The palace was sited on the southern side of the square; since two of the principal elements of a royal residence – the great hall and the chapel – were already in place around other sides of the square, the main purpose of the new building was to house matching lodgings for the king and his consort. There was therefore no need for the building to be on the expansive scale of Linlithgow. Nevertheless, it is a notably monumental structure. Set so close behind the western section of his father's forework that it was contiguous with the Prince's Tower at the western end of that forework (see Figure 10.12), it was of compact quadrangular plan, with a rectangular courtyard at its centre. At basement level, and possibly along part of the west side, it incorporated earlier structures, and this may have enforced the slightly irregular rhomboidal plan; but in all essential respects it was a new construction by James V.

The Stirling palace has inevitably suffered later modifications. Much of its west range was falling into decay by 1625, and was demolished later in that century; it was perhaps at the same time that the windows and doors of the west gallery towards the courtyard were altered and the stair into the courtyard suppressed. Around the turn of the seventeenth century the main porch, at the north-west corner of the building, was replaced by a smaller porch and stair to the governor's apartment in the attic storey. The formation of that apartment also required windows to be cut through the parapet. But, despite these changes, the main rooms of the lodgings still preserve their original inter-relationships and proportions. Those rooms are approached at ground-floor level, by a doorway at the top end of the façade towards the square – though the slope of the land means that there is a full storey beneath them at the eastern end of the building, where there is the most imposing façade. The two lodgings occupied the main floor of the north, east and south ranges. The sequence of rooms in each was a hall followed by an outer and an inner chamber; the inner chambers adjoin each other in the east range, and there were closets off each, though those of the queen are now destroyed.

Externally, the rectangular windows are capped by segmental tympana carved with '15'; they alternate with recessed sections of walling bridged by segmental multi-cusped arches at a higher level than the window heads (see Figure 10.24). The windows rest on a string course carved with winged angel heads, from which, in the recessed sections, there rise elaborate baluster shafts supporting statues. The wall-head parapet is crenellated and projects out on a deep cornice carved with foliage trails. In front of the merlons of the parapet, and corresponding with the niche statues below, are shorter balusters bearing smaller statues. Throughout the whole design there is a profusion of carving, with gargoyle-like corbels below all of the balusters and at the arch springings of the recessed sections. The richness of the surface modelling is further emphasised by the heavy roll mouldings which mark the changes of the wall plane.

In the complex and slightly irrational changes of wall plane, the stepping alternation of arched and lintelled wall articulation, and the lavish sculptural effects, there is a mannerist note which offers a Scottish parallel for works in some of the more advanced artistic centres. There could be no direct connection with the wilfully anti-classical rhythms of wall-faces seen in such contemporary Italian buildings as those designed by Giulio Romano for the Dukes of Mantua, or with the closely spaced alternation of windows and sculpture recesses seen in the Palazzo Spada in Rome. Nevertheless, it may not be fanciful to wonder if the questioning architectural spirit represented by those buildings has also had its impact on Stirling. But the net effect is very different, and not least because Stirling shows such an intermingling of the medieval and the classical; indeed, on first sight there is even something of the feeling of the great Anglo-Norman keeps in what can be read as a regular rhythm of broad shallow pilasters combined with the wall-head crenellation. Looking for more specific debts, the use of arches with bands of dropped cusps, together with baluster-like shafts, could reveal debts to Louis XII's east range at Blois.

Perhaps the most lasting impact of the exterior of the palace is created by the statuary, which shows considerable variety of style (see Figure 10.25).[60] The carver of some figures was striving for a degree of classicism, but others are deliberately grotesque or show an overstated realism. Some of the latter have a Germanic quality, and it has been shown that several were based on engravings of the planetary deities

FIGURE 10.24 (*above*)   Stirling Castle, the east face of the palace block.
FIGURE 10.25 (*left*)   Stirling Castle, one of the figures on the north face of the palace block.
FIGURE 10.26 (*right*)   Stirling Castle, one of the carved wooden roundels from the ceilings of the royal apartments in the palace block.

by Hans Burgkmair. A number of the corbels look like depictions of the more buxom members of James's court, and something of the same spirit is to be seen in some of the carved heads within roundels which once decorated the ceilings of rooms within the palace (see Figure 10.26).[61]

The basic form of the ceiling roundels is similar to those in the walls of the two courtyard façades at Falkland, and it may be significant that the wright Robert Robertson had worked at Falkland before being appointed to Stirling in 1541 (see Figure 10.20). However, as with the external statuary, several hands were involved in their carving, and it has been suggested that the French craftsman Andrew Mansioun, who was much involved in royal works from 1539, could have been one of them. The heads were removed from the ceiling in 1777 but, if the engraving published in *Lacunar Strevelinense* in 1817 was accurately based, they were set within a square grid of ribs.[62] One possible inspiration for such an arrangement could have been the roundels within coffering which decorate the stair vaults at Azay le Rideau in the Loire Valley. It is more difficult to suggest sources for the fireplaces in the main rooms, which have massive jambs carried on round or square shafts. However, the animal or human forms disposed around the capitals, in a way that is intended to reflect the massing of Corinthian capitals, could be a distant echo of the lesser capitals found in a number of the palaces of François I.

In the design of its façades the Stirling palace block is not the most architecturally sophisticated of the Scottish royal residences; that accolade must go to the courtyard façades of Falkland. Nevertheless, for all its idiosyncrasies, it represents a worthy climax to the palace building operations of the fourth and fifth Jameses. Considering the relatively limited resources of the kingdom, this was royal architecture on an impressive scale. After it, little other work on the royal residences was to be undertaken before the terminal date for this book. The death of James V – in 1542 – left Mary, a baby of only a few days old, as queen, and six years later she was sent to France as the future wife of the Dauphin. By the time she returned to Scotland, in 1561, the Reformation had already taken place. We know of some works carried out on her residences at the behest of the regents who governed Scotland in her absence, and the Earl of Arran seems to have been particularly active at Edinburgh Castle, where parts of the work carried out for him could still be incorporated in the palace block. But it was not to be until after James VI's marriage to Anne of Denmark in 1589 that there was to be a significant new wave of royal building, and that is outside the remit of this book.

Conclusion

The terminal date for this book is 1560, the year of the Reformation, and a date of profound significance for ecclesiastical architecture. Yet it is of nothing like the same relevance for secular architecture, since the seeds of many of the ideas which were to flourish in the later sixteenth and seventeenth centuries had already been sown by the middle decades of the sixteenth century, and there is therefore a strong sense of continuity.

The influence of the precocious experiments with Renaissance detailing seen in the royal works at Edinburgh in about 1500 and at Falkland, Holyrood and Stirling in the 1530s and 1540s, for example, was already beginning to be more widely disseminated. This was particularly the case in the secular works of the greater prelates, who for some time had been showing an awareness of the Renaissance ideas that they must have encountered on their European travels. As early as 1491 a Scottish archbishop, William Schevez of St Andrews, could be shown looking like a humanist scholar on a medal which was probably cast for him by the artist Quentin Matsys — as he passed through the Low Countries on his way to Rome.[1]

Later at St Andrews, the few surviving *ex-situ* carved fragments from Cardinal David Beaton's work on the castle (dating from before 1546) show sophisticated French-inspired work,[2] while the baluster shafts from the heraldic panels of Archbishop Dunbar's work on the gatehouse of the archiepiscopal castle at Glasgow (of before 1547) indicate a wish not to be outdone by his great rival.[3] On a larger scale the works of around the 1550s at St Andrews Castle and in the domestic buildings of the nearby St Mary's College show that Archbishop John Hamilton was to continue the discerning artistic patronage of his predecessor up to the eve of the Reformation.[4] Yet, if the education and travels of the prelates made them particularly fitted to follow the lead of the king in fostering the spread of Renaissance ideas before the Reformation, the magnates and burgesses were to continue this trend after it — as in Regent Mar's Stirling town house of 1570–2.[5] There was thus to be no real break in the gathering momentum of the Scottish Renaissance.

At a more domestic level, the way had already been paved before the Reformation for the greater convenience of planning which was to find its fulfilment in the ingenious later developments on the tower-house.[6] Perhaps the only likely impact of church reform here was in the transfer of church lands into secular ownership after 1560, and in the yet wider availability of education that was an aim of the reformers.

The secularisation of church lands may have encouraged a greater investment in domestic architecture than before, while the expansion of education possibly increased receptivity to new ideas. Moving on to more strictly military architecture, it is likely the only real bearing the Reformation had on the development of artillery fortification was that English aggression in the years leading up to it meant that English and French forces on Scottish soil constructed works on a scale, and to a degree of sophistication, which might not otherwise have been contemplated. Nevertheless, the operations of James V and Hamilton of Finnart at Blackness, Craignethan and Cadzow in the 1530s show that the Scots themselves already had a lively appreciation of the value of artillery works.

However, if the Reformation had only an indirect impact on secular architecture, its influence on ecclesiastical architecture was traumatic. For several decades it had been by no means certain that Scotland would follow England and parts of Scandinavia and Germany in rejecting Rome's authority over the church. Indeed, before his death in 1542, James V had consistently rejected the blandishments of Henry VIII to join him in reforming the church, favouring instead a continued political alliance with France and allegiance of the Scottish church to the papacy. There was much to be said in favour of this, apart from the fact that England was an unreliable friend. Since at least 1487 successive popes had been constrained to allow Scotland's kings a greater say in the appointment to high offices within the church, and the wish to retain Scotland's loyalty meant that ever more was likely to be on offer to a faithful son of the church. Beyond this, from the later 1540s the church was itself beginning to take limited steps to reform some of the more blatant abuses,[7] and in 1545 the Council of Trent – which set in motion the Counter-Reformation – began its first session.

Within Scotland there is less evidence than might be expected of a concerted and widespread call for reform after a first burst of enthusiasm in the 1530s. Nevertheless, acts of 1541, calling for greater respect for the church, show there was a continuing ground swell of unrest – particularly among groups in Fife, Lothian and Ayrshire. At the same time, although the leaders of the Scottish church were doing far too little to eradicate abuses – and doing that little too late – concessions to changing opinions were being made, as is evident from Archbishop Hamilton's *Catechism* of 1552. This summary of the faith ignored the authority of the papacy, and what it says about the mass and justification by faith would have been acceptable to many of the less extreme protestants.[8]

Official policy towards reform fluctuated after the death of James V. Under the regency of the Earl of Arran a more pro-English policy gave hope to some in the reforming party, even if Arran himself was forced by circumstances to be indecisive on a number of issues. A more overtly pro-French and Catholic policy was pursued after 1548, and especially when Mary of Guise became regent in 1554 – though even this was not as clear-cut as might have been expected. Mary of Guise went to considerable lengths to avoid antagonism of any group, and the case for toleration of the reforming party was strengthened because the throne of England was by then occupied by the Catholic Mary Tudor. For all of these reasons, while the need for

changes within the church must not be underestimated, when reform finally came in
1560, it was partly for political purposes and not simply because of the demands of
the protestant leaders.

It is difficult to gauge how far the possibility of reform affected the amount of
church building in the decades before 1560, but some new foundations, together with
the necessary investment in buildings to house them, were being made well into the
sixteenth century. A major establishment for Dominican nuns was founded at
Sciennes in Edinburgh in 1517, while a house for the Dominican friars was established
in Dundee in about 1521. The Edinburgh house of the Carmelites may have been
founded a few years later than that. Collegiate foundations also continued to be set
up, including that at Crail in 1517, and those at Haddington, Stirling, Peebles and
Aberdeen St Nicholas in the 1540s. These particular colleges were mainly in buildings
that were already largely complete; but at those of Our Lady in Glasgow of about
1525, at Biggar of 1545, and at the academic college of St Mary at St Andrews of
1537, the new foundations were probably all accompanied by new building works.[9]
Beyond these, it has been seen that there were still major building operations at several
of the cathedrals, abbeys and burgh churches some decades into the century. All of
this suggests that many churchmen and lay patrons still had sufficient confidence in
the future of their church to continue to build for it, and that for them there was little
sense of the church being balanced on the edge of an abyss.

There does seem, however, to have been an element of conservatism in those
ecclesiastical building operations that were in progress around the second quarter of
the sixteenth century. Even though many prelates were responding to the intellectual
stimulus of the Renaissance, and were introducing the latest ideas into the secular
buildings erected for them, these ideas seem to have been felt less appropriate for
churches. One minor exception is at Midcalder Church, of around the 1540s, where
at least one of the choir pinnacles has what appears to be acanthus-like foliage for its
crocketing.[10] But even at Biggar Collegiate Church, where Gothic forms were greatly
diluted, there is nothing specifically classical in the architecture.

Nevertheless, Renaissance forms do occasionally permeate into church fixtures and
furnishings. The sacrament house at Kintore, in Aberdeenshire, for example, is
flanked by baluster shafts.[11] Classical influences are also detectable in some tombs
and, significantly, the accounts for the tomb of James V in 1542 specified the use of
Roman letters.[12] Among surviving tombs there is an element of classicism in
the spandrel roundels of the monument to Alexander Ogilvie of Findlater at Cullen
Church in Banffshire, of about 1554.[13] The same is true of some wooden furnishings,
including panels said to have come from Seton Collegiate Church,[14] and the simplified
linenfold lower panels on the rood screen doors at Foulis Easter.[15] A related type of
linenfold panelling, incidentally, appears on the choir stalls shown in the scene of the
royal requiem in the book of hours which James IV gave to Margaret Tudor at the
time of their wedding in 1503.[16]

Any ecclesiastical building still in progress was presumably brought to an abrupt
halt in 1560, when the sacrifice of the mass was abolished as the central form of
worship, and the authority of the Pope was repudiated. And yet the situation within

the church remained fluid for many years to come. The office of bishop was continued and, though their authority was greatly reduced or completely removed at various times, it was only finally abolished within the established church at the Revolution of 1689. Beyond this, the monasteries continued to exist as land-holding corporations, if not as religious institutions, and most monks who so wished could pass the rest of their days enjoying their portions of the monastic income, within those parts of the familiar walls that were allowed to survive. Eventually, after most members of the communities had died, the majority of those monasteries which were not retained by the crown through the Act of Annexation of 1587 were erected into temporal lordships for the commendators. At the lower levels of the church, even in the parishes the Reformation introduced no way of disposing of priests who did not wish to comply with the new forms of worship, and it was possible for an incumbent to continue receiving much of his old income, while making no contribution to the life of the church. The only diminution they suffered was that in 1561 it was legislated that one-third of ecclesiastical incomes should be collected, partly to pay for reformed clergy, but also to increase crown revenues.[17]

Under such circumstances there was no money to pay for new church building. In any case, in some parts of the country there were already more churches than could be afforded, while most of the larger cathedral, monastic and burgh churches were not well suited to new forms of worship and those which were retained had soon to be reduced in size or subdivided. One of the first churches designed specifically to meet the needs of reformed worship was at Burntisland in Fife, where an innovative centralised building with simple classical detailing was erected over thirty years after the Reformation, in 1592.[18] This church, built when the church was passing through one of its more strongly protestant and presbyterian phases, pointed the way to a radically new approach to planning.

Burntisland, however, was a unique experiment, and the very few church buildings constructed over several generations to come, tended to be less revolutionary. Indeed, in some cases, and especially at phases when episcopacy was in the ascendant, it might seem there was a nostalgia for a more traditional approach. The model church built in 1621 by Archbishop Spottiswoode at Dairsie in Fife is the most extreme – and most charming – illustration of this, with its plate-traceried windows.[19] Several other examples could be quoted of the use of medieval forms in religious buildings. Among these are the traceried windows in the burial aisle at Oldhamstocks Church in East Lothian of 1581, in the chapel of George Heriot's Hospital in Edinburgh started in 1628, in the crossing arch at Holyrood Abbey nave of about 1633, in the private chapel at Fordell Castle of 1650, and in the Archerfield aisle at Dirleton Church of 1664.[20]

Looking at these buildings it might be thought that the impact of the Reformation on church design has been overstated, and that a Gothic vocabulary remained current for ecclesiastical buildings. However, the medievalism of these later buildings must be understood rather as a type of romanticism in which certain motifs were restated because of their particular connotations, with no intention of perpetuating Gothic forms as a whole in doing so. Dairsie has a fine Renaissance frame to its main doorway, for example, while the aisle at Dirleton has heavily baroque rusticated quoins. The contrast between the Gothic windows and the rest of the building is even more plainly evident in Heriot's Hospital, where in all other respects the designer was creating a modern building. Such self-conscious use of archaic motifs in fact emphasises just how completely Gothic was no longer a current idiom by the later sixteenth-century. Just as in an English parallel such as the library building of the 1620s at St John's College in Cambridge,[21] for example, by making certain architectural quotations it was possible to evoke specific religious or scholarly associations for those receptive enough to understand them.

It is pointless to speculate how soon the impact of the Renaissance would have transformed ecclesiastical architecture – in the way it was transforming the more advanced secular buildings[22] – if the Reformation had not intervened. Nevertheless, since our late medieval architecture showed a continuing need for contact with the larger world to maintain the stimulus of a regular infusion of new ideas, and since most of the areas to which Scotland looked were themselves adopting an increasingly classical architectural vocabulary, it could only have been a matter of time before Renaissance forms came to predominate. But, in the event, the Reformation inhibited church construction for an extended period and, when it began again, there could be no continuity with what had gone before.

Notes

These notes have been kept to what was considered an essential minimum. In addition to the citation of sources, however, they are intended to provide pointers to literature in which may be found fuller details about the buildings under discussion (although the interpretation of the evidence to be found in that literature may not necessarily be the same as that offered in this book). A list of abbreviations used for commonly cited titles appears at the start of the bibliography.

NOTES TO CHAPTER ONE

1   For a fuller account of the historical background to this period see Ranald Nicholson, *Scotland, the later Middle Ages*, Edinburgh, 1974, pp. 184–280.

2   For discussion of Scotland's trading links see the essays in Michael Lynch, Michael Spearman and Geoffrey Stell (eds), *The Scottish medieval town*, Edinburgh, 1988, and particularly David Ditchburn, 'Trade with northern Europe, 1297–1540', pp. 161–179, and Alexander Stevenson, 'Trade with the south, 1070–1513', pp. 180–206. See also a number of essays and maps in Peter McNeill and Ranald Nicholson (eds), *An historical atlas of Scotland c.400–c.1600*. St Andrews, 1975, and particularly A. A. M. Duncan, 'Foreign trade and the burghs 1327–31, 1362–66', pp. 63–4, and Athol Murray, 'Foreign trade and Scottish ports 1471 and 1542', pp. 74–5.

3   On trading links with the Low Countries see Cosmo Innes (ed.), *The ledger of Andrew Halyburton, 1492–1503*, Edinburgh, 1867; John Davidson and Alexander Gray, *The Scottish staple at Veere*, London, 1909; M. P. Rooseboom, *The Scottish staple in the Netherlands*, The Hague, 1910; Alexander Stevenson, *Trade between Scotland and the Low Countries in the later Middle Ages*, unpublished Ph.D. thesis, Aberdeen University, 1982. For outline accounts of artistic links see David McRoberts, 'Notes on Scoto-Flemish artistic contacts', *Innes Review*, vol. 10, 1959, pp. 91–6; Colin Thompson and Lorne Campbell, *Hugo van der Goes and the Trinity panels in Edinburgh*, Edinburgh, 1974, pp., 50–4; Richard Fawcett, 'Late Gothic architecture in the Low Countries: considerations on the influence of the Low Countries', *Proc. Soc. Antiq. Scot.*, vol. 112, 1982, pp. 477–96. On aspects of cultural links see, for example, John Durkan, 'Education in the century of the Reformation', *Innes Review*, vol. 10, 1959, pp. 67–90; R. J. Lyall, 'Scottish students and masters at the universities of Cologne and Louvain in the fifteenth century', *Innes Review*, vol. 36, 1985, pp. 55–73. On

aspects of the influence of the Netherlands on Scottish worship see passing references in David McRoberts, 'The medieval Scottish liturgy illustrated by surviving documents', *Transactions of the Scottish Ecclesiological Society*, vol. 15, 1957, pp. 24–40; James Galbraith, 'The Middle Ages', in Duncan Forrester and Douglas Murray (eds), *Studies in the history of worship in Scotland*, Edinburgh, 1984, pp. 17–32.

4   W. T. Oldrieve, 'Remains of David's Tower at Edinburgh Castle', *Proc. Soc. Antiq. Scot.*, vol. 48, 1914, pp. 230–70; *Exch. Rolls,* vol. 2, pp. cix–cx and 308.

5   *Exch. Rolls*, vol. 2, pp. 85, 113, 306, 477, 524, 551 and 621, and vol. 3, pp. 64, 80, 244, 667 and 676.

6   W. Douglas Simpson 'Dundonald castle', *Ayrshire Archaeological and Natural History Society Collections*, 2nd ser., vol. 1, 1947–9 pp. 3–15.

7   Gordon Ewart, 'The excavations at Dundonald Castle 1986–88', unpublished interim report (publication in Château Gaillard conference transactions, forthcoming).

8   For the Stewarts' landholding see G. W. S. Barrow, 'The earliest Stewarts and their lands', in id., *The Kingdom of the Scots*, London, 1973, pp. 337–61.

9   For drawings of the vault at Yester see MacGibbon and Ross, *Castellated and Domestic*, vol 1, pp. 117, 118 and 120.

10   William Fraser, *The red book of Menteith*, Edinburgh, 1880, vol. 1, pp. 471–96; MacGibbon and Ross, *Castellated and Domestic*, vol. 1, pp. 413–29; W. Douglas Simpson, 'Doune Castle', *Proc. Soc. Antiq. Scot.*, vol. 72, 1937, pp. 73–83; W. Douglas Simpson, *Doune Castle* (guidebook), Derby, 1974; R. Denys Pringle, *Doune Castle* (official guide), Edinburgh, 1987.

11   *Reg. Mag. Sig.*, vol. 1, no. 890 etc.

12   See Simpson, op. cit. note 10.

13   *Exch. Rolls.*, vol. 6, pp. i, 220, 380 and 482; G. P. Stell and M. L. G. Baillie, note on Darnaway roof, in W. D. H. Sellar (ed.), *Moray* (Scottish Society for Northern Studies), forthcoming.

14   For the career of Lewyn see John Harvey, *English medieval architects, a biographical dictionary down to 1550*, 2nd edn, Gloucester, 1984, pp. 181–4.

15   RCAHMS, *Roxburghshire*, 1956, vol. 2, pp. 407–11.

16   *Exchequer K. R. Accounts*, bundle 483, no. 32; the indenture is printed in L. F. Salzman, *Building in England down to 1540*, Oxford, 1952, pp. 457–9.

17   RCAHMS, *Dumfriesshire*, 1920, pp. 10–24; W. Douglas Simpson, 'The two castles of Caerlaverock', *Transactions of the Dumfriesshire and Galloway Natural History and Antiquarian Society*, vol. 2, 1936–8, pp. 180–204; B. H. St. J. O'Neil, *Caerlaverock Castle* (official guide), Edinburgh, 1952.

18   S. Rigold, 'Structural aspects of medieval timber bridges', *Medieval Archaeology*, vol. 19, 1975, pp. 71–74; M. G. L. Baillie, *Tree-ring dating and archaeology*, London, 1982, pp. 160–3.

19   RCAHMS, *East Lothian*, 1924, pp. 16–21; J. S. Richardson and C. J. Tabraham, *Dirleton Castle* (official guide), 3rd edn, Edinburgh, 1982.

20   G. S. Aitken, 'Bothwell Castle', *Journal of the Royal Institute of British Architects*, 3rd ser., vol. 9, 1904, pp. 413–26; W. Douglas Simpson, 'The architectural

history of Bothwell Castle', *Proc. Soc. Antiq. Scot.*, vol. 59, 1924–5, pp. 165–93; W. Douglas Simpson, 'Bothwell Castle reconsidered', *Transactions of the Glasgow Archaeological Society*, new ser., vol. 11, 1947, pp. 97–116; W. Douglas Simpson, 'The donjons of Conisborough and Bothwell', *Archaeologia Aeliana*, 4th ser., vol. 32, 1954, pp. 100–15; W. Douglas Simpson, *Bothwell Castle* (official guide), revised edn, Edinburgh, 1985.

21   RCAHMS, *Roxburghshire*, 1956, vol. 1, pp. 75–85; W. Douglas Simpson, *Hermitage Castle* (official guide), 3rd edn, Edinburgh, 1987.

22   See Harold G. Leask, *Irish castles and castellated houses*, revised edn, Dundalk, 1946, figs 79 and 80.

23   RCAHMS, *East Lothian*, 1924, pp. 61–7; C. J. Tabraham and J. S. Richardson, *Tantallon Castle*, Edinburgh, 1986.

24   *Works Accts*, vol. 1, pp. 198, 200, 227, 228, 235, 236 and 241; Iain MacIvor, 'Artillery and major places of strength in the Lothians and east Border', in David H. Caldwell (ed.), *Scottish weapons and fortifications 1100–1800*, Edinburgh, 1981, pp. 122–4 and 132–3.

25   D. Hay Fleming, 'Some recent discoveries in St Andrews', *Proc. Soc. Antiq. Scot.*, vol. 49, 1914–15, pp. 223–8; D. Hay Fleming, *Handbook to St Andrews*, St Andrews, 1924, pp. 90–9; RCAHMS, *Fife, Kinross and Clackmannan*, 1933, pp. 250–7; Stewart Cruden, *St Andrews Castle* (official guide), 3rd edn, Edinburgh, 1982; Richard Fawcett, *St Andrews Castle* (official guide), Edinburgh, 1992.

26   *Chron. Bower* (Goodall), vol. 1, p. 365.

27   RCAHMS, *Stirlingshire*, 1963, vol. 1, 249–54.

28   For discussion of the spread of tower-houses in Britain see N. J. G. Pounds, *The medieval castle in England and Wales*, Cambridge, 1990, pp. 276–94, and M. W. Thompson, *The decline of the castle*, Cambridge, 1987, pp. 21–7. For Irish tower-houses see Leask, op. cit. note 22, pp. 75–124.

29   H. L. Janssen, 'The archaeology of the medieval castle in the Netherlands: Results and prospects for future research', in J. C. Besteman, J. M. Bos and H. A. Heidinga (eds), *Medieval archaeology in the Netherlands*, Assen, 1990, particularly pp. 244–9. See also Frans Doperé and William Ubregts, *De donjon in Vlaanderen*, Leuven 1991.

30   For the history of the Douglas family see W. Fraser, *The Douglas Book*, Edinburgh, 1885.

31   RCAHMS, *Stewartry of Kirkcudbright*, 1914, pp. 28–34; Christopher J. Tabraham, *Threave Castle* (official guide), Edinburgh, 1989.

32   G. L. Good and C. J. Tabraham, 'Excavations at Threave Castle, Galloway, 1974–78', *Medieval Archaeology*, vol. 25, 1981, pp. 90–140.

33   For Dunnottar, see W. Douglas Simpson, 'The development of Dunnottar Castle', *Archaeological Journal*, vol. 98, 1941, pp. 87–98; W. Douglas Simpson, *Dunnottar Castle: historical and descriptive*, Aberdeen, 1968; for Craigmillar, see R. Denys Pringle, *Craigmillar Castle* (official guide), Edinburgh, 1990.

34   RCAHMS, *Peeblesshire*, 1967, vol. 2, pp. 243–61.

35   There is a useful summary of the documentation relating to Robert I's burial in S. M. Webster, *Dunfermline Abbey*, Dunfermline, 1948, pp. 34–5.

36   Harvey, op. cit. note 14, p. 229.

37   Michael R. Apted and Susan Hannabuss, *Painters in Scotland* 1301–1700, *a biographical dictionary* (Scottish Record Society), new ser., Edinburgh, 1978, vol. 7, p. 24.

38   D. Black, *The history of Brechin*, Brechin, 1839, p. 17.

39   Boece, *Vitae*, p. 24; see also Ronald G. Cant, *The building of St Machar's Cathedral, Aberdeen* (Friends of St Machar's Cathedral), occasional papers, no. 4, Aberdeen, 1976.

40   *Reg. Mag. Sig.*, vol. 1, nos 378 and 428; Reg. Aven., 229, fo. 188v.

41   MacGibbon and Ross, *Ecclesiastical*, vol. 3, pp. 338–43.

42   For easter sepulchres see Francis Bond, *The chancel of English churches*, Oxford, 1916, pp. 220–41; and Veronica Sekules, 'The tomb of Christ at Lincoln and the development of the sacrament shrine: easter sepulchres reconsidered', in *Medieval art and architecture at Lincoln Cathedral* (British Archaeological Association Conference Transactions for 1982), Leeds, 1986.

43   MacGibbon and Ross, *Ecclesiastical*, vol. 2, pp. 486–91; Cowan and Easson, p. 158; *Bldgs of Scot.*, Lothian, 1978, 446–7.

44   RCAHMS, *Fife, Kinross and Clackmannan*, 1933, pp. 152–3.

45   The fullest account of the architecture of Melrose is in RCAHMS, *Roxburghshire*, 1956, vol. 2, pp. 265–91; see also Frederick Pinches, *The abbey church of Melrose*, London, 1879.

46   *Cal. Docs Scot.*, vol. 4, no. 397; Cosmo Innes (ed.), *Liber Sancte Marie de Melros* (Bannatyne Club), Edinburgh, 1837, vol. i, p. 488.

47   The plan of Newbattle was inexpertly excavated between 1878 and 1894 for Lord Lothian and the findings published in J. C. Carrick, *The Abbey of St Mary Newbattle*, Selkirk, 1907, pp. 80–6. *Bldgs of Scot.*, Lothian, 1978, p. 36 suggests the rectangular aisled plan of the eastern limb should be interpreted as having had a rectangular eastern ambulatory. Kinloss also had a fully aisled eastern limb, although the disposition within that framework is unknown.

48   John Harvey, *The Perpendicular style*, London, 1978, p. 116.

49   Richard Fawcett, 'Scottish medieval window tracery', in David Breeze (ed.), *Studies in Scottish antiquity*, Edinburgh, 1984, pp. 154 and 182–4; see also I. C. Hannah, 'The penetration into Scotland of English late Gothic forms', *Proc. Soc. Antiq. Scot.*, vol. 64, 1929–30, pp. 149–55.

50   Richard Fawcett, *Later Gothic architecture in Norfolk*, University of East Anglia unpublished Ph.D. thesis, 1975, pp. 227–53.

51   For an analysis of Howden see Nicola Coldstream, 'St Peter's Church, Howden', in *Medieval art and architecture in the East Riding of Yorkshire* (British Archaeological Association conference proceedings for the year 1983), Leeds, 1989, pp. 109–20.

52   For a discussion of English net-vaults see Henning Bock, *Der Decorated style*, Heidelberg, 1962, pp. 50–70; and Jean Bony, *The English Decorated style*, Oxford, 1979, pp. 50–2.

53   *Chron. Bower* (Goodall), vol. 1, p. 369; F. J. Armours (ed.), *The original chronicle*

of Andrew of Wyntoun (Scottish Text Society), Edinburgh, 1903–14, vol. 6, pp. 309–12; *Exch. Rolls*, vol. 3, pp. 70 and 674.

54   Robert Branner, *St Louis and the court style*, London, 1965, p. 18.

55   *Chron. Bower* (Goodall), vol. 1, p. 363.

56   John Dowden, *The bishops of Scotland*, Glasgow, 1912, p. 27.

57   Myln, *Vitae*, p. 16.

58   *Chron. Bower* (Watt), vol. 8, p. 74.

59   R. M. Lemaire, *Les origines du style Gothique en Brabant*, pt 2, Antwerp and Zwolle, 1949.

60   For a survey of French late Gothic, see Roland Sanfaçon, *L'architecture Flamboyante en France*, Quebec, 1971.

61   For information on Dutch late Gothic see F. A. J. Vermeulen, *Handboek tot de geschiedenis der Nederlandsche bouwkunst*, vol. 1, The Hague, 1928; M. D. Ozinga, *De Gothische kerkelijke bouwkunst*, Amsterdam, 1953; Rijkscommissie voor de Monumentenbeschrijving, *Kunstreisboek voor Nederland*, 7th edn, Amsterdam, 1977; R. Meischke, *De gothische bouwtraditie*, Amersfoort, 1988. For information on Belgian late Gothic see A. L. J. Van de Walle, *Belgique Gothique*, Antwerp, 1971.

62   Colin Thompson and Lorne Campbell, *Hugo van der Goes and the Trinity panels in Edinburgh*, Edinburgh, 1974.

63   *Archaeologia*, vol. 31, 1846, pp. 346–9; there is a useful discussion of the case in G. G. Coulton, *Scottish abbeys and social life*, Cambridge, 1933, pp. 194–5.

64   *Cal. Papal Letters*, vol. 1, p. 553.

65   John Alexander Smith, 'Notes on Melrose Abbey, especially in reference to inscriptions on the wall of the south transept', *Proc. Soc. Antiq. Scot.*, vol. 2, 1854–7, pp. 166–75 and 295.

66   Peter McGregor Chalmers, *A Scots medieval architect*, Glasgow, 1895 represents the fullest attempt to reconstruct the career of John Morow, but is generally unconvincing.

67   The practice of permitting burials of lay folk within Cistercian churches had certainly begun by the thirteenth century; see Nicola Coldstream, 'Cistercian architecture from Beaulieu to the Dissolution', in Christopher Norton and David Park, *Cistercian art and architecture in the British Isles*, Cambridge, 1986, pp. 157–8.

68   J. Cameron Lees, *The abbey of Paisley*, Paisley, 1878; see also Nat. Art Survey, vol. 4, pl 17–39.

69   *Exch. Rolls*, vol. 3, p. 221.

70   His memorial is within that porch, though its original position is uncertain.

71   Reg. Aven., 259, fo. 471–2v.

72   *Reg. Mag. Sig.*, vol. 2, no. 133.

73   Nat. Art Survey, vol. 2, pl. 15.

74   Reg. Aven., 324, fo. 500.

75   Archbishop Eyre, 'The western towers', in George Eyre-Todd (ed.), *The book of Glasgow Cathedral*, Glasgow, 1898, pp. 289–90.

76   Peter MacGregor Chalmers, *The cathedral church of Glasgow* (Bell's cathedral series), London, 1914, p. 26; see also Chap. 2, note 24.

77   Cosmo Innes (ed.), *Registrum Episcopatus Moraviensis* (Bannatyne Club), Edinburgh, 1837, no. 303.

78   Ibid., no. 173.

79   Richard Fawcett, *Beauly Priory and Fortrose Cathedral* (official guide), Edinburgh, 1987; G. G. MacDowall, *The chanonry of Ross*, Fortrose, 1963.

80   Edmund Chisholm-Batten, *The charters of the priory of Beauly*, Edinburgh, 1877, p. 195.

81   MacGibbon and Ross, *Ecclesiastical*, vol. 2, p. 539.

82   David Laing (ed.), *Bannatyne Miscellany* (Bannatyne Club), Edinburgh, 1836, vol. 2, p. 109.

83   John Durkan, 'The sanctuary and college of Tain', *Innes Review*, vol. 13, 1962, pp. 147–8.

84   *Reg. Mag. Sig.*, vol. 2, nos. 1513 and 1694.

85   William B. D. D. Turnbull (ed.) *Extracta e variis cronicis Scocie* (Abbotsford Club), Edinburgh, 1842 p. 194; the contract with the plumber is in Cosmo Innes and Patrick Chalmers (eds), *Registrum Nigrum de Aberbrothoc* (Bannatyne Club), Edinburgh, 1849–56, fo. 42r., and is printed in L. F. Salzman, *Building in England down to 1540*, Oxford, 1952, p. 471.

86   Fraser, op. cit. note 29, vol. 1, pp. 349–50.

87   Registra Vaticana in Vat. Arch., 322, fo. 440v.

88   At his election as abbot in 1398 Alexander de Pluscardyne declared himself ready to repair the church and other buildings, S. R. Macphail, *History of the religious house of Pluscardyn*, Edinburgh, 1886, pp. 83–4.

89   *Cal. Papal Letters*, vol. 11, p. 330.

90   *Reg. Mag. Sig.*, vol. 1, no. 832.

91   R. W. Southern, *Western society and the church in the Middle Ages*, Harmondsworth, 1970, p. 300 ff.

NOTES TO CHAPTER TWO

1   RCAHMS, *Orkney*, 1946, pp. 113–41; Richard Fawcett, 'Kirkwall Cathedral: an architectural analysis', in Barbara E. Crawford (ed.), *St Magnus Cathedral and Orkney's twelfth-century renaissance*, Aberdeen, 1988, pp. 88–110.

2   James Hutchison Cockburn, *The medieval bishops of Dunblane and their church*, Edinburgh, 1959.

3   David McRoberts, 'Dunblane Cathedral under the Chisholms', *Journal of the Society of Friends of Dunblane Cathedral*, vol. 11, 1971, pp. 37–52.

4   David McRoberts, ' "The glorious house of St Andrew" ', in David McRoberts (ed.), *The medieval church of St Andrews*, Glasgow, 1976, pp. 63–120.

5   *Chron. Bower* (Goodall), vol. 1, p. 375.

6   *Chron. Bower* (Goodall), vol. 1, pp. 372 and 375–6.

7   Hector Boece, *Scotorum Historiae*, 2nd edn, Paris, 1574, fo. 348v–349.

8   David McRoberts, 'The medieval Scottish liturgy illustrated by surviving documents', *Transactions of the Scottish Ecclesiological Society*, vol. 15, 1957, pp. 30–6.

9   Royal patent of 15 Sept. 1507 for introduction of printing into Scotland, M. Livingstone et al. (eds), *Registrum Secreti Sigilli Regum Scotorum*, Edinburgh, 1908, vol. 1, no. 1546; printed in Leslie J. MacFarlane, *William Elphinstone and the kingdom of Scotland*, Aberdeen, 1985, pp. 236–7.

10   Reg. Aven., 320, fo. 599v.; John Durkan, 'The great fire at Glasgow Cathedral', *Innes Review*, vol. 26, 1975, pp. 89–92.

11   E. L. G. Stones, 'Notes on Glasgow Cathedral, the northern extension to the choir', *Innes Review*, vol. 21, 1970, pp. 144–7.

12   E. R. Lindsay and A. I Cameron (eds), *Calendar of Scottish supplications to Rome* (Scottish History Society), Edinburgh, 1934, vol. 1, 1418–22, p. 182.

13   Cosmo Innes (ed.), *Registrum episcopatus Glasguensis* (Bannatyne Club), Edinburgh, 1843, vol. 2, pp. 329–39; John Dowden, 'The inventory of ornaments . . . belonging to the cathedral church of Glasgow in 1432 . . .', *Proc. Soc. Antiq. Scot.*, vol. 33, 1898–9, pp. 280–329.

14   David McRoberts, 'The crossing area of Glasgow cathedral in the Middle Ages', *Annual Report of Society of Friends of Glasgow Cathedral*, 1967, pp. 9–12.

15   John Durkan, 'Notes on Glasgow Cathedral, the medieval altars', *Innes Review*, vol. 11, 1970, pp. 46–9.

16   John Durkan, 'Archbishop Robert Blackadder's will', *Innes Review*, vol. 23, 1972, pp. 138–48.

17   David McRoberts, 'Notes on Glasgow Cathedral, Our Lady of Consolation', *Innes Review*, vol. 18, 1966, pp. 42–5.

18   Joseph Bain and Charles Rogers (eds) *Diocesan Registers of Glasgow* (Grampian Club), Edinburgh, 1875, vol. 2, pp. 152–3.

19   Richard Fawcett, 'The Blackadder aisle at Glasgow Cathedral: a reconsideration of the architectural evidence for its date', *Proc. Soc. Antiq. Scot.*, vol. 115, 1985, pp. 277–87.

20   RCAHMS, *Argyll*, 1983, vol. 4, pp. 52 and 84.

21   David McRoberts, 'The Scottish church and nationalism in the fifteenth century', *Innes Review*, vol. 19, 1968, pp. 3–14.

22   See engravings in J. Collie, *Plans, elevations, sections, details and views of the cathedral of Glasgow*, London, 1835.

23   Archbishop Eyre, 'The western towers', in George Eyre-Todd, *The book of Glasgow Cathedral*, Glasgow, 1898, p. 277.

24   Hugh McBrien, *Excavations at the west front of Glasgow Cathedral*, Scottish Urban Archaeological Trust Ltd, Perth, unpublished interim report, 1988.

25   Robert Mylne, Edinburgh University Library Dc. 4. 32, p. 166.

26   Richard Fawcett, *Elgin Cathedral* (official guide), Edinburgh, 1991; Nat. Art Survey, vol. 3, pls 1–29.

27   James Skene (ed.), *History of the troubles and memorable transactions in Scotland and England* (Bannatyne Club), Edinburgh, 1828–9, vol. 1, pp. 83 and 376.

28   Myln, *Vitae*, p. 22.

29   Ibid., p. 23.

30   Ibid., various references pp. 27–58.

3 1   Boece, *Vitae*.

3 2   David Littlejohn (ed.), *Records of the Sheriff Court of Aberdeenshire*, (New Spalding Club), Aberdeen, 1904–7 vol. 1, p. 102.

3 3   W. D. Geddes, *Lacunar basilicae Sancti Macarii Aberdonensis* (New Spalding Club), Aberdeen, 1888; David McRoberts, *The heraldic ceiling of St Machar's Cathedral Aberdeen* (Friends of St Machar's Cathedral), occasional papers, no. 2, 1973; Grant G. Simpson and Judith Stones, 'New light on the medieval ceiling', in *The restoration of St Machar's Cathedral*, Aberdeen, 1991.

3 4   W. Douglas Simpson, 'The architectural history of the cathedral', in Charles D. Bentinck, *Dornoch Cathedral and parish*, Inverness, 1926, p. 396, and pl. facing p. 212.

3 5   W. Orem, *A description of the chanonry, cathedral and King's College of Old Aberdeen*, Aberdeen, 1791, p. 61.

3 6   Leslie J. Macfarlane, *William Elphinstone and the kingdom of Scotland 1431–1514*, Aberdeen, 1985, particularly pp. 290–391.

3 7   William Kelly, 'Alexander Galloway, rector of Kinkell', in *A tribute offered by the University of Aberdeen to the memory of William Kelly*, Aberdeen University Studies, no. 125, 1949.

3 8   David McRoberts, op. cit. note 33, p. 5.

NOTES TO CHAPTER THREE

1   A. A. M. Duncan, *Regesta Regum Scottorum, Robert I*, Edinburgh, 1988, no. 288.

2   Gordon Donaldson, *The Scottish Reformation*, Cambridge, 1960, p. 4.

3   Ian B. Cowan, *The Scottish Reformation*, London, 1982, pp. 37 and 41.

4   Cowan and Easson, pp. 23–5; Mark Dilworth, 'The commendator system in Scotland', *Innes Review*, vol. 37, 1986, pp. 51–72.

5   *Exch. Rolls*, vol. 4, pp. cxiii, 508, 563–4, 613, 621, 640 and 678; R. and S. Fittis, *Ecclesiastical annals of Perth*, Edinburgh, 1885, pp. 216–18.

6   James Maidment, *Chronicle of Perth* (Maitland Club), Edinburgh, 1831 (Redrawn in MacGibbon and Ross, *Ecclesiastical*, 1897, vol. 3, p. 110).

7   Cowan and Easson, pp. 143–56.

8   For Kinloss, see the life of Abbot Chrystall by Ferrerius in John Stuart, *Records of the monastery of Kinloss*, Edinburgh, 1872.

9   George Thomas Beatson, *The Knights Hospitallers in Scotland and their priory at Torphichen*, Glasgow, 1903; RCAHMS, *Mid and West Lothian*, 1929, pp. 234–7; *Bldgs of Scot., Lothian*, 1978, pp. 447–9.

1 0   James Watson, *Jedburgh Abbey and the abbeys of Teviotdale*, 2nd edn, Edinburgh, 1894; Nat. Art Survey, vol. 3, pl. 1–23; RCAHMS, *Roxburghshire*, 1956, vol. 1, pp. 194–209; Richard Fawcett, 'The abbey church', in Gordon Ewart and John Lewis, *The excavations at Jedburgh Abbey* (forthcoming).

1 1   RCAHMS, *Fife, Kinross and Clackmannan*, 1933, pp. 106–21.

1 2   *Exch. Rolls*, vol. 2, p. 300.

1 3   See, for example, Peter Chalmers, *A historical and statistical account of Dunfermline*, Edinburgh, 1844, pl. 16.

14 RCAHMS, *Edinburgh*, 1951, pp. 129–44; *Bldgs of Scot.*, Edinburgh, 1984, pp. 125–41.

15 RCAHMS, *Argyll*, 1975, vol. 2, pp. 99–115.

16 Edmund Chisholm Batten, *The charters of the Priory of Beauly*, Edinburgh, 1877; W. Douglas Simpson, 'The Valliscaulian priory of Beauly', *Antiquaries Journal*, vol. 25, 1955, pp. 1–18; Richard Fawcett, *Beauly Priory and Fortrose Cathedral* (official guide), Edinburgh, 1987.

17 I. B. Cowan and A. I. Dunlop (eds), *Calendar of Scottish supplications to Rome, 1428–32*, (Scottish History Society), Edinburgh, 1970, p. 72.

18 R. K. Hannay and R. L. Mackie (eds), *The letters of James IV* (Scottish History Society), Edinburgh, 1953, no. 289.

19 RCAHMS, *Peeblesshire*, 1967, vol. 2, pp. 203–9.

20 R. Renwick, *Peebles aisle and monastery*, Glasgow, 1897, app. 8, pp. 71–4.

21 Stuart, op cit. note 8, p. xli.

22 W. Douglas Simpson, 'The early Romanesque tower at Restenneth Priory, Angus', *Antiquaries Journal*, vol. 43, 1963, pp. 269–83.

23 Cowan and Easson, pp. 95–6.

24 Royal Commission on Historical Monuments of England, *London*, vol. I, *Westminster Abbey*, London, 1924, pls 129–40.

25 Cowan and Easson, p. 76.

26 Charles S. Romanes, *Selections from the records of the Regality of Melrose* (Scottish History Society), Edinburgh, 1917, vol. 3, pp. 217 ff.

27 J. Wilson Paterson, 'The development of Inchcolm Abbey', *Proc. Soc. Antiq. Scot.*, vol. 60, 1925–6, pp. 227–53; Richard Fawcett, David McRoberts and Fiona Stewart, *Inchcolm Abbey and island* (official guide), Edinburgh, n.d.

28 D. E. Easson and Angus Macdonald (eds), *Charters of the abbey of Inchcolm* (Scottish History Society), Edinburgh, 1938, pp. xvii and xxxii–xxxiii.

29 *Chron. Bower* (Watt), vol. 8, p. 44.

30 Reg. Supp., 398, fo. 194v.

31 *Auchinleck Chronicle*, quoted in John Durkan, 'Paisley Abbey and Glasgow archives: some new directions', *Innes Review*, vol. 14, 1963, pp. 46–53.

32 T. Thomson (ed.), *Auchinleck Chronicle*, Edinburgh, 1819, pp. 19–20.

33 Nat. Art Survey, vol. 4, 1933, pls 17–39.

34 W. M. Metcalfe, *Charters and documents relating to the burgh of Paisley*, Paisley, 1902, pp. 52–5.

35 F. C. Hunter Blair, *Charters of the abbey of Crossraguel* (Ayrshire and Galloway Archaeological Association), Edinburgh, 1886, pp. xxii–xxv; Cowan and Easson, pp. 63–4; Ian Cowan, 'Ayrshire Abbeys: Crossraguel and Kilwinning', *Ayrshire Archaeological and Natural History Society Collections*, vol. 14, 1986, pp. 268–9.

36 Richard Augustine Hay, *Scotia Sacra*, National Library of Scotland, Advocates Library MS 34.1.8.

37 Hunter Blair, op. cit. note 35, no. 55.

38   Nat. Art Survey, vol. 4, 1933, pls 1–16; RCAHMS, *Argyll*, 1982, vol. 4, pp. 49–114.

39   K. A. Steer and J. W. M. Bannerman, *Late medieval sculpture in the West Highlands*, RCAHMS, Edinburgh, 1977, pp. 108–9.

40   *Cal. Papal Letters*, vol. 8, p. 24.

41   Steer and Bannerman, op. cit. note 39, pp. 106–9.

42   John Dunbar, 'Some aspects of Scottish royal planning in the sixteenth century', *Architectural History*, vol. 27, 1984, p. 17.

43   David Knowles, *The religious orders in England*, Oxford, 1955, vol. 2, p. 12.

44   *Reg. Mag. Sig.*, vol. 4, no. 1567.

45   Ian B. Cowan, *The Scottish Reformation*, London, 1982, p. 28.

46   For Dryburgh, see J. S. Richardson and C. J. Tabraham, *Dryburgh Abbey* (official guide), 4th edn, 1987, p. 15; for Balmerino see James Campbell, *Balmerino and its abbey*, 2nd edn, Edinburgh, 1899, p. 296.

47   C. A. Ralegh Radford, *Crossraguel Abbey* (official guide), 3rd edn, Edinburgh, 1988, pp. 9–11.

48   RCAHMS, *Fife, Kinross and Clackmannan*, 1933, pp. 222–4.

49   W. Douglas Simpson, 'The Augustinian priory and parish church of Monymusk, Aberdeenshire', *Proc. Soc. Antiq. Scot.*, vol. 59, 1924–5, pp. 34–71.

50   Bower's responsibility for the fortifications is implicit in the statement at *Chron. Bower* (Watt), vol. 8, p. 136 that in 1421 'there were not then, as there are now, defences in the monastery'.

51   *Chron. Bower* (Watt), vol. 8, p. 136.

52   RCAHMS, *Argyll*, 1974, vol. 2, pp. 105–10.

53   RCAHMS, *Argyll*, 1984, vol. 5, pp. 232–4 and 241–3.

54   Designated as such on a plan by Robert Mylne, reproduced in R. S. Mylne, *The master masons to the crown of Scotland*, Edinburgh, 1893, between pp. 168 and 169.

55   Scottish Urban Archaeological Trust, *Abbot's House Dunfermline*, unpublished structure report, Perth, 1993.

56   RCAHMS, *Roxburghshire*, 1956, vol. 2, p. 287.

57   Hunter-Blair, op. cit. note 35, plate 29 and pp. 142–3.

58   Stuart, op. cit. note 8, pp. l–lxi; Michael R. Apted and Susan Hannabuss, *Painters in Scotland 1301–1700: a biographical dictionary* (Scottish Record Society), Edinburgh, new ser., 1978, vol. 7, p. 25.

59   William Fraser (ed.), *Registrum monasterii S. Marie de Cambuskenneth* (Grampian Club), London, 1872, nos. 92 and 207.

60   The relationship between the gatehouse and adjacent buildings was clarified by excavations in 1975; see T. M. Robertson, G. H. Williams, George Haggarty and Nicholas Reynolds, 'Recent excavations at Dunfermline Abbey, Fife', *Proc. Soc. Antiq. Scot.*, vol. 111, 1981, pp. 388–400.

NOTES TO CHAPTER FOUR

1   For brief accounts of the origins of the friars see R. W. Southern, *Western society and the church in the Middle Ages*, Harmondsworth, 1970, pp. 272–99, and C. H. Lawrence, *Medieval monasticism*, London, 1984, pp. 192–220.

2   For the introduction of the friars into Scotland see Cowan and Easson, pp. 115–42; see also William Moir Bryce, *The Scottish Grey Friars*, 2 vols, Edinburgh, 1909.

3   W. J. Lindsay, 'Digging up old Ayr', *Ayrshire Archaeological and Natural History Society Collections*, vol. 14, 1985, pp. 220–2.

4   Piers Dixon et al., report on Jedburgh Friary excavation (forthcoming). I am grateful to Dr Dixon, Mr John Dent and members of AOC Scotland for discussing their findings with me; J. A. Stones (ed.), *Three Scottish Carmelite friaries: excavations at Aberdeen, Linlithgow and Perth* (Society of Antiquaries of Scotland), monograph no. 6, Edinburgh, 1989.

5   RCAHMS, *Fife, Kinross and Clackmannan*, 1933, pp. 153–5; see also Jonathan Wordsworth, 'Excavations in Inverkeithing, 1981', *Proc. Soc. Antiq. Scot.*, vol. 113, 1982, particularly pp. 534–5.

6   Stones, op. cit. note 4, pp. 24–5.

7   Cosmo Innes (ed.), *Registrum Honoris de Morton* (Bannatyne Club), Edinburgh, 1853, vol. 2, no. 210.

8   A. R. Martin, *Franciscan architecture in England*, Manchester, 1937, pp. 19–21.

9   MacGibbon and Ross, *Ecclesiastical*, 1897, vol. 3, pp. 462–5; Jonathan Wordsworth, 'Friarscroft and the Trinitarians in Dunbar', *Proc. Soc. Antiq. Scot.*, vol. 113, 1983, pp. 478–89.

10   John Slezer, *Theatrum Scotiae*, London, 1693, pl. 10.

11   Cosmo Innes (ed.), James Gordon, *Aberdoniae Utriusque Descriptio* (Spalding Club), Aberdeen, 1842.

12   James Cooper, *Greyfriars Church Aberdeen: a word on its behalf*, Aberdeen, 1889; James Cooper, 'Greyfriars Aberdeen: one more word in favour of its retention and restoration', *Transactions of the Aberdeen Ecclesiological Society*, vol. 4, 1897–1903, pp. 89–99; James Cooper, 'Old Greyfriars Church Aberdeen: an account of the particulars brought to light in the process of its demolition', *Transactions of the Scottish Ecclesiological Society*, vol. 1, 1903–4, pp. 72–87; Bryce, op. cit. note 2, pp. 307–42; Richard Fawcett, 'The architecture of King's College Chapel and Greyfriars' Church, Aberdeen', *Aberdeen University Review*, vol. 53, 1989, pp. 102–26.

13   William Kelly, 'Alexander Galloway, rector of Kinkell', in *A tribute offered by the University of Aberdeen to the memory of William Kelly*, Aberdeen University Studies, no. 125, Aberdeen, 1949, pp. 26–8.

14   See Cooper, 1903–4, op. cit. note 12.

15   MacGibbon and Ross, *Ecclesiastical*, 1897, vol. 3, pp. 356–8.

16   A payment was recorded to the friars in *Exch. Rolls*, vol. 10, p. 523; for discussion of the foundation see Cowan and Easson, p. 131.

17   Cowan and Easson, p. 137.

18   MacGibbon and Ross, *Ecclesiastical*, 1897, vol. 3, pp. 296–309; *Bldgs of Scot.*, *Lothian*, 1978, pp. 431–2.

19   See Harold G. Leask, *Irish churches and monastic buildings*, Dundalk, 1960, vol. 3, pp. 89–112.

20   *Reg. Mag. Sig.*, vol. 1, no. 304.

21   *Reg. Mag. Sig.*, vol. 2, no. 1047; Cowan and Easson, pp. 120–1.

22   Nat. Art Survey, vol. 2, 1923, pls 38–41; RCAHMS, *Fife, Kinross and Clackmannan*, 1933, pp. 262–4; *Bldgs of Scot.*, *Fife*, 1988, pp. 404–5. I am grateful to Mr Neil Cameron for discussing his views on St Monans with me.

23   Cowan and Easson, pp. 119–20.

24   See David Hay Flemming, *Handbook of St Andrews and neighbourhood*, St Andrews, 1924, pp. 12–14.

25   Anthony Ross, *Dogs of the Lord* (exhibition booklet), Edinburgh, 1981, pp. 5–7.

NOTES TO CHAPTER FIVE

1   D. E. Easson, 'The collegiate churches of Scotland', *Records of the Scottish Church History Society*, vol. 6, 1938, pp. 193–215 and vol. 7, 1941, pp. 30–47; George Hay, 'The architecture of Scottish collegiate churches', in G. W. S. Barrow (ed.), *The Scottish tradition*, Edinburgh, 1974, pp. 56–70; D. E. R. Watt, 'Collegiate churches', in Peter McNeill and Ranald Nicholson (eds), *An historical atlas of Scotland*, St Andrews, 1975, pp. 78–80; Cowan and Easson, pp. 213–34.

2   G. W. S. Barrow, 'The clergy at St Andrews', in id., *The kingdom of the Scots*, London, 1973, pp. 212–32.

3   Cowan and Easson, pp. 46, 89 and 215.

4   RCAHMS, *Argyll*, 1992, vol. 7, pp. 174–86.

5   Stewart Cruden, 'Seton Collegiate Church', *Proc. Soc. Antiq. Scot.*, vol. 89, 1955–6, pp. 417–37.

6   *Cal. Papal Letters*, vol. 7, pp. 460–1.

7   Edinburgh Architectural Association, *Sketch book*, new ser., Edinburgh, 1887–94, vol. 2, p. 22.

8   M. R. Apted and W. Norman Robertson, 'Late fifteenth-century paintings from Guthrie and Foulis Easter', *Proc. Soc. Antiq. Scot.*, vol. 95, 1961–2, pp. 262–79.

9   Thomas Ross, 'St Triduana's well-house', *Transactions of the Scottish Ecclesiological Society*, vol. 3, 1910–11, pp. 238–46; Iain MacIvor, 'The King's Chapel at Restalrig and St Triduana's Aisle; a hexagonal two-storeyed chapel of the fifteenth century', *Proc. Soc. Antiq. Scot.*, vol. 96, 1962–3, pp. 247–63.

10   *Reg. Mag. Sig.*, vol. 2, no. 1329; *Exch. Rolls*, vol. 9, p. 540.

11   *Cal. Papal Letters*, vol. 14, pp. 211–13.

12   David Laing, 'Suggestions for the removal of St Margaret's Well . . . to a more favourable site', *Proc. Soc. Antiq. Scot.*, vol. 2, 1854–7, pp. 143–7.

13   MacIvor, op. cit. note 9.

14   W. Cramond, *The church and churchyard of Cullen*, Aberdeen, 1883; MacGibbon and Ross, *Ecclesiastical*, 1897, vol. 3, pp. 398–405; Cowan and Easson, p. 218.

15   David Laing, 'The Forrester monuments in the church of Corstorphine', *Proc. Soc. Antiq. Scot.*, vol. 11, 1874–6, pp. 353–62; *Bldgs of Scot.*, Edinburgh, 1984, pp. 522–4.

16   *Midlothian Chrs.*, pp. 293–304.

17   Reg. Supp., 397, fo. 173.

18   MacGibbon and Ross, *Ecclesiastical*, 1896, vol. 2, pp. 531–7; Reg. Aven., 304, fo. 541v and 335, fo. 223–223v.

19   W. Douglas Simpson, *The castle of Bergen and the Bishop's Palace at Kirkwall*, Edinburgh, 1961, pp. 26–7.

20   MacGibbon and Ross, *Ecclesiastical*, 1897, vol. 3, pp. 189–99; A. B. Dalgetty, *History of the church of Foulis Easter*, Dundee, 1933; Apted and Robertson, op. cit. note 8.

21   Reg. Supp., 439, fo. 272, and 1361, fo. 231v–232.

22   David McRoberts, 'The fifteenth-century altarpiece of Fowlis Easter Church', in Anne O'Connor and D. V. Clarke (eds), *From the Stone Age to the Forty Five*, Edinburgh, 1983, pp. 384–98.

23   David McRoberts, 'Scottish sacrament houses', *Transactions of the Scottish Ecclesiological Society*, vol. 15, 1965, pp. 41–2.

24   J. Russell Walker, 'Scottish baptismal fonts', *Proc. Soc. Antiq. Scot.*, vol. 21, 1886–7, pp. 442–5.

25   MacGibbon and Ross, *Ecclesiastical*, 1897, vol. 3, pp. 506–13.

26   *Reg. Mag. Sig.*, vol. 2, no. 3048.

27   J. Herkless and R. K. Hannay, *The college of St Leonard*, Edinburgh, 1905; Ronald Gordon Cant, *St Leonard's Chapel, St Andrews* (guidebook), 3rd edn, St Andrews, 1970; Ronald Gordon Cant, *The University of St Andrews*, 2nd edn, Edinburgh, 1970, pp. 28–33.

28   Ronald G. Cant, *The college of St Salvator*, Edinburgh, 1950.

29   Annie I. Dunlop, *The life and times of James Kennedy, bishop of St Andrews*, Edinburgh, 1950.

30   *Exch. Rolls*, vol. 7, pp. liii and 79; for discussion of the mace see David McRoberts, 'Bishop Kennedy's mace', David McRoberts (ed.) *The medieval church of St Andrews*, Glasgow, 1976, pp. 167–71.

31   See drawing in Robert Branner, *St Louis and the court style in Gothic architecture*, London, 1965, pl. 80.

32   Norman McPherson, 'On the chapel and ancient buildings of King's College Aberdeen', *Archaeologia Scotica*, vol. 5, 1880, pp. 416–52; William Kelly, 'Scottish crown steeples', 'King's College Chapel' and 'Some further notes on King's College Chapel', in *A tribute offered by the University of Aberdeen to the memory of William Kelly*, Aberdeen, 1949, pp. 34–75; Francis C. Eeles, *King's College Aberdeen*, Edinburgh, 1956; Leslie J. Macfarlane, *William Elphinstone and the kingdom of Scotland, 1431–1514*, Aberdeen, 1985, pp. 290–402; Richard Fawcett, 'The architecture of King's College Chapel and Greyfriars' Church, Aberdeen', *Aberdeen University Review*, vol. 53, 1989, pp. 102–26.

33 C. Innes (ed.), *The Ledger of Andrew Halyburton* 1492–1503, Edinburgh, 1867, pp. 183–4.

34 G. Patrick Edwards, 'William Elphinstone, his college chapel and the second of April', *Aberdeen University Review*, vol. 51, 1985, pp. 1–17.

35 C. Innes (ed.), *Fasti Aberdonenses* (Spalding Club), Aberdeen, 1854, p. lvii.

36 William Kelly, 'Carved oak from St Nicholas Church, Aberdeen', *Proc. Soc. Antiq. Scot.*, vol. 68, 1933–94, pp. 355–66.

37 William Geddes, 'Old Aberdeen', *Transactions of the Aberdeen Philosophical Society*, vol. 1, 1884, p. 18.

38 E. J. Haslinghuis and C. J. A. C. Peeters, *De dom van Utrecht*, De Nederlandse monumenten van geschiedenis en kunst, The Hague, 1965.

39 William Kelly, 'Scottish crown steeples', op. cit. note 32, pp. 34–48.

40 Boece, *Vitae*, p. 95.

41 MacGibbon and Ross, *Ecclesiastical*, 1897, vol. 3, pp. 351–6.

42 Cosmo Innes (ed.), *Registrum episcopatus Glasguensis* (Bannatyne and Maitland Clubs), Edinburgh, 1843, vol. 2, no. 483.

43 See the plan in the Hutton Collection in the National Library of Scotland, Advocates MS. 30.5.23, 28c

44 MacGibbon and Ross, *Ecclesiastical*, 1897, vol. 3, pp. 309–15; *Bldgs of Scot.*, *Lothian*, 1978, pp. 213–14.

45 Cowan and Easson, pp. 215–16.

46 John Lewis, *Yester Chapel*, 1991 (unpublished excavation report), 1991.

47 John Dunbar, 'The building of Yester House, 1670–1878', *Transactions of the East Lothian Antiquarian and Field Naturalist Society*, vol. 13, 1972, pp. 20–42, particularly pp. 31–2.

48 Nat. Art Survey, vol. 3, pls 60–3; *Bldgs of Scot.*, *Lothian*, 1978, pp. 192–4.

49 Cowan and Easson, p. 219.

50 Cowan and Easson, p. 218–19; *Bldgs of Scot.*, *Lothian*, 1978, pp. 143–4.

51 *Midlothian Chrs.*, pp. 328–31; Cowan and Easson, p. 225; *Bldgs of Scot.*, *Lothian*, 1978, pp. 409–17; for a valuable study of the founder's background see Barbara Crawford, 'William Sinclair, Earl of Orkney, and his family: a study in the politics of survival', in K. J. Stringer, *Essays on the nobility of medieval Scotland*, Edinburgh, 1985, pp. 234–53.

52 David Laing (ed.) *Bannatyne Miscellany* (Bannatyne Club). Edinburgh, 1855, vol. 3, p. 96; Reg. Supp., 747, fos 75–6.

53 Richard Augustine Hay, *A genealogie of the Sainteclaires of Rosslyn*, Edinburgh, 1835, p. 26; *Midlothian Chrs.*, p. xciv.

54 Hay, op. cit. note 53, p. 27.

55 Robert Anderson, 'Notice of working drawings scratched on the walls of the crypt at Roslin Chapel', *Proc. Soc. Antiq. Scot.*, vol. 10, 1872–4, pp. 63–4. For information on tracing floors see J. H. Harvey, 'The tracing floor in York Minster', 40th annual report of the friends of York Minster, York, 1969, pp. 9–13; appendix in L. S. Colchester and J. H. Harvey, 'Wells Cathedral', *Archaeological Journal*, vol. 131, 1974, p. 214.

56   For the royal acquisition of the earldom of Orkney see Barbara Crawford, 'The pawning of Orkney and Shetland', *Scottish Historical Review*, vol. 48, 1969, pp. 35–53, and Gordon Donaldson, 'Sovereignty and law in Orkney and Shetland', In David Sellar (ed.), *Miscellany Two* (Stair Society), Edinburgh, 1984, pp. 13–40.

57   Carried out for Mr Niven Sinclair; see also MacGibbon and Ross, *Ecclesiastical*, 1897, vol. 3, p. 153.

58   Daniel Wilson, 'St Ninian's suburb and the collegiate church of the Holy Trinity...', *Proc. Soc. Antiq. Scot.*, vol. 1, 1883–4, pp. 128–69; J. Colston, *Trinity College and Trinity Hospital*, 2 vols, Edinburgh, 1896–7; James D. Marwick, *The history of the College Church and the Trinity Hospital, Edinburgh, 1460–1661* (Scottish Burgh Records Society), Edinburgh, 1911; *Bldgs of Scot.*, Edinburgh, 1984, pp. 170–2; Nicholas M. McQ. Holmes, *Trinity College Church, hospital and apse*, Edinburgh, 1988.

59   *Midlothian Chrs.*; Cowan and Easson, p. 221.

60   R. K. Hannay and D. Hay (eds), *The letters of James V*, Edinburgh, 1954, p. 217.

61   Peter Blythe, 'The Trinity College affair', in Valerie Fiddes and Alistair Rowan, *David Bryce, 1803–1876* (exhibition catalogue), Edinburgh, 1976, pp. 42–5.

62   Edinburgh Architectural Association, *Sketch book*, Edinburgh, 1878–9, vol. 2, pls 11–18; RCAHMS, *East Lothian*, 1924, pp. 115–21; Stewart Cruden, 'Seton Collegiate Church', *Proc. Soc. Antiq. Scot.*, vol. 89, 1955–6, pp. 417–37; John Durkan, 'The foundation of the Collegiate Church of Seton', *Innes Review*, vol. 13, 1962, pp. 71–6; *Bldgs of Scot., Lothian*, 1978, pp. 425–8.

63   John Fullarton (ed.), Richard Maitland, *History of the House of Seytoun* (Maitland Club), Edinburgh 1829; see also Bruce Gordon Seton, *The House of Seton*, unpublished typescript, in National Library of Scotland, R.272a. It should be noted that Maitland numbers the Lords Seton differently from what is now regarded as correct.

64   Cowan and Easson, p. 226; Reg. Supp., 965, fos 203–203v, 966, fo. 9v.

65   MacGibbon and Ross, *Ecclesiastical*, 1897, vol. 3, pp. 205–14; RCAHMS, *Mid and West Lothian*, 1929, pp. 58–61; *Bldgs of Scot., Lothian*, 1978, pp. 152–5.

66   *Midlothian Chrs.*, pp. 313–9; Cowan and Easson, p. 218.

67   David S. Rutherford, *Biggar St Mary's: a medieval college church*, Biggar, 1946; MacGibbon and Ross, *Ecclesiastical*, 1897, vol. 3, pp. 343–9.

68   John Stuart (ed.) *Miscellany of the Spalding Club*, 1852, vol. 5, pp. 196 ff.; Cowan and Easson, p. 215.

NOTES TO CHAPTER SIX

1   For information on the origins and medieval history of the burghs see George Smith Pryde, *The burghs of Scotland, a critical list*, Oxford, 1965; A. A. M. Duncan, *Scotland, the making of the kingdom*, Edinburgh, 1975, chap. 18; Michael Lynch, Michael Spearman and Geoffrey Stell, *The Scottish medieval town*, Edinburgh, 1988; Elizabeth Ewan, *Townlife in fourteenth-century Scotland*, Edinburgh, 1990. For information on the history and topography of many of the leading burghs see the publications of the Scottish Burgh Survey.

2   Ian B. Cowan, 'The development of the parochial system in Scotland', *Scottish Historical Review*, vol. 44, 1961, pp. 43–55.

3   For one view of late medieval spirituality, see J. Huizinga, *The waning of the Middle Ages* (Peregrine edition), Harmondsworth, 1965; for a more balanced view see R. W. Southern, *Western society and the church in the Middle Ages*, Harmondsworth, 1970, chap. 7; for the situation in Scotland see Gordon Donaldson, *The faith of the Scots*, London, 1990, chap. 3.

4   Donaldson, op. cit. note 3, pp. 51–2.

5   Ian B. Cowan, *The Scottish Reformation*, London, 1982, p. 90.

6   For the proliferation of altars at one burgh church see W. E. K. Rankin, *The parish church of the Holy Trinity, St Andrews*, Edinburgh, 1955.

7   Geoffrey Stell, 'The earliest tolbooths: a preliminary account', *Proc. Soc. Antiq. Scot.*, vol. 111, 1981, pp. 445–53.

8   For details of the burgh collegiate foundations see Cowan and Easson, pp. 213–30.

9   Jim Inglis, *The organ in Scotland before 1700*, Schagen, 1991, pp. 9–10 and 49.

10   J. C. Lees, *St Giles' Edinburgh: church, college and cathedral*, Edinburgh, 1889; RCAHMS, *Edinburgh*, 1951, pp. 25–34; George Hay, 'The late medieval development of the High Kirk of St Giles, Edinburgh', *Proc. Soc. Antiq. Scot.*, vol. 107, 1975–6, pp. 242–60; *Bldgs of Scot., Edinburgh*, 1984, pp. 102–18.

11   Throughout this chapter information on the origins of the burghs is taken from Pryde, op. cit. note 1; information on the origins of the parishes is taken from Cowan, *Parishes*.

12   David Laing (ed.) *Registrum cartarum ecclesie Sancti Egidii de Edinburgh* (Bannatyne Club), Edinburgh, 1859, p. 24, printed in L. F. Salzman, *Building in England down to 1540*, Oxford, 1952, pp. 466–7.

13   *Registrum . . . Sancti Egidii*, op. cit. note 12, p. 32.

14   *Chron. Bower* (Watt), vol. 8, p. 86.

15   Nicholas M. McQ. Holmes, *St Giles Cathedral, Edinburgh: archaeological excavation 1981*, unpublished interim report. I am grateful to Mr Holmes for discussing his findings with me.

16   *Registrum . . . Sancti Egidii*, op. cit. note 12, pp. 106–7.

17   Ibid., pp. 203–7.

18   Lees, op. cit. note 10, p. 80.

19   Cowan and Easson, p. 220.

20   Richard Fawcett, *St John's Kirk of Perth* (guidebook), Perth, 1987.

21   See plan in Marion L. Stavert, *Perth, a short history*, Perth, n.d., p. 10.

22   Cosmo Innes (ed.) *Registrum de Dunfermlyn* (Bannatyne Club), Edinburgh, 1842, pp. 291–3, no. 413.

23   *Treasurer Accts*, vol. 1, pp. 121 and 323.

24   Ibid., p. 323.

25   See Chap. 2 note 32.

26   op. cit., Chap. 3, note 6; J. Cant, *Memorabilia of the city of Perth*, Perth, 1806 (redrawn in MacGibbon and Ross, *Ecclesiastical*, 1897, vol. 3, pp. 110 and 109).

27   RCAHMS, *East Lothian*, 1924, pp. 38–43; *Bldgs of Scot., Lothian*, 1978, pp. 230–5.

28 Joseph Stevenson (ed.) *Illustrations of Scottish history* (Maitland Club), Glasgow, 1834, pp. 75–6.

29 G. Donaldson and C. Macrae (eds), *St Andrews Formulare, 1514–46* (Stair Society), Edinburgh 1942–4, vol. 2, no. 435.

30 Robert Gourlay and Anne Turner, *Haddington* (Scottish Burgh Survey), Glasgow, 1977, p. 2.

31 J. Ferguson, *Ecclesia Antiqua*, Edinburgh, 1905; RCAHMS, *Mid and West Lothian*, 1929, pp. 213–17; *Bldgs of Scot., Lothian*, 1978, pp. 284–90.

32 Reg. Supp., 262, fo. 234.

33 Thomas Thomson (ed.), *Liber Cartarum Prioratus Sancti Andree* (Bannatyne Club), Edinburgh, 1841, p. xxxviii, no. 47.

34 *Treasurer Accts*, vol. 3, p. 205.

35 *Liber curiae capitalis Burgi de Linlithgw*, referred to in Ferguson, op. cit. note 31.

36 Thomas Ross, 'Stirling Parish Church', *Transactions of the Stirling Natural History and Archaeological Society*, 1913–14, pp. 115–36; RCAHMS, *Stirlingshire*, 1963, vol. 1, pp. 129–40.

37 *Exch. Rolls*, vol. 4, p. 210.

38 Ross, op. cit. note 36, p. 118.

39 RCAHMS, *Stirlingshire*, 1963, vol. 1, p. 130, note 3.

40 R. Renwick (ed.), *Charters and other documents relating to the royal burgh of Stirling, 1124–1705* (Scottish Burgh Records Society), Glasgow 1884, no. xxxvii; *Treasurer Accts*, vol. 3, p. 290.

41 R. Renwick (ed.), *Extracts from the records of the royal burgh of Stirling* (Scottish Burgh Records Society), Glasgow 1887, vol. 1, p. 38.

42 Cowan and Easson, p. 227; *St Andrews Formulare*, op. cit. note 29, vol. 2, p. 172.

43 Colin Gibson, 'St Mary's Church and tower', in Colin Gibson (ed.), *Historic Dundee*, Dundee, n.d., pp. 5–13; Sylvia J. Stevenson and Elizabeth P. D. Torrie, *Dundee* (Scottish Burgh Survey), 1988, pt 2, pp. 16–28.

44 W. Hay (ed.), *Charters, writs and public documents of the royal burgh of Dundee, 1229–1880* (Scottish Burgh Records Society), Dundee, 1880, p. 19–23.

45 James Cooper (ed.), *Cartularium Ecclesiae Sancti Nicolai Aberdonensis* (New Spalding Club), Aberdeen 1888–91; William Kelly, 'Carved oak from St Nicholas Church, Aberdeen', *Proc. Soc. Antiq. Scot.*, vol. 68, 1933–4, pp. 355–65; John Hunter, 'The church of St Nicholas, Aberdeen', *Proc. Soc. Antiq. Scot.*, vol. 105, 1972–4, pp. 236–47.

46 *Treasurer Accts*, vol. 2, pp. 89, 273 and 275.

47 John Stuart (ed.), *Extracts from the council register of the burgh of Aberdeen* (Spalding Club), Aberdeen, 1844, vol. 1, pp. 56–7 and 77–8.

48 Cowan and Easson, pp. 214–15; Cooper, op. cit. note 45. vol. 1, nos. cxxv–cxxvi, vol. 2, pp. 346 and 381.

49 W. E. K. Rankin, *The parish church of the Holy Trinity, St Andrews*, Edinburgh, 1955; *Bldgs of Scot., Fife*, 1988, pp. 380–2; Ronald Cant, *The parish church of the Holy Trinity, St Andrews* (guidebook), St Andrews 1992.

50 Cowan and Easson, p. 228; Reg. Supp., 286, fo. 221.

51 Rankin, op. cit. note 49, p. 33.

52 J. R. Walker, *Pre-Reformation churches in Fifeshire*, Edinburgh, 1885; RCAHMS, *Fife, Kinross and Clackmannan*, 1933, pp. 87–9; *Bldgs. of Scot., Fife*, 1988, pp. 160–2.

53 *Chron. Bower* (Watt), vol. 8, p. 84.

54 I. B. Cowan and A. I. Dunlop (eds), *Calendar of Scottish supplications to Rome* (Scottish History Society), Edinburgh, 1970, vol. 3, pp. 27, 140, 176.

55 MacGibbon and Ross, *Ecclesiastical*, 1896, vol. 1, pp. 372–5; Robert Gourlay and Anne Turner, *Rutherglen* (Scottish Burgh Survey), Glasgow, 1978, p. 5.

56 C. B. Gunn, *The book of Peebles Church, St Andrew's Collegiate Parish Church*, Galashiels, 1908; RCAHMS, *Peeblesshire*, 1967, vol. 2, pp. 209–11.

57 James A. Morris, 'The church of St John Baptist, Ayr', *Transactions of the Scottish Ecclesiological Society*, vol. 3, 1911–12, pp. 331–42; J. C. Carrick, *The tower of St John the Baptist at Ayr*, Ayr, 1913.

NOTES TO CHAPTER SEVEN

1 For discussion of the impact of the Reformation on medieval churches, see George Hay, *The architecture of Scottish post-Reformation churches*, Oxford, 1957, pt I.

2 For an account of the post-Reformation history of the Scottish church, see J. H. S. Burleigh, *A church history of Scotland*, Oxford, 1960, pts II to IV.

3 See the *Transactions* of that society, which was founded in 1886.

4 James Scott Marshall, *The church in the midst*, Edinburgh, 1983; *Bldgs of Scot., Edinburgh*, 1984, pp. 457–9.

5 *Treasurer Accts*, vol. 1, pp. cxxxi and 382.

6 RCAHMS, *Argyll*, 1974, vol. 2, p. 299.

7 William Fraser, *The red book of Grandtully*, Edinburgh, 1868, pp. 73–5.

8 William Kelly, 'Alexander Galloway, rector of Kinkell', in *A tribute offered by the University of Aberdeen to the memory of William Kelly,* Aberdeen, 1949, pp. 19–33.

9 Cowan, *Parishes*, p. 113.

10 David McRoberts, 'Scottish sacrament houses', *Transactions of the Scottish Ecclesiological Society*, vol. 15, 1965, p. 45–6.

11 J. Russell Walker, 'Scottish baptismal fonts', *Proc. Soc. Antiq. Scot.*, vol. 21, 1886–7, pp. 400–1.

12 McRoberts, op. cit. note 10, p. 46.

13 MacGibbon and Ross, *Ecclesiastical*, 1897, vol. 3, pp. 330–7; The 7th Duke of Atholl, *Chronicle of the Atholl and Tullibardine families*, 5 vols, Edinburgh, 1908, vol. 1, p. 7. For a view of the chapel in relation to the castle see the view in the Hutton Collection, National Library of Scotland, Advocates MS. 30.5.23, 126

14 Cowan and Easson, p. 229.

15 MacGibbon and Ross, *Ecclesiastical*, 1897, vol. 3, pp. 363–72; RCAHMS, *Outer Hebrides, Skye and the Small Isles*, 1928, pp. 32–7; *Bldgs of Scot., Highland and Islands*, 1992, pp. 623–5.

16   K. A. Steer and J. W. M. Bannerman, *Late monumental sculpture in the West Highlands*, Edinburgh, 1977, pp. 78–81 and 97–100.

17   RCAHMS, *East Lothian*, 1924, pp. 125–8; *Bldgs of Scot.*, *Lothian*, 1978, pp. 467–8.

18   Cowan, *Parishes*, p. 209.

19   P. Hume Brown, *Early travellers in Scotland*, Edinburgh, 1891, pp. 24–9.

20   William Dobie, 'Notes on Ladykirk parish', *History of the Berwickshire Naturalists' Club*, vol. 12, 1890–1, pp. 369–78; RCAHMS, *Berwickshire*, 1915, pp. 99–101.

21   *Treasurer Accts*, vol. 2, pp. lxxxiii–lxxxiv; vol. 3, pp. 86–8, 131, 161 and 295–9; vol. 4, pp. 44–5, 81, 284, 329, 379 and 446; *Exch. Rolls*, vol. 2, p. 276.

22   John Durkan, 'Archbishop Robert Blackadder's will', *Innes Review*, vol. 23, 1972, p. 139.

23   See the view in R. Stuart, *Views and notices of Glasgow in former times*, Glasgow, 1848, (reproduced in George Eyre-Todd, *The book of Glasgow Cathedral*, Glasgow, 1898, p. 102).

24   Joseph Robertson, 'Notice of a deed by which Sir James Sandilands . . . binds himself and his heir to complete the vestry and build the nave, steeple and porch of the parish church of Mid-Calder', *Proc. Soc. Antiq. Scot.*, vol. 3, 1857–60, pp. 160–71; MacGibbon and Ross, *Ecclesiastical*, 1897, vol. 3, pp. 279–87; *Bldgs of Scot.*, *Lothian*, 1978, pp. 322–4.

25   Cowan, *Parishes*, p. 25; C. Wordsworth, *Pontificale Ecclesiae S. Andreae*, Edinburgh, 1885, pp. x–xx.

26   Ian Cowan, *The Scottish Reformation*, London, 1982, p. 8; Margaret H. B. Sanderson, *Cardinal of Scotland*, Edinburgh, 1986, p. 84.

27   MacGibbon and Ross, *Ecclesiastical*, 1897, vol. 3, pp. 614–15.

28   Cowan, *Parishes*, p. 196.

29   A. M. Mackenzie, 'Arbuthnott Church', *Transactions of the Aberdeen Ecclesiological Society*, vol. 1, 1886–9, pp. 41–4; MacGibbon and Ross, *Ecclesiastical*, 1897, vol. 3, pp. 235–42; G. Henderson, *The kirk of St Ternan, Arbuthnott*, Edinburgh, 1962.

30   Wordsworth, op. cit. note 25.

31   *Reg. Mag. Sig.*, vol. 2, no. 2867.

32   A. P. Forbes, *Liber ecclesie Beati Terrenani de Arbuthnott*, Burntisland, 1864; W. MacGillivray, 'Notices of the Arbuthnott missal and psalter and office of the Blessed Virgin', *Proc. Soc. Antiq. Scot.*, vol. 26, 1891–2, pp. 89–104; W. M. Metcalfe, *The Arbuthnott manuscripts, a description*, Paisley, n.d.; *Trésors des bibliothèques d'Écosse* (Bibliothèque Albert Ier, exhibition catalogue), Brussels, 1963, pp. 20–2.

33   Charles Carter, 'The *arma Christi* in Scotland', *Proc. Soc. Antiq. Scot.*, vol. 90, 1958–7, p. 122.

34   George W. T. Ormond, *The Arniston memoirs*, Edinburgh, 1887, pp. 6–8; RCAHMS, *Mid and West Lothian*, 1929, pp. 1–2; *Bldgs of Scot.*, *Lothian*, 1978, pp. 117–18.

35   MacGibbon and Ross, *Ecclesiastical*, 1896, vol. 1, pp. 316–20; James Robertson, *The churches and churchyards of Berwickshire*, Kelso, 1896, pp. 98–104.

36 Durkan, op. cit. note 22, pp. 139 and 143.

37 RCAHMS, *Stirlingshire*, 1963, vol. 1, pp. 143–8.

38 *The New Statistical Account of Scotland, Perthshire*, Edinburgh, 1845, p. 1119.

39 William Duke, 'Notice of the fabric of St Vigeans Church, Forfarshire . . .', *Proc. Soc. Antiq. Scot.*, vol. 9, 1873, pp. 481–98; MacGibbon and Ross, *Ecclesiastical*, 1897, vol. 3, pp. 459–62.

40 *Registrum Nigrum* . . . , op. cit., Chap. 1, note 85. pp. 226 and 366.

41 MacGibbon and Ross, *Ecclesiastical*, 1896, vol. 1, pp. 196–204.

42 Cowan, *Parishes*, p. 154.

43 J. R. Walker, *Pre-Reformation churches in Fifeshire*, Edinburgh, 1885; MacGibbon and Ross, *Castellated and Domestic*, 1892, vol. 5, pp. 145–9; RCAHMS, *Fife, Kinross and Clackmannan*, 1933, pp. 130–2.

44 W. Douglas Simpson, *Ravenscraig Castle*, Aberdeen, 1938, p. 25.

45 James C. Roger, 'Notices of ancient monuments in the ruined church of St Mary, Rothesay', *Proc. Soc. Antiq. Scot.*, vol. 2, 1854–7, pp. 466–81.

NOTES TO CHAPTER EIGHT

1 For more detailed – but varying – views of the historical background, see Ranald Nicholson, *Scotland, the later Middle Ages*, Edinburgh, 1974, chaps 11–14 and 17–18, and Jenny Wormald, *Court, kirk and community, Scotland 1470–1625*, London, 1981, chaps 1–4. See also Jennifer M. Brown, 'Taming the magnates?', in Gordon Menzies (ed.), *The Scottish nation*, London, 1972, pp. 46–59. The impact on castle building of the historical and social circumstances of the time has been discussed in a number of valuable papers by Geoffrey Stell, including 'Architecture: the changing needs of society', in Jennifer Brown (ed.), *Scottish society in the fifteenth century*, London, 1977, pp. 153–83, and 'Late medieval defences in Scotland' in David Caldwell (ed.), *Scottish weapons and fortifications, 1100–1800*, Edinburgh, 1981, pp. 21–54.

2 T. Thomson and C. Innes (eds), *Acts of the parliaments of Scotland*, Edinburgh, 1814–75, vol. 2, p. 133.

3 Ibid., vol. 2, p. 346.

4 Ibid., vol. 2, p. 13.

5 *Reg. Mag. Sig.*, vol. 2, no. 2038.

6 R. S. Rait, *The parliaments of Scotland*, Glasgow, 1924, p. 195.

7 *Acts of the parliaments of Scotland*, op. cit. note 2, vol. 2, pp. 335–6.

8 David Laing (ed.), *Correspondence of Sir Robert Kerr*, 2 vols (Bannatyne Club), Edinburgh, 1875, vol. 1, p. 62. For the symbolism of military architecture see, for example, Charles Coulson, 'Structural symbolism in medieval castle architecture', *Journal of the British Archaeological Association*, vol. 132, 1979, pp. 73–90.

9 *Acts of the parliaments of Scotland*, op. cit. note 2, vol. 2, p. 244.

10 Geoffrey Stell, 'Kings, nobles and buildings of the later Middle Ages: Scotland', in Grant Simpson (ed.), *Scotland and Scandinavia, 800–1800*, Edinburgh,

1990, pp. 68–9; see also Joachim W. Zeune, *The long pause – a reconsideration of Scottish castle building*, unpublished typescript, 1984.

11   *Reg. Mag. Sig.*, vol. 3, nos. 1432 and 1675.

12   The relationship between the courtyard and tower-house at Spynie has been clarified by recent excavations carried out by Mr John Lewis, to whom I am grateful for discussing his findings with me; until those are published, the fullest account of the castle is W. Douglas Simpson, *The palace of the bishops of Moray at Spynie*, Elgin, 1927.

13   M. R. Apted, 'Excavations at Kildrummy Castle, Aberdeenshire, 1952–62', *Proc. Soc. Antiq. Scot.*, vol. 96, 1962–3, pp. 215 and 218.

14   W. Douglas Simpson, 'Urquhart Castle', *Transactions of the Inverness Gaelic Society*, vol. 35, 1929, pp. 51–82.

15   See, for example, Joachim Zeune, *Der schottische Burgenbau vom 15. bis zum 17. jahrhundert*, Marksburg über Braubach, 1989.

16   A valuable outline of castle building in the northern and western Highlands is provided by John Dunbar, 'The medieval architecture of the Scottish Highlands', in *The Middle Ages in the Highlands* (Inverness Field Club), Inverness, 1981, pp. 38–70. For more detailed studies of individual castles in the Western Highlands see RCAHMS, *Argyll*, 1971–92, vols. 1–7.

17   RCAHMS, *Roxburghshire*, 1956, vol. 1, pp. 44–5; H. G. Ramm, R. W. McDowall and Eric Mercer, *Shielings and bastles*, Royal Commission on Historical Monuments, England, 1970; Philip Dixon, 'Towerhouses, pelehouses and Border society', *Archaeological Journal*, vol. 136, 1979, 240–52; Tam Ward, 'Bastle Houses of the Anglo-Scottish Borders', *Fortress*, no. 5, 1990, pp. 35–43.

18   RCAHMS, *Roxburghshire*, 1956, vol. 2, pp. 421–2.

19   Ward, op. cit. note 17.

20   The fullest corpus of tower-house plans is still that provided by the five volumes of MacGibbon and Ross, *Castellated and Domestic*.

21   MacGibbon and Ross, *Castellated and Domestic*, 1887, vol. 1. pp. 237–43; RCAHMS, *Dumfriesshire*, 1920, pp. 186–7.

22   MacGibbon and Ross, *Castellated and Domestic*, 1887, vol. 1, pp. 233–7; RCAHMS, *Mid and West Lothian*, 1929, pp. 120–1.

23   Zeune, op. cit. note 15, fig. 33a.

24   Ibid., pp. 6–9 and fig. 3. See also MacGibbon and Ross, *Castellated and Domestic*, 1887, vol. 1, pp. 243–7; 1889, vol. 3, pp. 213–16; and 1892, vol. 5, pp. 279–84.

25   MacGibbon and Ross, *Castellated and Domestic*, 1889, vol. 3, pp. 173–83; Stewart Cruden, *The Scottish castle*, Edinburgh, 1963, p. 139.

26   Simpson, op. cit. note 12.

27   RCAHMS, *Argyll*, 1971, vol. 1, pp. 161–5.

28   RCAHMS, *Stewartry of Kirkcudbright*, 1914, pp. 56–9.

29   RCAHMS, *Fife, Kinross and Clackmannan*, 1933, pp. 155–7.

30   Ibid., pp. 50–2; Zeune, op. cit. note 10, p. 6.

31   W. Douglas Simpson, 'Edzell Castle', *Proc. Soc. Antiq. Scot.*, vol. 65, 1930–1, pp. 115–73; W. Douglas Simpson and Richard Fawcett, *Edzell Castle* (official guide), revised edn, Edinburgh, 1989.

32   MacGibbon and Ross, *Castellated and Domestic*, 1887, vol. 1, pp. 189–202; RCAHMS, *Mid and West Lothian*, 1929, pp. 120–6; *Bldgs of Scot.*, Edinburgh, 1984, pp. 538–43; R. Denys Pringle, *Craigmillar Castle* (guidebook), Edinburgh, 1990.

33   MacGibbon and Ross, *Castellated and Domestic*, 1887, vol. 1, pp. 328–35.

34   *Reg. Mag. Sig.*, vol. 2, no. 1.

35   MacGibbon and Ross, *Castellated and Domestic*, 1889, vol. 3, pp. 138–43; G. Watson, 'Cessford Castle', *Transactions of the Hawick Archaeological Society*, 1909, pp. 47–54; RCAHMS, *Roxburghshire*, 1956, vol. 1, pp. 128–31.

36   MacGibbon and Ross, *Castellated and Domestic*, 1887, vol. 1, pp. 314–17; Jonathan Wordsworth, 'Excavation at Auchindoun Castle, Moray District, in 1984', *Proc. Soc. Antiq. Scot.*, vol. 120, 1990, pp. 169–71.

37   MacGibbon and Ross, *Castellated and Domestic*, 1889, vol. 3, pp. 202–4 and 296–301.

38   Ibid., 1887, vol. 2, pp. 51–2, 52–4 and 79–82.

39   Ibid., 1887, vol. 1, pp. 335–44.

40   W. Douglas Simpson, 'Crookston Castle', *Transactions of the Glasgow Archaeological Society*, new ser., vol. 12, 1953, pp. 1–14.

41   MacGibbon and Ross, *Castellated and Domestic*, 1887, vol. 1, pp. 344–52; Nat. Art Survey, vol. 2, 1923, pls 31–7; RCAHMS, *Mid and West Lothian*, 1929, pp. 3–9; Stewart Cruden, op. cit. note 25, pp. 131–6.

42   *Reg. Mag. Sig.*, vol. 2, no. 157.

43   RCAHMS, *Fife, Kinross and Clackmannan*, 1933, pp. 3–4.

44   *Reg. Mag. Sig.*, vol. 3, no. 2460.

45   John Mooney (ed.), *The Kirkwall charters* (3rd Spalding Club), Aberdeen, 1952, pp. 131–57; RCAHMS, *Orkney*, 1946, pp. 345–50.

46   MacGibbon and Ross, *Castellated and Domestic*, 1892, vol. 4, pp. 51–5; Joachim Zeune, 'Perfecting the tower house', pt 2, *Fortress*, no. 11, 1991, p. 17.

47   Margaret H. B. Sanderson, *Cardinal of Scotland*, Edinburgh, 1986, p. 38.

48   See note 33.

49   MacGibbon and Ross, *Castellated and Domestic*, 1887, vol. 1, pp. 295–6; P. C. Deuholm, 'Excavations at Levan Castle, Gourock, 1966 and 1970–72', *Glasgow Archaeological Journal*, vol. 16, 1989–90, pp. 55–80.

50   MacGibbon and Ross, *Castellated and Domestic*, 1887, vol. 1, pp. 178–82; RCAHMS, *Fife, Kinross and Clackmannan*, 1933, pp. 316–19.

51   MacGibbon and Ross, *Castellated and Domestic*, 1887, vol. 1, pp. 409–13; RCAHMS, *East Lothian*, 1924, pp. 122–4.

52   R. Denys Pringle and J. S. Richardson, *Huntingtower* (official guide), Edinburgh, 1989.

53   Alastair M. T. Maxwell-Irving, 'Cramalt Tower: historical survey and excavations 1977–9', *Proc. Soc. Antiq. Scot.*, vol. 111, 1981, pp. 401–29.

54   RCAHMS, *Fife, Kinross and Clackmannan*, 1933, pp. 280–3.

55   See note 11.

56   Christopher Tabraham, 'Smailholm Tower: a Scottish laird's fortified residence
      on the English Border', *Château Gaillard*, vol. 13, 1987, pp. 227–38; Chris-
      topher Tabraham, *Smailholm Tower* (official guide), 2nd edn, Edinburgh, 1989;
      see also Christopher Tabraham, 'The Scottish medieval towerhouse as lordly
      residence in the light of recent excavation', *Proc. Soc. Antiq. Scot.*, vol. 118,
      1988, pp. 267–76.

57   W. Galloway, 'The Boyd papers' and 'Architectural description of Dean Castle',
      Archaeological and Historical Collections of Ayr and Wigton, vol. 3, 1882, pp.
      110–211; MacGibbon and Ross, *Castellated and Domestic*, 1887, vol. 1, pp.
      401–8; J. Hunter and J. F. T. Thomson, *Dean Castle* (guidebook), 1976.

58   MacGibbon and Ross, *Castellated and Domestic*, 1887, vol. 1, pp. 377–82;
      RCAHMS, *Fife, Kinross and Clackmannan*, 1933, pp. 202–7; *Bldgs of Scot., Fife*,
      1988, pp. 88–91.

59   RCAHMS, *Fife, Kinross and Clackmannan*, 1933, pp. 321–5; Stewart Cruden,
      Castle Campbell (official guide), 2nd edn, Edinburgh, 1984.

60   Richard Fawcett, 'Stirling Castle: the King's Old Building and the late medieval
      royal planning', *Château Gaillard*, vol. 15, 1990, pp. 175–93.

61   RCAHMS, *Mid and West Lothian*, 1929, pp. 47–51; Christopher Tabraham and
      W. Douglas Simpson, *Crichton Castle* (official guide), 2nd edn, Edinburgh, 1987;
      A. Rowan, 'Crichton Castle, Midlothian', *Country Life*, 7 Jan. 1971, pp. 16–19.

62   MacGibbon and Ross, *Castellated and Domestic*, 1892, vol. 4, pp. 311–16.

63   Sanderson, op. cit. note 47, pp. 136, 143 and 221–2.

64   W. Douglas Simpson, 'The architectural history of Huntly Castle', *Proc. Soc.
      Antiq. Scot.*, vol. 56, 1921–22, pp. 135–63; W. Douglas Simpson, 'Further
      notes on Huntly Castle', *Proc. Soc. Antiq, Scot.*, vol. 67, 1932–3, pp. 137–60;
      W. Douglas Simpson, *Huntly Castle* (official guide), 4th edn, Edinburgh, 1985.

65   Op. cit. note 31; see also Charles McKean, 'The House of Pitsligo', *Proc. Soc.
      Antiq. Scot.*, vol. 121, 1991, pp. 369–90.

66   W. Douglas Simpson, 'The development of Balvenie Castle', *Proc. Soc. Antiq.
      Scot.*, vol. 60, 1925–6, pp. 132–48; Margaret E. Root, A. N. Taylor, Iain
      MacIvor and J. S. Richardson, *Balvenie Castle* (official guide), 2nd edn, Edin-
      burgh, 1990.

67   RCAHMS, *Orkney*, 1946, pp. 142–8; W. Douglas Simpson, *The castle of Bergen
      and the Bishop's Palace at Kirkwall*, Edinburgh, 1961; W. Douglas Simpson and
      R. Denys Pringle, *Bishop's Palace and Earl's Palace, Kirkwall, Orkney* (official guide),
      5th edn, Edinburgh, 1991.

68   David H. Caldwell, 'A sixteenth-century group of gun towers in Scotland', *Fort*,
      vol. 12, 1984, pp. 19 and 23.

69   MacGibbon and Ross, *Castellated and Domestic*, 1887, vol. 1, pp. 366–76;
      RCAHMS, *Mid and West Lothian*, 1929, pp. 106–12; *Bldgs of Scot., Lothian*,
      1978, pp. 418–20; Richard Haslam, 'Rosslyn Castle, Lothian', *Country Life*,
      13 Apr. 1989, pp. 112–15.

70 Those drawings are reproduced in Haslam, op. cit. note 69.

71 MacGibbon and Ross, *Castellated and Domestic*, 1887, vol. 1, pp. 289–95; RCAHMS, *Fife, Kinross and Clackmannan*, 1933, pp. 155–7.

72 Op. cit. note 32; see also Geoffrey Stell, 'Late medieval defences in Scotland', in David H. Caldwell (ed.), *Scottish weapons and fortifications 1100–1800*, Edinburgh, 1981, pp. 45–7.

73 MacGibbon and Ross, *Castellated and Domestic*, 1887, vol. 1, pp. 146–9; R. Burns-Begg, *Lochleven Castle and its associations with Mary Queen of Scots*, Kinross, 1887; RCAHMS, *Fife, Kinross and Clackmannan*, 1933, pp. 296–8; N. Q. Bogdan, *Lochleven Castle* (official guide), Edinburgh, 1984.

74 MacGibbon and Ross, *Castellated and Domestic*, 1889, vol. 3, pp. 144–8; RCAHMS, *Mid and West Lothian*, 1929, pp. 12–15.

75 Simpson, op. cit. note 12, pp. 13–14 and fig. 2.

76 Neil Hynd and Gordon Ewart, 'Aberdour Castle gardens', *Garden History*, vol. 11, 1983, pp. 93–111.

77 Cosmo Innes (ed.), *Registrum episcopatus Moraviensis* (Bannatyne Club), Edinburgh, 1837, p. 429.

78 E. H. M. Cox, *A history of gardening in Scotland*, London, 1935, pp. 17–24 gives a number of references to castle gardens, though the view presented there is more negative than would now be acceptable.

79 Geoffrey Stell, 'The earliest tolbooths: a preliminary account', *Proc. Soc. Antiq. Scot.*, vol. 111, 1981, pp. 445–53.

80 Anne Turner Simpson and Sylvia Stevenson, *Historic Perth* (Scottish Burgh Survey), Glasgow 1982, p. 24; R. M. Spearman, 'The medieval townscape of Perth', in Michael Lynch, Michael Spearman and Geoffrey Stell (eds), *The Scottish medieval town*, Edinburgh, 1988, pp. 51–2.

81 N. Q. Bogdan and J. W. Wordsworth. *The medieval excavations at the High Street Perth 1975–76*, an interim report, Perth, 1978.

82 RCAHMS, *Edinburgh*, 1951, pp. lxii–lxvi and 120–1.

83 John Schofield, 'Excavations south of Edinburgh High Street, 1973–4', *Proc. Soc. Antiq. Scot.*, vol. 107, 1975–6, pp. 155–241.

84 RCAHMS, *Stirlingshire*, 1963, vol. 2, pp. 304–6; RCAHMS, *Peeblesshire*, 1967, vol. 2, p. 280.

85 Boece, *Vitae*, p. 98.

86 For fuller information on bridges see R. G. Inglis, 'The ancient bridges in Scotland and their relation to the Roman and medieval bridges in Europe', *Proc. Soc. Antiq. Scot.*, vol. 46, 1911–12, pp. 51–177; R. G. Inglis 'The roads and bridges in the early history of Scotland', *Proc. Soc. Antiq. Scot.*, vol. 47, 1912–13, pp. 303–33; Ted Ruddock, 'Bridges and roads in Scotland 1400–1750', in Alexander Fenton and Geoffrey Stell (eds), *Loads and roads in Scotland and beyond*, Edinburgh, 1984, pp. 67–91.

87 RCAHMS, *Fife, Kinross and Clackmannan*, 1933, pp. 250–7; Richard Fawcett, *St Andrews Castle* (official guide), Edinburgh, 1992.

88   J. C. Roger, 'Notices of sculptured fragments, formerly in the episcopal palace, Glasgow', *Proc. Soc. Antiq. Scot.*, vol. 2, 1854–7, pp. 317–29; A. H. Millar, 'The bishop's castle', in George Eyre-Todd (ed.), *The book of Glasgow Cathedral*, Glasgow, 1898, pp. 324–57.

89   MacGibbon and Ross, *Castellated and Domestic*, 1887, vol. 2, pp. 336–7; *Bldgs of Scot.*, *Highland and Islands*, 1992, pp. 568–9.

90   MacGibbon and Ross, *Castellated and Domestic*, 1887, vol. 1, pp. 508–14; Geoffrey Stell, 'Urban buildings' in Lynch, Spearman and Stell, op. cit. note 80, pp. 70–2.

91   MacGibbon and Ross, *Castellated and Domestic*, 1887, vol. 2, pp. 58–60.

92   Ibid., 1892, vol. 5, pp. 89–93; Ronald Cant, *Historic Elgin and its Cathedral*, Elgin, 1974, pp. 28–31.

93   J. F. S. Gordon, 'The prebends and prebendal manses of Glasgow', in Eyre-Todd, op. cit. note 88, pp. 378–94; J. D. Mackie, *Provand's lordship*, Glasgow, n.d.

94   Bogdan and Wordsworth, op. cit. note 81; Anne Turner Simpson and Sylvia Stevenson (eds), *Town houses and structures in medieval Scotland* (Scottish Burgh Survey), Glasgow, 1980; Aberdeen Art Gallery and Museums, *A tale of two cities, the archaeology of Old and New Aberdeen*, Aberdeen, 1987.

95   Corpus Christi College Cambridge, MS 171 fo. 265 (reproduced in *Chron. Bower* (Watt), vol. 6, frontispiece).

96   British Library, Cotton MSS, Augustus, I, ii, 56 (reproduced in RCAHMS, Edinburgh, 1951, fig. 59).

97   RCAHMS, Edinburgh, 1951, pp. lxvi–lxviii.

98   N. P. Brooks, 'St John's House, its history and archaeology', *St Andrew's Preservation Trust, Annual Report*, St Andrews, 1976, pp. 11–16; RCAHMS, Edinburgh, 1951, pp. 95–9.

99   Stell, op. cit. note 90, pp. 60–80.

100   E. K. Roy, K. J. H. Mackay and L. Corbett, *Alloa Tower*, rev. edn., Alloa (Clackmannan Field Studies Society), 1987.

101   See the views reproduced in Ian G. Lindsay and Mary Cosh, *Inveraray and the Dukes of Argyll*, Edinburgh, 1973, figs 5, 6 and 7.

102   MacGibbon and Ross, *Castellated and Domestic*, 1889, vol. 3, pp. 498–502 and 1892, vol. 5, pp. 115–16.

NOTES TO CHAPTER NINE

1   This section is particularly indebted to the work of Iain MacIvor, a valuable expression of whose views on certain aspects is found in 'Artillery and major places of strength in the Lothians and east Border', in David H. Caldwell (ed.), *Scottish weapons and fortifications, 1100–1800*, Edinburgh, 1981, pp. 94–152.

2   See T. F. Tout, 'Firearms in England in the fourteenth century', *English Historical Review*, vol. 26, 1911, pp. 666–702.

3   See Anthony Tuck, *Border warfare*, London, 1979.

4   Referred to in *Exch. Rolls*, vol. 6, p. 383.

5 Claude Gaier, 'The origin of Mons Meg', *Journal of the Arms and Armour Society*, vol. 5, 1967, pp. 425–31 and 450–2.

6 Christopher Tabraham and George L. Good, 'The artillery fortification at Threave Castle, Galloway', in Caldwell, op. cit. note 1, pp. 55–72.

7 W. Douglas Simpson, *Ravenscraig Castle*, Aberdeen, 1938; *Exch. Rolls*, vol. 7, pp. 1–liii.

8 RCAHMS, *Stirlingshire*, 1963, vol. 1, pp. 193–6.

9 MacIvor, op. cit. note 1, pp. 94–103.

10 Ibid., pp. 107–19.

11 James Gairdner et al. (eds), *Letters and papers, foreign and domestic of the reign of Henry VIII*, London, 1862–1932, vol. 3, pt ii, no. 1976.

12 Christopher Tabraham and J. S. Richardson, *Tantallon Castle* (official guide), 2nd edn, Edinburgh, 1986; MacIvor, op. cit. note 1, pp. 122–4 and 132–3; R. A. V. G. Mackay (ed.), Lindesay of Pitscottie, *The historie and cronicles of Scotland* (Scottish Text Society), Edinburgh, 1899–1911, vol. 1, pp. 330–3.

13 *Works Accts*, vol. 1, pp. 198, 200, 228 and 241.

14 MacIvor, op. cit. note 1, pp. 128–32; Iain MacIvor, *Blackness Castle* (official guide), 2nd edn, Edinburgh, 1989; *Works Accts*, vol. 1, pp. 123–5 and 129; *Acts of the Lords of the Council in public affairs, 1501–54*, R. K. Hannay (ed.), Edinburgh, 1932, p. 453.

15 The interpretation offered by W. Douglas Simpson, 'Craignethan Castle', *Transactions of the Glasgow Archaeological Society*, new ser., 1960, vol. 15, pp. 34–45 has been largely superseded by Iain MacIvor, *Craignethan Castle* (official guide), Edinburgh, 1978. See also Iain MacIvor, 'Craignethan Castle, Lanarkshire: an experiment in artillery fortification', in M. R. Apted, R. Gilyard-Beer and A. D. Saunders (eds), *Ancient monuments and their interpretation*, London, 1977, pp. 239–61, and MacIvor, op. cit. note 1, pp. 124–6.

16 The land was granted to him in 1532 by his father, the first Earl of Arran, *Reg. Mag. Sig.*, vol. 3, no. 1220.

17 R. Denys Pringle, ' "Cadzow Castle" and "the castle of the Hamiltons": an architectural and historical conundrum', *Château Gaillard*, vol. 15, 1992, pp. 277–94.

18 M. Livingstone et al. (eds), *Registrum Secreti Sigili Regum Scotorum*, Edinburgh, 1908–, vol. 2, no. 4191.

19 David H. Caldwell, 'A sixteenth-century group of guntowers in Scotland', *Fort*, vol. 12, 1984 pp. 16–17.

20 RCAHMS, *Fife, Kinross and Clackmannan*, 1933, pp. 250–7; Caldwell, op. cit. note 19, pp. 18–19; Richard Fawcett, *St Andrews Castle* (official guide), Edinburgh, 1992.

21 MacGibbon and Ross, *Castellated and Domestic*, 1889, vol. 3, pp. 430–2.

22 Op. cit. note 11, vol. 21, p ii, no. 380.

23 J. R. Hale, 'The development of the bastion, 1440–1534', in John Hale, Roger Highfield and Beryl Smalley (eds), *Europe in the late Middle Ages*, London, 1965, pp. 466–94.

24   H. M. Colvin et al. (eds), *History of the king's works*, London, 1982, vol. 4, pp. 694–726.

25   Belvoir Castle, Rutland letters, vol. 2.

26   Op. cit. note 24, pp. 702–4.

27   Ibid., pp. 708–13.

28   Ibid., pp. 722–5.

29   Ibid., pp. 713–17.

30   *Treasurer Accts*, vol. 9, p. 163.

31   RCAHMS, *Stirlingshire*, 1963, vol. 1, p. 184.

32   Gordon Ewart, 'Excavations at Stirling Castle, 1977–78', *Post-medieval Archaeology*, vol. 14, 1980, pp. 23–51. This possibility was first advanced by Mr Iain MacIvor.

33   *Works Accts*, vol. 1, pp. xxvii and xxxiv; R. S. Mylne, *The master masons to the crown of Scotland*, Edinburgh, 1893, p. 53 suggested the work could be attributable to the French mason John Roytell.

34   J. Bain et al. (eds), *Calendar of state papers relating to Scotland and Mary Queen of Scots,* 1547–1603, Edinburgh, 1898, vol. 1, p. 158; Andrew Saunders, 'The defences of the Firth of Forth', in David Breeze (ed.), *Studies in Scottish antiquity*, Edinburgh, 1984, p. 470; Stuart Harris, 'The fortifications and siege of Leith: a further study of the map of the siege in 1560', *Proc. Soc. Antiq. Scot.*, vol. 121, 1991, pp. 359–68.

NOTES TO CHAPTER TEN

1   *Exch. Rolls*, vol. 4, pp. cxxxix–cxli, 413, 565, 580, 603, 605 and 626.

2   Ibid., vol. 4, p. 579, and vol. 5, p. 66. I am grateful to Mrs Doreen Grove for discussing her views on this chamber with me.

3   Ibid., vol. 4, pp. 623 and 626.

4   Valuable – if in some aspects conflicting – accounts of the building of Linlithgow Palace are to be found in RCAHMS, *Mid and West Lothian*, 1929, pp. 219–31; *Bldgs of Scot., Lothian*, 1978, pp. 291–301; John Dunbar, 'Some aspects of the planning of Scottish royal palaces in the sixteenth century', *Architectural History*, vol. 27, 1984, pp. 15–24; R. Denys Pringle, *Linlithgow Palace* (official guide), Edinburgh, 1989. Measured drawings of the palace are published in Nat. Art Survey, vol. 4, 1933, pls 42–57.

5   *Exch. Rolls*, vol. 4, pp. cxxxv–cxxxix and 391, 415, 434, 449–50, 513, 529–30, 553–8, 579, 613 and 652.

6   Ibid., vol. 5, pp. lxxv–lxxvi, 2, 10, 21, 227, 266, 274, 338, 340, 346–7, 374, 458, 478, 538 and 686–7.

7   A. V. G. Mackay (ed.), R. Lindesay of Pitscottie, *The historie and cronicles of Scotland* (Scottish Text Society), Edinburgh 1899–1911, vol. 1, p. 200.

8   *Exch. Rolls*, vol. 7, pp. 189 and 452.

9   Ibid., pp. 617, 637 and 656; vol. 8, pp. 65 and 134.

10   For a detailed account of the reign and personality of James IV see Norman MacDougall, *James IV*, Edinburgh, 1989.

11 G. A. Bergeworth (ed.), *Calendar of letters, despatches and state papers relating to the negotiations between England and Spain*, London 1862, vol. 1, no. 210. The text is printed in P. Hume Brown, *Early travellers in Scotland*, Edinburgh, 1891, pp. 39–49.

12 J. Lesley, *The history of Scotland from the death of James I in the year* 1436 *to the year* 1561 (Bannatyne Club), Edinburgh, 1830, p. 78.

13 See sketch plans at fig. 1 in Dunbar, op. cit. note 4.

14 H. M. Colvin et al. (eds), *The history of the king's works*, London, 1982, vol. 4, p. 1.

15 *Treasurer Accts*, vol. 1, p. 94.

16 *Treasurer Accts*, vol. 2, pp. 347–59, 362, 366, 370, 391 and 440; vol. 4, pp. 279, 374, 379 and 446. See the useful summary of craftsmen involved in the work in Pringle, op. cit. note 4.

17 *Treasurer Accts*, vol. 2, p. 362.

18 See Charles J. Burnett, 'The act of 1471 and its effect on the Royal Arms of Scotland', *Proc. Soc. Antiq. Scot.*, vol. 105, 1972–4, pp. 312–15. I am grateful to Mr John Dunbar for reminding me of the significance of this act.

19 *Treasurer Accts*, vol. 1, p. 204; vol. 2, p. 439.

20 *Treasurer Accts*, vol. 2, pp. lxxx–lxxxii, 87, 269 and 273. A valuable discussion of the construction and planning of Holyrood is to be found in two articles by John Dunbar: 'The palace of Holyroodhouse during the first half of the sixteenth century', *Archaeological Journal*, vol. 120, 1964, pp. 242–54 and op. cit. note 4. I am grateful to Mr Dunbar for discussing his views on Holyrood with me.

21 John Leland, *De rebus Britannicis collectanea* . . . , London 1770, vol. 4, pp. 258–300.

22 Dunbar, op. cit. note 4, pp. 15–17.

23 *Treasurer Accts*, vol. 3, p. 86.

24 Ibid., vol. 2, p. 273–4.

25 For accounts of Falkland, see RCAHMS, *Fife, Kinross and Clackmannan*, 1933, pp. 135–42; Dunbar, op. cit. note 4; *Bldgs of Scot.*, *Fife*, 1988, pp. 212–17.

26 For accounts of Edinburgh Castle, see RCAHMS, *Edinburgh*, 1951, pp. 1–25; *Bldgs of Scot.*, *Edinburgh*, 1984, pp. 85–102; Historical Research Associates (Mrs Doreen Grove), *Edinburgh Castle, royal palace to people's palace* (unpublished typescript), 1989; Iain MacIvor, *Edinburgh Castle*, London, 1993.

27 *Treasurer Accts*, vols 2, 3 and 4 (scattered references).

28 Ibid., vol. 4, p. 279.

29 The most detailed account of Stirling Castle is RCAHMS, *Stirlingshire*, 1963, vol. 1, pp. 179–223.

30 Charles Rogers (ed.), *History of the Chapel Royal* (Grampian Club), Edinburgh 1882, no. 1. See also D. E. R. Watt (ed.), *Fasti Ecclesiae Scoticanae Medii Aevi* (Scottish Record Society), 2nd draft, Edinburgh, 1969, pp. 333–41; Cowan and Easson, pp. 226–7.

31 *Treasurer Accts*, vol. 2, pp. 85 and 277; vol. 3, p. 88; vol. 4, p. 44.

32 Aonghus MacKechnie, 'Stirling's triumphal arch', *Welcome* (Historic Scotland magazine), Sept. 1991.

33   This was revealed in the course of excavations in 1987and 1993.

34   *Works Accts*, vol. 1, pp. 310–11.

35   *Treasurer Accts*, vol. 1, pp. 238 and 357.

36   Richard Fawcett, 'Stirling Castle: the King's Old Building and the late medieval royal planning', *Château Gaillard*, vol. 14, 1990, pp. 175–93.

37   *Treasurer Accts*, vol. 1, pp. 277 and 306.

38   Ibid., vol. 2, pp. 82 and 381.

39   See comparative plans in H. M. Colvin et al. (eds), *The history of the king's works*, London, 1963, vol. 1, fig. 9, p. 44.

40   National Library of Scotland, Z2/18b.

41   W. Douglas Simpson, *Rothesay Castle* (official guide), Edinburgh, 1972.

42   *Treasurer Accts*, vol. 4, pp. 335 and 345.

43   For references to some of those masons see *Works Accts*, vol. 1, pp. xxx–xxxv; see also Robert Scott Mylne, *The master masons to the crown of Scotland*, Edinburgh, 1893, chaps 3 and 4.

44   *Works Accts*, vol. 1, pp. 1–103; Dunbar (1964), op. cit. note 20.

45   *Works Accts*, vol. 1, pp. 132–95.

46   Oxford, Bodleian Library, Gough Maps 39, fo. Iv, published in Mylne, op. cit. note 43, between pp. 148 and 149.

47   Colvin, op. cit. note 14, pp. 19–20 and 137, and pl. 10.

48   *Works Accts*, vol. 1, pp. xiii, 201–21, 243–63, 269–88 and 297–8.

49   John Dunbar, 'Falkland Palace', *The St Andrews area, proceedings of the* 137th summer meeting of the Royal Archaeological Institute, 1991, pp. 51–2.

50   Ibid. and John Dunbar, 'Some sixteenth-century French parallels for the Palace of Falkland', *Review of Scottish Culture*, vol. 7, 1991, pp. 3–8.

51   Dana Bentley-Cranch, 'An early sixteenth-century French architectural source for the Palace of Falkland', *Review of Scottish Culture*, vol. 2, 1986, pp. 85–95.

52   M. Livingstone et al (eds), *Registrum Secreti Sigilli Regum Scotorum*, Edinburgh, 1908–, vol. 1, no. 3523.

53   *Works Accts,* vol. 1, pp. viii, xiv, 115–31.

54   Ibid., pp. 325–6 and 328.

55   RCAHMS, *Stirlingshire*, 1963, vol. 1, pp. 184, 196–205 and 220–3.

56   *Works Accts*, vol. 1, pp. 327–8. I am grateful to Mr Iain MacIvor for discussing with me his views on the dating of the Stirling palace block, and of the role of Hamilton of Finnart in its construction, at a time when he was preparing a paper on this subject.

57   Op. cit. note 52, vol. 2, no. 3144.

58   Ibid., no. 4191.

59   For a view placing greater emphasis on Hamilton of Finnart's contribution, see Charles McKean, 'Finnart's Platt', *Architectural heritage*, vol. 2 ('Scottish architects abroad'), Edinburgh, 1991, pp. 3–17.

60   This is discussed in op. cit. note 55, pp. 220–3.

61 John Dunbar, *The Stirling heads*, 2nd edn, Edinburgh, 1975.

62 Jane Graham, *Lacunar Strevelinense*, Edinburgh, 1817.

NOTES TO CONCLUSION

1 See David McRoberts (ed.), *The medieval church of St Andrews*, Glasgow, 1976, pl. XIII.

2 David Hay Fleming, *St Andrews Cathedral museum*, Edinburgh, 1931, p. 184 and fig. 111.

3 A. H. Millar, 'The bishop's castle', in George Eyre-Todd, *The book of Glasgow Cathedral*, Glasgow, 1898, p. 332.

4 Richard Fawcett, *St Andrews Castle* (official guide), Edinburgh, 1992; David Hay Fleming, *Handbook of St Andrews*, St Andrews, 1924, pp. 33–5.

5 RCAHMS, *Stirlingshire*, 1963, vol. 2, pp. 285–9.

6 Joachim Zeune, 'Perfecting the tower house', *Fortress*, no. 10, 1991, pp. 24–30 and no. 11, 1991, pp. 14–28.

7 Ian Cowan, *The Scottish Reformation*, London, 1982, pp. 72–88.

8 Gordon Donaldson, *The Scottish Reformation*, Cambridge, 1960, p. 35.

9 For details of these foundations see Cowan and Easson.

10 See Joseph Robertson, 'Notice of a deed . . . to build the nave steeple and porch of the parish church of Mid-Calder', *Proc. Soc. Antiq. Scot.*, vol. 3, 1857–60, pp. 160–71, pl. XX.

11 MacGibbon and Ross, *Ecclesiastical*, 1897, vol. 3, fig. 1320.

12 *Treasurer Accts*, vol. 8, p. 143. I am grateful to Mr John Dunbar for drawing this reference to my attention.

13 MacGibbon and Ross, op. cit. note 11, fig. 1324.

14 Illustrated in National Museum of Antiquities of Scotland, *Angels, nobles and unicorns* (exhibition catalogue) Edinburgh, 1982, p. 108.

15 MacGibbon and Ross, *Ecclesiastical*, 1897, vol. 3, fig. 1119.

16 Illustrated in Duncan Macmillan, Scottish art 1460–1990, Edinburgh, 1990, pl. 12.

17 Gordon Donaldson (ed.), *Accounts of the collectors of thirds of benefices* (Scottish History Society), Edinburgh, 1949.

18 George Hay, *The architecture of Scottish post-Reformation churches, 1560–1843*, Oxford, 1957, pp. 32–4 and pls 2 and 29a.

19 Ibid., pp. 43–5 and pl. 9c.

20 Ibid., pls 3b, 5b, and RCAHMS, *Edinburgh*, figs 272 and 278.

21 Royal Commission on Historical Monuments (England), *London*, London, 1959, vol. 2, p. 197 and pls 235–6.

22 See Royal Incorporation of Architects in Scotland, *The architecture of the Scottish Renaissance* (exhibition handbook), Edinburgh, 1990.

Select Bibliography

The main bibliographical information in this book is contained within the notes, and can be found by following up references to the particular buildings or subjects through the index and from there to the notes themselves. The following is intended as no more than a guide to some of the principal or most readily accessible works which cover the period in Scotland.

ABBREVIATIONS USED FOR COMMONLY CITED TITLES

Bldgs of Scot.	*The buildings of Scotland*, regional volumes, Harmondsworth (for *Lothian, Edinburgh*) and London (for *Glasgow, Fife, Highlands and Islands*), 1978– .
Boece, *Vitae*	Hector Boece, *Murthlacensium et Aberdonensium episcoporum vitae* (New Spalding Club), Aberdeen, 1894.
Cal. Docs Scot.	J. Bain (ed.), *Calendar of documents relating to Scotland*, Edinburgh, 1881–8.
Cal. Papal Letters	W. Bliss et al. (eds), *Calendar of entries in the papal registers relating to Great Britain and Ireland: papal letters*, London, 1893– .
Chron. Bower	W. Goodall (ed.), *Johannis de Fordun Scotichronicon cum supplementis et continuate Walteri Bower*, Edinburgh, 1759; or Donald Watt et al. (eds), Aberdeen, 1987– .
Cowan, *Parishes*	Ian B. Cowan, *The parishes of medieval Scotland* (Scottish Record Society), Edinburgh, 1967.
Cowan and Easson	Ian B. Cowan and David Easson, *Medieval religious houses, Scotland*, 2nd edn, London, 1976.
Exch. Rolls	J. Stuart et al. (eds), *The Exchequer Rolls of Scotland*, Edinburgh, 1878–1908.
MacGibbon and Ross, *Castellated and Domestic*	David MacGibbon and Thomas Ross, *The castellated and domestic architecture of Scotland*, 5 vols, Edinburgh, 1887–1892.

MacGibbon and Ross, *Ecclesiastical*	David MacGibbon and Thomas Ross, *The ecclesiastical architecture of Scotland*, 3 vols, Edinburgh, 1896–7.
Midlothian Chrs.	*Charter of the Hospital of Soltre, of Trinity College, Edinburgh, and other collegiate churches in Midlothian* (Bannatyne Club), Edinburgh, 1861.
Myln, *Vitae*	Alexander Myln, *Vitae Dunkeldensis ecclesiae episcoporum* (Bannatyne Club), Edinburgh, 1831.
Nat. Art Survey	National Art Survey of Scotland, *Examples of architecture from the twelfth to the seventeenth centuries*, 4 vols, Edinburgh, 1921–33.
Proc. Soc. Antiq. Scot.	*Proceedings of the Society of Antiquaries* of Scotland, 1851– .
RCAHMS	Royal Commission on the Ancient and Historical Monuments of Scotland, County *Inventories*, Edinburgh, 1909– .
Reg. Aven.	Registra Avinionensia in Vat. Arch.
Reg. Mag. Sig.	J. Thomson et al. (eds), *Registrum Magni Sigilii Regum Scottorum*, Edinburgh, 1882–1914.
Reg. Supp.	Registra Supplicationum in Vat. Arch. (manuscript calendar of entries held by Glasgow University Scottish History Department).
Treasurer Accts	T. Dickson and J. Balfour Paul (eds), *Accounts of the Lord High Treasurer of Scotland*, Edinburgh, 1877–1916.
Works Accts	H. M. Paton et al. (eds), *Accounts of the masters of works*, Edinburgh, 1957– .

BIBLIOGRAPHICAL GUIDES

Ian B. Cowan, 'The medieval church in Scotland: a select critical bibliography', *Records of the Scottish Church History Society*, vol. 21, 1981.

P. D. Hancock, *Bibliography of works relating to Scotland, 1916–50*, 2 vols, Edinburgh, 1960.

Cyril Matheson, *A catalogue of the publications of Scottish historical and kindred clubs and societies, 1908–27*, Aberdeen, 1928.

David and Wendy B. Stevenson, *Scottish texts and calendars*, London and Edinburgh, 1987.

Charles Sandford Terry, *A catalogue of the publications of Scottish historical and kindred clubs and societies, 1780–1908*, Glasgow, 1909.

Bruce Webster, *Scotland from the eleventh century to 1603*. London, 1975.

GENERAL WORKS ON SCOTTISH MEDIEVAL HISTORY

Jennifer M. Brown (ed.), *Scottish society in the fifteenth century*, London, 1977.

Ian B. Cowan and Duncan Shaw (eds), *The Renaissance and Reformation in Scotland*, Edinburgh, 1983.

W. Croft Dickinson, Gordon Donaldson and Isabel A. Milne, *A source book of Scottish history, vol. 2*, 1424–1567, 2nd edn 1958. London.

Gordon Donaldson, *Scotland: James V – James VII*, Edinburgh, 1971.

A. A. M. Duncan, *James I*, Glasgow, 1976.

John Durkan, 'Education in the century of the Reformation', *Innes Review*, vol. 10, 1959, pp. 67–90.

Elizabeth Ewan, *Townlife in fourteenth-century Scotland*, Edinburgh, 1990.

Alexander Grant, *Independence and nationhood: Scotland 1306–1469*, London, 1984.

Inverness Field Club, *The Middle Ages in the Highlands*, Inverness, 1981.

R. J. Lyall, 'Scottish students and masters at the universities of Cologne and Louvain in the fifteenth century', *Innes Review*, vol. 36, 1985, pp. 55–73.

Michael Lynch, Michael Spearman and Geoffrey Stell, *The Scottish medieval town*, Edinburgh, 1988.

Norman Macdougall, *James III*, Edinburgh, 1982.

Norman Macdougall, *James IV*, Edinburgh, 1989.

Christine McGladdery, *James II*, Edinburgh, 1990.

Peter McNeill and Ranald Nicholson, *An historical atlas of Scotland, c.400–c.1600*, St Andrews, 1975.

Gordon Menzies (ed.), *The Scottish nation*, London, 1977.

Ranald Nicholson, *Scotland: the later Middle Ages*, Edinburgh, 1974.

K. J. Stringer (ed.), *Essays on the nobility of medieval Scotland*, Edinburgh, 1985.

John Warrack, *Domestic life in Scotland, 1488–1688*, London, 1920.

Jenny Wormald, *Court, kirk and community: Scotland 1470–1625*, London, 1981.

WORKS ON SCOTTISH MEDIEVAL ECCLESIASTICAL HISTORY

William Moir Bryce, *The Scottish Grey Friars*, 2 vols, Edinburgh, 1909.

J. H. S. Burleigh, *A church history of Scotland*, London, 1960.

G. G. Coulton, *Scottish abbeys and social life*, Cambridge, 1933.

Ian B. Cowan, *The parishes of medieval Scotland* (Scottish Record Society), Edinburgh, 1967. vol. 93,

——*The Scottish Reformation*, London, 1982.

——and David E. Easson, *Medieval religious houses: Scotland*, 2nd edn, Edinburgh, 1976.

Mark Dilworth, 'The commendator system in Scotland', *Innes Review*, vol. 37, 1986, pp. 51–72.

Gordon Donaldson, *The Scottish Reformation*, Cambridge, 1960.

——*Scottish church history*, Edinburgh, 1985.

——*The faith of the Scots*, London, 1990.

John Dowden, *The medieval church in Scotland*, Glasgow, 1910.

——*The bishops of Scotland*, Glasgow, 1912.

John A. Duke, *History of the church of Scotland to the Reformation*, Edinburgh, 1937.

Annie I. Dunlop, 'Life in a medieval cathedral', *Society of Friends of Dunblane Cathedral*, vol. 4, 1945, pp. 70–86.

——*The life and times of James Kennedy, bishop of St Andrews*, Edinburgh, 1950.

John Durkan, *William Turnbull, bishop of Glasgow*, Glasgow, 1951.

Duncan Forrester and Douglas Murray (eds), *Studies in the history of worship in Scotland*, Edinburgh, 1984.

Jim Inglis, *The organ in Scotland before 1700*, Schagen, 1991.

Alex R. MacEwen, *A history of the church in Scotland, vol. 1, 397–1546*, London, 1913.

Leslie J. Macfarlane, *William Elphinstone and the kingdom of Scotland, 1431–1514*, Aberdeen, 1985.

David McRoberts, 'The medieval Scottish liturgy illustrated by surviving documents', *Transactions of the Scottish Ecclesiological Society*, vol. 15, 1957, pp. 24–40.

——'Material destruction caused by the Scottish Reformation', *Innes Review*, vol. 10, 1959, pp. 126–72.

George Smith Pryde, *The burghs of Scotland, a critical list*, London, 1965.

Margaret H. B. Sanderson, *Cardinal of Scotland, David Beaton c. 1494–1546*, Edinburgh, 1986.

D. E. R. Watt (ed.), *Fasti ecclesiae Scoticanae medii aevi ad annum 1638* (Scottish Record Society), new ser., vol. 1, Edinburgh, 1969.

GENERAL WORKS ON SCOTTISH ARCHITECTURE

John G. Dunbar, *The architecture of Scotland*, 2nd edn, London, 1978.

Edinburgh Architectural Association, *Sketch books*, Edinburgh, 1875– .

John Gifford, *The buildings of Scotland: Fife*, London, 1988.

——*The buildings of Scotland: Highland and Islands*, London, 1992.

——Colin McWilliam and David Walker, with Christopher Wilson, *The buildings of Scotland: Edinburgh*, Edinburgh, 1984.

Francis Grose, *The antiquities of Scotland*, 2 vols, London, 1789–91.

Douglas Knoop and G. P. Jones, *The Scottish mason and the mason word*, Manchester, 1939.

Colin McWilliam with Christopher Wilson, *The buildings of Scotland: Lothian*, London, 1978.

R. S. Mylne, *The master masons to the crown of Scotland*, Edinburgh, 1893.

National art survey of Scotland, *Examples of architecture from the twelfth to the seventeenth centuries*, 4 vols, Edinburgh, 1921–33.

Royal Commission on the Ancient and Historical Monuments of Scotland, *Inventories*, Edinburgh, 1909– .

John Slezer, *Theatrum Scotiae*, London, 1693.

Elizabeth Williamson, Anne Riches and Malcolm Higgs, *The buildings of Scotland: Glasgow*, London, 1990.

WORKS WITH A PARTICULAR BEARING ON SCOTTISH MEDIEVAL ARCHITECTURE

Robert William Billings, *The baronial and ecclesiastical antiquities of Scotland*, 4 vols, Edinburgh, 1845–52.

David H. Caldwell (ed.), *Scottish weapons and fortifications, 1100–1800*, Edinburgh, 1981.

——'A sixteenth-century group of gun towers in Scotland', *Fort*, vol. 12, 1984, pp. 15–24.

Stewart Cruden, *The Scottish castle*, 2nd edn, London, 1963.

—— *Scottish medieval churches*, Edinburgh, 1986.

Philip Dixon, 'Towerhouses, pelehouses and Border society', *Archaeological Journal*, vol. 136, 1979, pp. 240–52.

John Dunbar, 'The medieval architecture of the Scottish Highlands', in Inverness Field
     Club, *The Middle Ages in the Highlands*, Inverness, 1981, pp. 38–70.
——'Some aspects of Scottish royal planning in the sixteenth century', *Architectural
     History*, vol. 27, 1984, pp. 15–24.
Richard Fawcett, 'Late Gothic architecture in Scotland: considerations on the influence
     of the Low Countries', *Proc. Soc. Antiq. Scot.*, vol. 112, 1982, pp. 477–96.
——'Scottish medieval window tracery', in David Breeze (ed.), *Studies in Scottish
     antiquity*, Edinburgh, 1984, pp. 148–86.
Ian C. Hannah, 'The penetration into Scotland of English late Gothic forms', *Proc. Soc.
     Antiq. Scot.*, vol. 64, 1929–30, pp. 149–55.
——'Screens and lofts in Scottish churches', *Proc. Soc. Antiq. Scot.*, vol. 70, 1935–6,
     pp. 181–201.
George Hay, 'The architecture of Scottish collegiate churches', in G. W. S. Barrow (ed.),
     The Scottish tradition, 1974, pp. 56–69.
David MacGibbon and Thomas Ross, *The castellated and domestic architecture of Scotland*, 5
     vols, Edinburgh, 1887–92.
——*The ecclesiastical architecture of Scotland*, 3 vols, Edinburgh, 1896–7.
Iain MacIvor, 'Artillery and major places of strength in the Lothians and the east Border',
     in Caldwell, 1981 (op. cit.), pp. 94–152.
W. Mackay Mackenzie, *The medieval castle in Scotland*, Edinburgh, 1927.
David McRoberts, 'Scottish sacrament houses', *Transactions of the Scottish Ecclesiological
     Society*, vol. 15, 1965, pp. 33–56.
Alastair M. T. Maxwell-Irving, 'Early firearms and their influence on the military and
     domestic architecture of the Borders', *Proc. Soc. Antiq. Scot.*, vol. 103, 1970–1,
     pp. 192–224.
Henry M. Paton (ed.), *Accounts of the masters of works for building and repairing royal palaces
     and castles, vol. 1, 1529–1615*, Edinburgh, 1957.
James S. Richardson, 'Fragments of altar retables of late medieval date in Scotland', *Proc.
     Soc. Antiq. Scot.*, vol. 62, 1927–8, pp. 197–224.
Geoffrey Stell, 'Architecture: the changing needs of society', in Brown, 1977 (op. cit.),
     pp. 153–83.
——'Late medieval defences in Scotland', in Caldwell, 1981 (op. cit.) pp. 21–54.
——'The Scottish medieval castle: form, function and evolution', in Stringer, 1985
     (op. cit.), pp. 195–209.
J. R. Walker, *Pre-Reformation churches in Fifeshire*, Edinburgh, 1885.
Tam Ward, 'Bastle houses of the Anglo-Scottish border', *Fortress*, no. 5, 1990, pp.
     35–43.
Joachim Zeune, *Der schottische Burgenbau vom 15. bis zum 17. Jahrhundert*, Marksburg über
     Braubach, 1989.
——'Perfecting the tower house: post-medieval Scottish castellated architecture',
     Fortress, no. 10, 1991, pp. 24–30, and no. 11, 1991, pp. 14–28.
——*The last Scottish castles* (International Archaeology, vol. 12), Buch am Erlbach,
     1992.

THE OTHER ARTS IN MEDIEVAL SCOTLAND

Michael R. Apted and Susan Hannabuss, *Painters in Scotland, 1301–1700: a biographical
     dictionary* (Scottish Record Society), new ser., Edinburgh, 1978, vol. 8.

Robert Brydall, 'Monumental effigies of Scotland from the thirteenth to the fifteenth century', *Proc. Soc. Antiq. Scot.*, vol. 29, 1894–5, pp. 329–410.

Duncan Macmillan, *Scottish art 1460–1990*, Edinburgh, 1990.

David McRoberts, *Catalogue of Scottish medieval liturgical books and fragments*, Glasgow, 1953.

——'Notes on Scoto-Flemish artistic contacts', *Innes Review*, vol. 10, 1959, pp. 91–6.

National Museum of Antiquities of Scotland, *Angels, nobles and unicorns: art and patronage in medieval Scotland*, Edinburgh, 1982.

James S. Richardson, 'Unrecorded Scottish wood carvings', *Proc. Soc. Antiq. Scot.*, vol. 60, 1927, pp. 384–408.

——*The medieval stone carver in Scotland*, Edinburgh, 1964.

K. A. Steer and J. W. M. Bannerman, *Late medieval monumental sculpture in the West Highlands*, Edinburgh, 1977.

Colin Thompson and Lorne Campbell, *Hugo van der Goes and the Trinity panels in Edinburgh*, Edinburgh, 1974.

University of Glasgow Department of Art History, *Rarer gifts than gold: fourteenth-century art in Scottish collections*, Glasgow, 1988.

J. Russell Walker, 'Scottish baptismal fonts', *Proc. Soc. Antiq. Scot.*, vol. 21, 1886–7, pp. 346–448.

Index